The Art of the Novel

The Art of the Novel

FROM 1700 TO THE PRESENT TIME

By

PELHAM EDGAR

NEW YORK / RUSSELL & RUSSELL

FIRST PUBLISHED IN 1933
REISSUED, 1966, BY RUSSELL & RUSSELL
A DIVISION OF ATHENEUM PUBLISHERS, INC.
L. C. CATALOG CARD NO: 66-13168
ISBN: 0-8462-0710-9
PRINTED IN THE UNITED STATES OF AMERICA

To My Sister Maud

PREFACE

It is presumptuous for a writer to assert the worth of his own wares: it is permitted to him to declare only his intentions. Much has been written on the novel in the past few years. It has come to be recognized at its best as an important branch of literary art, but its flexibility is such as resolutely to resist definition. The design of this book has been in Part One to set forth the essentials of fiction about which there can be no dispute. In what follows, great books and authors from 1700 to the present day are interpreted with a view to ascertaining what has been the main drift of fiction, and for the purpose of estimating current tendencies. A biographical and bibliographical section is appended which establishes the essential facts about the thirty-eight major authors presented and provides full material for further investigation of their work.

The book is issued in two editions. A feature of the College edition is a series of working suggestions that may form a satisfactory basis for class discussions and theme work.

PELHAM EDGAR

VICTORIA COLLEGE
University of Toronto

ACKNOWLEDGMENTS

In addition to acknowledgments made in the text I wish to thank Professor E. K. Brown of University College, Toronto, for the contribution of the chapter on Edith Wharton. I have made free use in the Aldous Huxley chapter of a graduate seminary paper by Mr. Earle Birney, and in the Conrad chapter of material prepared by another former graduate student, the late Professor G. H. Unwin of the Ontario Agricultural College, Guelph.

CONTENTS

PART ONE

PART TWO

Contents

PART ONE

THE ART OF THE NOVEL

CHAPTER I

PRELIMINARIES

The present book is not an organized study of fiction in the historical or biographical sense. The advantage is that many unimportant names can be disregarded. As for the disadvantages, these may properly be left for the reader to determine. If he is frivolously inclined, he may find too slender a stock of contemporary gossip and anecdote. If more serious, he may consider that not enough attention is paid to the intellectual content of fiction. My chief aim being to present a systematic study of the structural evolution of the English novel, it was necessary to emphasize its formal aspects, but in that effort it is hoped that the subject matter has not unduly suffered.

We must not undervalue this latter element, but I feel that the surest way to develop the instinct of "creative reading" is to fix our attention primarily on the way the author shapes and develops his material. None of the other values in the book are minimized. We are always free to estimate the range of the author's ideas, his fertility of invention in episode and character, and indeed we can achieve a due appreciation of his content only when we have become so to speak partners in his creative process. I have chosen therefore a few admittedly great books of the older time and a number of modern books which have some chance of survival, and have made as careful an examination as the case warranted of the manner in which the author has organized his theme.

It is an inductive method, but though it may lead to an occasional fruitful generalization I cannot flatter myself that it is a sufficient basis on which to found a philosophy of fiction. There is probably a formula, if one could work it out, for cheap effects and quick returns, but there is no sole and sovereign way by which a novelist may achieve a lasting result. Yet because fiction is the youngest of the literary arts, and therefore the most fluctuating, it does not follow that a consideration of its formal element is without its value. There are no fixed laws, it is true, beyond the compulsion to entertain the reader, but there are undoubtedly a number of devices which lead to that result and which are discoverable in the conscious or unconscious experimentation of the past.

The books that we shall explore have all produced their admitted effect. We must give their authors credit for knowing what effects they wished to produce, and for planning these effects. Sometimes they may have scanted their material, sometimes overworked it, sometimes even have misshaped it, and the books, otherwise handled, might have been better than they are. The choice of a subject is an author's concern; the reader should have something to say about the treatment, and the novelist's effort at communication is only complete when we can give our reasoned assent to both the matter and the manner. There is evidence that writers are increasingly anxious to say things not only in the way that is most congenial to themselves, but in what is conceivably the best way for the theme they have in hand. It is certainly desirable that the reader should repay their artistic intention by sharpening his powers of discrimination, and his enjoyment will be immeasurably enhanced if he can train himself to realize how the author has evolved his harmony. It is precisely here, where it is needed most, that appreciation lags furthest behind. If then we select a number of reputable books, and estimate them as *contrived* creations we are taking a step in the required direction. Mr. Percy Lubbock in his *The Craft of Fiction* has done this admirably for a few selected books, but he admits that his generalizations rest on too slender a basis. "My analysis of the making of a few novels," he writes, "would have to be pushed very much further before it would be possible to reach more than one or two conclusions in this connection. . . . I can imagine that by examining and comparing in detail the workmanship of many novels by many hands a critic might arrive at a number of inductions in regard to the relative properties of the scene, the incident dramatized, the incident pictured, the panoramic impression and the rest. In order to recreate them durably there is the one obvious way—to study the craft, to follow the process, to read constructively. The practice of this method appears to me at this time of day, I confess, the only interest of the criticism of fiction. It seems vain to expect that discourse upon novelists will contain anything new for us until we have really and clearly and accurately seen their books."

More numerous examples, if less deftly handled, are provided here, and in the final comment a tentative effort is made to reach some reasoned judgments on the material. We are far from finality yet, but if the method fails to achieve that "philosophy of fiction" which I have confessed to be as elusive as it is alluring, it still provides justifiable results. Perhaps not the least of these is to give the instructor not only a method of teaching but an opportunity of providing his class with workable themes. Dramatic form has been utilized in this fashion for centuries. So far as fiction is concerned we have been timid from ignorance, and have felt that a consideration of a few rhetorical expedients was the last word to be said on the question of form.

One reason of course for our uncertainty as to the permanent validity of any author's method of handling his material is to be found in the constant oscillation of literary fashion. At one time romance is in the ascendant, at another realism has the vogue. The author is brutally frank or prudishly reticent. He loves to preach or he abhors didacticism. He parades his own opinions or seeks to hide himself in the story. He paints with full broad strokes, or gets his effects by inference and innuendo, and substitutes suggestion for the full-flowered statement. At one time he affects the carefully patterned design, incidents dovetailed, characters grooved, and everything irresistibly moving to the inevitable conclusion, or again strives to simulate the haphazard incongruity and inconclusiveness of life. It is an amusing game to watch and an exhilarating game to play, and every participant is so serenely convinced that he, and he alone, is right, or at best the few readers and writers who are like minded with himself. Where shall we find leading in the labyrinth? It is all so puzzling, and literary revolutions are perpetually decapitating our crowned heads. George Eliot was once a sufficient queen, but among the "bright young people" of today she commands no loyalty. And there are so many reputations, slipping, slipping, or painfully balanced on their precarious pinnacles. Scott is hardly now defended even by the pundits of the critical world. Thackeray is suspect and Dickens only divides our suffrage. Meredith, once the idol of the intellectuals, is now a fallen god. In this welter of toppling renowns the strange fact emerges that Defoe and Fielding who first discovered the virtues of sustained prose narrative stand much nearer to the modern temper than the men our fathers and grandfathers knew. Dissatisfaction is, I suppose, one element of growth, and as such we should value it. But it is not evidence of our wisdom that in providing room for the urgency of the new we should make such a holocaust of the old. It does not promote the germination of the young bud to lop off the limb that bears it, nor is a tree advantaged by severing its roots.

These oscillations of fashion and recoils from tradition may be more profitably discussed when we have laid out our material. It is sufficient here to set forth in somewhat general terms the constituent elements of fiction—the bricks and mortar so to speak of the novelist's trade.

Chapter II

THE ESSENTIALS

The theme of a novel can generally be disengaged from the series of events that illustrate it. Tolstoy's *War and Peace* is a vast affair, but after all it is a book written about something which should be capable of being indicated with the utmost brevity. In the narrative of adventure and incident this may be difficult to do, but there is in most significant fiction a basic idea from which the book proceeds, and in every novel of power there is a necessary congruity between the subject and the mode of treatment. The scope for failure here is obviously great, and whether incompetence in the author is to be attributed to an unsatisfactory choice of subject matter or to ineffective treatment is a question too hypothetical to be here considered. Our concern is with the subject. How the author finds it is his own affair. His field is virtually the whole range of human activity. Aspiration, failure, achievement, the gamut of the passions, the form and feature of contemporary life, the complexity of individual problems—out of all this confused welter of experience the novelist must create his harmony. The problem is one of superfluity rather than defect, and recognizing this we shall be the less surprised if the faculty of wise choice is rare. We might indeed almost venture to affirm that the man who can originate a theme is already a novelist.

Assuming then that a workable subject has been found there remains for the author the task of communicating it with the minimum leakage of value. I have said that there is no sole and sovereign way of proceeding, which means that there is no established formula for producing a result. It is not a severe exaggeration to say that there are as many modes of treatment as there are subjects to be treated, but the essence of the matter is that for every subject there exists an appropriate form which it is the author's business to discover, and the reader's to understand. When we realize how varied are the elements of expression at the novelist's command we shall recognize how great is the margin of possible error, and how extensive also in an art that is still in its formative stage are the possibilities of untested combinations. This is the justification of innovation, for none of the other expressive arts save music offer so exciting an opportunity for fresh discovery and renewed experimentation.

Drama and Fiction. There are no dark continents to explore in drama. The mechanician will develop new effects, the dramatist a changed emphasis of tone, and the actor a few fresh attitudes and gestures, but as an art the drama is somewhat severely restricted to conditions long since established. Its effect, and a notable one, on fiction has been produced, for novelists have not recently learned the value of dramatic heightening and relief. But the counter-effect of fiction on drama is now in progress, and such development as drama is capable of will be derived from that source. We may note for example Bernard Shaw's attempt to combine the acting and the reading play—his contentious prefaces, his commentative embroideries on his text, and O'Neill's brave effort to exhibit the concealed thought processes of his characters.

It is unnecessary to rehearse here distinctions and differences which frequent repetition has made so familiar, and which we can in a sufficient degree establish for ourselves. It seems more important to inquire what we mean by saying that the novelist in quest of a certain effect has recourse to the methods of the dramatist. In how far may we legitimately use the term dramatic as applied to fiction? And what are the particular effects that flow from the dramatic resource?

Characteristics of Dialogue. A rough subdivision of fiction will resolve it into its dialogued and non-dialogued elements. The function of the latter we must reserve for a somewhat careful examination. It is sufficient here to note that the novelist in these spacious intervals has privileges that are denied to the dramatist. He narrates, he comments, he analyzes, he describes, and if he has utilized his opportunities aright he has adequately prepared the occasion for the appearance of his characters. In drama speech is the only available index, since the setting is inevitably a subordinate adjunct. In fiction there are many other ways of preparing and producing an effect, though the spoken word still remains the medium of highest intensity and significance. It is here too that the novelist approximates most closely to the objectivity of drama, and we may observe that the authors who prefer to reveal their characters rather than exhibit themselves incline strongly in the direction of dialogued fiction. Even in the narrative and descriptive portions of their work they simulate so far as possible the serene impersonality which drama imposes. For there is a legitimate sense in which description, analysis, and narration may be dramatically conveyed. This is a device, however, utilized only by the more subtle practitioners and needs for its due appreciation a markedly alert response from the reader's side. Examples would illustrate this expedient better than abstract assertion, though good examples in the present immaturity of fiction will be far to seek. The normal author is often aware of how readily the non-dialogued portions of his book go dead. But he does not realize sufficiently the possibility of enlivening them, and has no alternative other than to reduce them to the utmost and work his speech element to the furthest limit. This is capitulating to a difficulty too easily, and a wiser economy would not so readily sacrifice mediums of expression which confer on fiction its distinctive quality.

Every author must follow his natural bias, and it is a matter of interest to note how certain writers incline to the conversational and others to the pictorial manner of presentation. Before a book is read a glance of the eye will indicate where the preponderance lies. This visual test alone would inform us that Tolstoy, Dostoevsky, Jane Austen, and Dickens, for example, achieve their effects mainly by what their characters reveal in speech. They may be described therefore as rather scenic than pictorial in their method, whereas Thackeray is notably less lavish in his dialogued scenes. Seeking a large generalized result he achieves vividness by more laborious means. There is no need to accentuate his success—he was light-handed enough to disguise the labor,—but younger writers have preferred to follow what they conceive to be an easier road, with the result that most of our current fiction is over-dialogued. This was certainly the view of Henry James, who is not sufficiently recognized as the most intelligent experimentalist that fiction has known. Habitually he was inclined to an undue amplification of the pictorial side of his subject in his eagerness to set the scene for the appearance of his actors. But if he was unduly sparing of dialogue it was not because he undervalued its possible effectiveness, and as if for a wager he wrote one book, *The Awkward Age*, to test its capacity to carry the whole weight of the action. It was an instructive experiment, but not likely to be repeated.

A statement of the characteristics of sound dialogue

would not necessarily cover the case of any particular author who might conceivably escape from a standard too arbitrarily imposed. But the following general principles may constitute a convenient point of departure for any special example.

Dramatic Quality. Dialogue is the natural vehicle for dramatic effects. Other portions of fiction may be dramatically rendered, but speech is the normal medium. It is not to be understood that by "dramatic" is necessarily implied speech-interchange under the pressure of excitement. High tension passages will ordinarily be rendered in dialogue, but even the quietest verbal communication is properly to be described as dramatic.

Preparation and Relief. Speech is most effective when its occasions are adequately prepared by the various devices to which the novelist, as distinct from the dramatist, has access—analysis, description, narration. Dialogued scenes are also with advantage relieved and broken by these expedients, and it is the skill with which this is done that marks the proficient craftsman. Minor breaks in dialogue are necessitated by indications of the speaker. It is a teasing problem for even the good writer to make these indications at once clear and fresh. To avoid the recurrent monotonies of the "he said" and "she replied" variety, writers too frequently have recourse to irritating affectations—"she snapped," "she droned," "she tittered," "she blurted," or "said Wilson, nonchalantly flicking the ash of his cigarette." By contrast we welcome the straight-forward manner of Scott who accepts the "saids" and "replieds" as a matter of convenience, yet on occasion supplies a descriptive phrase to characterize the speaker or to visualize him more effectively for the reader. "Major Melville reddened even to the well-powdered ears which appeared beneath his neat military side-curls, the more so as he ob-

served Mr. Morton smile at the same moment. 'Mr. Gil-
fillan,' he answered with some asperity, 'I beg ten thousand
pardons for interfering with a person of your importance.'"

Naturalness. Naturalness is generally held to be a virtue
in dialogue, but this opens up the difficult question of how
closely fiction can or should approximate to actual conditions. Romance in its origins was an idealized attempt to
escape from reality. Men craved impossible situations,
and the language of narration also consorted with this
demand. Our art now creeps closer to natural conditions,
but if we examine even its most realistic examples we see
convention asserting itself on every hand. Speeches are
organized for effect as they are not in real life, and the
occasional note of sheer naturalness is a device like the
rest. Whoever spoke so brilliantly as a Meredith or Huxley
character? Yet if life is to be our pattern the flatness of
many a novelistic utterance provokes the question whether
a certain degree of heightening is not a privilege we willingly accord an author.

The employment of slang and dialect may be considered
here. The use of the former has the merit or disadvantage
of dating a book, for slang is peculiarly susceptible to the
fluctuations of fashion. To a discreet use of dialect there
can be no objection, but it does not seem wise to convert
fiction into a series of phonetic records.

Time Qualities of Dialogue. Conversational scenes normally bring the action into the immediate present. This
fact enables us to realize why novelists intent upon ex-
hibiting large tracts of time are compelled to elaborate
the descriptive and narrative portions of their work at
the expense of dialogue.

It is to be noted, however, that characters are always
privileged to talk about the past, and novelists frequently
utilize this opportunity of relieving themselves of some

portion of their narrative task. This is especially true of novelists who prefer to work dramatically.

Recovered Dialogue. Another device for harking back in time is the employment of what might be fittingly called "recovered dialogue." By this we understand speeches which the author arbitrarily reconstructs from the past, or speeches conveyed by the first personal character of the autobiographical novel. It is obvious that in the last named type the hero is always recollecting. A reference to *Moll Flanders* or *David Copperfield* will make this point sufficiently clear. In the epistolary novel conversations are also dramatically invented. Clarissa Harlowe and her friend Miss Howe constantly enliven their letters by remembered dialogue.

Range of Subjects in Dialogue. This will vary of course with the degree of mentality assumed in the speaker, and also to some extent with the intellectual interests of the author. Aldous Huxley is less concerned with the dramatic appropriateness of his dialogue than with the opportunity it affords him of emptying his mind of its content. Henry James had a mind presumably as rich in ideas, but concern for the unity of his theme restrained him from discursiveness. He has some voluble talkers like Gabriel Nash in *The Tragic Muse*, but what Gabriel says, and it is a great deal, has reference always to the topic of the book. Novelists who affect a looser structure permit themselves a wider range. The only compulsion here should be to maintain the characteristic quality of the individual speeches. But when the personages are fountains of ideas the principle of differentiation is difficult to apply. We are too manifestly then listening to the author's voice.

The Functions of Dialogue. First in order should be set the value of dialogue as an aid to characterization. Appearance, gesture, behavior are contributing indications, the presentation of mental and emotional processes through the medium of analysis is an effective factor in delineation, but speech remains the readiest and the liveliest medium of revelation. If in any novel the speech of one character could be set without detection upon the lips of another, this function of dialogue is wasted. Squire Western's words in *Tom Jones* could never be transferred to Allworthy, and in every syllable he utters he gives himself away completely. It is a severe test to apply to fiction, and few authors would surmount it in the length and breadth of their work. Another and an easier way in which speech may come to the aid of characterization is to make the qualities of any particular person the subject of general comment. Nothing indeed can be more natural than for people to discuss the virtues of other individuals, unless it may be considered still more natural for them to discuss their defects.

How important dialogue is in rounding off a situation may be tested by reference to innumerable examples. The quarrel scene towards the close of the first chapter in Lawrence's *Sons and Lovers* is led up to by narrative, and relieved by analytic touches. But it is the hot tongues flaming into speech that give the vivid culmination to the episode. Huxley's *Point Counter Point* in its opening chapter launches the incipient dissension between Walter and Marjorie. All the composite elements for building up a scene are requisitioned, but the words though few bear the greatest weight.

The Non-Dialogued Elements in Fiction. The important items to be considered here are Narrative, Plot, Pattern, Description, and Analysis.

The instinct for story-telling, and even more the instinctive delight we have in hearing a story told, are as primitive as any impulse that has gone to the making of litera-

ture. It would appear strange therefore to those unfamiliar
with the principles of literary growth that the emergence
of the novel should have been so long delayed, and, if we
grant the rooted primitiveness of the narrative instinct, it
is equally a matter of surprise that novelists are now beginning to question the virtue of the story element as a
legitimate source of appeal. The first puzzle has been sufficiently answered in the many available histories of the
novel. The second problem is not merely an affair of history. A constructive principle is involved, and we shall
perhaps encounter the explanation as we proceed to sift the
meaning of the terms "narrative," "plot," and "pattern."

Narrative. Narrative in its rudimentary form is capable
of definition. In its developed form something has been
added—the spirit of the narrator—which evades exact
analysis. Reduced to its simplest terms narrative is the
recounting of an episode, or a series of episodes in temporal
and causal sequence. Art begins with emphasis and arrangement, and a manipulation of reality will generally
serve its purpose better than a frank report of events that
merely happened. Actuality may be the starting point,
and a simulation of the actual the goal, but the inventive
faculty of the artist must be free to impose its own logic
on the episodes it discovers and combines. This is no more
true of the fantasticality of early romance than it is of the
disciplined realism of modern fiction. The episodes invented may be of a different order, but in both types imagination equally asserts its privileges.

This is not equivalent to saying that the narrative habit
has not changed with the lapse of time. By the eighteenth
century the vogue of the marvelous had passed; but episodic
adventures had not lost their power to stimulate the interest of the reader, and the work of Defoe persists to this
day to prove the enduring appeal of work conceived in

this spirit. There have been periodic revivals of the novel of incident and adventure. Even in our sophisticated age the type recurs, but with no indication that the naturalness, the freshness, and the vividness of Defoe will ever be surpassed.

Several considerations incline us to that opinion. Without denying the human qualities that underlie a typical Defoe narrative, and its multiplied touches of penetrating observation, we must recognize that the main interest develops from his report of what happened from point to point of his story. He concentrated all his power upon the incidents, and it is doubtful whether narrative so singularly self-supporting, so independent of contrived plot, analysis, and general reflection can ever be reproduced. As interest in character develops the zest for incident must decline.

There will always be room for the story-teller, but since the unadulterated yarn is so rare in modern literature, and generally so lacking in quality, it will serve our purpose best to study the narrative function in examples where narration is merely contributory to a larger result.

A novel is not a static creation, but is essentially restless and full of movement. Not only must the theme unfold itself, which gives us the idea in motion, but the characters too are in a state of perpetual oscillation, their exits and entrances must be provided for, and the author must constantly intervene to indicate the nature of their activity. What they are doing, why they are doing it, and how, is his perpetual concern. Narrative therefore has to deal not only with the large ordering of the action,—its motion in time and thought—but with an infinity of small detail that has no particular reference to the main action, and may indicate nothing more than the mannerisms or gestures of people in conversation.

"'Say nothing; not a word, not a word, my dearest madam,' urged Mr. Pluck. 'Mrs. Nickleby,' said that excellent gentleman, lowering his voice, 'there is the most trifling, the most excusable breach of confidence in what I am about to say; and yet if my friend Pyke there overheard it—such is that man's delicate sense of honour, Mrs. Nickleby—he'd have me out before dinner-time!'

"Mrs. Nickleby cast an apprehensive glance at the warlike Pyke, who had walked to the window, and Mr. Pluck, squeezing her hand, went on:

"'Your daughter has made a conquest—a conquest on which I congratulate you. Sir Mulberry, my dear Ma'am, Sir Mulberry is her devoted slave. Hem!'

" 'Hah!' cried Mr. Pyke at this juncture, snatching something from the chimney-piece with a theatrical air. 'What is this! What do I behold!' "—*Nicholas Nickleby*.

Action is here indicated, but strictly in subordination to the dialogue, and not for the purpose of shifting the story in place or moving it onward in time. We noted the device in our discussion of dialogue, and the varying skill of authors in turning its difficulties to advantage. The abundance of such intercalated passages in every novel compels our attention. But their contribution to the main action of the story is negligible, and they are often so pictorial in character as to be indistinguishable from description.

It is when we consider narrative in its larger aspects that its structural importance is revealed.

Narrative Perspective—The Handling of Time. A reader is not normally sensible of the difficult problem which the representation of time presents to the writer of fiction. He is often aware of the jolting passage of the years, when clumsy subterfuges are utilized to mask the problem, but when a book flows harmoniously he is not sufficiently conscious of the artful planning that has produced the smooth result. Though dialogue may on occasion be given a retrospective scope, and reflection be made to cast its illumination over the past, it is by the undramatic way of narrative that tracts of time are normally revealed. The older novelists freely used the story-tellers' privileges of clearing their stage of actors and appearing in person before their audience to announce the progress of events. Current writers for the most part adopt the same convention but with increasing reluctance, and if the "stream of consciousness" group have their way all the obligations of continuity and development will be annulled. Time will be annihilated, and past and present will merge themselves in the eternal now of the mind.

The Point of View in Narrative. The method of telling a story in most constant use is the third personal method. The author is responsible for the narration, the description, and the reflection, and loses his identity only in the dialogue. Even here he may not succeed in losing himself if he has a deficient dramatic sense. Next in frequency is the autobiographical method, where an important figure, not necessarily the most important character, assumes the responsibility of narration.

The point of view has such an important structural bearing that I shall dwell with some care on the characteristics of the main methods and touch lightly for the moment on the various modifications that have developed.

Narrative in the Third Person. Here the author is assumed to have complete knowledge of every circumstance affecting his characters, and can even enter their minds at will. For the analytic novelist access to the mental processes of characters is an obvious advantage, and this, therefore, is the habitual method of approach for such writers as George Eliot and George Meredith. But the dangers of "omniscience" are as obvious as the advantages. The author enjoys an almost unlimited freedom in the disposal of his material, yet there is always the risk of obtruding himself to the point of destroying his reader's illusion and deadening the vitality of his report. A convenient means of escape from this difficulty is for the author to set some barriers to his omniscience. Jane Austen's *Emma* may serve as an example of this. Miss Austen tells her story in the third person, but subordinates her point of view to that of Emma. Her mind is conveniently laid bare for us, but Jane Austen's knowledge of the other characters is confined to the reflections of Emma's consciousness. Jane Austen's art is as nearly instinctive as may be. A more conscious effort to secure the same advantages of substituted vision was made by Henry James in *The Ambassadors*, which remains the classical example of the dramatization of a consciousness. In this book the author is almost completely relieved of responsibility.

Narrative in the First Person. We must concede to authors in the preconscious days of fiction the privilege of calculating the effects they wished to produce. We may at least take for granted that they were all desirous of entertaining the audience they wrote for, though our modern mind may occasionally stumble at the terms and conditions of that entertainment. We cannot realize, for example, how so alert a nation as the French could have found liveliness in the prolixity of the romances with which de Gomberville, la Calprenède, and de Scudéry fascinated their century, and even the laborious fullness of the profounder Richardson can be justified only by the large leisure of a bookless and slow-moving age. Though the principle of liveliness may have always prevailed still progress was possible only when a better way of liveliness was found. And similarly with another fixed principle of fiction which changes its aspect with the movement of the years—the principle of credibility. Our ancestors were more gullible than we. An author had but to present his tale of marvels on his own responsibility to conquer the easy faith of his audience. Our credence now is more refractory, and concedes always less to the unsupported statement of an author manipulating his story as it were from the outside.

Daniel Defoe made no claim to be a theorist of fiction. Indeed he despised fiction as idle fabrication, and professed rather to be a chronicler of fact, a plain unvarnished reporter of the truth, a transmitter of things that happened. But this very lack of pretention, confining itself within the desire for vividness and verisimilitude, constitutes him, however unwillingly and unconsciously, a theorist of definite importance, since we can name no structural idea that counts for more in the general scheme of fiction than these principles of vividness and verisimilitude. The devices for securing them are many, but Defoe found instinctively the simplest of them all, and is the first important name in a long line of novelists who have chosen the method of autobiographical narration.

Despite its seeming simplicity and naturalness the first personal device presents the author with a full measure of difficulties, and to obtain a few advantages he must reconcile himself to sacrifices in other directions. Assuming its source in the desire for vividness and plausibility, by applying these tests we can readily estimate the gains and losses of the method. The man to whom things happened is reporting them. He is the pivotal center of the story, and our credulousness should have no further strain set upon it than to accept his version of the facts. But evidently his survey of the field is limited to a personal experience. He has not the all-seeing eye, the all-knowing mind of the unembarrassed third personal novelist, and many important and interesting things must have occurred beyond his range of vision. Whenever he wishes to report of these he must clumsily account for his knowledge. Some one had told him that something had happened to somebody else, and instead of relishing a first-hand experience we are then listening to a diminished version of surmised facts. Even within the range of his personal experience the narrator has obvious limitations set upon him. He is facing outwards to life, and is transcending the permitted scope of his observation if he concerns himself unduly with processes that lie beneath the surface—the thoughts, the motives, the emotions that govern the actions of his peopled world. His own reflections and surmises concerning them of course he can give us. But they can afford to be but shrewd guesses at hidden things, and he can enter into no serious rivalry with the analytic novelist. Nor can he with becoming grace deal too continuously with his own inner life. That he can transmit his own sensations more vividly than a novelist could report them the simple experiment of substituting "he" for "I" in any sensational passage may prove. But it would savor of priggishness if he exposed the operations of his own mind too consecutively.

Whatever be the cause of this dearth of self-analysis in the first personal form of narrative, whether it arises from fear of priggishness or from a desire to concentrate upon episode and adventure, it is unquestionably true that evasion of mental exposure has been a governing principle of this type of fiction to the present time. We have had to wait until our own day to witness notable deviations from the older practice. To Proust and Dorothy Richardson it seemed obvious that nothing could be more interesting or natural than for the narrating center of the book to make his own intelligence the controlling theme. The innovation is merely mentioned here, but we shall learn more about it when we consider some of the modern examples.

Enough has been suggested in a preliminary way on the point of plausibility. A concluding word may be added to what has already been said on the subject of vividness in this form of fiction. The narrator is of necessity constantly remembering and recreating scenes. The action is therefore always retrospective, all the conversations are reconstructed, and we can never surprise the central figure at the moment when events are making their impact upon him. And the main figure must remain at least in partial shadow. We may learn a great deal about him, but he can never turn upon himself the light from other revealing eyes. His tone, his gestures, his features are unrecorded; in short he can never become an *object* of observation.

There is loss and gain therefore in the matter of vividness, but the retrospective cast of the autobiographical story does not seriously impair the immediacy of its appeal, since the reader is perpetually reconstructing a past-present in his mind. We are perhaps now ready for the conclusion that every form has its possibilities and its limitations, its advantages for the obtaining of certain effects and its disadvantages if results are aimed at beyond its scope. When a writer like Proust arrives we are more chary in speaking of limitations, but though there is a pattern discernible in his work by those who seek it diligently it is doubtful if even he can overcome the inherent looseness of the autobiographic form. It is by its nature digressive, prolix, and episodic, and is an ill instrument for an author to employ whose mind is set upon compactness and a rounded coherence.

Narrative, Plot, and Pattern. We have noted as one of the characteristics of fiction the rapidity with which one element merges into another. For that reason I have attempted to describe rather than to define the dominant characteristics of dialogue and narrative, which to this point are the only aspects of fiction we have examined. But here the need of closer definition arises. Our critical vocabulary is so admittedly inadequate and vague that for the purpose of any particular book a writer must indicate with some approach to precision the meaning of his terms. By narration I would imply therefore *the devices by which an author communicates movement to his story*. It concerns itself largely with the selection and the ordering of incident, and under the existing conditions of the art the reader without protest submits to the control of the author in this phase of his activity. Our acquiescence depends in some measure upon the extent of his intervention. For that reason the wary author continually seeks to mask his identity, and we have noted some of the disguises he assumes to achieve that end. His control was formerly less subject to challenge. He could not only invent his series of exciting or illuminating incidents, but he could weave them into such a scheme of complications as to concentrate our interest throughout the first portion of his narrative in the gathering complexity of events, and excite our attention at the close with his skillful unraveling of the interwoven threads. Plotting we might therefore define as a *dexterous manipulation of the action for the purpose of stimulating curiosity*. It is obviously a phase of narrative, but just as obviously narrative may exist with a minimum of plotting. We should always be interested in what is happening, but we need not admit that this legitimate satisfaction of our curiosity is dependent upon an author's desire to bewilder us by his skill in complicating incident. What is legitimate in a mystery novel, and constitutes indeed its main interest, should not dominate our attention in other forms of fiction.

[24]

This statement is less arbitrary than it appears, for it sets no barrier upon the ordering of events in the interests of a comprehensive design where every item is contributory to the total effect, and it concedes a permitted license to the novelist to manipulate his events within modest limits for the purpose of stimulating the curiosity and exciting the suspense of the reader. The protest is merely against the tyranny of the plot and its insidious habit of diverting our attention from considerations that are more natural and more significant. In the drama plot and what I shall presently define as pattern are difficult to distinguish. Design and plot in the drama are almost indistinguishable terms; but the novel as it deviates further from the once dominating plot control of drama tends to depreciate the value of the intrigue element. The danger will present itself that in his desire to avoid an artificial compactness the novelist will proclaim looseness as a virtue and cultivate anarchy in the presumed interests of his art. But this is probably an unfounded fear, for no revolution in method will ever eliminate the need of shaping one's material into a recognizable design.

This brings us to the question of pattern, the significance of which term I have dimly indicated in the last sentence. I have defined it there as "recognizable design." It is, I fear, in our present confused sense of fiction an ideal definition, and I should have been nearer the truth if I had said the design which a competent writer intended to be recognizable but which the reader almost persistently refuses to perceive. Partly our incapacity, and partly our inattention is to blame. We can follow the pattern of an ode or a sonnet. We can grasp the sequence and the consistency of a play. These are forms that readily submit themselves to a comprehensive glance, but a novel is so vast in its scope, so shifting, and so seemingly amorphous in its structure that we content ourselves too readily with momentary effects at the expense of the total impression. The remedy lies with ourselves. The faultless novel does not exist and faulty ones abound, but every generation produces a score at least that are written with the conscience as well as the mind, and where these exist it repays us to follow in the author's footsteps. All his insight and all his skill have been directed to overcome the difficulties of his material. However genially he writes his effects have been planned, and every sentence is a note in the general harmony. We can make many valid excuses for failing to return his effort with effort. There are so many novels; there is so little time. We read the book for an hour one day, and by snatched intervals complete it in a week. How much of the author's calculated planning can our memories retain? We take refuge in the ready excuse that a novel is for recreation and not for labor, and a choked market is our further justification for neglect. Let us make these concessions to necessity, and still admit that if recreation is our aim we shall derive a quite unique pleasure from the rereading of a book of evident power in order to discover what the author put there, and what our first hurried contact failed to reveal. I do not minimize the value of first impressions. The elements of surprise and suspense which the book may contain can never be recovered in their freshness, but there is nothing else which repetition will not enhance, and innumerable niceties of design and cumulative effects will only then strike home to our minds. Of such subtleties is pattern fashioned.

Description. Here at last is a word that would seem to be self-defining. To describe is to stimulate in the reader a sense impression, visual, auditory, tactual, or olfactory, of the object observed, and therefore the mere report of our senses should suffice for a definition of the process. But while no special effort of intelligence is required to recognize description in its more manifest aspects, some alertness is necessary to note the subtle way in which it frequently interpenetrates narrative. We have already indicated the swift merging of elements in fiction, and the fusion point of description with narrative presents us with one of these minor problems of discrimination. This however is a distinction which we may leave to the rhetorician, and pass on to a consideration of the subject which will better repay our attention.

When fiction was establishing itself with Richardson and Fielding the cult of the picturesque had not yet dawned. Scenes, persons, and objects were sketched in with the barest sufficient detail. Obvious appearances were succinctly summarized, and authors were rarely tempted to elaborate a description for the sheer love of describing. Smollett is the exceptional man in his century who achieved his satiric end by the multiplication of telling details, but while there is much significance there is no lift of ecstasy in his descriptive art.

By the time of Scott, and largely indeed owing to his individual effort, the zest for romantic description was widely established. Jane Austen resisted the lure of the picturesque as a value to be sought and cultivated for its own sake. Carlyle fulminated against "view-hunting," as he contemptuously called it, but the authors of the period in England and in France overflowed in descriptive fervor. It was here they felt that they could accumulate their effects, and here above all that they could indulge their propensity for "fine writing." It was on the whole a dangerous tendency and threatened to wrench the novel from its true function of depicting incident or revealing personality. The realists of the succeeding generation— and more particularly in France—maintained the zest for

description, but were relatively careless of pictorial effect
in their conscientious effort to achieve significance. Flaubert succeeded in charging his significance with beauty,
but it was rather the example of Balzac that prevailed with
Zola and his naturalistic school. Unduly obsessed as they
probably were with the idea that men are the automatic
outcome of the two forces of heredity and environment,
the value of setting rose to the dignity of a philosophic or
scientific conception. For some odd reason they attributed
to these influences a prevailingly sordid tinge, with the
result that significance emerged for them only from circumstances of compelling horror and distress. Our mid-
century writers were for the most part free from these
obsessions. Thackeray and Dickens escaped the pressure
of science. George Eliot was measurably a victim, though
she struggled loyally to keep her little flame of idealism
alight. A superficial estimate might associate Hardy more
closely with the uncompromising and pessimistic realism
of the French naturalists. His characters too are enmeshed
in the coil of their environment. His setting therefore is
designed for significance, but we are conscious always of
the sensitive reaction of his pity, and his humor and feeling
for beauty no less than his compassion redeem his work
from any suspicion of sordidness. A closer approximation
to French naturalism we may find in Gissing and Arnold
Bennett. A study of the descriptive element in the latter's
work will reveal his tendency to accumulate detail, and
when we examine his method we may decide whether these
details are as he imagined them to be, significant, or as his
adverse critics judge them to be, irrelevant. He builds up
his masses admittedly with a light hand, but we shall be
compelled to ask whether they illuminate his human beings
or oppress them with the heavy shadows they cast.

As for the younger of the moderns, we can generalize

confidently with regard to certain clearly defined tendencies in the field of description. They have left far behind them the frank obviousness of the early writers. They abjure the pictorial lyric fervors of the romantics, and are indifferent to the more conscientious fullness of the realists. They are dubious of environmental influences, but they are sufficiently alive to the value of an appropriate setting if it is only for the purpose of creating that vague emanation from reality which we designate as atmosphere. The methods are almost as various as the individuals, but nearly always the desired effect is achieved with a most economical expenditure of words. One must be graphic, vivid, suggestive; and to achieve that end only the method that is swiftest in its results will suffice. If we must affix a label to this method "impressionistic realism" will serve as well as any other. In the work of D. H. Lawrence it reached a height of beauty that no former writer has achieved.

Much has been written on the elements of contact and divergence among the arts. It is a heavy question to ventilate here, but without pedantry we may examine a very obvious affiliation between the two forms of descriptive landscape that have words and paint respectively as their medium. An artist with a feeling for literature would be worth many philosophers as an æsthetic interpreter, and an unpublished paper of such an artist, Mr. C. W. Jefferys, R.C.A., has many ideas of definite importance. He notes the purely decorative purpose of the landscape of the early painters whose figure groups are rarely bathed in the same atmosphere. The drawing is usually either minute or unintelligent copying or vague generalization. Things are seen piecemeal, without perspective and void of envelope, so that the figures and the landscape background are not displayed under the same conditions of light and air, nor with a single focus. Atmosphere, sunlight and perspective, linear and aërial, were elements of representation that the painter was slow to learn, and he learned to paint them indoors before he mastered them in the open air.

In the developed landscape periods of both arts we may note fundamental elements of difference more readily than we can detect resemblances. Since literature is an art of sequence the writer is able to describe in detail the progress of an effect in nature, whereas the painter is confined to one transitory moment and can only suggest its preface and its sequel. The painter can look at his scene from only one fixed point, and must have but one focus or center of vision for his picture to which every item is contributory. The writer can sweep the horizon, and can shift his standpoint, but this very freedom leads him sometimes to crowd several pictures into one canvas, and to substitute what may be called a sequence of space for that sequence of time which is his legitimate sphere.

Again, painting being an art of space, the painter sees things as it were simultaneously, and in contact with each other. Hence he pays particular attention to their relations in juxtaposition. Colors exist for him not separately, but as affected by their neighbors, forms are observed only with regard to all the forms within the range of his fixed vision, or the limits of his pictorial composition. By its very limitations his art must be synthetic. The writer, dealing with an art whose essence is movement, passes from object to object, and focussing each in turn is apt to describe them as separate and unrelated. To the painter's eye by virtue of his experienced observation much of the color description in literature must seem to possess this disconnected character. Too often the writer paints colors, not color, and no skill can compensate him for the severe restrictions of the color vocabulary at his command. A painter luckily does not require to find names for his multifarious gradations of tone.

But if painting, in some respects, can convey a more concentrated and complete expression, literature can call upon a wider range of sensations. The painter appeals to but one sense, the writer addresses himself to all. The picture speaks directly to the eye alone, and though it may suggest by the association of ideas, it can report directly only what is seen. The written word records the evidence of all the senses, and conveys suggestions not only of the appearances of things, but of their sounds, scents, taste, and touch. This wide range is not without its dangers, and the force and unity of the literary picture are sometimes lost in the multiplicity of the sensations which the writer attempts to express.

We are in a position now to understand the tardy development of the landscape sense in fiction.

Defoe knows something of geography, he knows something of climate and natural resources; he has not a glimpse of landscape and only a blurred vision of scenery. His trees, like those of the primitive painters, are only trees. He mentions but few species and such only as are of service to him. His rocks are generalized rocks with serviceable caves. His sea-beach exists only to afford a landing place for his cannibal visitors and to receive the impress of that human footprint at which so many thousands have gazed. He is the practical, resourceful, pioneering Briton, who looks at the world with the eye of the trader and knows the value of property.

Fielding's *Tom Jones* is another out-of-doors book. Many of Mr. Jones's adventures take place on the highway, in the fields or woods, or in roadside inns, and he meets with a variety of weather. But there is really very little landscape setting: a road is merely a muddy road, or the wrong road, and the rain confines itself to the artistic function of wetting the hero to the skin. The views we are given are generally hill-top views. "They arrived at the bottom of a very steep hill. Here Jones stopped short, and directing his eyes upwards stood for awhile silent. At length he said, 'Partridge! I wish I was at the top of this hill; it must certainly afford a most charming prospect, especially by this light, for the solemn gloom which the moon casts on all objects is beyond expression beautiful, especially to an imagination which is desirous of cultivating melancholy ideas.' " A mitigating circumstance is that Jones is in love.

Wild and rugged scenery must wait for Scott. We recall Boswell's naïve desire to impress Dr. Johnson with the grandeur of his native landscape. The eighteenth century speaks in the doctor's reply—"that he had noted some considerable protuberances."

Scott, for all his sense of landscape values, does not compose his picture with more skill than Dickens or Charlotte Brontë. Meredith sees vividly, but too lyrically and metaphorically to achieve a firm effect. Hardy is the supreme word painter. He sums up in himself with noticeable additions all the virtues that landscape in fiction had so far developed. He has the firm contour that Meredith lacks. He is true to impression, he has scientific knowledge (something too much of this at times), his landscape is frequently steeped in romantic, legendary, or historical association, it has moods and a soul, it binds itself so intimately with its human inhabitants that they seem as native to it as the grass itself. Of all English novelists he seems to come nearest to the painter's view of landscape. He has true observation, he sees tones and colors correctly, and his color vocabulary indicates that he sees color as an artist does, that is relatively. His architectural training perhaps prompted him to construct his landscape with a profound knowledge of its anatomy, and his focus is rarely confused. His rendering of Egdon Heath is an often quoted instance of his power. The chapter in the same book, in which Eustacia dies, Gabriel Oak's sensing of the coming storm in *Far from the Madding Crowd*, and passages almost at random from *Tess of the Durbervilles* or *The Woodlanders* illustrate the qualities which this paragraph has assigned to him.

Analysis. The analytic curve in fiction can be plotted as clearly as the descriptive curve, but "analysis" is on the whole a more difficult matter to treat. We generally mean by the term the novelist's attempt to represent the motives and the conscious or unconscious thought processes of the characters to whom he sees fit to apply the test. It is therefore an important element in characterization. The extent and manner of its use differ greatly from age to age, and from author to author. Save for Richardson the eighteenth century is almost innocent of this device. It is an expedient sparingly used by Scott, more subtly and extensively by Jane Austen. Neglected by Thackeray and Dickens it is further developed by the Brontës, George Eliot, and Meredith. Henry James was still more lavish in its use, and in our time every novelist considers himself to be a qualified psychologist, interested mainly in the morbid anatomy of the soul, and threading his way through its obscurest labyrinths with at least an assumed confidence in his general direction.

Is it life then we ask or merely art which grows more introspective and analytic with the passing of the years? The novel is without denial increasingly addicted to analysis. Shakespeare's divination of motives was a glaring anachronism; but in fiction we need pass only from Defoe and Smollett to Henry James and Mrs. Virginia Woolf to realize the distance traversed. Our writers are satisfying therefore a growing desire for applied psychology, but we cannot rest so satisfied that they are reflecting the characteristics of the contemporary world. Indeed the multiplication of external physical and mechanical resources in modern life has made the habit of meditation more precarious than in the leisured past. We must therefore attribute our changed literary mood mainly to the pressure of scientific study in the region of psychology.

Something must be conceded also to the aid which analysis presumably offers to characterization. If we are convinced that fiction's most important function is to illustrate human character in action and in repose, in isolation and in association, we must welcome any new instrument of precision, provided we have faith both in its efficacy and in its manipulation. We are content to sacrifice something of the speed of action for the enriched knowledge we obtain of the actors. In our normal experience as human beings we have no opportunity to probe the depths of personality. We satisfy ourselves with sometimes clear but always limited conceptions of character. We can forecast a friend's reaction to certain circumstances, but our judgment of his probable behavior rests upon a rapid intuition. We do not formulate the psychic processes by which he governs his actions or shapes his verbal response to the situation. Moreover he is usually himself not aware of any such psychic preparation, and act and speech are with him alike instinctive. Our odd conclusion then is that a novelist essays to give us a completer rendering of character than our experience can offer, and further that this presentation, convincing as it may be, does not rest on any observed facts of our normal life. An occasional writer is aware of this and is content, for probability's sake, to make his thought index neither too consecutive nor too profound.

[34]

Among the interesting things, therefore, that the student of fiction should note is the differing quality of the analytic content, and the extent of its employment from book to book. The best practitioners are careful to limit themselves in this respect, and are content to "go behind" only a selected few of their characters. Miss Dorothy Richardson thinks herself entitled to dip into only one mind, Miriam's—or her own. Henry James gives us many important characters who are not analyzed at all—the Princess Casamassima and Milly Theale for example; and Mr. Galsworthy who never wearies of probing the harassed Soames Forsyte, not once permits himself to be directly familiar with Irene's consciousness.

The analytic process, then, for good or for ill has invaded the novel. We may conclude that skillfully used it reveals character more subtly if not more vividly than speech or narrative without its support can do. But everything in letters as in life is paid for with a price. Analysis does not seriously get in the way of dialogue, for being itself a kind of spiritual monologue it serves as a half way house to speech. But it paralyzes narrative vigor, and in its presence action languishes. This is a loss which for the ordinary reader has no adequate compensation. Such a reader will probably decide that Henry James gets excited by the wrong things, and will turn with infinite relief to the late lamented Edgar Wallace.

Before deciding how far dramatic effect suffers by the analytic invasion we must reconsider the legitimate relationship of drama to fiction, and also the varied forms that analysis is capable of assuming.

Let us be frank with ourselves and admit that drama and fiction are separate arts and cannot effectively be reconciled. The interaction of their influence is at once legitimate and possible, and it is obvious that the preponderant influence has been from drama to fiction rather than the reverse. Fielding was a dramatist before he was a novelist, and it was highly natural that when he girded himself for his greatest effort, *Tom Jones*, he should have utilized the expedients which his other craft had taught him. He may have conceived of the novel as a "comic epic in prose," but insensibly he availed himself of dramatic devices. His incidents are dramatic only in a farcical way, but his plot is essentially a dramatist's plot. It was no casual judgment of Coleridge's that ranked it with *Œdipus Rex* and *The Alchemist* as one of the three most perfect plots in literature. Exposition, complication, suspense, extrication would satisfy the pit's most exacting demands, were we to subtract something by reason of the necessitated leisurely movement which the amplitude of fiction requires. There can never be the same impact of immediacy, or the vividness of the flesh and blood presence.

Masters of the craft today set little value on these artificial complications of intrigue, and while they profess their eagerness to work dramatically they are relatively indifferent to the physical thrill which flows from exciting incidents. What justification then have they for assuming that they work with dramatic intention?

Their assumption seems to be that a novel is dramatic to the extent that the novelist lets the story unfold itself with the minimum of ostensible intervention from the once ubiquitous, ever present, and all knowing author. In dialogue this concealment is possible, and dialogue therefore counts as a major dramatic resource. It may be low-pitched and unexciting. It is sufficient that the voice be set in a ventriloquist key, and that the author's lips do not obviously move.

Description is dramatic to the extent that it becomes an experience of an actor in the piece. The presentation of

narrative action affords more dramatic difficulty in proportion as the author refuses the excitement of critical
situations. His resource then is only the milder shock of
an intellectual predicament, since moral predicaments have
lost their vogue.

The analytic problem remains. We have concluded that
analysis is hostile to action. Can it conceivably be made
dramatic is the question we now consider.

Here again our concern must be with the degree of the
author's ostensible intervention. He can achieve a species
of subjective objectivity if he occupies a character's mind.
It may be the zig-zag thinking we are offered of the psycho-
analytic group, or the more consecutive processes of the
Jamesian school; the claim is in either case that it is possible
to dramatize a consciousness.

Looking back over the field of fiction we can estimate
in how far this genuine illusion of inwardness has been
achieved. For the sake of argument we will consider the
effect to be weakly dramatic, though the theater offers remarkably few examples of the process. In the rudimentary
stages of analysis this inwardness was rarely attained.
Richardson's letter device was a good substitute, but his
contemporaries exemplify only the external approach to
states of mind. The occasions when we occupy a character's mind in Fielding are astonishingly rare. Perhaps
the author says that he will now tell us what Sophia is
thinking of, but it is patently the author telling us, and
he is very happy when he is off after other game. That
uncanny genius Jane Austen made a closer approximation
to analytic inwardness. George Eliot and George Meredith
were the earliest authors to make conscious and systematic
use of the device, and what was their practice? For a
paragraph we occupy a mind. Then the author sets us at
a slight remove, informs us merely of the cerebral state,

and is off on his own account with some generalized philosophic reflection that is purely excrescent from the story. Today a more consistent inwardness has the cry, but there occasionally comes a sufficiently modern author like Lawrence who does not shy at the old tradition. But his personal annotation is vivid, brief, and penetrating.

If I have not made out a satisfactory case for the dramatic possibilities of analysis, I have perhaps made sufficiently clear the extent to which unguarded analysis can be defiantly undramatic.

PART TWO

Chapter III

THE EIGHTEENTH-CENTURY ADVANCE

The intelligent people of Tudor England had standards of excellence which the modern mind sometimes finds difficult to grasp. Lyly's *Euphues* for example seems as monstrous to us today as our annual best seller would appear to an Elizabethan. And it is for us hopelessly antiquated for three sufficient reasons—the pedantry of its style, the strained absurdity of situations and incidents that purport to represent reality, and the undisguised zeal of its author for edification at all costs.

If we examine these reasons in order, we may readily discover the direction which fiction must take in order to rank on a level of importance with poetry and poetic drama which had reached a basis of perfection at a vastly earlier date.

Language is the instrument of literature, and for reasons I need not here explain (were it possible) our poetic speech had acquired its pitch and tune and flexibility while our prose was still heavy and uncertain in its movement. For the perfection of the prose instrument flexibility and clearness were required, and these were not a common possession until Dryden late in the seventeenth century made them current. Some people explain this by the growing influence of French writers who had long since mastered the art of prose expression, and yet another explanation is afforded by the constitution of the Royal Society and the demand for clearness of exposition which marked its proceedings. Whatever the cause, prose utterance more clear and flexible has never been found than in the works of Swift and Steele and Addison and Defoe, and in the Queen Anne writers in general.

The second point concerns the degree of realism in situation and incident. Fantastic romance is today the exception where it was once the rule, for fiction aims now at an intensification of reality rather than at an escape from the actual. If we must occasionally have our marvels we insist on recognizing them as marvelous. The general progress of fiction has been from the impossible through the possible to the probable, and we expect our novelists now to lie strenuously but to lie like truth. The anti-romantic, rationalizing, eighteenth-century mind made this transition possible, and it is therefore to this generative century that we shall be well advised to look for the germs of the modern novel.

Lyly's *Euphues* and Sidney's *Arcadia* are unreadable today for the third sufficient reason that their moral intention was too frankly proclaimed. We recognize freely enough that the novel at its best must concern itself with the discipline of life, but the modern reader is chilled to the marrow by the obtrusive sermonizing which appears to have been our ancestors' chief delight.

Nothing comes quite by chance in this hard-working world, and it is evident that the elements of the novel had to shape themselves by a process of gradual evolution. The final formula of perfection will of course never be discovered, because the elements of which the novel is fashioned are so numerous as to permit of almost endless combination, and the final flavor is always contributed by the personality of the author. No one man can be proclaimed as the ancestor of the modern novel, but it is safe to assert that three men were responsible for giving it a strong impetus in the modern direction. These three men were Defoe, Richardson, and Fielding, and each of them more or less accidentally blundered into fiction. Defoe had been a merchant, a pamphleteer and a politician for a long and harassed life, with always a journalist's keen scent for copy. He traveled down to Bristol one day to get Alexander Selkirk's story which people were talking about. When he was almost sixty he gave the world *Robinson Crusoe*, and finding fictitious narratives based on truth so easy he wrote between sleeping and waking *Moll Flanders, Colonel Jack, Captain Singleton,* and *Roxana*, the first and last of which are masterpieces of vivid narration which no modern writer has surpassed. Samuel Richardson was a successful printer with no thoughts of authorship more ambitious than the compiling of love letters for confiding servant girls. When he was fifty years of age a publishing firm asked him to prepare a kind of model letter-writer for the use of "those country readers who were unable to indite for themselves." Out of this proposal came *Pamela or Virtue Rewarded* (1740), and so dazzling was its success that there promptly followed *Clarissa* which took not only England but Europe by storm, and the gravely proper *Sir Charles Grandison*. Chance played an equal part in the advent of Henry Fielding. The drama was the chosen outlet of his energies, but Walpole's Licensing Act of 1737 closed his theater and diverted him to the desultory practice of law. Sheer annoyance at the brand of virtue inculcated in *Pamela* prompted him to write the rejoinder *Joseph Andrews* which began as a parody and found its own independent value when the inimitable Parson Adams entered the story. Fielding had now discovered his *métier*, and the element of chance no longer presided over the creation of *Jonathan Wild, Tom Jones,* and *Amelia*.

Defoe never intended to be nor thought himself a novelist. The term was one of discredit in his day. *Crusoe* he called an allegory. *Moll Flanders, Colonel Jack, Captain*

Singleton, The Journal of the Plague, and the *Memoirs of a Cavalier* he considered to be true histories, that is to say authenticated facts in an artistic setting. In his *Family Instructor,* novels and romances are grouped with plays and songs and "such like stuff." He had no concern with the deeper springs of human character, and of the art of combination he was equally innocent. Still his work registers a remarkable advance in the art of fiction which he professed to despise. And if we take him at his own valuation, not as a novelist but as a mere writer of lively memoirs, he still taught the novelist the most important item of his craft. In his ability to create the illusion of reality Defoe is a supreme master, and in the art of "grave and imperturbable lying" he has had no rival. It was from him that Swift learned the value of minute and seemingly trivial detail, and all subsequent masters of the realistic process are consciously or not his followers.

The old trick of moralizing survives, but with a curious twist in his work. *Moll Flanders* and *Roxana* are outspoken to a degree of frankness which modern fiction might envy, but the books are carefully peppered with edifying passages of high morality. Mr. Orlo Williams in *Some Great English Novels* has a good word to say on the subject:

"No doubt his public was more than satisfied, and failed, as he intended, to observe that, while artistically quite convincing, Roxana's heart-searchings are wholly devoid of any suasory effect, but show, on the contrary, that periods of nocturnal remorse will never cause the abandonment of completely successful daily practice. The twinges of the soul, as of the liver, have very transitory effects while things are going well. So far, then, by the ingenious importation of a conventional moral, Defoe indulged the childishness of mind which, in all of us and in all ages, long outlasts physical adolescence; but so far only. In all the rest of the things he recorded and in those he admitted, in his pauses and his rapid transitions, in his portrayal of manners, in his view of character, in the spare but firm simplicity of his prose and in the whole imaginative scale upon which he handles his narrative—he wrote as for minds which, like his own, had reached maturity. Such minds would not be deceived by specious triviality, but would respond to clean outline, significant detail and the delight of those deft but unexpected touches, the secrets of only great artists, which give life, unobtrusively and inimitably, to the work of art."

Chapter IV

RICHARDSON AND THE EPISTOLARY NOVEL

If we do not deal with Richardson in the measure of his deserts, it is only because the form he cultivated now seems dead beyond all hope of resuscitation. The books of this type that have had a somewhat precarious survival to the present day are Richardson's *Pamela, Clarissa,* and *Sir Charles Grandison;* Smollett's *Humphrey Clinker;* and Frances Burney's *Evelina.*

Pamela appeared in 1740, but we must reject the popular notion that this date is the birthday of epistolary fiction. Its antecedents go back a hundred years or more, and have been interestingly traced out by Singer in *The Epistolary Novel* and in a paper by Helen Sard Hughes in *The Manly Anniversary Studies.* Miss Hughes notes by way of preliminary the marked increase in letter writing consequent upon the establishment of an Inland Post System in 1635, and successive improvements which culminate in the organization in 1680 of the London Penny Post. Manuals of letter writing became increasingly popular. There is one, for example, by Angel Day (1586), "The English Secretarie, wherein is contayned a perfect method for the enditing of all manner of Epistles and familiar letters," and numerous manuals followed for the instruction of "young learners," "each degree of women," "a person of the meanest capacity," etc.

Richardson, we may remember, had constituted himself the scribe in ordinary of all the illiterate females in distress who applied to him for aid. "I cannot tell you what to write," said one girlish applicant, "but you cannot write too kindly." And so by an easy and natural gradation we come to the time when at the age of fifty he was invited by Messrs. Rivington and Osborn to compile a kind of model letter-writer for the use of "those country readers who were unable to indite for themselves." Thus *Pamela or Virtue Rewarded* came into the world and was described by its author as "a series of familiar letters from a beautiful young damsel to her parents, published in order to cultivate the principles of virtue and religion in the youth of both sexes."

Letter fiction for a hundred years before *Pamela* had based itself mainly on four stock conventions: (1) The rifled post-bag, (2) Letters of travel, (3) Letters between the friend in the country and the friend in the town, (4) The correspondence of lovers.

The first device yields no literary result of importance. The second was more fruitful in France than in England, in which last named country Smollett's *Humphrey Clinker* affords us the one distinguished example. The third convention is in part responsible for Miss Burney's *Evelina*. It is to the fourth device, the correspondence of lovers, that Miss Hughes attaches most importance for the genesis of the full fledged epistolary novel. Many titles of forgotten books are given, but more particular emphasis is laid on a paper by John Hughes in *The Spectator*, No. 375, of May 10, 1712. This is *The History of Armanda*, which gives mainly through the medium of letters, "A scene of distress in private life." Domestic interests are here combined with the love motive, so that Richardson's task nearly thirty years later was largely a matter of amplification. He is an originator in so far as he was the first writer to employ letters for purposes of narration on so extended a scale, and, may we not add? because he was the first writer of genius in England to utilize the device.

Let us consider now the degree of adaptability of the letter form to the purpose of fiction.

It is undeniably a natural mode of expression when postal facilities permit us to abridge distance, but many modifications of normal letter-writing are necessary if coherence and continuity are to be aimed at, and variety achieved. A good letter-writer pours himself out with comparative unreserve to a congenial correspondent. He writes of the major and minor concernments of his daily life, he describes, he comments, he jests, he prattles. But he does not weave a concerted story, and he never seeks variety by reproducing conversations at any length. Now the first thing one notes is that the letter novelist insists on certain conventional privileges. He must be allowed to tell a story with some continuity of development and some degree of complication. And also in order to secure variety he must combine the letters of various people, and render them dramatic by copious dashes of conversation. I think the reader concedes these conventions willingly enough, and responds quite as readily to the novelist's attempt to secure variety by the conversational device, and by the characteristically different flavor that he communicates to the many pens that he enlists in his service. The letter novelists of the eighteenth century are at one in their copious use of conversation. But they vary considerably in the value that they attach to plot interest, in the skill with which they contrive to make their letters flow naturally from the circumstances presented, and in the measure of their ability to differentiate the tone and style of their desk-chained victims. Richardson is more concerned than the others with extricating his main characters from a desperate situation, either happily as in Pamela's case or tragically as in Clarissa's. He gives us one main problem with infinite subsidiary modifications. The result is therefore of necessity monotonous, and he secures his intensity of effect by unremitting pressure on the same raw wound. Smollett has the faintest of plots in *Humphrey Clinker*, and Frances Burney's *Evelina* is relatively plotless until the highly conventionalized close when all the old melodramatic *clichés* are utilized for the happy solution.

Smollett is more successful than the others in varying the tone of his letters, and both Smollett and Frances Burney are more satisfactory than Richardson in the way their letters arise naturally out of the occasion. Smollett sets a small group of people on their travels, and quite spontaneously they give their friends descriptively vivid accounts of the episodes of their journey. The same place and the same conditions are often as not described, but there is no risk of confusing the accounts as given by Matthew Bramble, Lydia, Winifred Jenkins, or the Squire. Evelina writes copiously to her guardian, as she naturally should, to describe a young country girl's first sensations of town excitements. We cannot give Pamela or Clarissa the same justifications, and much unintentional comedy derives from Richardson's cumbersome efforts to account for their letter-writing ardor, or even to make it possible. They are both jealously guarded prisoners. Both devise ingenious postal arrangements, and both are capable of driving their pens with accelerated energy in the mid-throes of an emotional crisis. Pamela foresees this need of expression when she is removed from the kindly protection of Mrs. Jervis. The "good Mr. Longman gave me above forty sheets of paper, a dozen pens, and a little phial of ink, which last I wrapped in paper, and put in my pocket, with some wax and wafers." She falls on evil days with Mrs. Jewkes, and is compelled to a variety of

cunning evasions. "No sooner was her back turned, than
I set about hiding a pen of my own here, and another there,
and a little of my ink in a broken china cup, and a little in
another cup, and a sheet of paper here and there among
my linen; with a little wax and a few papers in several
places, lest I should be searched." The letters multiply
more rapidly than they can be despatched. "I begin to be
afraid my writings may be discovered; for they grow large.
I stitch them hitherto in my under coat, next my linen.
If this brute should search me! but I must try to please her
and then she won't."

The messenger by whom she often despatched her mis-
sives had betrayed his trust and she is soon aware that her
master has penetrated all her secrets. She writes so beau-
tifully that he urges her on to her beloved task, and even
when her father has arrived to protect her interests she
is prevailed upon to write to her mother a full report of
events which she will hear detailed on her husband's
return. It is the zest of an artist that now possesses her.
"I have got such a knack of writing, that when by myself, I cannot sit without a pen in my hand."

From this kind of clumsiness Miss Burney and Smollett
are free. Needless to say that from Richardson's incontestable merits they are likewise free. As a generating
influence no other English novelist can compare with him,
and this fact must weigh with us in our final estimate.
We remember some of the echoes of the praise that rang
through Europe. Rousseau asserted that nothing approach-
ing *Clarissa* had been written in any language. Diderot
is even more dithyrambic, and places the book on the
same shelf with Moses, Homer, Euripides, and Sophocles.
England had presently the rival reputation of Fielding to
consider, but the balance inclined in Richardson's favor
for a century, and it was not in a spirit of satire that Pope

exclaimed of *Pamela* that it "would do more good than many volumes of sermons." Richardson's importance then we must perforce concede, but it is an absorbed influence that he now wields, and it is only indirectly that he operates on the analytically inclined novelist of today. More actively influential in the sense that he is more constantly read is a novelist whose methods are as different as if a hundred years had divided them.

Chapter V

HENRY FIELDING AND *TOM JONES*

The prejudice against Fielding is yielding at last to a more reasonable sentiment. He is still a sealed book for readers who wince at Aristophanes and have no relish for Rabelais, who rashly identify vitality of animal spirits with licentiousness, and whose shrinking sensitiveness shivers at the gusty humors of this intemperate tribe.

Fielding, though less boisterously imaginative, is still of their line, and like them has failed of his effect precisely with those readers who would seem to have had most to gain from him. Even in his own day his frankness was not wholly acceptable, if we may judge from Richardson's ill-tempered comment on the "lowness" of his characters, and from the allegations and innuendos of personal misconduct set in circulation by his literary and political enemies. This legend of loose behavior reflecting itself in the wantonness of his books, or even naïvely transferred from the books to the life, bade fair at one time to establish itself as the fixed tradition. It required only to be exposed to be exploded, and this his latest biographer, Professor Wilbur Cross, has most effectively done. For their material, he tells us, Fielding's enemies drew largely from his own writings. "Many of the plays and all the novels took the reader into low life among people guilty of crime and all sorts of moral offences. Sex instinct was often perverted or subject to no control. . . . When hardly more than a boy he wrote as if he were the young Wilding of *The Temple Beau* and the Luckless of *The Author's Farce;* and in the poems which he then addressed to Sir Robert

Walpole he was the poor poet starving in a garret besieged by creditors. Subsequently all the follies and vices of Mr. Wilson, Tom Jones, and Captain Booth were transferred to him. Into his life must have come a Lady Bellaston, a Miss Matthews, and numerous other accidental women. . . . He was even identified with Jonathan Wild, as if he had been in his youth a pickpocket or a receiver of stolen goods. . . . He was in turn therefore not only every bad character in his works, but the bad qualities of all of them were combined by his enemies into an immoral monster who was labelled Henry Fielding. He might protest, as he often did, against this usage, but it was in vain. He was described as ill-natured and quarrelsome; he was a broken wit, a sponger on the great, a shifty politician ready to write on either side for money, a rake, a libertine, and a corrupt justice." His earliest biographer, Arthur Murphy, was an irresponsible scatter-brain, who sought to offset this malignity by anecdotal triviality. "When he had contracted," says Murphy, "to bring on a play, or a farce, it is well known by many of his friends now living that he would go home rather late from a tavern, and would, the next morning, deliver a scene to the players written upon the papers which had wrapped the tobacco in which he so much delighted." He adds that three mornings usually went to the making of a farce. Since his ordinary plays averaged nearly 20,000 words, not only must his speed of composition have been terrific, but his consumption of tobacco unprecedented, a simple calculation producing the result of 186 pipefuls a day!

Another anecdote from Murphy that has found its way into literary history indicates a lack of prudential restraint so characteristic of genius at large that we must regret the unreliability of its source. After his marriage to Miss Craddock, Fielding retired to the small estate at East Stour which he had inherited from his mother. It was his intention to bid farewell to the stage and all the follies of the town. "But unfortunately," continues Murphy, "a kind of family-pride here gained an ascendant over him, and he began immediately to vie in splendour with the neighbouring squires. With an estate not much above two hundred pounds a year, and his wife's fortune, which did not exceed fifteen hundred pounds, he encumbered himself with a large retinue of servants all clad in costly yellow liveries. For their master's honour, these people could not descend so low as to be careful in their apparel, but in a month or two were unfit to be seen; the Squire's dignity required that they should be new-equipped; and his chief pleasure consisting in society and convivial mirth, hospitality threw open his doors, and in less than three years, entertainments, hounds and horses, entirely devoured a little patrimony, which, had it been managed with economy, might have secured to him a state of independence for the rest of his life."

I confess that I fondly cling to those charming yellow liveries, which produce in their reckless multiplication so vivid a picture of indigent magnificence. To live as nearly within your means as a cramped income will permit you to do, and to labor without stop or stay to meet your obligations satisfies neither contemporary gossip nor the picturesque cravings of posterity. There is however just enough of credible legend surviving to save Fielding from the imputation of drab respectability, and there is no reason to suspect the truth of Lady Mary Wortley Montagu's account of her cousin many years after his death: "He loved his wife passionately, and she returned his affection; yet led no happy life, for they were almost always miserably poor, and seldom in a state of quiet and safety. All the world knows what was his imprudence; if even he possessed a score of pounds nothing could keep him from lavishing it idly, or make him think of to-morrow. Sometimes they were living in decent lodgings with tolerable comfort; sometimes in a wretched garret without necessaries; not to speak of the spunging-houses and hiding places where he was occasionally to be found."

Here is our justification, if we insist upon it, for reinstating those irresistible yellow liveries, which will not keep out of the picture, repaint it how we may. Our concern is quite obviously not with an ascetic, a saint, or an idealist, but with a man overflowing with the exuberance of life, the *homme sensuel moyen* of the eighteenth century, differentiated only from the normal type by the accident of genius. It is at once impertinent and inept to cavil at his manner of life. Alter his habit of thought, reduce the variety and vigor of his contacts, turn inward the gaze of those eyes which penetrated so piercingly into the spectacle of the world, and you will purge his books of much of their grossness, but in the process of purgation you will rob them also of those qualities which preserve so vividly for posterity the tone and temper of the age that produced them. The best criticism of Fielding has always insisted on this representative value of his work, and no authority carries more weight than that of Leslie Stephen, the most systematic and thorough student of eighteenth-century thought in our day. "Fielding announces that his object is to give a faithful picture of human nature. Human nature includes many faculties which had an imperfect play under the conditions of the time; there were dark sides to it, of which, with all his insight, he had but little experience, and heroic impulses which he was too much inclined to treat as follies. But the more solid constituents of that queer compound, as they presented themselves under the conditions of the time, were never more clearly revealed in any observer. A complete criticism of the English artistic literature of the eighteenth century would place Fielding at the centre and measure the completeness of other representatives pretty much as they recede from or approach to his work. Others, as Addison and Goldsmith, may show finer qualities of workmanship and more delicate sentiment; but Fielding more than anyone gives the essential—the very form and pressure of the time."

Let us dismiss therefore as mere idle impertinence and as chiefly false all the malevolent insinuations that have been leveled at Fielding in his character as a man, and concern ourselves as it is our duty to do with the books by which we truly know him. Are they gross we ask ourselves and are they immoral? Without casuistry I would assert that they are palpably gross, and at the same time unmistakably moral in intention and in effect. It is quite possible that a sensitive reader should be so repelled by their coarseness as to be blinded both to the intention and the result. Such a reader prefers, and one cannot argue with a temperament, to find his morality associated with a more refined representation of life. His personal scheme of morality may also be founded on a different scale of values, which would consign to the lowest depths of the Inferno such vices of exuberance and irrestraint as Dante's sinners expiate in the milder torments of the first circle. I can only answer that if Fielding is an immoral writer, our sentence of excommunication must be extended to embrace the reputations of many writers of genius who have profoundly influenced the course of the world's thought.

Coleridge had this problem in his mind when he made the following remark on Rabelais, which presents us with the clue to lead us out of the labyrinth. "The morality of his work is of the most refined and exalted kind; as for the manners, to be sure, I cannot say much."

If we are not too preoccupied with the non-essentials of morality, we shall not rashly conclude that an author who reproduces the manners of an age that is not so successful as our own in the arts of concealment is thereby incapable of appreciating the virtues that lift men above the level of the brute. It is pruriency and insincerity that are the unpardonable sin in art, the false conception, the perverted portrait. A monster of iniquity may thus be a moral creation, though it does not necessarily follow that his activities will make pleasant reading. The doctrine I have enunciated may seem to err on the side of liberality. May I add as a corrective that the viciousness and brutality of human nature are themes which only the profoundest minds should venture to explore, and also as a corollary that frankness and fearlessness lead art further along the path of truth than the timid evasiveness that shies at every specter by the wayside?

It is an interesting task to determine the qualities in an author that make for permanence. The works of fiction that have weathered the ages are fortunately not so numerous as by their multitude to baffle our investigation, and we may hazard therefore some general statements that will lead us towards a solution. The novel being a record of human activities, that author is assured of his certificate of immortality who can pour the fullest tide of life through his pages, who can create the most diverse world of credible human beings, and among these a few figures so genially conceived as to triumph over all known laws of mortality and decay. Fielding will survive because he has created such a world, and his Parson Adams is one of those companionable figures that posterity lodges in its heart.

A creative faculty so energetic as his generates not only

[57]

this large vision of reality but imposes upon it also those laws of harmonious adjustment which we call art. If we judge him on the mere ground of his executive capacity the importance of Fielding will tend rather to grow than to diminish. He was a pioneer who had to shape his own instruments to turn unbroken ground. He was in a sense a disciple of Cervantes, but the model that he proposed to himself to follow was a non-existent comic epic in prose which legend attaches to the name of Homer. His developed sense of the theater carried him successfully through his first venture *Joseph Andrews*. A native satiric gift nourished on the brilliant performance of Swift produced his second masterpiece *Jonathan Wild*, one of the best sustained examples of irony our literature contains. In *Tom Jones* he put forth his united powers, and few books in our language surpass it in the harmonious diversity of the qualities it combines. *Amelia* has its company of admirers, and though I refuse to concede with Thackeray its supremacy among the novels, it is still a solid angle-stone of his great quadrilateral.

Professor Saintsbury finds in these famous four all that was necessary for future fiction. That again is an estimate which demands important eliminations. Virtues of so positive a kind must somewhere pay their penalty. The breadth of his manner does not preclude many strokes of delicate observation, nor are sympathy or even tenderness alien to his robust common-sense philosophy. Yet many subtleties escape him, and Richardson rather than Fielding must rank as the ancestor of those who choose to explore the complexities of our tortured mortality. But our modern realists cannot afford to neglect an author whom neither timidity restrains nor pruriency incites, and a generation that is not wholly free from the taint of morbidity and in whom self-inquisitiveness has developed into a disease

[58]

may turn to Fielding with profit and find in him a salutary corrective.

In *Tom Jones* we seem to have arrived at one of the pivotal books of the century. It has such lively powers of resistance to the encroachments of time that I am heartened to present the following all too dry analysis.

Theme and Author's Intention. The author relates the life story of Tom Jones from childhood to early manhood, and it lies also within the scope of his purpose to present to his readers a comprehensive account of English life in the middle of the eighteenth century. He proposes to be perfectly frank in his exposition of contemporary manners, and to reserve to himself the privilege of moral comment where the indiscretions or knaveries of his characters demand it.

Conditions of Composition. We should bear in mind that Fielding began his career as novelist in definite rivalry with Richardson. His dramatic works had been forcibly ended by Walpole's Licensing Act of 1737. He then turned to law and journalism, and sketched the first draft of his *Jonathan Wild*, which appeared in the third volume of his *Miscellanies* in 1743, with portions obviously composed subsequent to the appearance of his first published novel *Joseph Andrews* (1742). This book was begun in conscious parody of Richardson's *Pamela or Virtue Rewarded* (1740). Fielding's detestation of hypocrisy compelled him to discover many elements of calculation in Pamela's vaunted chastity. His familiarity with dramatic technique prejudiced him also against Richardson's epistolary method of narration, and in *Tom Jones* (1749) we find the culmination of this moral and artistic protest. Appearing only a few months after *Clarissa* it cannot properly be considered a rejoinder to that famous book; but Richardson was always eager to communicate the details of his work to his circle of female friends, and we must remember that Fielding's sister Sarah was one of this confidential and admiring group. In this indirect way, therefore, he was aware of the contents of Richardson's masterpiece. The similarities of the plots in any event are scarcely less remarkable than the divergence of treatment. Clarissa elopes with the man she loves in order to escape an odious marriage. Lovelace reveals the full hatefulness of his character and the heroine dies of a broken heart. Sophia Western flees from home rather than marry the detested Blifil. Tom's reckless libertinage disturbs her, but he eventually proves his worth and is reconciled to his uncle and Squire Western. The happy end of this novel in the marriage of the two lovers is in designed contrast with the tragic close of *Clarissa*.

His General Method. The *Joseph Andrews* preface is an important document. Fielding announces there his intention of establishing a new type of fiction which he describes as a "comic epic poem in prose; differing from comedy, as the serious epic from tragedy: its action being more extended and comprehensive; containing a much larger circle of incidents, and introducing a greater variety of characters." He wishes to avoid the extravagance of burlesque except occasionally in the diction: "Surely a certain drollery in style, where characters and sentiments are perfectly natural no more constitutes the burlesque than an empty pomp and dignity of words, where everything else is mean and low, can entitle any performance to the appellation of the true sublime." . . . The Ridiculous only falls within my province in the present work" and "The only source of the true Ridiculous is affectation which proceeds from one of these two causes, vanity or hypocrisy." Fielding here announces himself as a comic satirist. If we turn to his Invocation Chapter in *Tom Jones* (Bk. XIII, Ch. I) we find him ranging himself confidently in the human family with which his genius gave him kinship: "Teach me, which to thee is no difficult task, to know mankind better than they know themselves. Remove that mist which dims the intellects of mortals, and causes them to adore men for their art, or to detest them for their cunning, in deceiving others, when they are, in reality, the objects only of ridicule, for deceiving themselves. Strip off the thin disguise of wisdom from self-conceit, of plenty from avarice, and of glory from ambition. Come, thou that hast inspired thy Aristophanes, thy Lucian, thy Cervantes, thy Rabelais, thy Molière, thy Shakespeare, thy Swift, thy Marivaux, fill my pages with humour, till mankind learn the good-nature to laugh only at the follies of others, and the humility to grieve at their own."

Organization. The novel is divided into three parts, each consisting of six books. The first six books lay the foundation of the story, and cover the time preceding Tom's birth to his unjust banishment by Allworthy. The second part describes the several adventures of Tom and Sophia on their journey from Glastonbury to London. Adventures abound and nearly all contribute to the development of the plot. The last six books cover but little time, but are replete with incident. Fielding had many problems left in suspense for his *dénouement.* He must punish Tom for his breaches of good conduct, reveal the fundamental goodness of his character, lay bare the intrigues against him, and disclose the mystery of his birth. All this is done with great art, and the book ends happily with the marriage of Tom and Sophia.

To this point the confidences that we have shared with the author have helped our understanding of the book and its intention. The intellectual lineage which he has established for himself, except for the dubious inclusion of

[61]

Marivaux who worked always for delicacy rather than breadth, prepares us for a somewhat liberal interpretation of the moral code with its attendant disregard of conventional decencies. His ambition to produce a comic epic in prose implies a regard for varied movement artfully organized (we have noted the three parts each with six book divisions), and it grants him also a permitted lapse into the region of burlesque. But he has curiously scanted his indebtedness to the method of drama which counts for so much in the fashioning of his plot with its elements of exposition, preparation, complication, surprise, suspense, and extrication. The book's controlled abundance is a constant source of power. For all its sprawling length it shows surprisingly little wastage of material. The incidents count generally for character and always for plot, and it is this economic adjustment that more particularly marks the dramatic relationship.

There are occasional flaws in the cunning of his arrangement, and twice at least in the book there is a notable maladjustment of episode and character. To create complications for Tom and Sophia he cannot permit the course of true love to run smooth. The Molly affair is drawn in to provide the necessary friction. The coarse gusto with which it is presented is so much dust thrown in the reader's eyes. We are entertained in varying proportion, but whatever the degree of our entertainment we cannot satisfactorily adjust the episode to Tom's psychology at that particular moment. The Lady Bellaston episode is disturbing but does not present a like problem, and it is not this I have in mind for my second example of a difficulty scanted. It is rather the matter of Tom's banishment from home, which had to occur for the story's sake, but which is not satisfactorily accounted for in terms of Mr. Allworthy's character. Blifil has some of the malignancy but none of the cunning of Iago, and Allworthy's benevolence suffers an incredible lapse.

Time Element. The author has managed his time scheme with skill to give the illusion of the natural sequence of events and the lapse of the years. The first six books cover a period of more than twenty years, the remaining twelve are confined to a period of forty-two days. Fielding was conscious of the difficulties he faced, and with a pleasantly malicious thrust at the labored copiousness of Richardson informs his readers how he proposes to deal with the problem of time. He refuses "to imitate the painful and voluminous historian who, to preserve the regularity of his series, thinks himself obliged to fill up as much paper with the detail of months and years in which nothing remarkable happened, as he employs upon those notable eras when the greatest scenes have been transacted on the human stage. . . . The writer, indeed, seems to think himself obliged to keep even pace with time, whose amanuensis he is; and, like his master, travels as slowly through centuries of monkish dullness, when the world seems to have been asleep, as through that bright and busy age so nobly distinguished by the excellent Latin poet. . . . Now it is our purpose, in the ensuing pages, to pursue a contrary method. When any extraordinary scene presents itself (as we trust will often be the case), we shall spare no pains nor paper to open it at large to our reader; but if whole years should pass without producing anything worthy his notice, we shall not be afraid of a chasm in our history; but shall hasten on to matters of consequence, and leave such periods of time totally unobserved. . . . My reader then is not to be surprised if, in the course of this work, he shall find some chapters very short, and others altogether as long: some that contain only the time of a single day, and others that comprise years; in a word, if my history sometimes seems to stand still, and sometimes to fly, for all which I shall not look on myself as accountable to any court of critical jurisdiction whatever: for as I am, in reality, the founder of a new province of writing, so I am at liberty to make what laws I please therein."

Handling of Incident. The happenings in this book are so numerous that recapitulation would be impossible. It is essentially a dramatist's plot,—Coleridge ranks it in ingenuity with the *Œdipus Rex* and *The Alchemist*—in which the incidents at once reveal character and complicate the action, with provision made in the *dénouement* for the ultimate resolution of all difficulties. Austin Dobson has referred to the intricate pattern of the book: "The incidents which, in Cervantes, simply succeed each other like scenes in a panorama, are, in *Tom Jones*, but parts of an organized and carefully arranged progression towards a foreseen conclusion. As the heroes cross and re-cross each other's tracks, there is scarcely an episode which does not aid in the moving forward of the story." The Man of the Hill episode is the one glaring irrelevancy, an inheritance from the digressive habit of the Cervantes tradition; the story of Mrs. Fitzgerald has some relation to the main theme, and the Mrs. Hunt interlude is designed, however unsatisfactorily, to counteract Sophia's prejudices occasioned by the unsavory Bellaston affair. Trifles like the bible, the bird, the horse, and the muff are compelled into the service of the story, and the headlong follies of the Upton Inn and the road have a further purpose than merely to excite our risibilities. A novel achieves distinction from the totality of its effects, among which the handling of incident is only one element. But we hazard the opinion that the appeal of *Tom Jones* largely derives from the masterly way in which the episodes are marshaled. They are interesting and amusing in themselves, they illustrate a period and characters in that period, and they are all interwoven into a complicated and masterly design.

Description. Fielding wrote before the zest for descriptive writing had developed. He gives us only the bare necessities of external aspects. Allworthy's Gothic house is lightly sketched in—all we know of Squire Western's is that it adjoined. We cannot visualize any of the characters—even Tom and Sophia are presented for the most part in general terms—each has a winning countenance, a frank expression, a charming smile. The two passages of set description—of Sophia in Book IV, Chapter II, and of Jones in Book IX, Chapter V seem generalized to the modern reader. Descriptive vigor is devoted to episodes rather than to persons or places. Minor characters are occasionally the subject of more precise reference. Mrs. Partridge (Bk. II, Ch. III) might have sat to his friend Hogarth, for we are informed that "she exactly resembles the young woman who is pouring out her mistress's tea in the third picture of the Harlot's Progress." The most biting portrait is of Captain Blifil (Bk. I, Ch. XI), but it wants the cutting edge of the modern satiric picture.

Author's Comment. Author's comment abounds in the novel. Obviously the initial chapters of the eighteen books are defiant deviations from the story, but are so arranged that they may be separately read: and indeed they are too good to miss. Scott's and George Eliot's comments are well known, the former erring on the extravagant side of praise: "Those critical introductions which rather interrupt the course of the story, and the flow of the interest at the first perusal are found, on a second or third, the most entertaining chapters of the whole work."

Fielding reserves to himself also the right to comment

at will on characters and incident. It is his story and he proposes to do what he pleases with it. Above all he is anxious to adjust the moral point of view of his readers to his own perspective of right and wrong. Tom's failings for example (which are exhibited with so much evident relish) are chastised, but we are informed repeatedly that they are the ingenuous indiscretions of exuberance and do not attack the source of virtue which flows from natural goodness of heart. Square's hypocritical perversions of the Shaftesbury doctrine are not so tenderly treated, and the varying grades of villainy from Blifil to Thwackum are not, after the modern manner, left to the inference of the reader.

Analysis. Analysis is slight and few of the situations breed reflections in the minds of the characters. The most extended piece of analysis is in Book V, Chapter III, where Tom estimates his chance with Sophia and is disturbed the while in his conscience by memories of Molly Seagrim and her desperate plight. Nor is Sophia's dilemma more intimately explored. In contrast to the morbidly analytic Clarissa Harlowe we are given a heroine into whose mind we are scarcely permitted to glance. In Book IV, Chapter XII, Fielding seems to have realized the necessity of an inward revelation, for Sophia in her predicament had really much to think about. The passage begins with a flourish: "We will, however, make the reader amends in disclosing what passed in the mind of Sophia." Needless to say, the promise is only sparsely fulfilled, and we are forced to the alternative conclusion either that Fielding was deficient in analytic skill, or that he felt that he had sufficiently wrought his picture and established his characters by other means. Analysis is obviously not a necessary element in his compositional scheme.

The book then lives by its narrative vigor, its author's

witty comment, and its rich and racy humanity. The part that illustrative incident has played in conferring this life quality is realized so readily by even the casual reader as not to demand further amplification. But the life-giving quality of the dialogue, the consummate skill with which the author contrives to make the characters "give themselves away" by their unseemingly unstudied utterances, are no less a sign of Fielding's genius than his invention of revealing incident. There is no "censor" standing sentinel on the lips of Partridge, or Western, or Mrs. Honour. There is illumination in every phrase of their coinage. No inhibitions constrain them, and no self-consciousness checks their exquisite absurdities. Thwackum and Square are in a measure conventionalized, for they are complementary representatives of rival theories, and Allworthy runs too readily perhaps into the predetermined mold of the typical "good man" of his century. The successful utterances, then, in the book are not colloquies, but torrents of speech. The give and take of modern dialogue was as yet undiscovered, and interchange of speech between the supposedly normal characters has not much relation to reality. It is rather a matter of surprise that Sophia and Tom so successfully survive their conversations.

Chapter VI

THE CONTRIBUTION OF STERNE

It is very difficult to catch hold of this slippery thing, the novel, by the tail. And when you may seem to have pinned down certain characteristics of a writer or a type you may well question what advantage you get beyond the dubious pedantic satisfaction of knowing that every author who is worth while differs from every author who is or is not worth while, and precisely by those phases of his genius which are least communicable. We thought we had discovered something important in the narrative art of Defoe, but if we are honest with ourselves we did not quite discover what it was, and to get the effect we are driven back upon the books themselves. That of course in itself is a result worth having, though it is rather disconcerting for the inquirer who starts out with false hopes of another kind of success. However, let us not give away our case completely. We can never find again the characteristic Fielding compound, but succeeding novelists need not miss all the hints he gave. If they want to build up a dramatist's plot they can go to no better master, or if they are careless of that kind of effect they will know at least by his example what to avoid. He will convince them that a Parson Adams is a good sort of character to have in a book, but he will throw them on their own generative energies to reproduce such another. Richardson will show them what powerful results can be pressed out of one situation pursued into its multitudinous ramifications, but they will wisely decide that his method entails too many sacrifices in other directions. His particular type of inwardness therefore will offer small attraction to the readers or writers of a later time. They will be interested in what he aimed at in the main—the immediate notation of the mind's recoil from the experience of the moment;—but they will reject with emphasis the clumsiness of his method.

A later writer of genius, Laurence Sterne, is concerned with "inwardness" in another way. He is the most evasive and volatile writer of his century, and we shall probably make a poor attempt at evaluating his real quality. Initially we may despair of estimating as a whole that fantastic fusion of single items which gives us the Shandyan product; but we have better hope of itemizing his genius in its separate characteristics.

And first, I think there is something useful to be said about his faculty of expression. Style, as Buffon tells us, is bound up in the man, and one quality which Sterne possessed in excess, his quivering sensibility, reflects itself in many characteristic passages that possess for the modern reader a flavor discernible in no other writer of his age. His sensitiveness is not wholly modern, inasmuch as certain aspects of life that affect us deeply seem beyond his range. He has no observable regard for landscape values, which if he had possessed his delicate phrasing could have reproduced in the most approved impressionistic manner.

But here is a passage well worth our study. I give it in excerpt, but it should be read in its entirety in the early pages of *A Sentimental Journey*, if we would get the full virtue of the personal reflection that is interwoven with the description. It concerns a Franciscan monk who has entered the room of a Calais inn to beg for his convent:

"The moment I cast my eyes upon him, I was predetermined not to give him a single sou; and accordingly I put my purse into my pocket—button'd it up—set myself a little more upon my centre, and advanced up gravely to him: I have his figure this moment before my eyes, and think there was that in it, which deserved better.

"The monk as I judged from the break in his tonsure, a few scatter'd hairs upon his temples being all that remained of it, might be about seventy—but from his eyes, and that sort of fire which was in them, which seemed more temper'd by courtesy than years, could be no more than sixty—Truth might lie between—He was certainly sixty-five; and the general air of his countenance, notwithstanding something seemed to have been planting wrinkles in it before their time, agreed to the account.

"It was one of those heads which Guido has often painted—mild, pale, penetrating, free from all commonplace ideas of fat contented ignorance looking downward upon the earth—it look'd forwards; but look'd, as if it look'd at something beyond this world. How one of his order came by it, heaven above, who let it fall upon a monk's shoulders, best knows; but it would have suited a Bramin, and had I met it upon the plains of Indostan, I had reverenced it.

"The rest of his outline may be given in a few strokes; one might put it into the hands of any one to design, for 'twas neither elegant or otherwise, but as character and expression made it so: it was a thin, spare form, something above the common size, if it lost not the distinction by a bend forwards in the figure—but it was the attitude of entreaty; and as it now stands presented to my imagination, it gain'd more than it lost by it.

"When he had enter'd the room three paces, he stood still; and laying his left hand upon his breast (a slender white staff with which he journey'd being in his right)—when I had got close up to him, he introduced himself with the little story of the wants of his convent, and the

poverty of his order—and did it with so simple a grace—
and such an air of deprecation was there in the whole cast
of his look and his figure—I was bewitch'd not to have
been struck with it—

"A better reason was, I had predetermined not to give
him a single sou."

The style of other novelists of the century, of the best
of them—Defoe or Fielding—is blunt by comparison.
Theirs is externalized expression, forthright and honest
and effective for the result they seek; Sterne's is inward,
subtle, insinuating, caressing, and by it he produces the
kind of spiritual portraiture which some of our modern
writers would achieve in Sterne's way if they could. It is
certain at least that Sterne's is a present and prevailing
example in a degree that is true of no other novelist of
his century.

In many other passages his words give the exact nuance
of attitude, tone, and gesture, with occasionally the inward
revealing phrase that flashes the whole portrait upon our
mind; and these are the qualities of his style which I shall
not say are most communicable but which are still the
most worth striving after. Of his extremer mannerisms
there is not so much good to be said, but these too are
part of the man, and bespeak his fantasticality, his pedantry,
and his conscious attempts at times to follow in the footsteps of Burton or of Rabelais, or brazenly to steal from
them.

His humor then is a complex product. The asterisks,
the blank or marbled pages, the absent chapters, the
tenderness, the coarseness, the hesitating indecencies, the
lightly-darting whimsicality, the lumbering pedantry, the
extravagant sentimentality, the never ending digressions,
the topsy-turvy defiance of time—all go to swell the main
account. Subtraction from the total sum is not for the

reader to make, who can allow himself at most the privilege of accepting or rejecting the offering on his own responsibility.

It is necessary here to speak only of certain phases of his humor, indicated in the imperfect enumeration above, and which may be held to have some continuous value for fiction. His typographical eccentricities need not concern us, nor his sentimentality, nor his pedantry, nor the peculiar type of indecent suggestion which has proved more offensive to delicate readers than the franker coarseness of Fielding or Smollett. These are elements of his work that have not perpetuated themselves, or have at least been disguised beyond all possibility of recognition. But his habit of digression and his wilful disregard of time sequence are matters of more present import. Let us first note what he has to say on his own account, remembering as we must that the digressive habit was already deeply rooted in fiction. Fielding halts *Tom Jones* for forty pages to recount the history of the Man on the Hill, and Smollett inserts an interlude of one hundred and eighty-six pages in his *Peregrine Pickle*. But Sterne had no apparent sympathy for solid digressions of this stamp. They must be airily handled, and also they must for all their seeming inconsequence bear some relation to the major theme. Swift's *Tale of a Tub* offers a nearer analogue to Sterne's way. Here is his artistic justification of his practice.

"For in this long digression which I was accidentally led into, as in all my digressions (one only excepted) there is a master stroke of digressive skill, the merit of which has all along, I fear, been overlooked by my reader,—not for want of penetration in him,—but because 'tis an excellence seldom looked for, or expected indeed, in a digression; and it is this: That tho' my digressions are all fair, as you observe,—and that I fly off from what I am about, as far, and as often too, as any writer in Great Britain; yet I constantly take care to order affairs so that my main business does not stand still in my absence.

"I was just going, for example, to have given you the great outlines of my uncle Toby's most whimsical character;—when my aunt Dinah and the coachman came across us, and led us a vagary some millions of miles into the very heart of the planetary system: Notwithstanding all this, you perceive that the drawing of my uncle Toby's character went on gently all the time; not the great contours of it,—that was impossible,—but some familiar strokes and faint designations of it, were here and there touch'd on, as we went along, so that you are much better acquainted with my uncle Toby now than you was before.

"By this contrivance the machinery of my work is of a species by itself; two contrary motions are introduced into it, and reconciled, which were thought to be at variance with each other. In a word, my work is digressive, and it is progressive too,—and at the same time.

"This, Sir, is a very different story from that of the earth's moving round her axis, in her diurnal rotation, with her progress in her elliptick orbit which brings about the year, and constitutes that variety and vicissitude of seasons we enjoy;—though I own it suggested the thought, —as I believe the greatest of our boasted improvements and discoveries have come from such trifling hints.

"Digressions, incontestably, are the sunshine;—they are the life, the soul of reading! take them out of this book, for instance,—you might as well take the book along with them;—one cold eternal winter would reign on every page of it; restore them to the writer;—he steps forth like a bridegroom,—bids All-hail; brings in variety, and forbids the appetite to fail.

"All the dexterity is in the good cookery and the management of them, so as not to be only for the advantage of the reader, but also of the author, whose distress in this matter, is truly pitiable: For, if he begins a digression,—from that moment, I observe, his whole work stands stock still; and if he goes on with the main work,—then there is an end of his digression.

". . . This is vile work. . . . For which reason, from the beginning of this, you see, I have constructed the main work and the adventitious parts of it with such intersections, and have so complicated and involved the digressive and progressive movements, one wheel within another, that the whole machine in general, has been kept a-going; and, what's more, it shall be kept a-going these forty years, if it please the fountain of health to bless me so long with life and good spirits."

Can it be possible that Sterne has detected a vice in his genius for which he invents this humoristic corrective, or is he giving us here a conscientious protest against the well-made book as his age and subsequent ages understood it? He gives us another prescription of excellence elsewhere which chimes sufficiently well with the above advice—"to begin with writing the first sentence, trusting to Almighty God for the second." And his expatiation on time in Book II, Chapter VIII is a similar assertion of artistic freedom. Were we committed to the principle of regularity which had been asserting itself in English fiction for generations before the advent of Sterne, his diverting and highly successful experiment might have been more disconcerting than it is, and we should have had to satisfy ourselves as best we might with his assurance that a cunningly concerted plan underlies his apparent planlessness, and that his seeming lawlessness is under bondage to the highest law he recognizes—the law of his own genius. He was plainly dissatisfied with what was being done in his day. He wrote the *Sentimental Journey* in undisguised protest against the humorless solidity of Smollett's *Travels through France and Italy*, and *Tristram Shandy* is evidence that he was thoroughly uninterested in current attempts to convey through fiction a diversified account of contemporary manners. His interest was in a few characters, chosen for their individual virtues rather than for their representative value, and every stroke of his work however digressive in seeming was cunningly devised to display their interactions.

The question comes back again to the old principle of unity and design; for when an author is imaginatively at one with his theme he can introduce into it nothing that is unrelated. Where Sterne may sometimes seem to stray into sheer extravagance, the fault lies either in our defective perception, or else his brain was tired, his invention flagged, and he dipped his bucket into some other's well.

We may turn to this eccentric novelist for light on one further æsthetic problem. After all it is the irregular writers who challenge our judgments most, and Sterne in the eighteenth and Joyce in the twentieth century are if not the greatest at least the most provocative artists of their age. The question I refer to is the subjectivity of the artist, the extent to which his personality may be disguised and the extent also to which it may be profitably indulged. The excellent book is one that appears to have an independent life of its own. Homer passes, his history is mythical, but his book lives. Shakespeare is almost equally legendary, and we can build up a Shakespearean body of opinion only by inference and surmise. One was an epic and the other a dramatic writer you may say, and anonymity was one of the conditions of their art. Should a novelist be similarly limited in personal expression? Flaubert proclaimed a serene independence from the world of his own creation. As an artist he must love it, as a man he was permitted to despise it. His contention was extravagant, but it has borne some fruit in the effort of the best succeeding novelists to refrain from personal comment, and to allow the book to operate directly on the mind of the reader. Flaubert was the first man to theorize on the subject and to make a self-conscious effort towards impassivity. But more than a hundred years earlier Defoe had produced books more solidly objective, and because less obviously organized by the arranging mind of the artist therefore more serenely impersonal than Flaubert's picture of life. Autobiographical narrative offers a ready natural disguise for the author, and Richardson's epistolary device confers the same opportunity for concealment. Fielding is perpetually reminding us that he is responsible for the story he tells, but his unabashed comment is made acceptable to the reader by the humor with which it is conveyed. When we reach Sterne we encounter an author who succeeds by some queer magic in writing a story that has an independent life of its own and yet is saturated throughout with his personal opinions, whims, and prejudices. If the practicing novelist of today thinks he can display himself so brazenly he does so at his peril unless his genius has a like protean quality. Sterne felt that he could defy the whole race of formula-bound critics by virtue of a fire that was in him. "Of all the cants which are canted in the canting world—though the cant of hypocrites may be the worst—the cant of criticism is the most tormenting!

"I would go fifty miles on foot, for I have not a horse worth riding on, to kiss the hand of that man whose generous heart will give up the reins of his imagination into the author's hands—be pleased he knows not why, and cares not wherefore.

The Contribution of Sterne

"Great *Apollo!* if thou art in a giving humour—give me—I ask no more, but one stroke of native humour, with a single spark of thy own fire along with it—and send *Mercury*, with the *rules and compasses*, if he can be spared, with my compliments to—no matter."

Tobias Smollett in a generative sense is definitely less important than the four major novelists of his century. As documentary evidence of the manners of his age he yields a richer harvest than Defoe, Richardson, Fielding or Sterne. But it is mistaken zeal that would rank his contribution on a parity with theirs. Without him English literature would possess in Defoe and Fielding quite adequate patterns of narrative vigor, and in Fielding an author who was not content to squander incident with reckless unconcern. Acknowledging the same allegiance to Cervantes and LeSage Fielding revealed in his art an economy unknown to his more impetuous contemporary, less willingness to expand farce beyond its legitimate limits, less concession despite his frankness to the grosser reaches of realism, and above all a greater sensitiveness to the demands of form. Measured by the standards set by subsequent fiction the great four maintain their identity and their value. Smollett is merely a not unimportant historical item.

Goldsmith, Fanny Burney, and the Gothic romancers bring the century to a close. The last are never read, Fanny Burney's *Evelina* is taken on trust, but *The Vicar of Wakefield* still remains one of the most popular novels in the language written by the creator of the most popular play and one of the most popular poems of its century. Such a combination is beyond the reach of accident, and to lay impious hands upon such an author would be the height of folly. Vicars do not grow on every hedge, and we are still as open to the charm of the book that reveals this particular vicar, as our fathers were and their fathers before them. It is a disconcerting book to deal with. Almost everything seems to be wrong and yet turns out in the result to be astoundingly right. Can it be that it triumphs by reason of its faults? or shall we rather say that its virtues are so vital that the faults are powerless against them? Poetry, a sense of comedy, humaneness, and the magic of deftly ordered words are qualities that inhere in the center, and are capable of establishing their own sufficient form. The technical misdemeanors lie on the surface, and the flimsy conventions that Goldsmith so confidently employed may even be said to contribute to the calculated effect.

Chapter VII

SIR WALTER SCOTT

The present age is probably unjust to Scott. For fifty years his supremacy in fiction was unchallenged, and no novelist has ever exerted so immediate or so wide an influence. He is said to be out of fashion now. He has not the liveliness of attack which appeals to the young reader of today, nor the reflective depth which maturer minds demand. The items of detraction might readily be multiplied, and yet we should still be forced to account reasonably for his outstanding reputation, and not conclude too hastily that all his peculiar virtues having been absorbed by his successors there is no need to return to the original source. Let us rather hope that there is still a fund of entertainment in those books that stand in serried and forbidding rows on our fathers' shelves, and that it is unwise to dismiss him as a mere historic figure.

For the moment our concern is with him in that capacity. Time has so winnowed the heap that we are not prepared to realize the mass of fiction, inconsiderable only by relation to the mad productivity of our own time, which poured from the press when Scott began to write. But it was undistinguished work. In spite of the scattered fine examples that the eighteenth century had to show, the novel was hardly yet considered a respectable branch of literature. When Scott had given a distinguished status to the novel the only valid excuse he could proffer for his anonymity was his obstinacy and his humor, but his original concern had been for his reputation. It is a minor merit perhaps to have rendered the novel respectable: his genuine merit was to have given it a new direction.

For no writer can we advance the claim of complete originality, and historical novels of a kind had existed for a century and a half before Scott's advent. Illustrious historic names embellished grotesquely improbable actions which satisfied the romantic desires of an age that lacked all discriminating sense. Defoe, our first master of realistic narrative, is here again a pioneer, and in his *Memoirs of a Cavalier* gave a hint, which was slow to be followed, of how fiction might occupy the past and make it present to the imagination. The eighteenth century developed historic studies and built up a mass of antiquarian detail which was still perhaps too undigested to be utilized by the writer of fiction. In any event until Scott appeared the effort was not made, though it is interesting to note that our first great master of historic fiction had no original ambition in that direction.

This point deserves some emphasis. If you read Scott's "General Preface" to the Waverley novels you will discover that his primary intention was to emulate Miss Edgeworth, to attempt something "for my own country of the same kind with that which Miss Edgeworth so fortunately achieved for Ireland—something which might introduce her natives to those of a sister Kingdom, in a more favourable light than they had been placed hitherto, and tend to procure sympathy for their virtues and indulgence for their foibles. I thought also, that much of what I wanted in talent might be made up by the intimate acquaintance with the subject which I could lay claim to possess, as having travelled through most parts of Scotland, both Highland and Lowland; having been familiar with the elder, as well as more modern race; and having had from my infancy free and unrestrained communication

with all ranks of my countrymen, from the Scottish peer
to the Scottish ploughman. Such ideas often occurred to
me and constituted an ambitious branch of my theory,
however far short I may have fallen of it in practice."

Incidentally this passage may afford an example of Scott's
not infrequent clumsiness as a manipulator of language,
but its importance for us is in the fact that Scott before
launching into fiction considered himself well equipped
to be an illustrator of manners, and that in this direction
his main ambition lay. We recognize of course the fullness
of his historic knowledge and his developed sense of the
characteristics that differentiate one age from another.
Yet it is a fact of some significance that not until his fourth
novel, *Old Mortality*, did he venture behind the limits of
oral tradition, and in many of his subsequent books, *The
Bride of Lammermoor* and *The Heart of Midlothian* for example,
he chose to remain on this relatively familiar ground.

His first adventure in historic romance was accidental,
as were apparently so many of his literary beginnings,
and was not of a character which permitted him to cherish
hopes of success in that field. In the year 1807–1808 he
patched up at John Murray's request an unfinished romance
of Joseph Strutt called *Queen-Hoo-Hall*. It was a tale of
the Henry VI period, and despite its extreme erudition, or
perhaps by reason of it, was not in Scott's opinion successful. Earlier attempts had suffered from the too little, this
from the too much of history. "I thought I was aware of
the reason (of his failure), and supposed that, by rendering
his language too ancient, and displaying his antiquarian
knowledge too liberally, the ingenious author had raised
up an obstacle to his own success. . . . I conceived it
possible to avoid this error; and by rendering a similar
work more light and obvious to general comprehension,
to escape the rock on which my predecessor was ship-

wrecked. But I was, on the other hand, so far discouraged by the indifferent reception of Mr. Strutt's romance, as to become satisfied that the manners of the middle ages did not possess the interest which I had conceived; and was led to form the opinion that a romance, founded on a Highland story, and more modern events, would have a better chance of popularity than a tale of chivalry. My thoughts returned more than once to the tale which I had actually commenced, and accident at length threw the lost sheets in my way." The reference is to his tentative beginning of *Waverley* in 1805, the discovery of the lost chapters in a writing desk, and the feverish completion of the work in a few summer weeks of 1814.

I said above that Scott has earned the twofold merit of making the novel respectable and giving it a new direction. His vast popularity justifies the first assertion. The second demands some examination for proof. The obvious thing to say is that it was his example which made possible and engendered a number of world-famous books whose main motive was the lively resuscitation of the past. His reputation first leaped across the channel where his technique with minor modifications found echo in de Vigny's *Cinq Mars*, Mérimée's *Chronique du règne de Charles IX*, and almost the whole range of Dumas's work. The method aborted in the brilliant but faulty *Notre Dame de Paris* of Hugo, who was no more capable of learning his lesson from Scott than he was of capturing the spirit or the manner of Shakespeare. Manzoni in Italy with his *I Promessi Sposi* was a more satisfactory disciple, and Germany in Feuchtwanger's *Jew Süss* has recently given us a work which in cumulative power and subtlety of penetration yields to none of its predecessors. English examples from Bulwer, Thackeray, Kingsley, and a host of lesser moderns come readily to mind.

What then were Scott's discoveries and how closely did he adhere to them in practice?

First in degree of importance was his determination to write period stories across whose pages great personages might occasionally stride, but who should not be permitted to absorb the maximum of interest. He wove his romance around secondary characters who imposed no factual obligations upon his invention, but left it free to explore the characteristic qualities of the age in which his scene was laid. His main preoccupation was always with manners, and his comparative failures were in those books where he was compelled to substitute antiquarian studies for the keener inspiration of personal contact or living tradition. Of his older revivals only *Old Mortality* and *Quentin Durward* are of like value with his more intimate eighteenth-century studies. His secondary contribution therefore to the technique of historic fiction is a negative one. If the vivid presentation of the manners of an epoch is the writer's main consideration, his difficulties multiply as his time scale extends, and revivals of far distant periods can rarely in the human sense be successful. An occasional brilliant result cannot offset the innumerable failures, and it is to the misdirected ambition of authors that we owe the present lapsed popularity of historic fiction.

Let us now examine some characteristic novels with an eye particularly directed to their technical qualities. I take two books which deal with eighteenth-century life, *The Bride of Lammermoor*, a structural success, and *The Heart of Midlothian*, a potentially finer novel spoiled in the making, and one book *Quentin Durward* where Scott has written entertainingly and convincingly of a remote period and a country not his own. This group reveals his strength and weakness and indicates his range as well as any others we might have chosen. The first two are novels of manners with mild historic attachments of recent date. *Quentin Durward* is a genuine creation of the historic imagination exercizing itself upon material furnished by the record of Philip de Comines who happens to be also an actor in the story.

The first two novels are products of the years 1818–1819. *The Heart of Midlothian* was written in the first accesses of a malady that reached its height during the composition of *The Bride of Lammermoor*. His agony had become so violent that the latter portions of this book were dictated from his sick-bed. James Ballantyne vouches for the extraordinary fact that when the published volume was put into his hands "he did not recall one single incident, character, or conversation which it contained." The fact is the more extraordinary when we reflect that this novel has the deserved reputation of being the finest in point of composition that bears his name. Scott prided himself on what he was wont to call his hab-nab and at-a-venture style. "I never could lay down a plan or, having laid it down, I never could adhere to it; the action of composition always diluted some passages and abridged or omitted others, and personages were rendered important or insignificant, not according to their agency in the original conception of the plan, but according to the success or otherwise with which I was able to bring them out. I only tried to make that which I was actually writing diverting and interesting, leaving the rest to fate."—*Journal*. The inconsequence was perhaps not always so diverting as he hoped, and nowhere else has Scott so marred an occasion for being convincingly and consistently great as in *The Heart of Midlothian* which we will now consider.

This novel revolves round the central figure of Jeanie Deans, and we can trace the origin and evolution of the story by the fortunate preservation of a letter from a Mrs. Thomas Goldie of Dumfries which Scott reproduces in his introduction. It gives a vivid description of an old woman, Helen Walker, who had so interested the writer that she determined to follow up her story and "discover what was extraordinary in the history of the poor woman. Mr. ——said there were perhaps few more remarkable people than Helen Walker. She had been left an orphan, with the charge of a sister considerably younger than herself, and who was educated and maintained by her exertions. Attached to her by so many ties, therefore, it will not be easy to conceive her feelings when she found that this only sister must be tried by the laws of her country for child-murder, and upon being called as principal witness against her, the counsel for the prisoner told Helen that if she could declare that her sister had made any preparations, however slight, or had given her any intimation on the subject, such a statement would save her sister's life, as she was the principal witness against her. Helen said, 'It is impossible for me to swear to a falsehood; and whatever may be the consequence I will give my oath according to my conscience.'

"The trial came on, and the sister was found guilty and condemned; but in Scotland six weeks must elapse between the sentence and the execution, and Helen Walker availed herself of it. The very day of her sister's condemnation she got a petition drawn up stating the peculiar circumstances of the case, and that very night set out on foot to London.

"Without introduction or recommendation, with her simple (perhaps ill-expressed) petition, drawn up by some inferior clerk of the court, she presented herself in her tartan plaid and country attire to the late Duke of Argyle, who immediately procured the pardon she petitioned for, and Helen returned with it, on foot, just in time to save her sister."

A novelist is not often given a better opportunity. Life here provides him with a significant incident teeming with possibilities, and crying out for dramatization. A little world has to be created round Jeanie the central figure. She was an orphan in the world of fact, but our author will hardly resist the temptation of justifying the strict integrity of her conscience by inventing a true-blue Presbyterian father. He had been annoyed by the adverse criticism of his Covenanters in *Old Mortality* and he was determined as he said "to tickle off" another. Douce Davie Deans is more than a challenge to his critics, for his weight definitely counts in the story, and it is only when he dies that it takes on its extravagantly melodramatic character. The shadowy figure of the original Effie must be firmly outlined, and a flesh and blood lover must complete the circle of the inner characters. I am considering the novel in its early chaotic state as it was beginning to take shape in its author's mind. Certain scenes of the original clamored for expansion, others must be invented, and these must necessarily engender casual figures on the periphery of the story and yet logically involved in the action. Jeanie's journey on foot to London must be made circumstantial and her misadventures on the way must not be merely casual. Having achieved her goal there is the interview with Argyle to be arranged, the audience with the Queen and Lady Suffolk to be invented, and the return journey to be organized by a more secure and comfortable method than the original provided. Having arrived home with the pardon the story naturally closes, and it was out of pure and misjudged bravado that Scott began to wind up another romance.

Let us now retrace our footsteps along the pathway of

the actual novel, and note the author's failures and successes. Until the unfortunate close the faults are almost inconspicuous. The opening is admittedly dull with the kind of sportive dullness that Scott permits himself before the heat of narrative energy has possessed him; and even when we have got rid of the quite superfluous lawyers he still refuses to satisfy our desire for liveliness. His aim is to establish a setting for the man we shall later discover to be Effie's lover, and to that end he somewhat laboriously builds up events leading to and associated with the Porteous riots. George Robertson emerges from these episodes as the shadowy villain of the piece, enigmatic and unsatisfactory at the outset, and crudely out of drawing at the melodramatic close. Effie's little world is further built up by a description of the Saddletree household where she has been living unvexed by the careful eyes of Jeanie and her father. The narrative begins to move effectively when Butler, the schoolmaster parson and Jeanie's patient lover, learns of Effie's desperate plight in prison. The conduct of the story proceeds now in Scott's best vein, with the dramatic liveliness, drollery of dialogue, and natural pathos that constitute his real greatness. Where he has to establish a setting for the Deans and Butler families there is no superfluity of retrospective narrative, but he invents a new Squire Western in miniature to enliven us. The death scene of old Dumbiedikes has no edification to recommend it, but its explosive energy makes it memorable. "After these contradictory instructions, the Laird felt his mind so much at ease that he drank three bumpers of brandy continuously and 'soughed awa', as Jenny expressed it, in an attempt to sing, 'De'il stick the minister.'"

The story dips back in time to deal with these family matters, and to account for the dumb infatuation of the young Laird of Dumbiedikes' wooing. We are given this brief and sole description of Jeanie's appearance: "She was short and rather too stoutly made for her size, had grey eyes, light-coloured hair, a round good-humoured face much tanned with the sun, and her only peculiar charm was an air of inexpressible serenity, which a good conscience, kind feelings, contented temper, and the regular discharge of all her duties, spread over her features." Effie's charms speak more eloquently to the eye. We have them presented in sufficient detail and the liveliness of their effect upon all but the constant Laird. "Even the rigid Presbyterians of her father's persuasion, who held each indulgence of the eye and sense to be a snare at least, if not a crime, were surprised into a moment's delight while gazing on a creature so exquisite,—instantly checked by a sigh, reproaching at once their own weakness, and mourning that a creature so fair should share in the common and hereditary guilt and imperfection of our nature. She was currently entitled the Lily of St. Leonard's, a name which she deserved as much by her guileless purity of thought, speech, and action, as by her uncommon loveliness of face and person."

The story returns to Effie in prison. With her meditations Scott is characteristically not concerned, but prefers to concentrate on circumstances connected with her fate. Butler had met her seducer, Robertson, had prevailed on Jeanie to meet him alone at night at Muschat's Cairn, and when returning to see Effie is detained in the Tolborton for his unwilling share in the Porteous riot. Scott is generally clumsy from undue explicitness in manipulating a double action. We are present on the heath at the interview of Jeanie and Robertson, which is interrupted by a wild song invading the midnight stillness and then several chapters intervene to account for the singing. Back in the prison again we are rewarded by meeting the genial des-

perado Ratcliffe and Madge Wildfire, the most picturesque
and poetic of doited females. It is her crazy song (so copiously introduced) that gives Robertson the opportunity
to escape. The book then passes into a series of admirably
contrived dramatic scenes and episodes—Jeanie's visit to
her sister in prison, the trial and Effie's condemnation,
Jeanie's heroic journey to London, her interviews with
Argyle and the Queen—all these presented with an easy
assurance of power that should compel the most grudging
admiration. Coincidence may seem too prominent in
Jeanie's waylaying by Madge's vagabond rabble, but old
Meg had her own reasons for balking the purpose of her
journey. The meeting with Robertson, now George Stain-
ton, in his father's parsonage, is less excusable in reason.
Whenever that unfortunate man appears plot exigencies
prevail over naturalness, but the intrusion is only momentary. The London part is excellent. The return journey
is broken by only one episode, extraordinary but memorable, the death of Madge Wildfire. Here we should purge
our minds of captiousness, and be grateful for once to the
undisciplined strangeness of the romantic imagination.

The story, as I have said, naturally ends with Jeanie's
return with the pardon. Lady Louisa Stuart, a friend of
Scott's, wrote to him the last necessary word. She praises
his skill in subordinating Effie to the admirable Jeanie.
She finds the Edinburgh lawyers of the introduction tedious
and thinks that Mr. Saddletree "will not entertain English
readers." The conclusion flags; "but the chief fault I have
to find relates to the reappearance and shocking fate of
the boy. I hear on all sides, 'Oh, I do not like that!' I
cannot say what I would have had instead, but I do not
like it either; it is a lame huddled conclusion. I know
you so well in it, by-the-by! You grow tired yourself,
want to get rid of the story, and hardly care how."

In *The Bride of Lammermoor* Scott projected in his central character a potential Byronic figure, handsome, disinherited, gloomy, brave, in fact the typical *beau ténébreux* of romantic fiction. Edgar Ravenswood is too destitute in his own person of the elements of mystery and criminal possibilities to furnish forth the complete type, but the novel of which he is all but the titular hero is still a most satisfactory romantic achievement. With every provision made for these essential features it departs from type only to its advantage, for it has solid compositional virtues which Scott and his fellow romantics seem rarely to have aimed at, and more rarely achieved. It is a triumph of tonality. Notable scenes and episodes are not multiplied as in the novel we have been considering, but every slightest touch is a note in the general harmony. In Caleb Balderstone there is a straining perhaps for comic effect. Scott was guiltily aware that he had ''sprinkled too much parsley on his chicken.'' But we want nothing else modified. A profounder writer might have given more reflective depth to Edgar. In the *Hamlet* grave scene the diggers are naïvely subtle, but Hamlet manages to have his say. In Scott's parallel scene his sexton is much the more potent spirit. Lucy Ashton's qualities might also have been extended, but for the purposes of a not too ambitious narrative both Edgar and Lucy amply suffice. They are designed to be children of fatality, and no great multiplication of incident is necessary to precipitate their doom. Its portents are clear enough in the supernatural mutterings of the uncanny hags, and in Alice's less tainted vision. This is the atmosphere-creating element in the book, and in this phase of it success or failure lay. Scott found success.

To classify novels by their subject matter is to establish as many varieties as there are themes in the world. But we can work loosely by a few rough divisions,—adventure books, mystery books, detective stories—and make some headway in organizing novels in respect of their emphasis on character or incident, or of their inclination in the direction of sheer fantasy or realistic representation. Though we have followed no such arrangement, I am willing to make some concessions in favor of the historical novel, for it is possible that we shall discover here a few governing principles which may come as near to being laws as fiction can tolerate. And to discover such principles we are well advised to consult the practice of Sir Walter Scott especially as illustrated in so artistically sound a narrative as *Quentin Durward* presents.

We may recognize as historical such novels as dip behind oral tradition to a merely documented age. A vivid historic sense fortified by sound erudition would seem therefore to be one prerequisite of success. The erudition too must be lightly borne and at least appear effortless. Scott, as we have seen, had early learned his lesson that a massing of antiquarian details upon the loose fringe of a story would blur the outlines of the picture. Doubtless the antiquarian died hard in him, but by the time he came to write his *Quentin Durward* (1823) he knew how to compromise between exactitude and liveliness, and for any swerving from precision satisfy his conscience with a note. Experience too had taught him how to make room in his story for the great historic figures without whom his theme would be shorn of much of its significance, and to give them salience without smothering our interest in the titular hero. Quentin is a genuine entity, and Scott's inventive faculty was certainly not wasted upon him, as on most of his pallid hero types. He bears with him a kind of woodland freshness, and is an admirable foil to the sinister and sophisticated king. Louis is certainly the triumph of the book, which takes on almost a Thucydidean quality in his crafty encounter with Charles the Bold. The German author of *Der Teufel* has made a subtler approach to an enigmatic character, but Scott is sufficiently life-like for his purpose. His character-triumphs lie elsewhere, and the somewhat grudging concessions of centenary critics has granted him almost supremacy in the range of his secondary figures. His philosophy, his style, his structure they condemn, but even the reservation of praise they bestow will serve to carry his name through another century.

Chapter VIII

JANE AUSTEN

Jane Austen's reputation unlike that of Scott is still in the ascendant. Extravagant claims have doubtless been made for her, and to allege for example the Shakespearean quality either of her ideas or their expression is to render her a disservice. With Chaucer's temper of mind there is a more obvious affinity. The playful malice and sympathetic irony of these seldom-associated writers stamp them as of the same spiritual family. But here again Jane Austen's defect in poetic quality and the narrowly realistic cast of her imagination forbid us to press the comparison. Cowper, Crabbe, and Scott were the only poets she relished, and they give the measure of her capacity in that direction. But the critics will take no warning. Macaulay reiterates the Shakespearean heresy. Mr. Saintsbury, who had a reputation for caution to sustain, assures us that "we shall have another Homer before we see another Jane," and Guizot, equally level-headed, sends us back to the great Athenian age for a parallel. Mr. Saintsbury's pious ejaculation yields no meaning. No great writer is reproduced, but whereas the Homeric form is irrecoverable, there is something in Jane Austen's art that can be perpetuated. She has nothing to give the epic-minded novelist who works for breadth rather than for intensity of effect, but she is a model of almost unapproachable perfection for the writer who is content to limit his material, to work like herself with a delicate brush on a miniature disk of ivory. It was this admirable proportioning of means to end and the consequent elimination of all superfluous content that suggested Guizot's Athenian parallel.

She had very early taken the measure of her capacity. She recognized in herself no aptitude for general ideas, and no impulse in the direction of social or political problems. Her interest in human nature was her only discoverable asset, and the types she preferred to study were removed from contact with the noisier activities of the world. "Two or three families in a village are just the subjects to work on." She arrived at her theme by unconscious preference rather than by design, and her method of handling the theme was instinctive as had been its choice. What makes her so interesting is that she has achieved an admittedly great result while foregoing many of the more obvious resources from which a novelist usually derives his power. She has written in short what we might call the "essential" novel, with most of the customary accessories eliminated. Moral or philosophical reflection, elaborated description, erotic complications she dispenses with as readily as she abstains from all contact with the world of affairs, and yet contrives to write books which are neither starved nor unnatural, and which are emphatically of the age that produced them. A brief examination of the structural design of *Emma* will reveal her habitual method of procedure.

The author's intention was evidently confined to giving an entertaining account of the life of a small group of upper middle class people in the Surrey countryside about sixteen miles from London. The period was contemporary, that is about the date of Waterloo. Emma Woodhouse was chosen as the center of the group, and the story was to occupy only so long a space of time as was necessary to show Emma's futile attempts at getting other people married, and to bring the frustrated match-maker unsuspectingly to the brink of matrimony.

There is nothing in the bare announcement of the theme to promise a successful result. The staunchness of Miss Austen's reputation is therefore something of a puzzle. The easiest way out of the difficulty would be to admit, were such an evasion of the problem permissible, that she was a woman of genius whose reactions to life were singularly fresh and interesting. She absolutely possessed her simple world and abundantly loved it with certain ironic reservations that give salt and savor to her observation. Rarely obtruding a personal comment she still contrives to make us subtly aware of her point of view, and it is for the most part a point of view that wins our amused assent. Fiction meant for her the representation of a small group of individuals linked by the compelling interest which all feel for whatever concerns the others. She is rarely the dupe of their behavior and even when she seems to share their queer timidities and reservations our inhibition-shattering modern world can still find its amusement in them. Her characters are possibly too clear in outline, their conduct too confidently controlled to bring them into relationship with modern efforts at portraiture, but the moderns of the future may not always be enamored of the irrational and the unexpected, while Jane Austen's safe and entertaining sanity will still be secure of a hearing.

Jane Austen's opening chapters are an interesting study. They are marked by their liveliness of attack. A few author's comments on the chief characters, their appearance and disposition, a hint perhaps of the conditions surrounding them, and they are launched upon the stream of talk. Here Jane Austen is in her element, and dialogue always remains the articulating principle of her art. Let us superficially examine some of these beginnings.

Pride and Prejudice opens with a brief and apposite generalization, and forthwith Mr. and Mrs. Bennet are revealing themselves in argument. The skillful chapter closes with the author's opinion of the pair: "Mr. Bennet was so odd a mixture of quick parts, sarcastic humour, reserve, and caprice, that the experience of three and twenty years had been insufficient to make his wife understand his character. Her mind was less difficult to develop. She was a woman of mean understanding, little information, and uncertain temper. When she was discontented, she fancied herself nervous. The business of her life was to get her daughters married; its solace was visiting and news."

Sense and Sensibility is the most gradual of Jane Austen's books in its development. It opens with a chapter of explanatory and retrospective narrative with some interspersed author's comment on the Dashwood family group. The second chapter, though but scantily attached to the story, is excellent conversational comedy—its theme John Dashwood's eager desire to give his step-sisters each a thousand pounds, tempered by his wife's progressively diminishing suggestions until a compromise is reached in an occasional present of game. It is not until the third chapter that the characteristic conversational contacts are made.

Conversational liveliness is again deferred in *Northanger Abbey* until the second chapter. The first one entertains us with the account of Catharine Morland's childhood, giving us a skillful selection of just so many characteristic items as are needed to establish a personality.

Mansfield Park spends four pages on information to the reader before the characters begin to act their parts, and *Persuasion* is equally economical of its expository preliminaries. The first chapter of *Emma* introduces to us Emma Woodhouse, her father, and the Westons. Miss Austen has the art to make her characters almost completely self-revealing, but at the outset she is willing to give the reader some assistance and nudges his elbow ever so gently to turn him in the right direction. Emma we are forthwith told was "handsome, clever, and rich, with a comfortable home and happy disposition." A further preliminary hint is given that she had been accustomed to having "rather too much her own way," and was inclined "to think a little too much of herself." It is obviously not the intention of the author to explore the depths of her consciousness. Emma's emotional range is limited, and to present her as a creature of aspirations and despairs would have involved Jane Austen in the kind of intensity of which she knew herself to be incapable, and which, if we may judge from her amusedly ironic attitude to all enthusiasms, she did not greatly admire. Mr. Woodhouse is one of the choice specimens from her museum of oddities, and once the story is in motion every word he utters is an amplification of the formula the author discovers for him in her opening pages. He had been "a valetudinarian all his life, without activity of mind or body . . . and though everywhere beloved for the friendliness of his heart and his amiable temper, his talents could not have recommended him at any time. . . . He was a nervous man, easily depressed; fond of everybody that he was used to, and hating to part with them—hating change of every kind. Matrimony, as the origin of change, was always disagreeable; and he was by no means yet reconciled to his own daughter's marrying, nor could even speak of her but with compassion, though it had been entirely a match of affection." He is worrying now about the loss of Miss Taylor who has just been married from his house. "Emma smiled and chatted as cheerfully as she could, to keep him from such thoughts;

but when tea came, it was impossible for him not to say exactly as he had said at dinner—

" 'Poor Miss Taylor! I wish she were here again. What a pity it is that Mr. Weston ever thought of her!'

" 'I cannot agree with you, papa; you know I cannot. Mr. Weston is such a good-humoured, pleasant, excellent man, that he thoroughly deserves a good wife; and you would not have had Miss Taylor live with us forever, and bear all my odd humours, when she might have a house of her own?'

" 'A house of her own!—but where is the advantage of a house of her own? This is three times as large; and you have never any odd humours, my dear.' "

The same method is followed with the other characters in the book—Mr. Knightley, Frank Churchill, Mr. and Mrs. Elton, to name only those who count for the story, and Miss Bates, whose perennial prattle is its own justification. The conversation it must be noted is not always in the same degree character-revealing. Some prevailing oddity as in Mr. Woodhouse and Miss Bates, or some perversion of nature as in Mrs. Elton is necessary to achieve that result. Knightley is announced to us as a cheerful person, which belies the monitory solemnity of his talk. He is forever taking Emma to task in a grave pedantic way, and we cannot be supremely interested in the progress of a love affair which is so studiously unromantic and unimpassioned.

Our conclusion then as to the dialogue is that Jane Austen derives most of her fine effects from that source. She takes no advantage of the opportunities it offers for dramatic intensity, for there are in her books no sharp collisions of angry and determined people in violent altercation. But in a milder comic way her dialogue has not been surpassed as a revealing medium. It strikes a happy mean between naturalness and art, and even when it is least expressive it serves the story by lessening the narrative responsibilities of the author.

We now turn to the narrative, descriptive, and reflective portions of her work. We have seen how terse are the narrative and descriptive summaries which usher in her dialogued scenes. A word may be added as to the quality of her descriptive writing. Jane Austen is essentially anti-romantic and she unconsciously shared Thomas Carlyle's antipathy for the prevailing "view-hunting" of current literature. There is for example an excursion to Box Hill with not a word of the countryside. Mr. Knightley's grounds were more to her taste. "It was hot; and after walking some time over the gardens in a scattered, dispersed way, scarcely any three together, they insensibly followed one another to the delicious shade of a broad, short avenue of limes, which, stretching beyond the garden at an equal distance from the river, seemed to finish the pleasure grounds. . . . It was a charming walk, and the view which closed it extremely pretty. The considerable slope, at nearly the foot of which the Abbey stood, gradually acquired steeper form beyond its grounds; and at half a mile distant was a bank of considerable abruptness and grandeur, well clothed with wood; and at the bottom of this bank, favourably placed and sheltered, rose the Abbey-Mill Farm, with meadows in front, and the river making a close and handsome curve around it.

"It was a sweet view—sweet to the eye and the mind. English verdure, English culture, English comfort, seen under a sun bright without being oppressive."

This last paragraph absolves Jane Austen from the charge of insensibility to natural effects, but for the most part her concern is for the state of the weather. It is not the timidity merely of her characters but her own sensitiveness that found terror in the snow and discomfiture in the rain.

Descriptions of personal appearance are not numerous, nor are they marked by any effort at subtlety. We can visualize only two of the people in *Emma*, and but imperfectly. Moral qualities count for more in the author's presentation. This much suffices for Harriet Smith: "She was a very pretty girl, and her beauty happened to be of a sort which Emma particularly admired. She was short, plump and fair, with a fine bloom, blue eyes, light hair, regular features, and a look of great sweetness." Emma's appearance is conveyed in a conversation between Knightley and Mrs. Weston. The former says: "I do not know what I could imagine, but I confess that I have seldom seen a face or figure more pleasing to me than hers. But I am a partial old friend."

"Such an eye!—the true hazel eye, and so brilliant!—regular features, open countenance, with a complexion—oh, what a bloom of full health, and such a pretty height and size, such a firm and upright figure! There is health not merely in her bloom, but in her air, her head, her glance. One hears sometimes of a child being 'the picture of health'; now Emma always gives me the idea of being the complete picture of grown-up health. She is liveliness itself, Mr. Knightley, is not she?"

Jane Austen has here anticipated the newer method of dramatized description, yet it is profitable to note the contrast of her forthright statements with the more impressionistic methods of the modern writer. It is obvious that since she wrote a distinct advance has been made in the direction of flexibility and fineness of notation.

Interior details are as economically conveyed as the aspects of persons and places. The environmental solicitude of a later generation imposes no obligation upon Jane

Austen, yet we are not always conscious that her characters are insufficiently established, and we take into our minds a most convincing picture of the day by day routine of their lives. It would be a malicious criticism that said it is not difficult to envisage dullness.

Miss Austen is not prone to analysis, and here again as in the element of description the divergence of method in modern fiction has been extreme. Even before the fashion of psycho-analysis had introduced such disturbing elements into our mental processes novelists had been widening and deepening the channels in which the thoughts of their creatures flowed. Dickens and Thackeray were perfunctory in their analysis, but George Eliot, Meredith, and James extended its possibilities so far that but for the advent of the Freudian psychology the limits of advance would seem to have been reached. In *Emma* we are but momentarily in Mr. Knightley's mind, and what we share of Emma's more constant reflections is not of high importance. Her mind works on direct and simple lines, consecutively if not powerfully, and always at the prompting of some casual incident of the day.

Neither in description nor in analysis is Jane Austen a notable pioneer, yet such is the firmness of her method that despite her limitations she will always remain a valuable center of reference in any structural consideration of the novel.

Chapter IX

AUSTEN AND THACKERAY

If we pass on from Miss Austen to Thackeray it is not by reason of any affinity between them. Indeed there are no two writers of fiction more dissimilar than Jane Austen and Thackeray, and it is, therefore, because contrasts are often as instructive as comparisons that the transition from the one to the other is made. Their juxtaposition will prove at least that a medium of expression must be very flexible which admits great effects from methods so diverse. It is futile to quarrel with a novelist for the way that he achieves his results. Give Jane Austen a wider range and she would cease to be Jane Austen and the world would be sensibly the poorer. Circumscribe Thackeray, expunge his diverting gossip, and make his actors talk instead of their creator, and we should miss the Thackerayan flavor which flows from qualities that it would be rash to name in the absolute either good or bad. All this we must admit, for the results are there to prove it. Every writer's manner must evidently suit himself, and all the vices of indifferent writing are not chargeable to weakness in the structural plan. Yet while the great affair is to achieve your effect, and while no prescription of method will atone for lack of genius, we cannot resist the impression that some novelists succeed by virtue of their abundant sense of life rather than by the manner in which they manipulate the material they so copiously possess. The question arises whether their success would not have been more absolute had they concerned themselves in equal measure with the form and substance of their work. Between Thackeray's range and Jane Austen's there can be no comparison, but whereas Jane Austen applied every ounce of her strength Thackeray was often recklessly wasteful of his power. It is futile I repeat to quarrel with the result, but we may reasonably ask whether Thackeray provides a formula which a writer of less abundant genius could afford to follow. From *Henry Esmond*, his greatest artistic achievement, every novelist who can may take his profit, and every reader his enjoyment. Here are none of the loose ends and extraneous interruptions which confront us in his other novels, but we are conscious always of a firm impersonal control, and as we close this book we are sensible of a harmony that fuses every detail with its compelling rhythm. It is such a model of perfection for the historic novelist as even Sir Walter Scott has not given us, and we can but regret that Thackeray has done nothing so flawless for the benefit of the novelist who deals with the material of contemporary life.

The contacts of Austen and Thackeray are obviously not so numerous as the contrasts. Utterly divergent as they are in style they may yet be confidently named together for the distinguishing purity and ease of their diction. As writers in this narrow rhetorical sense they have not been surpassed. They may be associated also for their kindred anti-romantic tendency, though the naturally unsentimental Jane is the more consistent in her opposition to the prevailing vogue. She never relaxed into pathos and could not have been described like Thackeray as a cynic with a tear in her eye. In each novelist, to conclude this matter of approximations, the range of analysis has the dual limitation of narrowness and shallowness. Yet Thackeray is the more perfunctory. We are permitted to see with Emma's vision or Elizabeth's, but the shutters of

Rebecca's mind are resolutely closed, and Amelia and Dobbin have apparently nothing to reveal.

The contrasting features of their art are more evident. Jane Austen's self-effacement is almost complete. In *Northanger Abbey* (Ch. V) she swerves from her story for two pages to give us her own opinion of the value of novels. Outside of this passage it would be difficult to discover more than a casual phrase here and there of author's comment. She intervenes to narrate, and to give the reader his initial direction, and then allows the characters to work out their mild destinies. Thackeray prides himself on being the most unabashed of showmen, and usurps the creator's privilege of comment upon his own creation. He is the omniscient author who has access to all secrets. "If, a few pages back, the present writer claims the privilege of peeping into Miss Amelia Sedley's bedroom and understanding with the omniscience of the novelist all the gentle pains and passions which were tossing upon that innocent pillow, why should he not declare himself to be Rebecca's confidant too, master of her secrets, and seal-keeper of that young woman's conscience?" His comment is continuous. Rebecca is employing all the resources of an *ingénue* to ensnare Jos's affections: "It was an advance, and as such, perhaps, some ladies of indisputable correctness and gentility will condemn the action as immodest; but, you see, poor dear Rebecca had all this work to do for herself. If a person is too poor to keep a servant, though ever so elegant, he must sweep his own rooms; if a dear girl has no dear mamma to settle matters with the young man, she must do it for herself. And oh, what a mercy it is that these women do not exercise their powers oftener! We can't resist them, if they do. Let them show ever so little inclination, and men go down on their knees at once; old or ugly, it is all the same. And this I set down as a positive truth. A woman with fair opportunities, and without an absolute hump, may marry *whom she likes*. Only let us be thankful that the darlings are like the beasts of the field, and don't know their own power. They would overcome us entirely if they did." Characteristic of Thackeray again, but a less personal aspect of the commentative tendency, is the parallel anecdote which he frequently introduces to illustrate some new phase of the action.

It is presumptuous perhaps in the face of the multitude of readers who delight in these congenial overflows to animadvert on Thackeray's zest for intervention. To share such brilliant confidences is a privilege which his admirers would not willingly forego. We are not usually admitted, they say, to such intimate contact with greatness, and conversation of this quality is not heard on an ordinary day. It is impossible to argue away a prejudice, but the contrary opinion at least deserves a hearing. The philosophic comment of George Eliot and Meredith will be dealt with in due course, as will be also the dramatized discursiveness of writers like Aldous Huxley. Their digressive tendencies may be dangerous, but they do not lie in quite the same category. Thackeray's asides are admittedly clever, but they have been scored legitimately on several grounds. Clever as they are, do they rise to the level of his narrative and dramatic presentation? Have we the assurance that he is lending us the aid of a powerful and penetrating intelligence to interpret the life he so lavishly depicts, or do we imagine ourselves listening to the gossip of an enlightened man of the world, a super clubman with a plate-glass mind?

Everyone must decide for himself as to the intrinsic merit of these asides, but the structural method they imply is more than an affair of personal preference. A principle of

construction is involved, and we must allow some weight
to the fact that neither Thackeray's confidential habit
nor the philosophic generalizing of Eliot or Meredith
have been perpetuated in the best modern fiction. Thackeray so charms us by the lightness of his touch that
we may be momentarily unaware of the insinuating effect
of his personality on the story he tells. And yet the
story indubitably suffers. We cannot be dupes of the author's feigning when he constitutes himself the central
figure in an action where he plays no rôle. Let him disguise himself as a participant—let him even be the focus
point of the action as in *Esmond*—and his report will have
credence. The reader has an infant's mind and does not
wish his illusion shattered. The novelist must be like
Defoe a master of "grave imperturbable lying." His world
must be a self-supporting world poised on its own axis,
and any rude tilting will reverse the poles of our imagination. His characters should bear their own credentials,
and if their creator cuffs their ears and berates them as
Thackeray inclines to do their errant behavior is less
plausible, and we feel that they are defrauded of the right
to speak and act for themselves. It is not much better
when he approves, for then the goodness of Amelia becomes insipid, and the virtue of Dobbin ridiculous. Chapter LXIV of *Vanity Fair* is an indefensible blemish in a
great book. We concede the concessions to prudery as a
mark of the Victorian convention, but no Victorian compromise compelled the wanton branding of Rebecca which
is compressed into the same opening paragraph: "We
must pass over a part of Mrs. Rebecca Crawley's biography
with that lightness and delicacy which the world demands—the moral world, that has, perhaps, no particular
objection to vice, but an insuperable repugnance to hearing
vice called by its proper name. There are things we do

and know perfectly well in Vanity Fair, though we never speak them: as the Ahrimanians worship the devil, but don't mention him: and a polite public will no more bear to read an authentic description of vice than a truly refined English or American female will permit the word 'breeches' to be pronounced in her chaste hearing. And yet, madam, both are walking the world every day, without much shocking us. If you were to blush every time they went by, what complexions you would have! It is only when their naughty names are called out that your modesty has any occasion to show alarm or sense of outrage, and it has been the wish of the present writer, all through this story, deferentially to submit to the fashion at present prevailing, and only to hint at the existence of wickedness in a light, easy, and agreeable manner, so that nobody's fine feelings may be offended. I defy anyone to say that our Becky, who has certainly some vices, has not been presented to the public in a perfectly genteel and inoffensive manner. In describing this siren, singing and smiling, coaxing and cajoling, the author, with a modest pride, asks his readers all round, has he once forgotten the laws of politeness and showed the monster's hideous tail above water? No! Those who like may peep down under waves that are pretty transparent, and see it writhing and twirling, diabolically hideous and slimy, flapping amongst bones, or curling round corpses; but above the water line, I ask, has not everything been proper, agreeable, and decorous, and has any the most squeamish immoralist in Vanity Fair a right to cry fie? When, however, the siren disappears and dives below, down among the dead men, the water of course grows turbid over her, and it is labour lost to look into it ever so curiously. They look pretty enough when they sit upon a rock, twanging their harps and combing their hair, and sing, and beckon to you to come and hold the looking glass; but when they sink into their native element, depend on it those mermaids are about no good, and we had best not examine the fiendish marine cannibals, revelling and feasting on their wretched pickled victims. And so, when Becky is out of the way, be sure that she is not particularly well employed, and that the less that is said about her doings is in fact the better.''

Balzac's Valérie Marneffe required no such marginal comment. A reader occasionally asks for the privilege of making deductions from the facts.

A final contrast is to be noted between the two authors we have been considering. Jane Austen's inclination is for the dramatic or scenic display of her subject; Thackeray's emphasis is on the pictorial or panoramic aspects of his theme. His scenes are memorable for their rarity, and his big occasions have an intense, sometimes even a melodramatic, quality that has no counterpart in Jane Austen's quiet art. Examine his dramatic moments—Rawdon's discovery of Steyne and Rebecca, Esmond's encounter with the Chevalier, and you will realize that these are the drama of incident where actions not words explode. When material is so copious as Thackeray's we tend to gather general impressions rather than particular memories. His parcel of facts bulks large from the multiplication of the outer wrappings. He seldom isolates a situation to develop its full dramatic value, and when this big exception occurs the scene has an accidental salience that compels our attention by its very unexpectedness. It is much the same with his pictorial effects. We call him a pictorial rather than a dramatic writer, but our visual sense is not frequently stimulated by the quality of his descriptions. We remember Esmond in the choir stalls of Winchester Cathedral, and we thrill at the picture of Beatrix, taper in hand, coming down the stairway at Walcote. These pictures like the dramatic scenes are memorable for their isolation. His descriptions are usually not of the aspects of persons, things, or places. They are voluminous annotations rather of separate social items which by their inexhaustible multiplication acquire a cumulative value. His marginal comments are more copious than the text, and a journey that is really short turns out to be an endless and fortunately a delightful voyage.

His technical masterpiece is beyond question *The History of Henry Esmond* (1852). While there are reasons to justify the opinion that in this book Thackeray attained the highest reach of his art, it may at least be affirmed with confidence that in no other novel has he discovered a theme where the flaws and eddies of a naturally vagrant talent are so effectively controlled by the strong sweep and current of his design. He flings always a wide net, and looseness is the law of his genius even when a coherent compactness would have yielded a more adequate result. But in *Esmond* we are not conscious of this disharmony, and as we read and re-read the book we feel that the free pictorial treatment he has devised, with its occasional flashes of dramatic intensity, is not only the method best adapted to his genius, but is also the method inherent in the theme itself. It is one of the instances in literature, as rare as they are precious, where manner and matter are inseparably blended, and if questions are raised in the following pages as to the efficacy of some of the devices employed they will be advanced for the most part only to evoke the justifying answer.

It might be urged for example that Thackeray, so emphatically a man of the current hour, was ill advised to cast his subject back one hundred and fifty years. He lacked Scott's fervent intimacy with the past, and had not the historic imagination of many romantic writers of the second rank. It is true that Thackeray could find his footing only in a familiar world, but by a lucky accident his mind accommodated itself with more ease and intimacy to the age of Anne than to the Victorian period into which he happened to be born. He was the pioneer of all eighteenth-century enthusiasms, and the historic research to which he applied himself for the purpose of his novel was but supplementary to the knowledge of the tone and temper of the age which he had acquired by intimate contact with its literary records. He may be said to have tasted the *Tatler* and the *Spectator* with his morning coffee, and Swift and Gay and Prior were his daily diet. There is therefore but little artifice in the eighteenth-century flavor of his style, and few modifications of his natural utterance were necessary to secure his illusion. Clarity of construction, a plain and even formulation of his thought would represent Thackeray's idea of expression no less correctly than that of Swift. He has of course here and there swerved from the classical restraint which his chosen arbiters of style had imposed upon him. His expression at times takes on a glow which marks him in spite of himself the child of a romantic age. I might refer the interested reader to various passages of description which are more heightened and detailed than anything furnished by his prototypes, and the opening page of Book III, Chapter VI will give him an example of emotional utterance for which he will find no parallel in that age of dignified discretion.

Satisfied therefore of Thackeray's competency to deal adequately with the period of his choice we may proceed to a more detailed consideration of his plan and purpose.

He had chosen his age. His business now was to find a story which should combine the intimacies of private life with the excitement of public affairs. Confining himself to the domestic sphere he would have labored in vain to match the living portraiture of Fielding and Smollett. A Squire Western or an Abraham Adams could never issue from the mind of a mere historian, but the perspective of time gave him on the other hand advantages denied to the contemporary observer. He was sailing on a well-charted sea, and could gauge the strength of the conflicting currents. If therefore he could discover some narrator who had lived in the full press of these excitements and might be moved in his reminiscential old age to set down the record of the stirring events that had already shaped themselves as history the result would combine the merits of immediate observation with all the advantages that derive from a knowledge of the accomplished fact. Such a recorder was found in the person of Henry Esmond, who in the leisure of his Virginian retreat sets down the story of his early days for the benefit of his descendants.

With the choice of this narrator Thackeray's main difficulties were solved, and he provided himself with a point of view that accorded singularly with his own. By temperament and conviction a Hanoverian Whig Thackeray's artistic instinct swayed him to the less reasonable side. There lay romance, there lay poetry, and there of necessity lay his story. So Esmond while the tale lasts is a declared Jacobite, less by conviction than by family affiliation, but when he sets down the record of his life the time of his disillusionment has arrived. It cannot be said that the narrative is unduly warped by this political bias save in one glaring instance at the crisis of the book. Esmond has to be weaned at once from Beatrix and from the Jacobite cause. Thackeray defies the truth in a measure that we may condone by bringing the Chevalier secretly to England while his sister was still alive, but there is no justification beyond the doubtful needs of the narrative for the wanton

[111]

misrepresentation of his character. James Edward was never a dissipated libertine, but, for a Stuart, amazingly sober, continent, and dull. Esmond's estimates of Swift and Marlborough may be harsh, but have some support in truth. The point we urge with emphasis is that an historic novelist may manipulate facts with relative impunity, but he is under severe compulsion to deal honestly with the characters of his historic figures.

Henry Esmond was born in 1678. The Memoir was supposedly completed by 1744, though a phrase from the preface "My years are past the Hebrew poet's limit" would set it as late as 1750. It takes on therefore the character of a long retrospect, and were it to proceed with perfect naturalness it would consist almost entirely of narration, description and reflective comment. How uncomfortably Dickens would have moved in this thick undramatic medium! and even Thackeray who worked always for breadth rather than intensity of effect found it necessary to break the strictly memoir tone by passages of recovered dialogue which bring us into immediate contact with events as they occur. By their relative infrequency they are the more memorable. Indeed in point of dramatic intensity the *Esmond* of Thackeray cannot be said to be markedly inferior to his other books, for it is always under compulsion that he sets a scene and permits his actors to vent their passion in words.

The form of a novel is conditioned by the relation which the author assumes towards his story. He may constitute himself the authoritative center of reference. All his characters are then projected on the same plane, though of course the author is free to graduate our interest in them as he deems them more or less worthy of attention. The important ones he analyzes by external comment, explores their consciousness, sets snares for their feet, traps for their hearts, and multiplies opportunities for their triumph or discomfiture. Save for the analytic element this is the primordial form of narrative—the story-teller who knows and the audience greedy for information. Let us consider now the advantages and difficulties which Thackeray encountered by substituting for himself a narrator who not only tells the story but has enacted it. Instances so multiply as to make selection difficult. I may therefore begin with such results of his choice of method as require only to be mentioned to be understood. The exploration of a few chapters will set us on our way.

The preface to the book is ostensibly furnished by Esmond's Virginian daughter, Rachel Warrington. This gives to the fiction that follows the desired element of credibility, but something more is aimed at than merely to conquer our credence. One handicap of the autobiographical form is that the narrator tends to be left in shadow. Everything to be sure in the narrative relates to him, and we enter his mind through his reactions to events and persons, but he cannot present himself objectively, and we miss in his portrait the salience of externalized figures. Beatrice we realize more vividly by Esmond's reflexes than if an impersonal author had sought to render her, but our conception of Esmond is vague and inferential. The daughter's introduction and footnotes added by her to the text are designed therefore to give us this necessary outside view of Esmond's character and appearance.

Esmond now takes pen in hand, but before initiating his narrative avails himself of old age's moralizing privilege. Author's asides are not usually to be commended, and Thackeray is an unrepentant sinner in this respect. But his memoir form legitimizes the device, and the moral comment flows in the stream of the story. . Thackeray's own views are naturally strained through Esmond's mind. The reflections are apt and penetrating, and the narrative would be the poorer for their omission.

Esmond is a boy of twelve when the story opens with the arrival in Castlewood of Francis, the new viscount, his wife Rachel, Beatrix, their daughter of three or four, and Francis the baby of two. The impression which Rachel makes upon him is lively after more than fifty years: "The new and fair lady of Castlewood found the sad lonely little occupant of this gallery busy over his great book, which he laid down when he was aware that a stranger was at hand. And, knowing who that person must be, the lad stood up and bowed before her, performing a shy obeisance to the mistress of the house.

"She stretched out her hand—indeed when was it that that hand would not stretch out to do an act of kindness, or to protect grief and ill-fortune! 'And this is our kinsman,' she said; 'And what is your name, kinsman?'

" 'My name is Henry Esmond,' said the lad, looking up at her in a sort of delight and wonder for she had come upon him as a *Dea certe*, and appeared the most charming object he had ever looked on. Her golden hair was shining in the gold of the sun; her complexion was of a dazzling bloom, her lips smiling, and her eyes beaming with a kindness which made Harry Esmond's heart to beat with surprise."

This passage has more value than appears on the surface, for it adjusts our point of view at the outset to the charm and graciousness of Rachel, and to the precocious gravity of the boy who is her junior by eight years. The author's problem will be to lead us through the subsequent years of Esmond's infatuation for the daughter to his marriage with the mother; and infinite and almost successful are the pains he takes to accommodate us to this strange adjustment of his affections.

The dialogue is scanty in this first chapter. The second is devoted entirely to a narrative account of the Castlewood family. The third dips back into Esmond's earlier childhood, when Father Holt takes him from Ealing to Castlewood where his putative father Thomas has just taken possession of his estate. Until Chapter VI the story concerns itself wholly with this early period in which we get an impression of perpetual Catholic plotting, are given an adequate description of Castlewood, and are made acquainted with the droll Isabel who figures as the Dowager Countess in the later portions of the story. Chapter VII links up in time with Chapter I, and is chiefly in the vein of reminiscential narrative. Again the graciousness of Rachel is in evidence, her devotion to her husband, and her growing suspicion of his faithlessness to her. When Harry brings smallpox to the house from having petted the blacksmith's daughter, Rachel shows an unsuspected capacity for temper in a sharp colloquy with the peccant youth. Beatrix and her father have fled the contagion, Rachel and Henry suffer and recover, she with her beauty ravaged, and he with spirits even more than usually depressed. Having damaged her beauty to achieve her husband's complete alienation, the author has to mend it again like Amelia's broken nose in Fielding's story. He could not afford to have her too crushingly eclipsed by Beatrix's growing radiance. Later passages will convey to the reader through Dick Steele's enthusiastic report a conviction that her beauty is wholly restored—a romantic adjustment that Thackeray's generation demanded.

The next chapter takes Esmond to Cambridge. His life there is merely generalized, but the episode serves to make us naturally aware of the passage of time, a purpose that justifies also the heavy blocks of campaigning narrative later in the book. Thackeray's handling of the time element is masterly throughout. He makes minor chronological blunders here and there and his manipulation of dates is sometimes confusing, but few books give us so charmed a sense of the wash and ripple of the years. It is a bold thing to single out one element from so many that co-operate to produce a great effect, but if the harmony of this book derives from one source more than another it is assuredly from the tenderness of its retrospective vision. While reading we may be uncomfortably conscious that Thackeray was unwilling to leave anything out which might count for fullness of impression—the campaigning chapters and the too conscientious introduction of notabilities suffice to make the point—but these fade in the afterglow of memory, and the poetry remains.

Chapter X

A GROUP OF DICKENS'S NOVELS

The world is so immeasurably in Dickens's debt, and so firmly do his finer qualities root themselves in his defects, that it is difficult to determine where admiration should end and criticism begin. Our concern being largely with the technical processes of his art we shall not lie open to the charge of intellectual snobbery if we take occasion to point out that in a constructional sense Dickens was often his own worst enemy. He was one of the anomalies of literature who would seem to have produced a great result by defective means, and if that is true he is a standing menace to the academic critic who would be well advised before dismissing him to revive his own faltering sense of humor.

It is fortunately but a half truth. Dickens's great effects were obtained only when the artist was perhaps unconsciously working within him; his failures were for the most part the result of a deliberate but misguided intention. Striking as the result was, it might conceivably have been more impressive—and here we are treading on dangerous ground—if he had been a shade more self-critical and intelligent. For mass appeal his method was beyond reproach. By its means he had gained a vast audience, and he knew every trick of the game for holding their attention. They wanted sentiment, they wanted satire, and they wanted fun. They had an unquenchable thirst for mystery, and an inappeasable zest for horrors. Sensationalism was the soul of the cheap miscellanies by which literature reached the mid-Victorian multitude, and all these alluring stimulants Dickens poured them in brimming measure. We may be sure that he found nothing nauseating in the draught. The more fastidious Thackeray might protest, but Dickens had the market. He was the universal provider. He may have created the desire, but what was demanded he gave; and if his dear public objected to the turn a story was taking no artistic scruples deterred him from meeting their desire. Seventy thousand people subscribe to *Master Humphrey's Clock*, thinking it a new novel by Boz. When they discover their mistake the list shrinks. When they are given *The Old Curiosity Shop* the list grows. *Martin Chuzzlewit* is doing badly at home. Dickens announces a visit to America (which has nothing to do with the original plan of the book, if it had a plan) and the sales miraculously rise. Mrs. Mowcher was degenerating. The original Mrs. Mowcher protests and she becomes a reformed character. Instances could be multiplied. It is all very clever, but what becomes of the artistic conscience? Dickens we may be sure did not greatly care, and it would not be just to him to say that the motive was purely mercenary. It was rather that he loved his public, and they naturally repaid him in kind.

Another thing they craved was the rousing excitement of a good story with multiple crises and mystifying suspense. So Dickens sought to give them that, and we find the tyranny of the artificial plot imposing itself upon him increasingly as his career advances. There is no story in *Pickwick*, and it is not very curiously contrived in *Oliver Twist* and *Nicholas Nickleby*, his next two ventures. We have noted how loosely fashioned it was in *Martin Chuzzlewit*. When we reach *Dombey and Son* it is another matter; and since this book passes currently as his best constructed novel we may profitably examine it.

The theme of the book is the vice of pride and its disastrous consequences. Before its downfall pride must have its victim. It will dominate for a season, but we may trust Dickens before the close to redress the balance, and following the heavenly hint throw down the mighty from their seats and exalt the humble and meek. Under the pressure of that prescription his story will be shaped and his mimic world fashioned; and if any intrusive characters insist upon appearing Dickens will labor hard at any cost of probability to give them some spurious attachment to his plot scheme.

Little Paul is one of the generative figures in the book. Intrinsically pathetic and interesting in himself whatever the pedants may say, he is also a touchstone of all the virtues and vices in others, and the pivotal center of Dickens's accustomed attack upon educational methods. Paul therefore necessitates Dr. Blimber and Dr. Blimber gives us Toots, who apart from his function as an inoffensive fun-maker will be useful in rounding off the happy marriages at the end.

Now Paul, being predestined for an early death, must be provided with a sister to carry on the story when he has gone, for obviously a renewal of interest will be as necessary as it is difficult. And thus Florence emerges, and it is not for lack of hard-working intention on her creator's part that we may not be violently interested in her. She is an example of suffering goodness, craving love and receiving it while Paul lives, but steadfastly refused affection from her father, and driven from his house by such a blow as a drunken carter might have dealt an aggravating wife.

Florence must naturally have her vacuum world filled, and Susan Nipper for a beginning is the happiest of solutions—a most alert and forceful character with not a trace of the infant-adultism that besets so many of Dickens's comic creations. She is thoroughly grown-up even from the moment when we meet her as a child of fourteen, and though she has nothing more to do with the story than to marry Toots at the end, she is one of those intrusive characters who are capable of standing on their own feet, and justify themselves by merely existing.

There must be more people of course. Envisaging the happy end we must have a lover in preparation, and that gives us Walter with his entourage, old Solomon Gill and Captain Cuttle.

Solomon and Captain Cuttle are good specimens of the infant adult, the former sparsely characterized, the latter amply provided with the tics and mannerisms by which Dickens's least convincing comic creations may be recognized. Cuttle does not go very deep or very far, but is amusing when he combs his hair with his hook. There is no great reach of humor in the Gargantuan watch or the preposterous hat, but they occur so often that they perhaps have some deep meaning which escapes us. Walter is one of the good young men who evidently gave his inventor trouble. He is sufficiently colorless as he stands. It had been the author's intention when he sent him away to the Barbadoes to exhibit him in a series of discreditable escapades after the Smollett manner. His imagination was competent for the task, but he knew that his audience would shy away from a sullied lover, and refrained. There was room for plenty of villainy in the book without Walter, and when he disappears and his ship is lost we are comfortably assured that some convenient spar will be provided to keep him afloat until he receives his next cue for entrance.

Such is the provision made for Florence.

Pride is an isolating vice, but Mr. Dombey's solitude cannot afford to be left complete. While young Paul lives he is sufficiently occupied, yet even in those early days we are prepared for the continuous manifestation of his hateful qualities. His sister Mrs. Chick and the adoring Miss Tox are not sufficient. It will certainly be a good idea to give him a second wife, not meekly acquiescent like his first martyr, nor such an idolizing subservient as Miss Tox would have proved to be, but a character who could match him on his own ground of hardness and pride. Edith Grainger, less tartarly and venomous than the typical Dickens shrew, but coldly determined and icily vindictive, is the preordained successor. Major Bagstock, that most insufferable of army bores, is her discoverer. "Old Joey" brings Edith Grainger and Dombey together to checkmate Miss Tox's designs on the proud financier, and here we say good-bye to all probability. Individual scenes will have strokes of the minute realism of which Dickens was a master, but the whole scheme of the book from this point rests on a false and wildly improbably human basis. It is conceivable that Dombey might have thought that Edith's beauty would adorn the head of his table. The most reckless romantic imagination could not conceive Edith's submitting to her mother's pressure to marry Dombey. The marriage that follows breeds still grosser improbabilities. The disputes and bickerings we accept as inevitable, but the manner of Carker's intervention, the crying inconsequence of his character, and the whole Alice Marwood episode are hardly on the level of third-rate romantic invention. The climax of absurdity is reached when Edith Dombey leaves her house as the apparent paramour of the man she despises more cordially even than her own husband, if a still more inconceivable climax is not provided by the untasted supper in the Dijon hotel.

Were we searching for a classic example of the plot running away with the story we need look no further, and after this does it much matter what conclusion is reached?

Carker has a gruesome taking off, for no penny-a-liner could get his lurid effects with more melodramatic *brio* than Dickens. His inexperienced hand had already shown its cunning with Bill Sikes, and there is scarcely a book that follows which has not its chamber of horrors. Peals of wedding bells ring out for the good, and Dombey, bankrupt and imbecile, has no power remaining to resist his daughter's devotion.

We may assert with confidence that Dickens wrote his flourishing *Finis* to this book with a sense of utmost artistic satisfaction. I have suggested what a thorn in the flesh he is to the formalist. The book not only succeeded with the multitude, but even the alert readers of his day accepted the platitudes with equanimity and the absurdities with delight, and acclaimed the book as a triumph of constructional art. We of a later and, as we think, wiser generation are confident that the book is badly done, but are constrained to the somewhat sad conclusion that exuberance, vitality, and creative energy seem to be a very sufficient substitute for art. We perhaps too timidly hope that these essential qualities might conceivably be more effectively operative with a subtler æsthetic control. Otherwise the whole problem of design is empty of meaning.

We have been examining a typical novel of Dickens's maturity. Let us now more briefly glance at his first novel *Oliver Twist*, less complicated and tyrannical in its plot, but with the tendencies of his later fiction already in lively evidence. These fall into obvious headings:

Pathos. A tender child in a den of thieves.

Mystery. Who is Oliver Twist?

Sensationalism. Monk's disease-blasted face; the death of Sikes; the death of Fagin.

Author's moralizing comment; as for example this as typical of many passages:

Ch. xxx. "It was a solemn thing, to hear, in the darkened room, the feeble voice of the sick child recounting a weary catalogue of evils and calamities which hard men had brought upon him. Oh! if when we oppress and grind our fellow-creatures, we bestowed but one thought on the dark evidences of human error, which like dense and heavy clouds, are rising, slowly it is true, but not less surely, to Heaven, to pour their after-vengeance on our heads; if we heard but one instant, in imagination, the deep testimony of dead men's voices, which no power can stifle, and no pride shut out; where would be the injury and injustice, the suffering, misery, cruelty, and wrong, that each day's life brings with it!"

There is much of this fustian in Dickens. Is it because of our lack of moral earnestness that we fail to relish it?

Realism Genuine and Spurious. Characteristic always of Dickens are topsy-turvy or violently unreal situations presented with the most acute visual accuracy. We should remember that Reade and Collins and even Disraeli and Kingsley, sharing his view that the novel is an effective instrument of social regeneration, shared also his view that evil conditions should be reproduced with no mitigation of their gruesome detail. Of this group Dickens was the most visually gifted, and when he ceases to be real it is either because he cannot refrain from introducing the melodramatic admixture that distorts his picture, or because his Victorian conscience refused to tolerate the cruder excesses of criminality and blasphemy that his situations demanded. It is therefore most delicately conveyed to us that Nancy is Sikes's mistress, and the latter is once permitted to vent his rage with the violent exclamation: "Wolves tear your throat!" Our modern realists would be less delicately evasive.

[123]

Dramatic Intention. Dickens had little time or inclination to theorize upon the novel, but he has pronounced a few general working principles of more æsthetic scope than the mere pleasing of an unlettered public. Of these the most important and the most reiterated was the compulsion to let the story tell itself. In his simple way he got to the heart of the modern problem which recognizes the same necessity, and theoretically at least he anticipates the twentieth-century distrust of auctorial intervention. His own ineptitude saved him from some of the difficulties of our psychological age. It was with a clean conscience that he rejected analysis, and with a certain knowledge of his own capability that he substituted dialogue as the revealing medium. He recognizes the need of conditioning his characters by physical and local description, but is in his happiest vein when he is able to leave them to their own devices. This theory should, but with Dickens unfortunately does not, exclude moral commentary on the author's part; and it also throws upon him the obligation of making speech so characteristic that not only will types and classes be distinguished, but individuals within these classes will have also their clear note of differentiation. In this respect *Oliver Twist* is not a good example of his power. We have observed the restraint in the colloquies of his criminals, where theory and practice were probably justified in parting company; and portions of his polite dialogue—I may instance Harry Meglie's interviews with Rose—are singularly colorless and flat. That the speech element is still so effective in his novels is merely another of the anomalies with which Dickens's genius confronts us.

Before dipping again into the stream of English fiction let us consider the contribution of the two most important American novelists of the mid-century period.

CHAPTER XI

NATHANIEL HAWTHORNE AND
THE SCARLET LETTER

For a generation Hawthorne was the only writer of fiction who could return a portion of America's debt to England, and his particular contribution was not a new technique but a new mentality. Apart from his penchant for symbol and a somewhat extended use of external commentary there is little in his narrative manner that distinguishes him from his English predecessors. It is the Hawthorne tone that is the novelty. Other novelists may have been more tragically-minded than Hawthorne. None surely had ever been so temperamentally depressed, and none had ever carried the cult of joylessness to such curious and, strange to say, such exquisite conclusions. For he is a fastidious and refined writer, and compels in us a reluctant æsthetic delight in physical distress and spiritual deterioration.

He is sufficiently conscious of his own peculiarities. "It is odd enough," he once wrote to a friend, "that my own individual taste is for quite another class of novels than those which I myself am able to write. If I were to meet with such books as mine by another writer, I don't believe I should be able to get through them. Have you ever read the novels of Anthony Trollope? They precisely suit my taste; solid and substantial, written on the strength of beef and through the inspiration of ale, and just as real as if some giant had hewn a great lump out 'of the earth, and put it under a glass case with all its inhabitants going about their daily business, and not suspecting that they were made a show of."

He is an interesting example of the type known in our day as a defeatist, and in his discomfiture he can achieve only a mildly ironic revenge upon the life that has baffled and beaten him. The strain of morbidity and shy aloofness in his nature made him at once eager for joy and incapable of attaining it, and all his writings are eloquent of this spiritual dislocation. Mr. Van Wyck Brooks has called him the "most deeply planted of American writers, who indicates more than any other the subterranean history of the American character." I suppose the reference here is to America's Puritanic inheritance, and the racial characteristic of enjoying pleasure sadly. The haunting sense of sin and the gloom of moral responsibility count for much, we admit, in Hawthorne's work, but we cannot assert these to be representative of the present American temper, and when we come to estimate the writings we are uneasily aware that they do not even represent the temper of the man himself. He is admittedly an artist of more than average merit, but we are constantly sensible of the fact that his representation of life tarries far in the rear of his own intellectual advance. He was compelled to proffer what his mind did not wholly accept, and his partial emancipation from the Puritanic coil bred in him a genuine distaste for his own achievement. He wanted sun and air and movement and liberation from constraint, and was compelled to give us studies in morbidity and gloom from which all joyousness or capability of joy have departed.

The Scarlet Letter is artistically the most satisfying of his longer stories. The author ascribed its popularity to the initial chapter where with something less than Lamb's whimsicality and poetry he rehearses his memories of the Salem Custom House. He confers a dubious authenticity upon his narrative by the fabled discovery there of Hester Prynne's identical scarlet letter with an attached explanatory document. Characteristically he launches his story proper with the emblematic symbol of a rose-bush, which might serve, he hoped, "to symbolize some sweet moral blossom, that may be found along the track, or relieve the darkening close of a tale of human frailty and sorrow." Hester's scarlet letter is such another symbol, the scaffold in the market place, the stream which divides her from her daughter when she and Dimmesdale have their momentous meeting in the wood, and the rather preposterous meteor which spreads its flaming A across the sky. If we add the mysterious A which Dimmesdale has branded over his heart we have reached the end of symbols, but have not indicated the constancy of their recurrence nor the elaboration with which the author develops their significance. I have not claimed for Hawthorne any marked originality as a technician, but while there is nothing revolutionary in his allegorizing trick it may serve to exemplify his most definite innovation in narrative method. It is a dangerous expedient, and not likely to perpetuate itself.

For the rest his mode of procedure is sufficiently conventional, and I must repeat that his power derives from the peculiar cast of his mentality, and the fascination with which certain moral problems attracted and repelled him, so that he was constrained to be their unwilling and relentless historian.

Hester has sinned against the Puritanic code. How will she expiate her crime? Dimmesdale has been her paramour in the far-off happy time. How will his conscience fare, and his priestly nature reconcile itself with a hidden vice? Everything in a sense has happened before the story begins, and only the tortured writhings of conscience remain to be exploited. The investigatory torch is applied to each in turn, but it is on the victim who has not made expiation that its light burns most fiercely. For added torment the injured husband is supplied, and his moral deterioration splits the interest of the story by still another factor. Indeed so important does this third member of the trinity seem to the author that he lends us his explicit aid for interpretation of his case. "Old Roger Chillingworth, throughout life, had been calm in temperament, kindly, though not of warm affections, but ever, and in all his relations with the world, a pure and upright man. He had begun an investigation, as he imagined, with the severe and equal integrity of a judge, desirous only of truth, even as if the question involved no more than the air-drawn lines and figures of a geometrical problem, instead of human passions, and wrongs inflicted on himself. But, as he proceeded, a terrible fascination, a kind of fierce, though still calm, necessity seized the old man within its gripe, and never set him free again until he had done all its bidding." A few years of inquisitorial probing of his victim's plight, and this is the author's summary of the degradation wrought on his soul substance: "In a word, old Roger Chillingworth was a striking evidence of man's faculty of transforming himself into a devil, if he will only, for a reasonable space of time, undertake a devil's office. This unhappy person had effected such a transformation, by devoting himself, for seven years, to the constant analysis of a heart full of torture, and deriving his enjoyment thence, and adding fuel to those fiery tortures which he analyzed and gloated over."

These are interpretative expedients that belong to a vanished age of fiction, and no less than the antiquated presentation of sin and expiation demand some degree of imaginative adaptation on the part of the modern reader. What we miss most perhaps is the lack of sun and circulation in the book. A narrow segment only of life is presented to our gaze. What was old Roger doing when he was not gathering herbs or anatomizing Dimmesdale's soul, or Dimmesdale when he was not preaching or pressing his hand over his heart, or Hester when she was not sewing or prattling with her elfin child? There are necessary contacts of course between the three, but even upon these interviews the horizon broods with oppressive closeness.

Chapter XII

HERMAN MELVILLE AND *MOBY DICK*

Superlatives are as common now about Melville as they were rare when they would have counted most. They abound too on foreign soil, and indicate a quality of universality in his genius that gives him almost solitary rank among his countrymen. We should fare ill if we sought to treat him as mere novelist. He certainly thought as little of the craft as Defoe, and was a maker of books sometimes because he needed money, and once at least because great ideas demanded release. This does not mean that profound implications are confined to *Moby Dick*. Anywhere we may be prepared to encounter significance, but once only in his life was a whole book drenched in power so that the most unregarded page registers in the total impression.

An enumeration of items in *Moby Dick* might imply a careless disdain of cohesion; but if we read the book with insight this false view corrects itself, and every seeming digression will be found to relate itself to the dominant idea. What that idea may be is another matter. It is a cloudy spiritual symbol that will find as many interpretations as there are commentators, as there are readers, and it is one of the virtues of the book that no one can impose upon us his individual explanation. Even the shallowest among us can realize that here is an author who is confronting ultimate problems courageously if not triumphantly, and in the measure of our own adventuring minds we can read our way into his meanings.

Much humor goes with his seriousness and his poetry,

and when Ishmael stuffs a shirt or two into his old carpet-bag, tucks it under his arm, and starts for Cape Horn and the Pacific we are quite ready to journey with him. New Bedford is the jumping off place for Nantucket where he is to find his whaler, and quaint things befall him there. The Queequeg encounter is touched with incomparable comic zest, and then we are in the heart of high seriousness with Father Mapple's sermon on Jonah as spoken in the whalesman's chapel.

The next originals we encounter are Captains Peleg and Bildad, the managing owners of the "Pequod," who reveal a swift firmness in characterization that any novelist might envy. They pilot the ship into the open and are let over the side. "Ship and boat diverged; the cold, damp night-breeze blew between; a screaming gull flew overhead; the two hulls wildly rolled; we gave three heavy-hearted cheers, and blindly plunged like fate into the lone Atlantic."

Though our course may be set for mystery and terror we are brought back reassuringly to the shores of matter of fact in a dissertation on the dignity of whaling, and still are in the region of normal circumstance in the author's masterly survey of the "Pequod's" three mates, Starbuck, Stubb, and Flask. Grimness and fantasticality enter in with the presentation of the three harpooners, the cannibal, the Indian, and the black, and the stage is then set for Ahab's first appearance.

"It was one of those less lowering, but still grey and gloomy enough mornings of the transition, when with a fair wind the ship was rushing through the water with a vindictive sort of leaping and melancholy rapidity, that as I mounted to the deck at the call of the forenoon watch, so soon as I levelled my glance towards the taffrail, foreboding shivers ran over me. Reality outran apprehensions; Captain Ahab stood upon the quarter-deck."

[131]

The gray hairs, the seamed scarred face, the grim immobility of the ivory leg firm-fixed in its augur-hole on the deck,—so Ishmael and we behold him standing erect and looking straight out beyond the ship's ever-pitching prow. "There was an infinity of firmest fortitude, a determinate, unsurrenderable wilfulness, in the fixed and fearless, forward dedication of that glance. Not a word he spoke; nor did his officers say aught to him; though by all their minutest gestures and expressions, they plainly showed the uneasy, if not painful, consciousness of being under a troubled master-eye. And not only that, but moody stricken Ahab stood before them with an apparently eternal anguish in his face; in all the nameless overbearing dignity of some mighty woe."

Ahab and the whale are the master symbols of the book. With the former tension is never relaxed. His set purpose has a maniacal ferocity that has had no counterpart in literature since Lear stormed upon the heath. Moby Dick his antagonist has the same isolation of power, but it is one of the curious features of this book that his fellow whales are mere mammalia to be chased and hacked and hewed, to provide their stores of ambergris, oil, and spermaceti, and to furnish matter for the technical descriptions where we falsely imagine the author to have sunk his prophetic intentions in a merely practical enthusiasm. It was more truly the greatness of his general conception that justified and even necessitated these details as part of his larger symbolic design. Strenuous indeed must be the dominant idea that could exercise such compelling force, and how strenuous his own words inform us: "How then with me, writing of this Leviathan? Unconsciously, my chirography expands into placard capitals. Give me a condor's quill! Give me Vesuvius' crater for an inkstand! Friends! hold my arms! For in the mere act of penning my thoughts of this Leviathan, they weary me, and make me faint with the outreaching comprehensiveness of sweep, as if to include the whole circle of the sciences, and all the generations of whales, and men, and mastodons, past, present, and to come, with all the revolving panoramas of empire on earth, and throughout the whole universe, not excluding its suburbs. Such, and so magnifying, is the virtue of a large and liberal theme! We expand to its bulk. To produce a mighty volume you must choose a mighty theme. No great and enduring volume can ever be written upon the flea, though many there be who have tried it."

A strange book indeed and a strange man. At eighteen he ships before the mast for a short sea voyage, and returns from Liverpool to a round of teaching drudgery. When twenty-one he boards a whaler, traverses the South Seas, and deserts his ship to live among the Marquesas cannibals. He escaped to further adventures in the South Pacific, and in 1843, aged twenty-four, shipped for home on board the frigate "United States." It was these seven years that furnished forth the plain narratives of *Typee*, *Redburn*, *Omoo*, and *White Jacket*, and that bred the perturbations of spirit from which the mightier *Moby Dick* was born. We are not more puzzled than Melville himself at this fierce and unexpected evolution of energy. Midway through his masterpiece he writes to Hawthorne: "My development has all been within a few years past. I am like one of those seeds taken out of the Egyptian pyramids which, after being three thousand years a seed, and nothing but a seed, being planted in English soil, it developed itself, grew to greenness, and then fell to mould. So I. Until I was twenty-five I had no development at all. From my twenty-fifth year I date my life. Three weeks have scarcely passed, at any time between then and now, that I have not unfolded within myself. But I feel that I am now come to the utmost leaf of the bulb, and that shortly the flower must fall to the mould."

This is a premonition which the forty almost sterile years that followed raise to the dignity of true prophecy. In his decay as in his development there is something strangely abnormal about Melville. It is easy to say that he had written himself out, as if having discharged so rich a cargo there was nothing left in the hold. There were riches still in the depths, but though his mind had kept its power it had lost its tone. Something between Hamlet's melancholy and Timon's misanthropy made expression savorless for him to the end. Great creative work is always an effort towards equilibrium, and Melville's attempt at adjustment had ended in failure. I do not refer of course to the lack of appreciation of the book, but to his failure to find his own spiritual bearings. He had left out the half of creation. His books are womanless, and his married life did not carry him far on his quest. Abstract philosophers can dodge the personal equation, but as soon as you put human beings into your books they must be allowed to function. They exist for Melville, but always to whet his dissatisfaction. His women, as I have said, are almost ciphers, and there are no currents of sympathy cementing his men, nor even currents of hate to divide them. Ishmael and Queequeg swear eternal friendship, but when the book is launched we are in the play of eternal forces for which mere human relationships have no significance. A dehumanized hate and defiance are pitted against an implacable impersonal malignity. There is no room for normal contacts, though the ship carries three sane mates, and three uncontaminated savages. Where relationships are allowed to develop they will be denaturalized, and Ahab the monomaniac of the idea will be permitted some access of tenderness only for the sinister Fedellah or the imbecile Pip.

The academic question "Is *Moby Dick* a novel?" should be reduced now to its proper level of importance. There is a rush of narrative energy when the author cares to use it, a rich power of characterization when he cares to use it, fine qualities of description, and reflective depth. These duly combined are the constituent elements of fiction, but I should prefer to recommend *Moby Dick* as one of the great books of the century than as one of the great novels.

With the Brontës and George Eliot we now resume our account of English developments.

Chapter XIII

THE BRONTËS

The hunger and thirst for particulars of the lives and habits of celebrities is inappeasable. It is a legitimate if slightly vulgar curiosity, and to protest against the desire to satisfy it would be unavailing. But we are entitled to question the efficacy of this biographical method in revealing the essential truth about an author. Up to a certain point it is reliable and satisfactory. Beyond that it is mischievous and misleading, for it tends to divert our attention from the work of art to circumstantial detail of no conceivable relevance. Mr. E. M. Forster has said that all great literature tends towards anonymity. This leans too far in the other direction, for every work of power carries the spiritual signature of its creator. But it would not enhance our appreciation or understanding of the *Iliad* to know that Homer had sprained his ankle in the year 800 B.C., or had been jilted by the village beauty. It would be an excellent bit of luck, apart from the financial return, to find a lost manuscript of Shakespeare, for that would relate itself much more truly to his genius than any further discovered details about his second-best bed. We are too inclined, I think, to make a man's art run in the same groove as his daily life. A relationship there is of course, but it is rather a remote parallelism than an identification, and we should always realize the degree of detachment that obtains between a work of art and the known habits of a man's day by day existence, or even the character front he displays to the world. Music and painting are naturally more detached than is literature which concerns itself more with the ordinary details of living, but even with the poet, the novelist, or the dramatist there is in his creative mood an unescapable something which defies registration in terms of his normal existence. We may interpret the novel or the poem, but its genesis will escape us, and more particularly will our attempt to explain it in terms of the author's environment be unavailing. What conceivable contact is there between the mundane Coleridge and the transmundane creator of *The Ancient Mariner*, and dare we affirm that the poem suffers by this lack of cohesion? The man had not even been to sea when he wrote it, but Mr. Lowes in *The Road to Xanadu* has tracked down many strange books he had read since boyhood, and has forced us to admit the importance at least of mental backgrounds, whatever else we reject as relatively indifferent. A bee is a queen bee by the food it eats, and we might detect a similar chemic virtue in the cerebral nourishment of genius had we the skill to apply the test. But unfortunately the source hunter is too much of a pedant to follow up his clues, and therefore this critical approach usually ends in a blind alley.

If we consider the case of the Brontës the appositeness of these remarks will be evident. The source hunter has luckily not been very busy, but their little plot of life has been tracked and retracked by plodding biographical feet until all semblance of a path has been obliterated. Our human curiosity is satisfied, but our intelligence is insufficiently fed. The strange and fascinating books they wrote do not emerge from the lives they led. They were in debt of course to their many predecessors who had shaped their instrument of fiction, but we must relinquish as idle speculation any attempt to explain their books in terms of Haworth Rectory, a half-blind and irritable father, a derelict and disreputable brother, and gusty northern moors. Or at best by a process of inversion we may hope to account for these books as their angry effort to escape from a hated environment, and to project themselves into an atmosphere where their minds could freely breathe. Sublimations and inhibitions are words that have drifted down to us from the Freudian vocabulary, but they are not without their application to these frustrated, eager, and angry sisters. Innocent and repressed, their imagination has a masochistic twist exhibited with sufficient clearness in their masculine types. The secondary males are mild enough, but masterfulness is the note of the major figures, tempered by a strain of gentleness in Rochester and Paul Emanuel, but innocent of any hint of mercy in Emily's implacable Heathcliff. The mild curates they knew at home could not generate this breed, and Paul's prototype Monsieur Héger is only a faint adumbration of the vital figure he suggested.

The mention of M. Héger leads to a consideration of another point where Brontë criticism is apt to stray. No novelists have ever worked upon a slenderer fund of experience, and the most attenuated hint of reality might on occasion be summoned to furnish forth the full-bodied picture. Hints with them are portents. Undoubtedly Charlotte was more in debt to these faint innuendos than her more daringly original sister—for the work-a-day world does not readily engender Heathcliffs—but even her gentler blood resented the imputation that she had made copy of her friends, her enemies, and her casual acquaintances. Hints and suggestions she developed of course from the only world she knew, but if M. Héger could have recognized himself in the Paul Emanuel of *Villette*, he must have experienced a vast expansion of pride at his enhanced consequence and vitality. He went down to the grave a mere three score and ten mortal. The death notice of Paul Emanuel has not yet been announced.

Mr. Clement Shorter after specifying every character in *Shirley* spends ten pages in identifying the localities and characters of *Jane Eyre*. He has satisfied our innocent curiosity, but has the good sense to conclude: "We may readily thrust aside, however, all these inquiries as to 'Keys' to *Jane Eyre*, and go to the real heart of the book, which is quite independent of plot and prototype. It is in reality as original a novel as was ever submitted to the judgment of the reading public." With this safeguard we may admit the peculiarly derivative element in her portraiture of persons and places, and pass on to other considerations.

Our concern is with the specific quality of her contribution to the form and content of fiction. Her subject matter can scarcely be said to be more extended than that of Jane Austen. She does not aspire to be polemical or informative. There is nothing markedly original in her method of attack, for she adopts without question the old rambling plotless mode of narrative in the first person. She is feminine enough not to be interested in physical adventure, yet sufficiently of her time to luxuriate in the mildly supernatural, and to risk on occasion such morbidly romantic situations as we encounter in *Jane Eyre*. Her real intentions can be divined in her expressed antipathy to Jane Austen, whom she evidently found tame and commonplace and passionless. *Pride and Prejudice* for example is "An accurate daguerrotyped portrait of a commonplace face; a carefully fenced, highly cultured garden, with neat borders and delicate flowers, but no glance of a bright vivid physiognomy, no open country, no fresh air, no blue hill, no bonny beck." This is partly true, but Jane can survive and even thrive upon the stricture. What follows is still more vindictive and therefore perhaps more illustrative of Charlotte Brontë's ambition: "The passions are perfectly unknown to her; she rejects even a speaking acquaintance with that stormy sisterhood. What sees keenly, speaks aptly, moves flexibly, it suits her to study, but what throbs fast and full, though hidden, what the blood rushes through, what is the unseen seat of life, and the sentient target of death, that Miss Austen ignores." "Though hidden" is the revealing phrase, for the signs and evidences of passion in Charlotte are compelled to pulsate beneath the surface, and suffer the check of all the conventional decencies. The only liberty with the proprieties one can discover in her work is that Jane at a given moment sits on Rochester's knee. We must therefore infer the "fast and full throb" from the alarmed protests of her own more sensitive generation.

If checked in the expression of passion by the prejudices of her time she more effectively supplies the other defect she had noted in Jane Austen. There have been few writers in our language with a more subtle and exquisite descriptive touch than she possesses. The wildness of the moors had entered into her blood, and more potently into Emily's. She has the genuine artist's eye, and color and contour are rendered with a precision and delicacy that none of her contemporaries could match. Her figurative speech has a like felicity, and if we asserted only that she combined the qualities of the poet and the artist we might seem to be giving her sufficient praise. These qualifications constitute her a great writer. But it is her powers of characterization that still more effectively perpetuate her reputation.

It is said that Emily died standing up in the parlor, refusing to go to bed, but leaning one hand upon the table. Literal truth or not this expresses Emily Brontë's resolute spirit, and reveals in her an almost unexampled capacity for suffering. It is these qualities that are transferred to her book, and make *Wuthering Heights* if not supreme among English novels still defiantly unique. It is undoubtedly too morbid and humorless to reach the highest excellence, but it has had no predecessor, and can have no successor until another Emily Brontë appears. As a link in the chain of English fiction it has therefore much less importance than a later solitary and defiant book, Butler's *Way of All Flesh*, which propagated a multitude of novels of like kind but less power.

An anonymous Hogarth essayist has explored the technique of *Wuthering Heights* to prove with what close precision all the dates and circumstances were calculated, and how cleverly this young girl had utilized the laws of property to support her intrigue. His findings are sound and useful as far as they go. They enable us at least to appreciate the skill with which the details are contrived, but we cannot by their aid account for the strange impressiveness of the book.

Let us summarize the tale before discussing how it gets itself told.

Two families, the Earnshaws and the Lintons, are involved. The elder Earnshaw has two children, Hindley and Catharine, and a few years before his death he introduces into the house a gypsy-like waif of a boy, Heathcliff, who is bullied by the older boy, Hindley, and befriended by Catharine. The Lintons of the neighboring Thrushcross Grange have also a boy and girl, Edgar and Isabella. When old Earnshaw dies, Hindley brings back a wife to Wuthering Heights, who dies in a year leaving a son, Hareton. At fifteen Catharine Earnshaw, still loving Heathcliff, becomes engaged to Edgar Linton for obviously mercenary reasons. Heathcliff disappears, and returns with a mysteriously acquired education and money, six months after Catharine's marriage. He installs himself at Wuthering Heights where he obtains a strange ascendancy over Hindley who has fallen into dissipated ways, and seeks also to terrorize the inoffensive Edgar Linton, who has married the woman he loves. His first act of vengeance is to elope with Edgar's sister Isabella, whom he treats with the utmost brutality, and brings back to Wuthering Heights. His passion for Catharine still possesses him. Catharine, after a stormy scene at Thrushcross Grange, gives birth to a daughter of the same name and dies. Isabella runs away from Heathcliff and produces a sickly child, Linton. This makes a third generation of young people, Hareton Earnshaw, Linton Heathcliff, and Catharine Linton, who now figure very actively in the story.

Years pass by and Catharine is trapped into a marriage with Heathcliff's sickly son, Linton. When the story opens she is a young widow at Wuthering Heights, her mother and father dead, and Heathcliff in possession of both properties. The plot now revolves round three people, for death has taken the elder Catharine Earnshaw, her husband Edgar Linton, his sister Isabella (Heathcliff's wife), their son Linton who had died at seventeen after the forced marriage with the younger Catharine, and Hindley Earnshaw the former owner of Wuthering Heights. It obviously requires much dexterity on author's and reader's part to straighten out the symmetrical entanglements of this highly genealogical romance. In the sequel Heathcliff dies, and Catharine at the book's close is to marry the regenerated Hareton Earnshaw.

Now, how is it all done?

A shadowy person called Lockwood has leased Thrushcross Grange from Mr. Heathcliff in the year 1801. He pays a visit to his landlord, and we learn immediately that there is something decidedly queer about the house and its inhabitants. The latter are Heathcliff the surly owner, Hareton Earnshaw an uncouth young man of twenty-three, and an interesting looking girl of seventeen, whom the visitor at first assumes to be Mrs. Heathcliff. Lockwood is storm-bound, and in his room at night he reads a record of the past that whets his curiosity. It was the elder Catharine's bitter commentary on events of twenty-four years ago, when her brother Hindley had brought a wife home after his father's death. This so whets his curiosity that when he reaches Thrushcross Grange he plies his housekeeper with numerous questions, and presently re-signs the narrative almost continuously into her hands. It is of course highly dramatized and copiously furnished with dialogue. It has reference to the past of twenty years before. In Chapter X we return to the present with Lockwood for a moment, and then Mrs. Dean again re-freshes his sick-bed, if refreshment is the right word, with details that carry the story down to the previous winter. Lockwood intervenes for a moment in Chapter XXV, but Mrs. Dean is a difficult woman to stop. Her last install-ment gives us the account of young Catharine and herself being inveigled into the Heathcliff house, and detained there while Catharine's father is dying in the other house. Catharine is forced to marry Linton Heathcliff—though no details of this are given—and escapes in time to hear her father's last words. The sickly Linton dies leaving under compulsion everything to his father, and Catharine lives on with the morose Heathcliff and the untamed Hareton Earnshaw, with Zillah and Joseph as kitchen companions.

Lockwood intervenes for a chapter, visiting the Heights to say that he will not renew his lease of Thrushcross Grange, and will pay for the balance of his twelve months' term. We can realize now how understandingly he can view the three with Mrs. Dean's narrative in his mind. He returns in the September of the following year, and Mrs. Dean fills the gap of the intervening months with the account of Heathcliff's last moody days, and Hareton's regeneration by Catharine, the only touch of light in the somberest of books. It is narrative at white heat, but it is only on reflection that we realize the inconsequence of putting it on Mrs. Dean's lips. But of course by that time she had had a lot of practice.

The book is too great to treat with levity, and the last remark was made seriously enough. We are uncomfortable whenever we think too closely of Mrs. Dean's intervention, and some of the confessions she reports could not conceivably have been made to her, could not conceivably have been made to any witness however enlightened. Heathcliff is morbid to the verge of insanity we admit, but he is taciturn and strong, and the one thing he holds sacred is the hate-love for Catharine whose earth-bound spirit has haunted him for twenty years, and whom he has haunted too with his love revenge since her death. What he did in the grave-yard was a secret that no mortal being could have wrenched from him, and it is straining convention to the breaking point to permit him to convey these gruesome details to a servant who despised and hated him. But they have to be conveyed, and Mrs. Dean transmits them to Lockwood, who transmits them to us. Poor Lockwood of course had broken down long since as an interlocutor, and no other substitute than Mrs. Dean was possible under the conditions which Emily Brontë had imposed on herself.

But the book survives this formal flaw. Are there other more serious impediments to the story's full effectiveness? Some readers will detect a curious break in the interest when the first Catharine dies. The story is hers and Heath-cliff's, and when she fades out of the book at a very early stage, subordinate figures must occupy the scene. What do we really care about Catharine the Second, or Linton Heathcliff, or Hareton, or the shadowy Lockwood? They are visible actors on a stage that is dominated by Heath-cliff and a ghost. If the story fails, and assuredly it does not fail, it will be because their mimic posturings distract our attention from the main actors. A shade less energy in the primary conception of the story, and it would have broken hopelessly long before the middle point was reached. But because the book came out of a deep spiritual or demonic experience this dislocation does not occur. What this experience was is Heathcliff's or Emily's secret. Certainly literature does not record so strange a love. It is wholly unreal and abnormal, but it has a ghostly po-tency. The only real things in the book are the moor-wind that blows through its pages, the ghostly moon, the spectral trees. Its strange virtue is that perhaps it is the unreal things that count for most,—the unrealities of a caged spirit making its dash for freedom. Emily had never loved, evidently knew nothing about love's actualities, but her Gondal poems reveal to us a Byronic demon lover, and Heathcliff is that man, at times her lover, and at times her tortured self.

Chapter XIV

GEORGE ELIOT

That George Eliot's direct influence is no longer active does not cancel her importance as a molder of English fiction. Indeed the fact that an influence has been absorbed and diffused is an indication that is was worth assimilating, and this is for our purpose the main consideration.

If we were searching only for affiliations and dependences it might be difficult to indicate George Eliot's importance in her craft. She is, when we strike the balance, decidedly more a creditor than a debtor. Something she owed to Fielding and something less to Scott, but so far as her own contemporaries are concerned she was perpetually pulling in a contrary direction. She stands for nothing almost that is to be found in the novels of Dickens, Thackeray, or George Sand. It is definitely less difficult to indicate successors who reaped from her sowing. Henry James was no one author's disciple, but of the blended influence of Balzac, Mérimée, Turgénev, and George Eliot he was himself consciously aware; and a novelist who can claim James as a transmitting medium is assured of a vicarious immortality were his books forever unopened on our shelves.

It was her philosophy and powers of observation that impressed James rather than her art. "It is to this union of the keenest observation with the ripest reflection, that her style owes its essential force. She is a thinker, not, perhaps, a passionate one, but at least a serious one; and the term can be applied with either adjective neither to Dickens nor Thackeray. The constant play of lively and vigorous thought about the objects furnished by her observation animates these latter with a surprising richness of colour and a truly human interest. It gives to the author's style, moreover, that lingering, affectionate, comprehensive quality which is its chief distinction, and perhaps occasionally it makes her tedious."

Thought, not observation, is the differentiating element that sets George Eliot apart from her predecessors. Fielding and Sterne had a characteristic way of looking at life, but philosophical considerations are certainly not their primary concern, whereas George Eliot is never satisfied to render emotion or action undetached from their intellectual implications. She is, then, the first of our novelists to be preoccupied with ideas, and had she possessed the art of fusing these in her narrative her reputation today would be incontestably higher than it is. Her characters were rarely designed as purveyors of thought in themselves, but rather as the laboring victims of forces which the author was constrained to explain. Ideas, then, are superimposed upon the story, and though they are frequently just and penetrating we are conscious too often of the pedantic weight that her expression is forced to bear, and of the inartistic cleavage that leaves so wide a gap between the theme and its manipulation. Her endowment as a novelist was great, and we should have no quarrel with her intention of intellectualizing fiction did this leave free scope for the exercise of her natural gift. There is justification in our modern view that fiction should be a self-contained and self-supporting art. The theme may contain a great idea or the germs of many ideas, but the actors in the story should take care of these with the least possible aid from an ostensible author. Analysis within limits has sufficiently justified itself, and George Eliot deserves much credit for the extension of its sphere; but the superimposed commentary with which she weighted down the novel is a virtue neither in her own work nor Meredith's who followed where she led.

Meredith invoked a divinity whom he very inaptly named the Comic Spirit to preside over his court of correction. George Eliot invoked a grimmer mentor,—the inexorable God of conscience and duty, with the result that no novelist of her day or since can vie with her in the high seriousness of her moral intention. Her own revolt against convention seems oddly enough to have made her nervously sensitive to the claims of passion, and this spiritual alarm of hers has an equal share with her reflective habit in checking the spontaneous flow of her narrative and the natural evolution of her characters. A dark shadow with monitory finger at its lips haunts her pages. In its presence we are shudderingly aware of the immense responsibilities that flow from our most unregarded actions, as if some vast world-conscience were bearing in upon our defenseless lives, and we grow conscious of "the inexorable law of human souls, that we prepare ourselves for sudden deeds by the reiterated choice of good or evil that gradually determines character."

This is a heavy weight for any novelist to carry, but George Eliot bears up bravely beneath it. It is this moral burden rather than any problem born of art which made the writing of each successive book a renewal of anguish. There would seem to be some happy middle way for the novelist between irresponsibility and the reverse, which George Eliot never found. In her the scientific moralist was always at odds with the artist, and we are constrained to wonder whether a novelist may not sometimes be handicapped by brains. The intellectual power that lay behind the excellent *Middlemarch* was greater than that which went to the making of *Henry Esmond*, but it is not therefore

a better novel, and *Daniel Deronda* where her mind is most
in evidence is her least satisfying achievement with the
possible exception of *Romola* which is perhaps not intelligent enough.

A happier balance of intelligence and art is to be found
in her first two novels which are so well known as to
require no detailed analysis. Much of what has been said
has reference both to *Adam Bede* and *The Mill on the Floss*,
though the direct freshness of her observation and her
rustic humor have freer play here than in the later books.
One aspect of her work they illustrate better than their
more labored successors. She did not inaugurate the representation of simple manners. Fiction before and since has
been rich in democratic types, but it is doubtful whether
such a degree of understanding sympathy had ever existed
before. The French realism of her day was wholly dispassionate when it was not ironic or brutal, and the French
critic, Brunetière, scored a triumphant point against his
countrymen when he contrasted their callousness with the
uncondescending tenderness of a writer whose observation
was not one whit less discerning by reason of its sympathy,
nor less convincing by virtue of the humor with which it
was conveyed. Her procedure is clearly enough indicated
in her first story *The Sad Adventures of the Reverend Amos Barton*, and if we set the following statement beside a similar
one in Hardy's *Woodlanders* an interesting sequence will be
established. Here is George Eliot speaking: "The Rev.
Amos Barton, whose sad fortunes I have undertaken to
relate, was, you perceive, in no respect an ideal or exceptional character, and perhaps I am doing a bold thing to
bespeak your sympathy on behalf of a man who was so
very far from remarkable,—a man whose virtues were not
heroic, and who had no undetected crime within his breast;
who had not the slightest mystery hanging about him,

but was palpably and unmistakably commonplace; who was not even in love, but had had that complaint favourably many years ago. 'An utterly uninteresting character!' I think I hear a lady reader exclaim—Mrs. Farthingale, for example, who prefers the ideal in fiction; to whom tragedy means ermine tippets, adultery, and murder; and comedy, the adventures of some personage who is quite a 'character.'

"But, my dear madam, it is so very large a majority of your fellow-countrymen that are of this insignificant stamp. At least eighty out of a hundred of your adult male fellow-Britons returned in the last census are neither extraordinarily silly, nor extraordinarily wicked, nor extraordinarily wise; their eyes are neither deep and liquid with sentiment nor sparkling with suppressed witticisms; they have probably had no hair-breadth escapes or thrilling adventures; their brains are certainly not pregnant with genius, and their passions have not manifested themselves at all after the fashion of a volcano. They are simply men of complexions more or less muddy, whose conversation is more or less bald and disjointed. Yet these commonplace people—many of them—bear a conscience, and have felt the sublime prompting to do the painful right; they have their unspoken sorrows, and their sacred joys; their hearts have perhaps gone out towards their first-born, and they have mourned over the irreclaimable dead. Nay, is there not a pathos in their very insignificance—in our comparison of their dim and narrow existence with the glorious possibilities of that human nature which they share?

"Depend upon it, you would gain unspeakably if you would learn with me to see some of the poetry and the pathos, the tragedy and the comedy, lying in the experience of a human soul that looks out through dull gray eyes, and that speaks in a voice of quite ordinary tones."

Hardy requires less space to reach the same conclusion.

[150]

He describes the scene of *The Woodlanders* as "one of those sequestered spots outside the gates of the world where may usually be found more meditation than action, and more listlessness than meditation; where reasoning proceeds on narrow premises, and results in inferences wildly imaginative; yet where from time to time, dramas of a grandeur and unity truly Sophoclean are enacted in the real, by virtue of the concentrated passions and closely knit interdependence of the lives therein."

There is a clear-cut issue here with the theories of such a man as D. H. Lawrence with his professed contempt of the commonplace, or with the practice of Wells who multiplies from novel to novel talking replicas of himself. Eliot and Hardy hold secure rank as thinkers, and they are condemned therefore by the mental limitations of their characters to labor hard for their intellectual result. George Eliot may have been conscious of this, for with every book she wandered further away from her theoretic starting point. But she never abandoned the sympathetic quality of observation which constrained Brunetière to regard her as the most satisfying nineteenth-century novelist. His conclusion was all the more readily reached because he found her a convenient stick wherewith to cudgel his enemies.

CHAPTER XV

GEORGE MEREDITH*

Meredith's themes and characters represent a philosophy
of life that he had early formulated, and that underwent
no marked change with the addition of years. In this
connection we may note the singular discrepancy of his
general views with those that moved his age. Politically
there are contacts, but elsewhere the severance is marked,
and he is of the nineteenth century only by the dates of his
birth and death. This deviation, more than the actual
validity of his thought, stamps him as an original if not
powerful thinker. I shall abstain from any anticipatory
exposure of this philosophy, preferring to gather it from a
brief examination of a few typical books. The result will
be in one sense monotonous by virtue of the recurrence of
the same ideas, but his method of attack is sufficiently
varied to make him technically interesting, if not in the
highest degree significant.

He began with *The Shaving of Shagpat*, an admirable
exercise in poetic phantasy, and followed this three years
later, in 1859, with his first full-length novel, *The Ordeal
of Richard Feverel*. This certainly is a book once valued
above its merits, with much teasing cleverness, and an
infusion of mawkishness and psychological absurdity that
he permitted himself in no later novel save once in another
over-praised book, *Diana of the Crossways*. The misapplied
cleverness of *Richard Feverel* is to be found in the aphoristic
utterances of the "Pilgrim's Scrip," so characteristically
Meredithian and therefore so discrepant as the product of

the blundering baronet's mind. From the sworn foe of sentimentality we are not prepared to accept the May Queen mawkishness of the whole Clara episode by which Meredith obviously meant to move our sympathies. And the tragic conclusion fails of its designed effect by reason of its most unconvincing preparation. Richard is presented as an imperfect character shaping for strength,—a type of frequent recurrence in the subsequent novels. But while we accept his intended weakness we cannot by any effort permit this weakness to explain his prolonged desertion of Lucy. *Richard Feverel* is then a great book marred in the making, but the psychological flaw is not alone responsible for its failure. Apart from this there is a fatal dislocation between theme and treatment. To the end of his career two mutually hostile impulses dominated Meredith. By turns a poet and a social critic he rarely succeeds in fusing these diverse strains, and in *Richard Feverel* the difficult harmony was not achieved.

He is studiously not a poet in his next story *Evan Harrington*. Readers who possess the requisite biographical background cannot afford to look on this book as merely the brilliant *jeu d'esprit* which captivates the uninformed. Rubbing salt into a raw wound is not a cheerful performance, but in spite of the self-immolation the story sparkles.

In *Sandra Belloni* (1864) Meredith definitely ranges himself with the major novelists of our language, for here the Shelley and the Congreve strains in his nature are no longer in collision. In fact neither is much in evidence, for the lyricism is subdued and the snip-snap of social repartee is reduced to a minimum. He is content to register the moods and actions of his characters, so ordering events as "to give the scene in the fullest of their blood and brain under stress of a fiery situation." He has given us in Sandra the first of a remarkable series of feminine portraits, and even if she is the embodiment of an idea, the philosophy does not distort the picture. She represents actually several things. She is a study of nascent musical genius, but more particularly she is a type of a genuine passionate nature, simple, sincere, but yet profound, in contrast with the veering sentimentality and sheer worldliness of the people who influence her destiny. Her creator indeed goes near to sacrificing her at times in the interest of this contrast, and there is something too much of the Pole sisters with their "nice shades and fine feelings" for even a spacious book to carry. A writer of course must always round out his world; he must have his pawns and queens and castles, but the pieces on his board should move in unison, and he should always know when it is wise to sacrifice a pawn. Wilfred Pole is definitely in the picture and finely drawn. He is an extension of the Richard Feverel study, a youth of excellent possibilities, but whose character still needs to pass through the searing test of some fiery ordeal for purification and strength. Pericles too is functional and admirably rendered. He is not a recurring type like Merthyr Powys, the silent man of action with forceful feelings in the grip of a strong intelligence. Merthyr and his fellows are always in the middle thirties and generally Welsh. But the greatness of the book is Sandra, and her admirers are not satisfied when as Vittoria she loses her identity in a national cause. Meredith was handling matter here that was better adapted to memoir form. He was not a master of historic fiction, and if we wish to assure ourselves of his power as a narrator it is better illustrated in a remarkable novel that appeared in 1871, *The Adventures of Harry Richmond*.

There is no mistaking the infectious quality of this book, nor its surprising originality. The critical world has been busy of late putting Meredith in his supposed place—a minor one. Well, *Sandra Belloni* is emphatically not a minor book, and *Harry Richmond* is just as unique in our literature as *The Egoist*, and in spirit and method poles apart. Hardy wrote books of varying value, the good almost regularly alternating with the bad. Yet there is not a surprising difference in the manner of his good and his bad product. In Meredith there is the same range of quality, but his genuinely good books are surprisingly unlike in the method of their attack and in the result achieved.

We find ourselves confronted with two opinions of puzzling contrariety. His recent biographer Mr. Priestley concedes him small value as a narrator. Henry James thought his structural sense uncertain. Mr. E. M. Forster, who does not care for his philosophy, nor for the general run of his characters ranks him in his *Aspects of the Novel* as "the finest contriver that English fiction has ever produced." The confusion arises from not regarding the whole scope of his work. No novel has a finer rush of narrative energy than *Harry Richmond* while preserving at the same time a relative sobriety in the episodes. The word "adventures" is in the title, but Meredith keeps always on the hither side of sensationalism. There is no appreciable slackening of the tide from start to finish, and this is the more remarkable as the book opens with a scene of high tension where that most glorious of mountebanks, Richmond Roy, demands from the irascible squire an interview with his wife, and his quest denied carries off his boy Harry in the dead of night.

This opening chapter is author's narrative. Harry Richmond then takes up the pen, and writes Meredith's first and only autobiographical romance. This is to be regretted if for no other reason than that the form here chosen excluded the teasing mannerisms that please only the devotee, and released in him an unsuspected fund of narrative energy. Mere adventure never gets the upper hand. In this book the episodes are always controlled, and its character-revealing incident gives it a depth that first personal narrative rarely attains. Mr. Percy Lubbock's criticism is hardly to the point when he avers that because of this method of presentation we receive only a blurred image of the titular hero. Harry Richmond conveys his impressions with ample intelligence, but he is much more than a mere registering medium, and our continued interest in his fortunes is proof that he has all the salience that a recording hero requires. Nor should we forget that it is through his medium that we are privileged to know Squire Beltham and Richmond Roy. What more should we desire?

If *Harry Richmond* is the freest *The Egoist* is the firmest in structure of all Meredith's books; and combining the two we become aware of the surprising extent of Meredith's range. Here with an irreducible minimum of incident he is concerned with the exposition of an idea, which in the interests of fiction he must vitalize with every known expedient that art commands. He has produced a masterpiece of compression and expansion, and only not a satisfying masterpiece because, like most subjects of anatomical experiment, the victim of the vivisection does not succeed in walking away from the operating table. The knife cuts deep but it kills.

In *The Egoist* the philosopher in Meredith first freely asserts himself. He had ridden his sentimental hobby in *Sandra Belloni*, but the Poles are a subordinate issue in the book. Here for the first time he expresses his rooted mistrust of male egoism with its attendant consequence of feminine subjugation, and rarely in the future will he be found to wander far from these conjoined themes. His poetry reflects them as constantly as the novels, and it is their dominance which breeds the monotony that even his diversified cleverness fails to overcome.

Squire Beltham and later Everard Romfrey of *Beauchamp's Career* are superb egoists from whom Meredith does not withhold his sympathy. Why then does he let loose all the imps of comic scorn on Willoughby's offending head? The answer to the question will present us with the key to Meredith's social philosophy.

As a student of society he is not peculiarly disturbed by the shortcomings of the existing social order. He would like a touch more of radicalism in politics, but he is concerned no more than Hardy is with a readjustment of class distinctions. Beltham and Romfrey despite their lack of imagination and their imperviousness to ideas appeal to him for their strong individual quality. They are genuine survivals of the age when "egotism built the house," the typical "Barbarians" whom Matthew Arnold condemns yet almost condones in his *Culture and Anarchy*. Sir Willoughby, the spoiled darling of a too easily admiring world, is a spurious upstart, and the sparkling comedy he provokes is designed to make him ridiculous. The comedy succeeds, but is a cure effected? Not with Sir Willoughby, we should answer, for he is impervious. But something is gained if the candid reader is constrained on finishing the book to take himself less seriously, and without sacrificing his individuality to abate something of his claims upon the world. The unconscious comedy of this salutary book is that it was written by one of the supreme egotists of the age, another proof that the man of genius writes best from his own experience.

With the possible exception of *Beauchamp's Career* it is Meredith's structural triumph, but even here he refuses to work consistently as an artist. One example will suffice. Clara Middleton has returned from her abortive visit to the railway station. The situation is as dramatic as one would wish, for Willoughby is insistent on receiving the letter that Clara had left for him to be opened at twelve. After some fine paragraphs analyzing the egotistic temperament which halt the action with our consent, we are confronted with the following comment that labors desperately in its wit:

"The quality of the mood of hugging hatred is, that if you are disallowed the hug, you do not hate the fiercer.

"Contrariwise the prescription of a decorous distance of two feet ten inches, which is by measurement the delimitation exacted of a rightly respectful deportment, has this miraculous effect on the great creature man, or often it has: that his peculiar hatred returns to the reluctant admiration begetting it, and his passion for the hug falls prostrate as one of the Faithful before the Shrine: he is reduced to worship by fasting.

"(For these mysteries consult the sublime chapter in the Great Book, the Seventy-First on Love, wherein nothing is written, but the Reader receives a Lanthorn, a Powder-cask and a Pick-axe, and therewith pursues his yellow-dusking path across the rubble of preceding excavators in the solitary quarry: a yet more instructive passage than the over-scrawled Seventieth, or French Section, whence the chapter opens, and where hitherto the polite world has halted.)

"The hurry of the hero is on us," etc., and with this twinge of conscience the action is again rudely jolted into its rut.

The passage is dull to read, but it goes far to explain why with such magnificent equipment Meredith has few readers and fewer disciples.

The readers came with *Diana of the Crossways* (1885), induced largely by the assumed identification of the heroine

with a well-known society name. This assumption has
since been proved baseless, and we have the author's dis-
claimer in all the later editions. "A lady of high distinction for wit and beauty, the daughter of an illustrious
Irish House, came under the shadow of a calumny. It has
latterly been examined and exposed as baseless. The story
of 'Diana of the Crossways' is to be read as fiction."

It is a brilliant but faulty study, with psychological
flaws that cannot be reconciled with reality, and while
it is a brave defense of woman's claim for larger freedom
it wears a hopelessly old-fashioned air to readers of a
generation that has seen the claim achieved. The brilliant
Diana was supposed to have sinned against society. Her
sense of decency having been shocked by Sir Lukin Dunstane's bold attempt to kiss her, she marries Mr. Warwick
in self-defense. She fills the intellectual void in her life by
a Platonic friendship with an old statesman (Lord Mel-
bourne?) who had the reputation of an amorous past. Beset with calumnies she makes a brave front against the
world with Emma Dunstane's friendship and her pen to
aid her. Dacier, the brilliant young statesman, is attracted
into her circle, and only an accident prevents her from
eloping with him. Her books begin to bring her fame,
and when Dacier returns to her again, she traffics with city
editors in his political ideas. For she is not only eager for
money to support her lavish hospitality, but has the vanity
to prove that a woman's brain can cope with men in their
chosen field of business and politics. After a dinner party
Dacier returns to find Diana alone. In his enthusiasm he
conveys to her the cabinet secret of the imminent repeal
of the corn laws. As his reward he presses her hand with
some warmth. A few months before they had been on the
point of eloping, but now Diana is outraged, and dismissing
Dacier goes at midnight to surprise the editor Tonans with

her news. It was partly her need of money that prompted her, partly her resentment of Dacier's extreme familiarity, and partly her desire to impress Tonans with the extent of her political knowledge. Disastrous consequences follow, and when Diana recovers from her prostration Redworth is at hand to restore her to sanity and happiness. For "Redworth believed in the soul of Diana. For him it burned, and it was a celestial radiance about her, unquenched by her shifting fortunes, her wilfullness, and, it might be, errors. She was a woman and weak; that is, not trained for strength. She was a soul; therefore perpetually pointing to growth in purification. The something sovereignly characteristic that aspired in Diana enchained him. With her, or rather with his thought of her soul, he understood the right union of women and men, from the roots to the flowering heights of that rare graft. She gave him comprehension of the meaning of love: a word in many mouths, not often explained. With her, wound in his idea of her, he perceived it to signify a new start in our existence, a finer shoot of the tree stoutly planted in good gross earth; the senses running their live sap, and the minds companioned, and the spirits made one by the whole-natured conjunction. In sooth a happy prospect for the sons and daughters of Earth, divinely indicating more than happiness; the speeding of us, compact of what we are, between the ascetic rocks and the sensual whirlpools, to the creation of certain nobler races, now very dimly imagined."

I have always felt that the ascription of Paganism to Meredith is a misleading assumption if it is supposed to imply a frankly animalistic basis for his philosophy. An Earth worshipper he certainly was, and he is obviously free from all theological entanglements, but his earthiness has a heavenly tint, and the glow of this passage and of innumerable passages in his verse is inspired by racial hopes that Paganism never uttered, and that Christianity sets beyond the range of human achievement. He finds justification for this belief in the very constitution of human nature with its basic trinity of body, mind, and spirit to point it on its upward way—"the tree stoutly planted in good gross earth; the senses running their live sap, and the minds companioned, and the spirits made one by the whole-natured conjunction."

This Earth-mother is an all-sufficient divinity for Meredith. She breaks us on her wheel, but her castigation purifies and strengthens. With her amplitude of time she can afford to work slowly, and though boundless in her resources of power and beauty, she seems content to use us as instruments of her purpose. Meredith's preferred characters always exhibit imperfection shaping to strength, and if he concentrated his attention more particularly on woman-kind it was because of their greater potentialities for growth in a hitherto man-possessed world. His touchstones of value in the individual are constantly the possession of a vivid sense of the poetry of earth, and the recognition of the virtues of a humanly constituted society. We are at once therefore creatures of convention and nature, and Willoughby's professed contempt for a world he despised and feared and his blunted perceptions of beauty would seem to set him beyond all possibilities of regeneration. Diana blunders, too crassly as we have said for a woman of her fine intellectual temper and warmth of heart, but the root of growth is in her. It might seem indeed as if all her extravagant misdemeanors were deliberately planned by Meredith to indicate the disabilities under which emerging woman must perforce suffer. "She was a woman and weak; that is not trained for strength. She was a soul, therefore perpetually pointing to growth in purification."

Beauchamp's Career (1875) is the only book of Meredith's with a tragic outcome, and it differs from all save *Vittoria* in the importance it accords the political theme. But neither tragedy nor politics are so implicit in this volume as to demand consideration from one or the other standpoint. It is a genuine novel of human relationships, and might be regarded most satisfactorily by contrast with *The Egoist* as a study in selflessness. It was Meredith's favorite among his novels. He describes it as the story of one "born with so extreme and passionate a love for his country, that he thought all things else of mean importance in comparison. . . . This day, this hour, this life, and even politics, the centre and throbbing heart of it, must be treated of: men, and the ideas of men, which are actually the motives of men in a greater degree than their appetites: these are my theme." A supplementary comment asserts that Beauchampism stands for nearly everything which is "the obverse of Byronism, and rarely woos your sympathy, shuns the statuesque pathetic, or any kind of posturing. His faith is in working and fighting." If Beauchamp is Byron's antithesis, Shelley, with the genius and the poetry left out, may serve as his prototype. There is the same unflinching devotion to humane ideals, the same careering enthusiasm, the same proselytizing ardor, the same stiffness in opposition, the same comical unpracticality unaware of the amusement and disturbance it evokes, the same capacity to fascinate and disturb, and whether by chance or design the same unnecessary death. In their proneness to hero-worship they are akin, but if Shelley ultimately discovered the feet of clay in his deity Godwin, Beauchamp never swerved from his devotion to his Carlylean mentor, Dr. Shrapnel. Such is the character whom Meredith has set in conflict with the socially secure world of his own family circle. Prejudice is pitted against prejudice, and the fanaticism of the reforming spirit is arrayed against the more comfortable but no less determined fanaticism of traditional opinion. Of this nature is the struggle of Beauchamp with the world, but it is complicated by the further strife of the hero's love passions with obligations that seem to him more sacred and imperative.

The author's problem is to preserve our attachment to Beauchamp in despite of blunders that would make an ordinary character ridiculous and perversities that would rob him of our sympathy. That he has definitely succeeded in keeping him magnetic indicates something more than mere mastery of method, but without this deftness of construction his genius would have labored hard to achieve his result. It is a book that one might well choose to illustrate the triumph of all the conventional methods of presentation that the novel had accumulated in a hundred years, but one device in aid of characterization foreshadows modern practice. Beauchamp we come to know by restrained author's comment, by act, and by speech. Analysis is largely absent since he is too unselfconscious to be much interested in what is happening inside. But our regard for him and our knowledge of his value is intensified by the influence he exerts on the people with whom he comes in contact,—on Shrapnel and Romfrey, and on those unforgettable women, Renée, Cecilia, and Rosamund Culling.

In the books that follow mannerisms accumulate and composition weakens. Hardy returned to poetry after the two major triumphs of *Tess of the D'Urbervilles* and *Jude the Obscure*. Meredith's exit from fiction was less triumphant, and duty rather than inclination takes us to the pages of *One of Our Conquerors*, *Lord Ormont and his Aminta*, and *The Amazing Marriage*. Flashes of the old power are there, but the books are not landmarks in our literature.

Chapter XVI

THOMAS HARDY *

We arrive at Thomas Hardy whom many competent judges affirm to be the greatest novelist our literature has produced,—the one man whom we can confidently set beside the Russian giants Tolstoy and Dostoevsky. Since we are not peculiarly concerned with such nice distinctions of merit we can afford to accept the fact of his greatness, and permit time and the judgment of the world to assay his ultimate value. One of the unfortunate effects of the emergence of a great reputation is that it so frequently involves the decline of another, and indeed it seems to imply a waste of mental values that appreciation should so systematically induce depreciation. As Shakespeare advances Ben Jonson declines, and with Pope's eclipse Wordsworth emerges. Are we not justified in seeking for some saner adjustment, and because we concede the superlative value of a Hardy must we perforce abate something of our esteem for a Meredith? For we have undeniably swapped prophets in crossing a stream, and the substitution has not brought us appreciably nearer to the farther shore.

There is, with much divergence, a curious parallelism in the literary careers of these two dominant figures. In each case the first love is poetry, and both having somewhat grudgingly given their middle years to fiction return at the close again to poetry. With both writers too the poetry is a necessary complement to the prose, and any attempt at appreciation would be inadequate that failed to treat them as mutually explanatory.

* Passages quoted by permission of Harper & Brothers, New York.

But here parallelism ceases and divergence begins. Whereas they were both dominant for a period the ascendancy of Hardy had been more continuous. Must we account for this by his philosophy or his art? Has he found some new mode of expression that has permitted fiction to accommodate itself to the ever present demand for variety? Or is it merely that his uncompromising view of human destiny, harsh yet tender, despairing yet courageous, relates itself better than the aggressive optimism of Meredith to the temper of our age?

I think it is the point of view rather than the novelty or the skill of the presentation that accounts for Hardy's continued vogue, but when our mental habit changes, as change it must, it is the sheer artistic perfection of three books that will carry his reputation into the future. Other novels of his will live for the human values they contain, but *The Return of the Native*, *Tess of the D'Urbervilles*, and *Jude the Obscure* have not only human values and philosophy, but also consummate executive power to sustain them.

I choose an exquisite yet less consummate book, *The Woodlanders*, to exhibit some of Hardy's prevailing characteristics as a novelist. It was a favorite book with him, and many readers echo his preference; but it is chosen here because it represents so adequately both his weakness and his strength. If its examination forces us to the too facile conclusion that flaws in construction are of no consequence when buttressed by such surplusage of power as Hardy can bring to bear on a theme that moves him, then technical perfection is an affair of chance or accident, and we waste our time in seeking to appreciate it as readers, or as novelists to achieve it.

The merits of this book are, I grant, greatly in excess of its defects, and of these not the least is the poetry and power of its descriptive passages. Description is something that the modern author dreads. So often it has been otiose and inept, so often has it been a mere excuse for fine writing which defeats its own end, and so often has it been indulged at the expense of the human interests of the book, that he concedes it at most an illuminating phrase or two and passes on. Romantic and realist had so exhausted the possibilities of description, or perhaps had so failed to realize them that the modernist's only resource is an affected bareness or at most a grudging concession. But Hardy for good or for ill was never afraid of an out-worn convention. He had both courage and knowledge, and when it was necessary to borrow the painter's art, he wrought in form and color with consummate sureness of his effects. It is not mere literary pictures that he gives us. The bones of the structure are there, the firm lines of the composition; but set in the midst of these and growing from their very substance are the human beings for whom the scene exists.

Whether harmonious outgrowths of the soil or rebels to the landscape, they are inextricably involved in it, so that Hardy's problem was to discover characters whose intense localization should not impair their universal significance. To that end he reduced humanity as Words-worth did to its simplest terms in the justified belief that the elemental chords of our nature vary but little from note to note of the scale. It is a limitation upon his great-ness that he could not discover the core of primitiveness beneath a polished surface, but sophistication perplexed him, and that is why his Marty Souths are a triumph and his Mrs. Charmonds without substance or significance.

The Woodlanders is a characteristic Hardy novel because it possesses these elements of strength and weakness. Two of his great books, *The Mayor of Casterbridge* and *Jude the Obscure* achieve tonality by other means than by a nature setting. *The Woodlanders* has the poetic quality and pervading atmosphere that unifies the action of *The Return of the Native* and *Tess of the D'Urbervilles*, with the substitution of woodiness for heath and pasture land. We are in the heart of the forest country in the two opening paragraphs, and presently we find the tree as a symbol of destiny in the superstitious dread of Marty South's father whose terrors are a survival of the animistic folk lore from which the primitive modern mind is never wholly free.

Hardy is not a nature-worshipper in the Wordsworthian sense, and has said contemptuous things of "Nature's holy plan." The concentration of bitterness is in the passage where Grace Fitzpiers looks out from Giles's hut to a scene of death and strife which has no elements of consolation for her troubled mind: "She continually peeped out through the lattice, but could see little. In front lay the brown leaves of last year, and upon them some yellowish green ones of this season that had been *prematurely blown down by the gale*. Above stretched an old beech, with vast arm-pits, and great pocket holes in its sides where branches had been removed in past times; a black slug was trying to climb it. Dead boughs were scattered about like ichthyosauri in a museum, and beyond them were perishing woodbine stems resembling old ropes. From the other window all she could see were more trees, in jackets of lichen and stockings of moss. At their roots were stemless yellow fungi like lemons and apricots, and tall fungi with more stem than stool. Next were more trees close together, *wrestling for existence, their branches disfigured with wounds resulting from their mutual rubbings and blows*. It was the struggle between these neighbours that she had heard in the night."

Grace's relations with the politer world have dulled in her the fine sensitiveness to nature contacts that is possessed by the true woodlanders, Giles and Marty. These two never seek out transcendental meanings in the external world, but like Gabriel Oak of an earlier book they are wood-wise and weather-wise, and they understand nature because they are so genuinely a part of her.

"The casual glimpses which the ordinary population bestowed upon that wondrous world of sap and leaves called the Hintock Woods had been with these two, Giles and Marty, a clear gaze. They had been possessed of its finer mysteries as of commonplace knowledge; had been able to read its hieroglyphs as ordinary writing; to them the sights and sounds of night, winter, wind, storm, amid those dense boughs, which had to Grace a touch of the uncanny, and even of the supernatural, were simple occurrences, whose origin, continuance, and laws they foreknew. They had planted together, and together they had felled; together they had, with the run of the years, mentally collected those remoter signs and symbols which seen in few were of runic obscurity, but all together made an alphabet. From the light lashing of the twigs upon their faces when brushing through them in the dark, they could pronounce upon the species of the tree whence they stretched; from the quality of the wind's murmur through a bough, they could in like manner name its sort afar off. They knew by a glance at a trunk if its heart were sound; and by the state of its upper twigs the stratum that had been reached by its roots. The artifices of the seasons were seen by them from the conjuror's own point of view, and not from that of the spectator."

It is this affinity with nature and one another that prepares us for the tenderest passage that even Hardy has written—the lament of Marty over Giles's grave with which the book closes.

The poetry of this book has more to say to us than the

conduct of the story. As a designer Hardy is markedly unequal. Abercrombie is perhaps too lavish and Beach too sparing of his praise. *The Return of the Native* is one of the most masterly designs in our fiction, if one reads it only to its original conclusion, and this in spite of the fact that it abounds in the narrative tricks and conventions of which we are more adversely aware in the less successful books. We have too often a feeling of alien artifice at war with a simplicity that is surely more native to the man, and the effects he admittedly gets are achieved with much unnecessary labor. The machinery creaks and groans to produce a result which would assuredly have been greater with the expenditure of less obvious effort. Having chosen simple characters he feels that he must supply the excitement of extraordinary situations. Thus *The Woodlanders* gives us Fitzpiers concealed in Mrs. Charmond's garret, and Grace concealed in Winterborne's hut, and an infinite amount of circumstantiality is set on foot to explain the reasonableness of these surprising episodes. To bring people together and to separate them he sets up a train of events that clutter the action rather than advance it. In such circumstantiality this book like the others abounds. Our modern writers may lack Hardy's deep views on human destiny, but they are free at least from this explanatory vice.

Though he is prolific of incident he still practices something of the economy that Fielding used in the dramatically contrived epic plot of *Tom Jones*. The mildest event Fielding cherishes for ultimate service, as witness the recurring muff that seems so harmless an article of attire when we first encounter it. It is in somewhat the same way that Hardy utilizes Marty's letter that betrays the secret of Mrs. Charmond's glorious crown of hair. There is no such excuse to be made for the egregious stranger who announces himself midway through the book to Giles as "an Italianized American; a South Carolinian by birth." Fielding even when most humorously inclined never presented us with a lay figure so preposterous. Of course Mrs. Charmond has to get herself murdered somehow to permit Grace and Fitzpiers to reunite, and it would almost seem as if Hardy despised the mechanics of novel writing that he should resort to so cheap a device.

Other minor flaws there are in a book which comes so near to being a masterpiece. His simple characters are never out of focus, but his difficulties with Fitzpiers and Mrs. Charmond are obvious and are reflected not only in his personal comment upon them, but in the pedantic things he permits them to say. Fitzpiers has crawled to his paramour's house after being hurled from his horse by his angry father-in-law. He pours his heart out to Felice Charmond, and his natural broken phrases presently turn to what we must suppose to be the accents of culture— "I can never go back to Hintock—never—to the roof of the Melburys! *Not poppy nor mandragora will ever medicine this bitter feud.*"

One has a sense almost of guilt in calling attention to minor lapses like these. They are not infrequent, but we may afford to look upon them as surface defects which prejudice but do not destroy the general high value of his work. A more searching criticism that applies to all his books, good and bad alike, must now be met.

He is accused, then, of too often presenting humanity in sorrier plight than the general circumstances of life would seem to warrant. This charge might rest against all writers who work by preference in the field of tragedy. The aggravation of the charge is that Hardy is never content to let nature take its course, but perpetually loads the dice against his hapless characters to suggest a certain malignity rather than mere indifference in the destiny that controls the world. If the charge is partly true, and his multiplied coincidences would seem to confirm it, Hardy's overflowing pity for human suffering goes far to redeem it. In any event the tragedy of *The Woodlanders* is not markedly controlled by chance, but it does systematically represent us as the playthings of circumstance, as creatures governed by the deterministic pressure of forces beyond our control. Hardy has been metaphysically satisfying to the generation that nourished itself upon scientific determinism. That generation is now passing away, for the pressure of modern science is in another direction. That is why I said that the future may satisfy itself with Hardy the artist rather than with Hardy the thinker. His intellect will be measured by the superb *Dynasts*, his art by *The Return of the Native*.

CHAPTER XVII

THE ESSENTIAL NOVELIST?
HENRY JAMES*

There is no question here of a rehabilitation of Henry
James. He is, to be sure, at the moment more taken for
granted than read, but his reputation is for all that secure,
and he holds the anomalous position, in spite of all neglect,
of being in a formative way the most important novelist
of his time. What he lacks and what he possesses we may
now all too briefly examine.

Some of the objections against his work are generalizations without point or depth. Mr. Van Wyck Brooks for
example in his *Pilgrimage of Henry James* elaborates the
specious argument that a writer who abandons his country
is invariably shorn of his strength. Hardy, we might agree
would not have written so convincingly if he had shifted
his base to Scotland or America, but the material in which
James worked could not be found concentrated in a hundred square miles of heath and meadow. There were rare
moments in which he felt that he had not adequately
nourished his genius, as we may gather from a letter to
his brother William cautioning him to guard his children
against the dangers of the uprooted state and urging him
to permit them "to contract local saturations and attachments in respect to their *own* great and glorious country,
to learn, and strike roots into, its infinite beauty, as, I
suppose, and variety. . . . Its being their own will
double their *use* of it."

As a generalization we can admit the truth of Mr. Brooks's

* Passages quoted by permission of Scribner's Sons, New York.

[172]

contention that the home-keeping novelist has a better chance and possesses his material more securely than one who flees from his native responsibilities. But as a particularization for James's individual case the argument imperfectly applies. In the first place he was possessed of as much American material as he could absorb, and he confidently employed that limited amount. And again we must realize that a man's country is not always or necessarily the country of his birth. We must distinguish between our natural and our spiritual home, and every circumstance of the young James's upbringing turned his mind and inclinations Europewards. As he matured these affinities strengthened. What increasingly interested him were the developed forms of civilization, the rich accretions which time and tradition alone can give.

Civilization in the making is exciting, but that could never be peculiarly James's affair except as affording the artistic relief of contrasted types. So we may conclude that James followed the law of his own genius, and even if he never succeeded in taking the hue of his adopted surroundings he was the better fitted to instruct the Englishman or the Frenchman in aspects of their own civilization worth recording, but which by excess of familiarity had escaped their attention.

Mr. H. G. Wells's ascription of triviality to James demands a sharper protest, for it rests on a perverse misapprehension of the function of the novel. It is a form, we grant, that may be bent to many and legitimate uses, but the more you deviate from its essential conditions the more dangers you incur. If you work outwards from a core of human interest you can be argumentative, didactic, reformatory, sociological, and many things besides, but always at the peril of the artistic integrity of your process. James neglects these excrescent attachments of fiction, and concentrates all the powers of his intellect on the artistic presentation of human behavior under conditions designed to reveal character at the maximum of intensity that situations on the hither side of tragedy may bear. It is by virtue of these abstentions, and by his supreme concentration on the central interest that we venture to name him the "essential" novelist. His work is the most rigidly "canalized" we know, with never a leak in the firm cement of its masonry, and never a deviation in the mathematical directness of its flow. Such Euclidean exactness is teasing to many readers, but while we can understand Mr. Wells's impatience at the supreme concentrative process of the novels and their apparent defect in general interest, we must again insist that their themes are of such importance as to escape his too casual imputation of triviality. At the worst he is occasionally more orotund and magnificent in manner than a slight occasion may warrant, wrapping a simple situation round with a bewildering web of words.

Other criticisms have more sanction in the facts, for every author must have the defects of his qualities. The sheet must always be balanced, and if we get something in abundance we pay for it somewhere else. Thus if we have no stint of the refined subtleties that extreme culture provides, we may be prepared for a deficiency in the raw materials of human nature. Henry James, then, is accused of not being primitive enough, of doing scant justice for example to such elemental characters as abound in the novels of George Eliot and Hardy. Such characters are certainly not James's chosen field, and he would be ill at ease with a peasant or laborer on his hands; but a survey of his work will show that he is not utterly deficient in simple types, and that he occasionally "does" them well. They are merely not in his general scheme, any more than the sophisticated business man in his office, or the professional man at his desk. We find the business man bewilderedly roaming Europe, in which lost state he is sufficiently convincing, and there is the study of a professional man, Sir Luke Strett in *The Wings of the Dove*, that is one of the minor successes of the book. The objection then we shall let pass as a valid one, making merely the reservation that if elemental qualities are in question an author sufficiently skilled can discover them beneath all the obscuring folds of civilization. It is a more exacting problem, but James went far towards solving it.

It is in his later books that James imagined himself to have found his true direction. They were the fruit of prolonged observation and ceaseless concern for the art of presentation. But the subtlety which went to their making, and certain stylistic peculiarities which developed when Miss Bosanquet's type-writer was substituted for his own pen, combined to limit the circle of his audience until ultimately his books became the delight only of the curious and courageous reader. His complaints on this ground are comical when they are not pathetic. He knew that his range of observation had widened, and that he had learned by repeated experimentation, so he fondly imagined, every technical device for revealing the latent values of a theme. But as his power grew his readers vanished, and this brings us to the very heart of the James problem. Is it possible, we ask ourselves, that a subject may be overworked? Does life leak out when art comes in, and will the novel of the future be lighter in its elaboration and more genially careless in its effects? I do not like to think so. I feel that the public has been too easily frightened, and that the last books are definitely and demonstrably finer than the first. But also we must realize that Henry James was a pioneer two hundred years after his art had been first established, and though there may be something stiff and constrained in his movements his successors may profit by his labors, and gain ease and freedom from his example.

No purpose would be served by dwelling on the early books which, save for the very earliest, are none the less delightful reading for being somewhat belatedly in the expiring romantic tradition. Transition dawned in *The Portrait of a Lady*, and deepened in *The Princess Casamassima*. After *The Tragic Muse* (1889) came a period when he confined himself to dramatic writing and the composition of short stories. It was during this season of abstention from major novel writing that his later theories of fiction germinated, and they find their first untrammeled manifestation in a half-length novel, *The Spoils of Poynton*, which appeared in 1896. From then onward he was almost painfully conscious of the effect he wished to produce and of the means of producing it. If this new discipline had entailed a loss of spontaneity we might well regret the change, but we find rather an increase of compositional ardor, and an inspirational glow that is lacking in the naïver works of his early prime. A further interest is engendered by the remarkable variety of method from book to book. A uniform style binds them together, but apart from their rhetoric each book is a new experiment in design. The cunning with which they are contrived demands closer attention than we are usually willing to bring to fiction. There are so many dodges that even with the commentary of the prefaces we are likely to miss not a few. Mr. Lubbock comes valiantly to our aid in his masterly analysis of *The Ambassadors*. For the other books we must rely unfortunately on our own more limited insight.

One of these, *The Wings of the Dove*, I propose to go into with some care. For some of the remainder I limit myself to the briefest annotation merely to indicate the variety of attack which differentiates them.

We know that James habitually found his incentive in a theme, and fitted his characters to his subject rather than the subject to the characters. One illustrative figure at the most might be a twin birth with the idea. The genesis of *The Spoils of Poynton* is known. A dinner-table conversation had given him the suggestion of a woman who in her husband's life-time had made his house beautiful with objects that her taste had brought together, and who after his death faces the prospect of losing the things she loved by the marriage of her son with a girl who could not value them. I can think of no other novelist who would have been thrilled with the possibilities of such a theme, but it entered James's imagination and he achieved a minor masterpiece.

We shall not follow all the steps by which it grew. It is sufficient to say that he rejected the subsequent detail which life provided in this particular instance, and allowed himself to be swayed by what he regarded as the superior logic of the imagination. His task was to create the world of people, and the smaller and more workable this world the better, that might allow the idea its unimpeded growth. Mrs. Gereth's identity once firmly established necessitated the inevitable kind of son and prospective daughter-in-law to complicate the action. But it was when he had discovered Fleda Vetch that the supreme precipitation of all the elements was possible. Everything now becomes drama reflected through her personality, and she blessedly permits the author to retreat into his inscrutable background. It was under such impersonal conditions that James's creative imagination most liberally worked, and these were to be the law of all his future compositions.

To organize a theme round some pivotal center, to find the requisite balance for all its conflicting forces and by a skillful distribution of emphasis to reveal the harmony that lies at the heart of complexity, these are preoccupations which can be exhibited only on a miniature scale within the brief compass of *The Spoils of Poynton*, and the next half-length novel, *What Maisie Knew*, is only another short step forward in the main direction. We find more to our purpose in *The Awkward Age* the deft workmanship of which even James has not surpassed.

The book was something in the nature of a challenge. Some of his converted dramas, *The Outcry* and *The Other House* we may instance, fell naturally into the conversational mold. We may entertain the view that every subject has its appropriate form of presentation, but *The Awkward Age* was cast in dialogue mainly because James was dissatisfied with the disordered way in which dialogue was employed in current fiction. There seemed no inevitable reason other than this for his choice of the scenic method. He had always maintained the high virtue of dialogue. It is the novelist's main dramatic resource, but its highest effect is gained when it is prepared by all the devices which the novelist, unlike the dramatist, has at his disposal. He was now determined to prove that speech even deprived of these supports is competent to bear the whole weight of the action, and he chose a drawing-room comedy as his testing medium. His success was indeed extraordinary. It would not be correct to say that there is no deviation from dialogue. There are brilliant thumb-nail sketches identifying the characters, but except for these there is nothing but speech—no narrative, no description beyond the barest indication, no analysis, and no general reflection. Yet the story gets itself in movement, and the characters develop themselves in sharpest outline. James felt that he had never surpassed the presentation of Mrs. Brookenham. The general reader is perhaps more impressed by Nanda, and is as fully seized of the characters of Mr. Longdon,

Vanderbank, the Duchess, and Mitchy. In sheer cleverness James has never surpassed this sparkling ironic comedy, but it is doubtful if he has profited by his own example, for the dialogue of his later books, fine though it is, has not the same liveliness or revealing quality.

We must beware of regarding James as a mathematician delighting only in pure form. He cultivates form always in the interest of substance, holding it as an affair of conscience that his human material should have the finest rendering that art can contrive. There is always an interblending of the two aspects, and his meaning is missed when we fail to grasp this fusion. If I have emphasized the formal element in James it is because he valued its heightening possibilities more than any of his contemporaries, who are so often artists as it were by accident. But the human values we must never slight, and one might hazard the opinion that if James had been endowed with a richer sense of life he would have been incomparably the greatest novelist who ever lived. What we have is fine enough to be thankful for, and in a relative way we may say that he has made the fullest use of the gifts he possessed.

And these gifts on the human side are not small. He did not touch life on so many sides as others one might name, but his perceptions within their limitations are still very fine and true. He has not more humor than would fill his sails with the gentlest breeze, but there is in him a blending of tenderness and irony that is almost unique in our literature, so rarely do these two qualities co-exist. *The Awkward Age* and *What Maisie Knew* exhibit this combination to perfection, but not more perfectly than *The Wings of the Dove* to which we now turn.

Here the tenderness is provided for in the circumstance of James's personal experience. His life abounded in friendships, but whether he was capable or not of the intensities of passion still the woman once existed whom he might have loved. It was his cousin Mary Temple, whom in his caressing retrospective way he commemorates in his autobiographical memoir, and whom he revives for us in the tragic figure of Mildred Theale. "She was absolutely afraid of nothing she might come to by living with enough sincerity and enough wonder; and I think it is because one was to see her launched on that adventure in such bedimmed, such almost tragically compromised conditions, that one is caught by her title to the heroic and pathetic mark. . . . One may have wondered rather doubtingly what life would have had for her, and how her exquisite faculty of challenge could have worked in with what she was likely otherwise to have encountered or been confined to. None the less did she in fact cling to consciousness; death at the last was dreadful to her; she would have given anything to live—and the image of this, which was long to remain with me, appeared so of the essence of tragedy that I was in the far-off aftertime to seek to lay the ghost by wrapping it, a particular occasion aiding, in the beauty and dignity of art."

So much for the tenderness. What humor there is flows entirely from Mrs. Lowder whose ponderous effectiveness is lightly rendered. But the hilarity is not excessive, and the irony is withheld until the closing pages when Kate touches the triumph of her treachery to find Milly's pale ghost rising between her and the consummation of her desire.

I have not yet discussed style in its rhetorical aspect. With James this would be a grave omission, for with respect to the choice and manipulation of words, and in the harmonious fall of his periods he is a sufficient master. In qualities of actual writing he bears it away from all his rivals. He is consistently finer than Meredith or Hardy, and there are in him more pages that we dwell on for the sheer beauty of the expression. Infelicities there are of course, but these are mainly constructional, such as his multiplied parentheses, and a mannerism that grew upon him of willfully misplacing his prepositions. It would require an expert grammarian to analyze the following sentence from *The Wings of the Dove:* "It was the handsome girl alone, one of his own species and his own society, who had made him feel uncertain; of his certainties about a mere little American, a cheap exotic, imported almost wholesale and whose habitat, with its conditions of climate, growth and cultivation, its immense profusion but its few varieties and their development, he was perfectly satisfied." There is perhaps nothing more radically wrong in this sentence than a mere suspended meaning. But there is no need to multiply these trifling but teasing peculiarities. His greatness as a writer stands out the more prominently because alone among his contemporaries he had the courage of length. There is a conspiracy of brevity among our writers, and whatever value for beauty there is in the sustained period we have lost. When James is at his best the great wash of his words flows like a tide into all the emotional recesses of his subject, and we are willing then to forgive the occasional heaviness and the not infrequent over-elaboration.

The Wings of the Dove has as much of this verbal music as any of his novels, and the construction of the fable, though less subtle and successful than he had hoped, bears every evidence of the accustomed Jamesian care. The focal center of the book is obviously the exposition of Milly Theale's predicament. What are the difficulties to be encountered, and what the best ways of circumventing them? She is to be made delicate, because it is of the essence of the book that life shall elude her, and rich and sensitive because she must have at her command all the possibilities that life can offer. Experiences must be invented to reveal her qualities, and characters devised to generate these experiences and reflect her influence.

These conditions James readily enough fulfilled, but he "got off" as we say to a brilliant but disastrous start, if a proportional distribution of interest was to be attained. In other words he built up the Kate Croy and Densher background so elaborately that he did not leave himself sufficient space to move round in the crucial second half of his book. And apart from this loss of the true perspective, he ran the risk of establishing two centers where one was intended. He has therefore to labor very hard to keep Milly Theale in the foreground of our interest, and that he has succeeded is as great a tribute to his manipulative skill as his triumph in *The Ambassadors* where his original plan required no such rectification. Mildred Theale will stand no rough handling, and her creator's solicitude keeps us perhaps at too respectful a distance from her, as the strong arm of the law restrains the curious crowd from too close an approach to the royal presence. He is always remembering and applying the Polonius dictum "by indirection to find direction out." To Mrs. Humphry Ward he wrote of "that magnificent and masterly *indirectness* which means the only dramatic straightness and intensity." And again to Mrs. Ward with particular reference to the present book: "I note how again and again I go but a little way with the direct—that is, with the straight—exhibition of Milly; it resorts for relief, this process, wherever it can, to some kinder, some merciful indirection; all as if to approach her circuitously, deal with her at second hand, as an unspotted princess is ever dealt with; the pressure all round her kept easy for her, the sounds, the movements regulated, the forms and ambiguities made charming. All

[182]

of which proceeds, obviously, from her painter's tenderness of imagination about her, which reduced him to watching her, as it were, through the successive windows of other people's interest in her." This process of indirection is not new with James. He had practiced it before in his presentation of the Princess Casamassima. But he is now more confirmed in his use of the method and in his belief in its efficacy. It entails certain sacrifices. We cannot inhabit the mind of a character so treated. Only twice in the book—at Mrs. Lowder's first dinner-party, and after the second visit to Sir Luke Strett—are we permitted to participate at any length in the operations of Milly's consciousness, and our participations even in her conversations are but sparsely conceded. James has obtained an effect, but whether the greatest possible I am not convinced. Mr. Galsworthy has accorded the same treatment to Irene Forsyte, but she is not central in his picture. "Successive windows" are all very well, but we feel ourselves somehow cheated of the great scene when Densher visits the dying girl, and we are granted only the pallid after-report of the interview. Of all the Jamesian innovations this is the most questionable.

Chapter XVIII

JOSEPH CONRAD*

From James to Conrad the transition is easy and natural. No question of discipleship is involved, but the older author felt that beneath all differences in theme and method there was between them at least the community of the artistic conscience, and Conrad in his turn has expressed the full measure of his personal obligation.

He began to write with a definite theory of the novel which he formulated in his preface to *The Nigger of the Narcissus* (1898). Any subsequent change in his books is a superficial change of method but not of artistic purpose. He repudiates philosophy and science in art and emphasizes the importance of imagination. "Imagination," he says, "and not invention is the supreme master of art as of life." Similarly, he forswears all books with a thesis: "The ethical view of the universe involves us at last in so many cruel and absurd contradictions . . . that I have come to suspect that the aim of creation cannot be ethical at all. I would fondly believe that its object is purely spectacular; a spectacle for awe, love, adoration, or hate, if you like, but in this view—and in this view alone—never for despair! Those visions, delicious or poignant, are a moral end in themselves. The rest is our affair—the laughter, the tears, the tenderness, the indignation, the high tranquillity of a steeled heart, the detached curiosity of a subtle mind— that's our affair."—*A Personal Record.*

This impersonal attitude sets him apart from most English writers, and consequently from a great many readers.

* Passages quoted by permission of Doubleday, Doran, Inc., New York.

There is in his work, as Abel Chevalley writes "no general idea, no claim, doctrine, protestation or social satire, no political or religious tendency." His characters are intensely individual, and since they come often from the ends of the earth, they have little in common with the general reader of fiction. They form no basis for possible generalization, they are not social types as the Forsytes, Britlings, or Clayhangers. In his impartiality and detachment he breaks with romanticism, which abhors "The detached curiosity of a subtle mind." On the other hand he has no kinship with those realists who, as one writer puts it "serve up a slice of life with the same indifference as an innkeeper serving up a slice of veal." His imagination beautifies and ennobles the sordid facts and relates them to the whole of life. *Almayer's Folly* marks the beginning of the present *rapprochement* between romanticism and realism. In fact Conrad's nature was essentially romantic. His life both in action and in literature was that of one who deliberately rejected the safe and easy way and sought out difficulty and adventure. One can understand the feelings of that earnest young tutor of his who after arguing with his pupil all over the Bernese Alps, suddenly picked up his knapsack and exclaimed: "You are an incorrigible, hopeless Don Quixote. That's what you are!"

This poetic view of life is, however, combined with a stern artistic conscience. He distrusts the emotions, or rather he distrusts their effect upon himself. He cultivates the high objectivity of Flaubert and submerges his own sympathies and antipathies so far as this is possible for a novelist. A great reader and confessed admirer of Dickens, he yet clearly perceives the dangers of emotionalism and arms himself against them. This he says specifically: "Yes! I too would like to hold the magic wand giving that command over laughter and tears which is declared to be the highest achievement of imaginative literature. Only, to be a great magician one must surrender oneself to occult powers, either outside or within one's breast. . . . The danger lies in the writer becoming the victim of his own exaggeration, losing the exact notion of sincerity, and in the end coming to despise truth itself as something too cold, too blunt for his purpose."—*A Personal Record.* Conrad's work may well serve as a corrective to the bad "sympathetic art" prevalent among English writers. His purpose is to evoke genuine emotion and like a poet to show the beauty and color of life, but to present it with absolute truth. So, like Marlowe, he assumes "that slightly mocking expression with which he habitually covers up his sympathetic impulses of mirth and pity." We may call him a romantic realist, which is to say that he is romantic in his vision of life, realist in his presentation, and thus more akin to the Russians of his own generation than to their mid-century predecessors in France.

Still following Conrad's critical lead we must note his almost Wordsworthian interlinking of the senses with the imagination, and his intense feeling for what he calls "human solidarity." "All art appeals primarily to the senses, and the artistic aim when expressing itself in written words must also make its appeal through the senses, if its high desire is to reach the secret spring of responsive emotions . . . my task, which I am trying to achieve, is, by the power of the written word, to make you hear, to make you feel—it is before all to make you see. That—and no more, and it is everything. If I succeed you shall find there according to your deserts: encouragement, consolation, fear, charm—all you demand and, perhaps, also that glimpse of truth for which you have forgotten to ask."

Conrad's use of the senses as the chief medium for revealing character is carried to a degree not hitherto reached in fiction. It is not merely an evocation of externals, but a revelation of inner qualities through the senses. He is gifted with adequate powers of mental and moral dissection, but he conceals his instruments and shows only the result. He avoids long, detached analysis, preferring to let his characters show themselves in action, snatches of speech, in the casual comments of others, in a hundred subtle ways, direct or indirect. His methods are difficult to analyze because they resemble the manifold, delicate, almost imperceptible processes by which in actual life we get to know our fellows. Actions, incident, scene and setting, words, thoughts and impulses are all co-ordinated to create the total impression. It might be argued that this method of presenting character through action and environment more than through speech and thought, is suitable only to the psychology of rather primitive people; but Conrad uses it to create an astonishing variety of characters, ranging from passionate savages like Almayer's Malay wife, through infinite gradations to highly sophisticated and cynical characters, like Axel Heyst, or dreamers like Razumov. From a technical point of view this ability to present a clear, intellectual conception of character chiefly through the senses is one of the most striking and original features of Conrad's art.

The third article of Conrad's creed is, to use his own words "the subtle but invincible conviction of solidarity—which binds together all humanity—the dead to the living and the living to the unborn." His work does not rest on any foundation of race or class but on the whole of human nature. Incidentally he is one of the best interpreters of racial character, because having known on his voyages an infinite variety of national types he estimates them all quite impartially. There are representatives from every quarter of the globe: Frenchmen, Englishmen, Americans,

Swedes, Norwegians, Russians, Dutchmen, Germans, Italians, Spaniards, Malayans, Arabs, Chinamen, and negroes. Moreover in each nationality it would be possible to find within the range of his books individuals of the highest and lowest types; for instance among Germans, Stein and Schomberg, among Englishmen Lord Jim and the horrible Jones of *Victory* or the more contemptible Donkin of the *Nigger of the Narcissus*, among Malays Dain and the execrable Babalatchi. All these characters are rendered with equal intensity, they all have their part in a "universe whose amazing spectacle is a moral end in itself."

In the early Conrad books, based on his life on ship and in the ports of eastern seas, the poetic quality is predominant, and the style is lyrical and passionate. In the later books he achieves a more impersonal attitude, and the style consequently becomes more restrained. At the same time his imagination assumes a greater creative burden since he is dealing here with characters and scenes springing less directly from personal experience.

In order to achieve this impersonality Conrad appointed Marlowe narrator-in-chief, and after Marlowe a host of others. Always conscious of his romanticism and always afraid of it, he sought to give authenticity by creating eyewitnesses and using the method of *Oratio recta*. Marlowe is of course the author, unshackled by earthly fetters, and free to roam at will on the Conrad planet. Sometimes he assumes a distinct personality of his own, but in *Youth* and *Heart of Darkness*, he is just another name for Conrad. Let us glance briefly at how the substitution works in the best known of his early stories *Lord Jim*.

The hero we remember reached a crisis in his life when with the remainder of the white crew he abandoned a cargo of heathen pilgrims on an apparently sinking ship. The ship however does not sink, and Lord Jim is on trial

when Marlowe spies him in the court. The first part of
the story Conrad himself has never surpassed for vividness.
Marlowe makes friends with the youth, wins his confidence, and can thereby sway us as readers to some understanding sympathy not with the offense itself, but with
the suffering victim of an irretrievable deed. Jim lives now
only for a chance to wipe out the disgrace with some act
of sacrifice. The irony of his life is that he is one of those
simple souls—common enough indeed—who continually
see themselves the heroes of imaginary conflicts, who
desire above all things that men should admire their brav-
ery and strength. Jim is indeed brave enough in actuality,
but he is cursed with a lively imagination; and his habit
of dreaming robs him in a crisis of the power to act quickly
and decisively. All this is admirably told in the form of
an after-dinner yarn by Captain Marlowe to an appreciative
circle on a hotel verandah, with whiskies, cigars, deck-
chairs, and all the time in the world. As long as Marlowe
is talking about the inquiry the method is perfect; but
when he takes up the sequel, the subsequent career of Jim,
his erratic dashes to this and that place to shake off his
memories, his life deep in the forest among the natives,
his devotion to them, and the inevitable *beau geste* with
which he dies, it does not seem to work so well. In the
first place Conrad has to labor hard to keep the two parts
in contact. Jim is not the sort of chap who writes letters,
and moreover he chooses the most outlandish places in
which to work out his atonement. Marlowe sees him occasionally, hears chance remarks about him, and finally has to
follow him to his sylvan retreat. He has to go on telling
the story himself, and in order to keep up the emotional
pressure he must create a whole series of romantic connections, a love story for Jim, a trusting native population for
him to lead, friendships with stately native chiefs, and all

the paraphernalia of a new social environment. In this latter part, then, Marlowe's narrative does not ring true; to avoid an anti-climax the sequel is made as romantic as possible, and at the same time to give it authenticity Marlowe still tells it from the point of view of the eye-witness. Let anybody apply to *Lord Jim* the simple test of memory: the scene on the Patna will remain, but how much of the sequel?

Before leaving the group of earlier books I must mention the sea-tales, *Youth, Typhoon*, and *The Nigger of the Narcissus*. In these Conrad's triumph is beyond question. The theme in each case is the same—the behavior of ordinary seamen under extraordinary emotional and physical stress. There is no plot, even in *The Nigger of the Narcissus*, which is the only one of the three long enough to call a novel. The incidents of a single voyage provide the material of this story, which is told by a member of the crew not named. The central figure is the negro, James Waite, who ships knowing that he is dying of consumption and takes to his bunk early in the voyage, from which point of vantage he exerts a sinister domination over the whole ship, and stirs up ill-feeling between officers and crew. The sailors admire their officers, but, being simple souls, they are deeply touched by the helplessness of this black giant, and they resent the unsympathetic attitude of their superiors. Then the "Narcissus" runs into a storm. And what a storm! In all the literature of the sea there is nothing to compare with it except perhaps its vivid counterpart in *Typhoon*. In the tremendous conflict officers and crew again achieve a common viewpoint; and as the body of James Waite is committed to the deep his dark influence passes away on a fair sea breeze.

Nostromo shall be our representative of Conrad's developed manner. As has been indicated we shall find it notably less fervent and poetic than the earlier books, and because of this matured restraint and the creative labor it cost him it remained to the end the author's favorite among his books. Its neglect was to him a surprise and a disappointment. "*Nostromo* is my best book; it is more Conrad than anything I have written . . . that is, in the sense that it embarks on my greatest imaginative adventure and involved the severest struggle. No work cost me so much and achieved, gave me such satisfaction. . . . Yet it did not succeed with the public. They will not have my poor *Nostromo;* they prefer *Lord Jim.*"—*Living Age*—Feb. 6, 1926.

In *A Personal Record* Conrad talks of the tremendous strain of writing *Nostromo*. He says that the place described is imaginary but absolutely true. He constructed the landscape stone by stone, tree by tree, house by house; Nostromo, the Goulds, Monygham, Avellanos, Viola, and all the others of that living group were children of his brain, and into them he blew the breath of life. The intensity of the creative effort has left its mark on the book; it is a hard story to read, but when finished leaves something of that vibration of the spirit which we feel on putting down *Othello* or *King Lear*.

The narrative matter of the book is essentially romantic. The problem was to give it the authentic flavor and to convey the true color of emotion. Conrad's method here is a combination of naturalism and the romantic-realism of the Russians. One can see quite clearly the fusing of the two methods in this extraordinary book. The town of Sulaco, set between mountains and gulf, is made very real and substantial. The people and their customs, the lumbering carriages full of señoras and señoritas, the gay crowds in the streets on the fiesta, the pale pink and white houses with their balconies, and further back the immense *campo* with its patient Indians and its thieving bandits—all the

vast background of fertile nature and pullulating humanity
is driven home into one's consciousness in a gradual accumulation of significant detail. Behind it, again, is the
poetic symbolic quality which connects Sulaco with the
whole of life, and makes its story a part of immemorial time.

In this novel there is a large amount of expository or
introductory material to be handled before the drama can
produce its full emotional effect. The growth of the mine,
its significance to both country and individual, the mingling of races and the background of each individual life,
all these things must be known if the book is to have any
more value than a mere adventure story. It stands to
reason that this expository part cannot be communicated
entirely through the "eye-witness" method of *Lord Jim*.
There must be generalized narrative by the author, and
as a matter of fact there is a considerable quantity. Conrad
suggests that the tale is told by some old resident of Sulaco.
For instance the eighth chapter (Part 1) begins: "Those of
us whom business or curiosity took to Sulaco in those
years before the first advent of the railway can remember
the steadying effect of the San Tome mine upon the life
of that remote province." There is, however, no attempt
to identify the narrator, and these indications are rare.
They are just sufficient to impart even to the direct narrative the general flavor of reminiscence.

The narrative is also broken by short snatches of dialogue
by various characters, Captain Mitchell, Giorgio Viola, or
full-length conversations, such as that between Gould and
Emilia (pp. 67 *et seq.*). Through the first part of the book
(to p. 246) there is a constant change of point of view,
rather delicately managed. Thus the political background
is constructed chiefly in the reminiscences of Captain
Mitchell, sometimes in his actual speech, sometimes in
direct narrative which is given the effect, however, of

coming from the Captain. The racial background of the Italian community is created in the musings of old Giorgio Viola in like manner. And the history of the mine and its present significance are conveyed through Mrs. Gould's personality in the same mingling of direct and indirect narrative and selected fragments of conversation. In this first part of the novel there are some dull passages, for example, the fifth chapter (Part 1), which is taken up with the ceremony of starting that "progressive and patriotic undertaking," the building of the railway. It is given mostly in the impressions of Sir John, an uninteresting official who thereafter drops completely out of view. This laborious accumulation of "atmosphere" imposes a considerable concentration on a reader, and, no doubt, accounts for the unpopularity of *Nostromo*—which, incidentally, was first published in serial form in *T. P.'s Weekly*, much to the consternation of its simple-minded subscribers.

Nostromo is one of the most striking examples of what Henry James called "the enforced collection of oratorical witnesses." The events of the revolution in Sulaco itself are described in a letter written by Decoud to his sister in Paris. He is in Giorgio Viola's inn, after having been fighting for forty hours. "An awful restlessness had made him its own, had marked him with all the signs of a desperate strife, and put a dry sleepless stare into his eyes." The letter is introduced to create the illusion of reality, and the scene of the writing, the movements of Decoud, and the interruptions themselves are wrought in to secure the basis. "Decoud paused to light a cigarette, then with his head still over his writing, he blew a cloud of smoke *which seemed to rebound from* the paper. He took up the pencil again." Mr. J. M. Robertson writing in *The North American Review* (September, 1918) points out (as an old journalist) that this narrative must have taken at least seven hours in the writing, that it was written by a man exhausted by forty hours of continuous exertion without food, and that, in a word, it is frankly impossible. Nevertheless it is at least as convincing as the protracted yarn of Marlowe in *Lord Jim* which must have occupied, at the lowest estimate, fifteen hours; but there is considerable truth in Mr. Robertson's criticism. In the pursuit of actuality and the effacement of the "omniscient author" there is always the danger of an overcharge.

Captain Mitchell is one of the principal narrators, but the point of view is continually shifting from one to the other of the characters. Considering the reaction, which is the important thing, *Nostromo* achieves a greater reality than does *Lord Jim*, being closer to the method of life where impressions are gained through various intermediaries, though the final impression may be ordered and harmonious. Mr. Conrad is interested, as he says, in making you hear, feel, and see. There is no doubt that his method gives actuality and vividness.

A word as to the curious chronology of Conrad's books, illustrated in *Nostromo*. In the third chapter there is the description of a riot. Then we are taken back eighteen months to the starting of the railway. Still in reverse, the story next takes up the career of the elder Gould and the early history of the San Tome mine. It is not till page 160 that the story gets fairly under way, and even then it pursues a zigzag course to the end. The reason is, of course, that Conrad is not interested in what happened so much as in how and why it happened. He is willing to tell the end of a story first provided he can make you understand the color and quality of events and their relation to character. Mr. Robertson (quoted above) has an excellent paragraph on this point, which I take the liberty of reproducing in full.

Joseph Conrad

"It is his supreme merit that his idiosyncrasy of background painting, though it is out of balance for readers not similarly disposed, never really curtails the ultimate aim of presenting character. The same intense vision plays upon that; and the business of back-grounding is applied psychically no less than physically. Every incident, every adventure, is fused in recollection. Every notable personality is made to grow upon us; there is rarely a preliminary 'character-sketch': We must come to know the persons in the book, for the most part, as we know them in life, by gradual intercourse; backward-looking revelations come only after we have become acquainted with the man as he lives. Dr. Monygham in *Nostromo* is a typical case; we meet him a dozen times, with hints of a past many times withheld, till at the stage of his actual entry into the plot it is all told with a concentrated intensity that suggests a novel used up for an incidental record."

It is hardly to be questioned that this curious method of going backwards and forwards over the events, while it interrupts the continuous thread of narrative, enables us to know the characters thoroughly and to realize their inner reactions to those events. It has a sound psychological basis.

Chapter XIX

EDITH WHARTON*

How far a high and original creative talent can accommodate itself to the rôle of disciple is evidenced in the interesting case of Edith Wharton. To Henry James "almost the only novelist who has formulated his ideas about his art," Mrs. Wharton's debt is almost incomputably great. To his theory and practice of the craft of fiction, she owes what is surest and finest in her technique; and, moreover, many of her individual works would not be just what they are, were it not for certain strangely similar works of Henry James. The trifocal presentation of the tale in *Twilight Sleep*—with its three focal characters members of one family and inmates of one New York house—is in a fine sense a later version of *Washington Square* where the focal characters are in the same relation to one another. The picture of the Faubourg Saint Germain in *Madame de Treymes* owes as much to *The American* and *Madame de Mauves* as it does to direct observation. The mode in which Kate Clephane's problem in *The Mother's Recompense* is put before her takes the critical reader back to thread the more tortuous complexities of *The Golden Bowl*. From beginning to end *The Reef* is Jamesian: it is inconceivable that this novel would have its special virtue if Henry James had not developed his later manner.

Henry James twitted Mrs. Wharton on her admiration for George Eliot, "perhaps born with the richest gifts of any English novelist since Thackeray," and her resemblances to "that most excellent woman," as he demurely

* Passages quoted by permission of D. Appleton-Century, Inc., New York.

called her. To less perceptive eyes than his a comparison between the two suggested itself in the superficial but striking likeness between *The Valley of Decision* and *Romola*. Even if these two novels were fundamentally alike, the relation established between Mrs. Wharton and George Eliot would be slight, for *The Valley of Decision* is altogether unlike Mrs. Wharton's other works. It is clearly off-center. Where she most significantly resembles George Eliot is in her ability—an ability she has had from the beginning—to transcend the limitations of her sex. Like George Eliot she is at ease in a man's world. When she narrates in the first person, the narrator is in almost every case a man. She carries off her men to Abner Spragg's office or to Newland Archer's library or to John Campton's studio and they are as vivid, as characteristic, as genuine as in a drawing-room or a summer-house. In two technical respects she is greatly George Eliot's superior. She has liberated herself from "the purely artificial necessity of the double plot." Throughout the novels of Dickens, George Eliot, Trollope and the majority of their contemporaries, "this tedious and senseless convention persists, checking the progress of each series of events and distracting the reader's attention." Mrs. Wharton was too astute a pupil of Balzac, Flaubert, and Turgénev to let such a convention pass unquestioned. She permits no bifurcation of interest in her fiction, no parallelism of development.

She finds fault with George Eliot on a second count of "continually pausing to denounce and exhort." It is not the morality, but the crudity of its presentation which repels her. For she too is profoundly and pertinaciously occupied with moral issues: her morality is not excrescent but inherent. George Eliot goes to the middle class for the substance of her best works; and in temper her work is middle-class. But widely as Mrs. Wharton's fiction differs from hers in substance and temper, their presuppositions are the same—a constituted social order of which each individual is a part and may be a center, a civilization and a culture against which heroic individuals must rebel but will be grievously wounded in rebelling, a morality which emerges from the social order and the civilization and cannot be imposed upon it.

"The two central difficulties of the novel," says Mrs. Wharton "have to do with the choice of the point from which the subject is to be seen, and with the attempt to produce on the reader the effect of the passage of time." On the matter of time, Henry James, Mr. Percy Lubbock and Mrs. Wharton have written often and at some length; but the matter is so intractable that none of the three has made much of it. With the other matter "the question of the point of view—the question of the relation in which the narrator stands to the story," as Mr. Lubbock formulates it, they have been more successful than any other theorists of fiction.

It may almost be said that Mrs. Wharton begins where Mr. Lubbock leaves off or—to put it more equitably— that Mr. Lubbock gives us the schema of a theorist and Mrs. Wharton the comments and counsels of a practitioner. Mr. Lubbock's principal conclusion is the supreme value of "the story that is centred in somebody's consciousness, passed through a fashioned and constituted mind—not poured straight into the book from the mind of the author, which is a far-away matter, vaguely divined, with no certain edge to it." A "fashioned" story he finds to be "of stronger stuff than a simple and undramatic report." The whole of his great book *The Craft of Fiction* may be considered a preparation, illustration and elaboration of that conclusion.

That conclusion Mrs. Wharton assumes; and she contents

herself with indicating the difficulties inherent for the craftsman in the method of narration through "reflecting consciousnesses." Is it better tactics, she inquires—and this is her most important addition to Mr. Lubbock's investigation—for the novelist to limit himself to one center of vision, to one focal character, or should he permit the center of vision to shift "from one character to another, in such a way as to comprehend the whole history and yet preserve the unity of impression?" "It is best," she says "to shift as seldom as possible, and to let the tale work itself out from not more than two (or at most three) angles of vision, choosing as reflecting consciousnesses persons either in close mental and moral relation to each other, or discerning enough to estimate each other's parts in the drama, so that the latter, even viewed from different angles, always presents itself to the reader *as a whole.*" It is implicit in this formula, I think, that Mrs. Wharton sees no virtue whatever in the multiplication of focal characters,—for her two are better than three, and one is better than two. Such a novel as Mr. Hergesheimer's *Java Head* with its ten angles of vision, or such a poetic fiction as *The Ring and The Book* with ten and the author's own would seem to her to impose an illicit strain upon the reader. I have quoted Mr. Lubbock's remark that the focal novel is superior to the non-focal because it has been "passed through a fashioned and constituted mind"; and what it gains in such a passing is unity of tone and definiteness of outline—harmony and proportion. But if parts of the novel have been passed through one mind and other parts through another, how can the whole acquire the desiderated harmony and proportion? They may be acquired, Mrs. Wharton points out, if the reflecting consciousnesses are in "close mental and moral relation to each other," approximating, that is to say, a unity. *The*

Reef is an exquisite example of such a relation: there is no strain, no harassing process of readjusting one's vision when the reader turns from the consciousness of Anne to go behind the character of Darrow. *Hudson River Bracketed* with the shift from Vance to Halo is a more audacious enterprise: at their first meeting the gap between them is huge, and in the early chapters of the novel there is a distinctly perceptible strain in shifting one's vision. When there are three focal characters as in *Twilight Sleep*—three characters of quite unrelated intelligences and emotions although they are father, mother, and daughter, there is no marked harmony or proportion. The novel would lose little and gain much if it were direct narrative. The closeness of moral relation between Lily Bart and Lawrence Selden saves *The House of Mirth* from so harsh a verdict; but Gerty Farish, the third focal character, is hopelessly disparate from them, and to see either of them from her point of vision is to imperil the wholeness of her conception of them; and to make matters worse, we are permitted occasional peeps into the consciousness of still a fourth character, Lily's aunt, a character as remote from Lily and Lawrence as from Gerty.

In the greater novels of her middle years—in *The House of Mirth*, *The Reef*, and *Ethan Frome*—Mrs. Wharton practiced with the happiest result her creed of economy in dialogue. It would be difficult to exceed her economic skill in *The Reef* where she uses very freely the long intricate unspoken soliloquy so dear to the later Henry James. If she is less economical of dialogue in her later novels, there is compensation in her steadily growing art for revealing character in conversation. She has cunningly diversified her very turn of sentence to bring out what is at once significant and peculiar in the speaker. With almost any New Yorker she always succeeds, whether her personage be aristocrat, pseudo-aristocrat or plutocrat, conventional or individual, dainty or robust or florid, old or young, man or woman. With her New Englanders also she succeeds,—with the farmers in *Ethan Frome* and the villagers and outcasts in *Summer*, with the Bostonian Adelaide Painter in *The Reef*. With her French characters, notably with those in *A Son at the Front* and *The Custom of the Country*, she is so excellent as to have no English or American superior unless it be Conrad in *Lord Jim*. Her competence is no less when she represents the speech of Americans whose spiritual home is Europe; from *Madame de Treymes* to *The Children* she has illuminated them in their conversation; and a very fair measure of her success with Ellen Olenska (née Mingott) issues from dialogue. She has made herself the accomplished mistress of the modes and syncopated rhythms of speech which have developed since the war; and these she employs with aptness and accuracy in *Twilight Sleep*, *The Children*, and *Hudson River Bracketed*.

Commenting (in *The Bookman* for May, 1905), on Mr. Howard Sturgis's novel *Belchamber*, at a time when *The House of Mirth* must have been in the foreground of her mind, Mrs. Wharton wrote: "A handful of vulgar people, bent only on spending and enjoying may seem a negligible factor in the social development of the race; but they become an engine of destruction through the illusions they kill and the generous ardour they turn to despair." Replace the words "generous ardour"—which are apt for Lord Belchamber rather than for Lily Bart—by "genuine aspiration" and you have the formula of *The House of Mirth* and the temper in which it was written. It speaks well for the discrimination of 1905 and 1906 that so pungent a social criticism, so acrid a tragedy, so shapely a work of art, should have been a best seller.

Despite Mrs. Wharton's endeavor to narrate with serene objectivity the encounter of Lily Bart with the forces of society, one feels from beginning to end that there is a prisoner in the dock. It is not the "captured dryad" as Mrs. Wharton calls Lily more than once: it is not even the collection of social mountaineers against which she is pitted. It is—to borrow the title of one of Mrs. Wharton's later novels—"the custom of the country." It was the custom of the country that led the smart set of New York to be complacent accomplices in the wrecking of a life which was, however uncertainly, a life given to a quest for beauty.

Few books can have so surprised an author's public as did *Ethan Frome* in 1911. For more than a decade Mrs. Wharton's fiction had dealt exclusively with metropolitan and cosmopolitan society, with a world whose pivots were money and luxury and art and beauty; with each passing year she had proved herself more and more the novelist of civilization; yet in *Ethan Frome* she accomplished something as bleak and simple as a sketch of Sara Orne Jewett. It was as bewildering as if Henry James had written of the villagers of Rye or Mr. Cabell of the negroes of Richmond.

There is no question that *Ethan Frome* is of all Mrs. Wharton's works the most certain to endure. One can go further: there is nothing in the work of Henry James or of W. D. Howells that has a better chance of survival. Eleven years after its first publication, in her introduction to the reprint of *Ethan Frome* in *The Modern Students' Library*, Mrs. Wharton frankly said: "It was the first subject I had ever approached with full confidence in its value, for my own purpose, and a relative faith in my power to render at least a part of what I saw in it." Her faith and confidence were not misplaced. The only significant reader who found it a disappointment was Henry James.

It is probable that what disappointed Henry James was the peculiar organization of the novelette, perhaps, too, the fact that it was a novelette rather than a novel. Of her decision to confine the story to a novelette Mrs. Wharton says:

"The problem before me, as I saw in the first flash, was this: I had to deal with a subject of which the dramatic climax, or rather the ante-climax occurs a generation later than the first acts of the tragedy. This enforced lapse of time would seem to anyone persuaded—as I have always been—that every subject (in the novelist's sense of the term) implicitly *contains its own form and dimension*, to mark Ethan Frome as the subject for a novel. But I never thought this for a moment, for I had felt, at the same time, that the theme of my tale was not one on which many variations could be played. It must be treated as starkly and summarily as life had always presented itself to my protagonists: any attempt to elaborate or complicate their sentiments would necessarily have falsified the whole. They were, in truth, those figures, *my granite outcroppings;* but half-emerged from the soil and scarcely more articulate." In a word the evolution of the novelette is abrupt, jagged, truncated to emphasize the granitic inarticulate quality of its characters. It is not a novel because its characters are not fluent or complex to the degree that the novel requires. How firmly Mrs. Wharton is convinced of the propriety of the novelette form for such a theme and such a type of character is shown by her restriction of *Summer,* her only other New England story of any length, to the dimension approved for *Ethan Frome*. The perfect air of reality in these stories is the product of the most cunning and deliberate art.

The House of Mirth is at once a studied portrait of a single character and a sketch of the manners of a versatile and numerous group—sometimes indeed the division of interest perturbs an avid reader and may even lead him to doubt the clearness of the intuition from which the novel issues. In *The Reef*, published in 1912, there is no such division. "The problem which Mrs. Wharton at last reached in *The Reef*," says Mr. Percy Lubbock, "is that of the squarely faced, intently studied portrait; and the portrait she produced is surely, on the whole, the most compellingly beautiful thing in all her work." One assents to Henry James's comment, more apposite to the last book than to any other part of the novel, that "there remains with one so strongly the impression of its quality and of the unspeakably *fouillée* nature of the situation between the two principals (more gone into and with more undeviating truth than anything you have done). . . ." One assents but not without a perception that, as Professor Lovett says, the novel dwindles into a chronicle of purely intramental events, sacrificing as Henry James was glad to do, the values of dramatic impact for those of psychological elaboration. One's estimate of *The Reef* is deeply engaged in one's estimate of *The Ambassadors*, *The Wings of the Dove*, and *The Golden Bowl*. It is Mrs. Wharton's greatest discipular work.

Mrs. Wharton's friendly admiration for Roosevelt is well known: to his memory she wrote the most moving of her elegies. The principle of her social criticism is not far removed from the better principles of his social action. She would relate the life of the aristocrats of New York to the life of the nation, stirring in them a sense of social responsibility. She would relate it also to the intellectual and artistic life of the world, committing these aristocrats to a vast general culture and a response to æsthetic stimulation keen enough and sure enough to guide the nation and contribute to the guidance of the world. She would broaden and deepen and diversify the currents of aristocratic life so that instead of the "innocence" of the seventies or the animality of the twenties there should be conscience and balance. In a word she would make of the aristocracy of New York what the hopeful imagination of Henry James made of the aristocracy of England and the American expatriates;—she would make of it a world of Chad Newsomes and Milly Theales. The mention of Henry James suggests his wish that Mrs. Wharton should be tethered in her own backyard; that backyard was the aristocratic life of New York. It is about that backyard that she has written her most significant social criticism, of aristocrats and for aristocrats to be sure, but in a mood of scarcely stifled rage against their complacency in weakness and ease.

No other American aristocrat has addressed the members of his class in such a mood. Indeed it is not easy to find an analogue to Mrs. Wharton's mood anywhere. One thinks of Thackeray only to remember how often his incurable sentimentality deflects the aim of his satire and negates the apparent intention of his social criticism. The early novels of Jane Austen are comparable; but the staid authoress of *Mansfield Park* would not have repeated the satires of her youth—her respect for religion would have deterred her from drawing another Mr. Collins and her respect for the gentry would have shrunk from the audacity of conceiving another Lady Catherine. And the satire of Jane Austen is purely devastating: no ideal is implicit in its sneers. One must, as in so many other places, go outside English fiction to find a kindred body of work. Turgénev is perhaps the true analogue for Mrs. Wharton: in *Rudin*, in *A Month in the Country*, in *Fathers and Sons*—to name but three of his books—is to be found the same kind of intelligence, addressing itself in the same kind of medium, to the same kind of task. Henry James was not the only American novelist who "went abroad and read Turgénev."

CHAPTER XX

JOHN GALSWORTHY *

The influences which shaped Mr. Galsworthy's art are more variously blended than we have found them in Mrs. Wharton. "I was writing fiction for five years before I could master even its primary technique." The gap between *Villa Rubein* (1900), Galsworthy's first book of any consequence and *The Island Pharisees* is four years, and as yet the finished craftsman has not announced himself. Mastery of his art was definitely achieved in 1906 with *The Man of Property*, the first novel, whether so designed or not at the outset we cannot say, of the imposing Forsyte Saga, which embraces six full-length novels and a number of interludes. Soames Forsyte seems capable of as many resuscitations as Sherlock Holmes. The author's death only has closed the series. It is this imposing array of Saga novels by which his stature will be measured in the future, and upon them therefore we can afford to concentrate our attention. His remaining books are important, but in a minor degree. Three of them, *The Dark Flower*, *Beyond*, and *Saint's Progress* are love stories with the erotic motive less discreetly veiled than in the *Saga*. In others like *Fraternity* and *The Patrician* the class-conscious Galsworthy balances with his usual deftness and lack of definition the social issues of his day. As we read them we concede something to the Edinburgh Reviewer's remark that "it is not so much life that he sees as the problems which life raises."

There is no dearth of human values in the *Forsyte Saga*. Before considering these and the manner of their pres-

* Passages quoted by permission of Scribner's Sons, New York.

entation let us remind ourselves of the matter of the various books.

The Man of Property. It is the summer of 1886. The whole Forsyte clan are assembled at Old Jolyon's to celebrate the engagement of his grand-daughter June to the penniless architect Bosinney.

We learn of the growing estrangement between Soames and his wife Irene. The story accentuates this and marks the growth of love between Bosinney and Irene. June, still loyal to her fiancé, secures him a commission to build Soames a house at Robin Hill. Altercations develop on the subject of cost, and Soames ultimately brings action. Bosinney is not present to defend his case. He had been run over in a fog and killed. Accident or suicide? He had heard from his mistress Irene that Soames had exercised his marital rights over her, and hence his distraught wanderings in the fog. Irene had left her husband obviously to elope with Bosinney. The close of the book finds her again in her husband's house, only to leave again that night.

A minor episode is worked into the story—the reconciliation of Old Jolyon with his son after an estrangement of fourteen years.

Indian Summer of a Forsyte. Date, the early nineties. Old Jolyon left alone in Robin Hill ruminates. His son and June are in Paris. He finds Irene one day sitting on a log in the coppice. The rest of the interlude is an idyll of friendship between the two. It closes with Old Jolyon's death.

In Chancery. Uncle Roger dies in the year 1899, and the Boer War breaks out. Soames still hankers after the wife who had deserted him, and twice he tries to bring her back only to learn the measure of her hate for him. His main desire is a son to inherit his name and property. Annette, a pretty French girl in a Soho restaurant owned by him, is a mere *pis-aller*, but baffled of Irene he divorces her with Young Jolyon as corespondent, and marries the second choice. When the times comes for her to bear a child, he must decide whether the baby shall be sacrificed and the wife saved, or the risk taken with the knowledge that no more children can be born. He makes the Soamesian choice, and Fleur who plays such a prominent part in the later Saga comes into the world. It is at this time also that James Forsyte dies.

Soames gets out of chancery. His sister Winifred tries ineffectually to shake free of Montague Dartie, and this minor issue takes many pages in the telling. Another deviation is the love affair of young Val Dartie with Jolyon's daughter Holly. Jolly is killed in the Boer War. Val and Holly marry in Africa, and a son, young Jon, is born to Irene and Jolyon.

Awakening. A brief interlude dealing with the childhood of young Jon. Time has moved on to 1909.

To Let. A gap of twenty years from *In Chancery*, and we are in post-war England. The main concern is the love episode between Fleur and Jon. From out the fatal loins of those two foes a pair of star-crossed lovers take their life. Fleur learns the truth of their parents' past before he does, but conceals it. Jolyon before he dies writes a long letter explaining everything, and after his death Jon without pressure from his mother realizes that he must give up Fleur. Michael Mont is waiting in the background, to take her, as the slang phrase goes, on the bounce. Galsworthy's phrase with its added dignity means the same thing. "The young man, Mont, had caught her on the rebound, of course, in the reckless mood of one whose ship has just gone down."

So ends the original *Forsyte Saga*. Three full-length novels and two interludes make up *A Modern Comedy*.

[208]

John Galsworthy

The White Monkey. Mont is a publisher, and Fleur who has apparently lived down her disappointment is bent on creating a highly modern salon. Up-to-date types flit in and out of the book. One of them, the poet Wilfred Desert, is sufficiently in love with Fleur to tell his best friend Mont the blunt fact. He presently fades away and the danger passes. The book abounds in minor characters and minor episodes. There is the publishing clerk Bicket who is dismissed for petty thieving, and becomes a toy balloon seller. Also his wife Victorine who secretly amasses funds for their migration to Australia by posing in "the altogether." And Soames is director of a company whose manager defaults—an episode apparently designed to show Soames's business acumen and determination. The White Monkey, which gives the book its name, is a picture symbolizing the confusion and disillusionment of the period. Of connected story there is nothing. What we have is a somewhat unsuccessful rendering of modern life with the puzzled and ageing Soames as a figure of reference.

A Silent Wooing. Jon consoles himself in South Carolina with Anne Wilmot.

The Silver Spoon. It is the end of 1924 when her brother Francis alights at Fleur's door, an unsophisticated young American who at least can soothe her restlessness with news of Jon. Fleur and the irrepressible Michael are getting on well enough with a young heir to help them, and Jon and his mother Irene are no longer foreground figures. For a later climax it was necessary to keep them alive, and hence the somewhat shadowy justification for Francis's appearance. The main episode of a slender story is the suit for damages brought by Marjorie Ferrar against Soames. This is worked out in the closest detail. Soames wins his case by the crude device of aspersing Marjorie's moral character, but his victory spells Fleur's social defeat, and to salve her feelings he takes her round the world.

Passers By. Michael has joined them in the States. Irene and Jon are in the same hotel, but Fleur is saved by Soames from meeting them.

Swan Song. It is 1926, the year of the General Strike. Fleur has recovered from the Marjorie Ferrar's check by gathering another set about her. Jon with his wife is in England, and throughout the book Fleur manœuvers to recapture his love. At the moment of victory she loses him, and her distracted state is responsible for the cigarette end that burns the house and kills her father.

The abstract is brief, but the story runs to 1668 pages and consumes 700,000 words! What shall we say of the alleged modern tendency to brevity, and what, in view of the author's pronounced seriousness of purpose, of the supposed modern craving for bright superficiality? We are indeed broken on the wheel! Balzac was comprehensive, and aspired to be the social historian of an age. But his single books are short, and connected only by the casual reappearance of a few characters. Proust is monumental. Romain Rolland is monumental, even our gay lamented Arnold Bennett consented to the practice of the trilogy, and now Mr. Hugh Walpole is following in Galsworthy's path with romantic narrative that demands a century or more to accomplish its leisurely revolution.

Mr. Galsworthy ranges from 1886 to 1926, and has spared us the fevered interval of the Great War. His ambition is announced in two prefaces, which after all are only a partial statement of his intention. In the first preface he disclaims the idea that his Saga is a scientific study of a period; "it is rather an intimate incarnation of the disturbance that Beauty effects in the lives of men."

The prudish reader will be shocked to discover that Irene and Bosinney, the social rebels, stand for the principle of Beauty. The love of beauty interweaves itself with the possessive property instinct in Old and Young Jolyon, but its infiltration into Soames's life expresses itself only in his passion for pictures, which still remain for him a value in the property sense. By a stroke of irony he is killed at last by one of his own pictures, to represent symbolically, as the author says, the old Greek proverb: "That which a man most loves shall in the end destroy him."

By the time he came to write his second trilogy he was more ambitious, and if the truth must be told succeeded less. "To render the forms and colours of an epoch is beyond the powers of any novelist, and very far beyond the powers of this novelist; but to try and express a little of its spirit was undoubtedly at the back of his mind in penning this trilogy." His device of making Soames, as a figure of reference, the binding link of his whole creation is well defended: "In the present epoch no early Victorianism survives. By early Victorianism is meant that of the old Forsytes, already on the wane in 1886; what has survived, and potently, is the Victorianism of Soames and his generation, more self-conscious, but not sufficiently self-conscious to be either self-destructive or self-forgetful. *It is against the background of this more or less fixed quantity that we can best see the shape and colour of the present intensely self-conscious and all-questioning generation.* The old Forsytes—Old Jolyon, Swithin, and James, Roger, Nicholas, and Timothy—lived their lives without even asking whether life was worth living. They found it interesting, very absorbing from day to day, and even if they had no very intimate belief in a future life, they had very great faith in the progress of their own positions, and in laying up treasure for their children. Then came Young Jolyon and Soames and their contemporaries, who, although they had imbibed with Darwinism and the 'Varsities, definite doubts about a future life, and sufficient introspection to wonder whether they themselves were progressing, retained their sense of property and their desire to provide for, and to live on in their progeny. The generation which came in when Queen Victoria went out, through new ideas about the treatment of children, because of new modes of locomotion, and owing to the Great War, has decided that everything requires revaluation. And, since there is, seemingly, very little future before property, and less before life, it is determined to live now or never, without bothering about the fate of such offspring as it may chance to have. Not that the present generation is less fond of its children than were past generations—human nature does not change on points so elementary—but when everything is keyed to such pitch of uncertainty, to secure the future at the expense of the present no longer seems worth while.''

The future will certainly assign a higher value to the first trilogy than to the second, and partly as we hinted because where the author did not aspire too self-consciously to render a period he succeeded, whereas the modernism that he hoped to seize escaped him. His account is ragged and unconvincing, and for its adequate presentation demanded a lighter hand than his. His purpose was perhaps too conscious, and many a lesser writer who breathes the atmosphere as his native air can persuade us to better effect. Marjorie Ferrar's trial scene, though it leaves its stain of meanness on Soames and Fleur, is the most revealing thing in the later books, but many of the other episodes serve to increase the bulk rather than to enhance the significance of the story. The General Strike exists only to give Fleur occupation and to bring her and Jon together, and many fads and 'isms might well have been dispensed with. Michael Mont who promised so well as a character is swamped by these and becomes the bore he is not. Fleur measurably survives her vagaries and is the best single delineation of the later trilogy. Irene who had been so delicately if evasively rendered fades out of the picture, and her son Jon is but imperfectly revived. In point of characterization the earlier books are definitely superior, and they fuse better into a single harmonious impression.

The first written of these, *The Man of Property*, is in respect of technique a remarkable advance on the *Villa Rubein* of six years before. In the interval Galsworthy had read his Henry James and Turgénev to advantage, and he may be said now almost to have perfected his craftsmanship, which means getting the greatest effect out of what you have to say. There are some minor defects, which noted we may pass on to larger considerations. Old Jolyon is meditating at the opera (they are great ruminators in Forsyte land), and his thoughts turn to his son Jolyon from whom he had been estranged. Into the heart of this mental soliloquy the author pops a narrative comment, and then, blunder of blunders, introduces two verbatim letters with everything included but the address and the postage stamp. A strange thing surely to carry in one's mind! When the rumination resumes we are out of step.

Another minor misdemeanor is the account of Bosinney's distraught wandering in the fog. The author wants to lighten his task of narration, so Bosinney's blind footsteps are dogged hither and thither by George Forsyte. He had seen Bosinney first in an underground station, speaking to Irene through a carriage window. What he had heard had devastated him. Then in the blinded streets the purport of the message is made clear: "Brought to a stand-still in the fog, he heard words which threw a sudden light on these proceedings. What Mrs. Soames had said to

Bosinney in the train was now no longer dark. George understood from those mutterings that Soames had exercised his right over an estranged and unwilling wife in the greatest—the supreme act of property."

We accept under question Bosinney's suicide or accidental death. We cannot admit the clumsiness and unreality with which the cause of his distraction is conveyed.

These, as we have said, are minor blemishes. In every other respect, in characterization, comment, dialogue, description, analysis the book is masterly, and the fusion of all these elements produces a harmony too rare and much to be desired in fiction.

Old Jolyon, James, and Soames are presented in the traditional manner of latter day fiction, with a slight deviation noted in the mode of analysis resorted to as occasion offers, and in the surprising frequency of these occasions. Analysis here both aids characterization and represents a period, and the former end is obtained by keeping it resolutely keyed down to the intellectual and spiritual pitch of the individual. The ruminations of Soames from first to last would fill a book, and in spite of their frequent dullness they justify themselves if faithfulness in characterization is a virtue.

Irene is carefully shielded from the light, and she is an admitted experiment in the Jamesian art of indirect presentation. James always maintained that a superior intensity might be derived from a character so sheltered from direct observation, and whose effect upon others is the main measure of its value. We may concede the virtue of this method of presentation in conjunction with the more habitual way, but it tends to throw the person in 'shadow. Irene does not possess the vitality commensurate with her destructive power, and when the book closes she is but a distant and pathetic memory.

[214]

The French critic Chevalley has commented on Mr. Galsworthy's consummate use of dialogue, and enforces his opinion by an examination of the chapter entitled "June's Treat." Here Soames, Irene, June, and Bosinney sit down to their ill-assorted but thoroughly Forsytian dinner. It is the sheer perfection of the art of preparation. If read in detachment the words will have no great significance, but familiar as we are with the general situation each word and each interlinear comment is charged with meaning, and the inter-spaced silences are as eloquent as speech.

Another chapter, "Drive with Swithin," is worth examination for the subtle way in which Galsworthy intermingles the various phases of the narrator's art. We are given first a full-bodied description of the portly Swithin, a touch of dialogue, and a touch of rumination. Then he is on the driving seat, and suddenly we have his after-account of the episode at Timothy's. The drive continues, and we are again suddenly switched to a scene between Irene and Soames on the previous Saturday. The drive is on again with more Swithin ruminations, not profound but eminently in character. Then a later account of the matter to his Aunt Juley, and the phaëton arrives at Robin Hill. Here the narrative for a few pages resumes its direct course under the author's manipulation. Swithin is sleeping at the top of the rise, and to him thus sleeping comes a vision of two lovers in the coppice below. Twice again we are shifted to Swithin's after-report of the occasion. Then the drive home with frightened horses: " 'Are we going to have an accident, Uncle Swithin?'

"He gasped out between his pants, 'It's nothing; a little fresh!' 'I've never been in an accident.'

" 'Don't you move!' He took a look at her. She was smiling, perfectly calm. 'Sit still,' he repeated. 'Never fear, I'll get you home!'

"And in the midst of all his terrible efforts, he was surprised to hear her answer in a voice not like her own:

" '*I don't care if I never get home!*' "

Here is the maximum of economy with the maximum of effect, with a few tense revealing words at the dramatic climax. If this were a book on rhetoric I might entitle it "A Model Chapter," and present it in its entirety for the study of all aspiring novelists. Even the rebels to tradition would find their profit here, so skillfully is the balance held between positive statement and suggestion, and so varied and subtly interwoven are the devices that give it power.

The future will juggle with the reputations of Galsworthy, Wells, and Bennett. These may have a fuller sense of life, but he is the surer artist, and his report of human nature, if less wittily entertaining, is as reliable within its limits.

Chapter XXI

H. G. WELLS AND THE MODERN MIND

The cap is too large for him, and far from a perfect fit for me, but here as well as anywhere else the attempt may be made to indicate some of the more striking differences between old and new thinking, and particularly as they affect the novel. Changes in form are easy of recognition. It is so much more difficult to trace the metabolism of ideas that I prefer a concrete approach to the subject, and have chosen a passage out of Richardson's *Sir Charles Grandison* that will reveal how the world has altered in its attitude towards fundamental things. It is a proposal of marriage in the forms.

A hundred pages have dwelt upon the initial difficulties, and more particularly upon Sir Charles's Italian complications. Then long orations required to be made to the uncle, the aunts, and the grandmama, and finally the culminating scene is staged. Miss Harriet Byron had given a modest hint of her inclinations.

"I wanted, I thought, just then, to shrink into myself.

"He kissed my hand with fervour; dropt down on one knee; again kissed it—'You have laid me, Madam, under everlasting obligations: and will you permit me before I rise—loveliest of women, will you permit me to beg an early day?—I have many affairs on my hands; many more in design, now I am come, as I hope, to settle in my native country for the rest of my life. My chief glory will be to behave commendably in the private life. I wish not to be a *publick* man; and it must be a very particular call, for the service of my King and country united, that shall draw me out into publick notice. Make me, Madam, soon the happy *husband* I hope to be. I prescribe not to you the time: but you are above empty forms. May I presume to hope it will be before the end of a month to come?'

"He had forgot himself. He said he would not prescribe to me.

"After some involuntary hesitations—'I am afraid of nothing so much, just now, Sir' said I, 'as appearing to a man of your honour and penetration, affected. Rise, Sir, I beseech you! I cannot bear——'

"'I will, Madam, and rise as well as kneel to thank you when you have answered a question so very important to my happiness.' Before I could resume, 'Only believe me, Madam,' said he, 'that my urgency is not the insolent urgency of one who imagines a lady will receive as a *compliment* his impatience. And if you have no scruple that you think of high importance, add, I beseech you, to the obligation you have laid him under to your condescending goodness, (and add with that frankness of heart which has distinguished you in my eyes above all women) the very high one, of an early day.'

"I looked down—I could not look up—I was afraid of being thought affected—yet how could I so soon think of obliging him?

"He proceeded—'You are silent, Madam!—Propitious be your silence! Allow me to inquire of your *aunt*, for your kind, your condescending acquiescence. I will not now urge you farther I will be all hope.'

"'Let me say, Sir, that I must not be precipitated. These are very early days.'

"Much more was in my mind to say; but I hesitated—I could not speak. Surely, my dear ladies, it was too early an urgency, and can a woman be so unobservant of custom,

[218]

and the laws of her sex?—Something is due to the fashion in our dress, however absurd that dress might have appeared in the last age, (as theirs do to us) or may in the next; and shall not those customs which have their foundation in modesty, and are characteristic of the gentler sex, be intitled to excuse, and more than excuse?''

Sir Charles gets even more insistent, and after a further series of impassioned orations ''he clasped me in his arms with an ardour—that displeased me not—on reflection.—But at the time startled me. He then thanked me again on one knee. I held out the hand he had not in his with intent to raise him; for I could not speak. He received it as a token of favour; kissed it with ardour; arose; again pressed my cheek with his lips. I was too much surprised to repulse him with anger; but was he not too free? Am I a prude my dear?''

Unfortunately we are embarrassed in our search for a modern equivalent. It simply does not exist. Neither life nor fiction has any counterpart. Over a century ago Jane Austen gave us Mr. Collins's wooing of Elizabeth Bennet, but she and Elizabeth both realized the comedy of the situation. The forms of love and marriage have changed beyond recognition; birth is now obstetrical, and death a physiological horror. Never again will Paul Dombey or Little Nell be permitted to die. It is either short shrift with a bullet through the heart—Thackeray was modern there—or if you are allowed a death bed the dying process will be neither pathetic nor romantic. Bennett's unmasking of the solemnity of death in *The Old Wives' Tale* is symptomatic of our age. We have indeed gone so far in the reverse direction that a discreet return to idealism may soon arrive.

Each succeeding generation is justified in esteeming itself modern. The pre-selfconscious ages are naturally not in question.　But Chaucer felt himself, and justifiably, a modern. The Elizabethan verve was a new birth. "Brightness fell from the air," and the most confirmed traditionalist spoke with an accent of originality.　We may be sure that the contemporaries of Addison felt that they had reached the acme of elegance, urbanity and ease; and they were conceivably right, for literature since then has suffered a notable roughening of the edges.　Our Victorians, whether in England or America, are supposed to have been righteously self-satisfied,—complacent children of a new dispensation, of a world that had triumphantly mastered the mechanics of life.　We of our particular modern world, for all our crude outspokenness, lack something of their confidence.　Their affirmations are our denials, and with our immeasurably enhanced range of knowledge and command of material resources, we are much more sceptical of solutions than they.　But of this at least we may be confident—that no age in the recorded history of the world has suffered so violent an upheaval in opinion and tradition, in theory and in practice, in the outward and inward habit of our lives, as we in our brief day have witnessed.

Ultimately for our salvation we must produce a novelist with power to correlate these bewildering results, but for the moment the intensive specialization of many generations appears to have widened the breach between the artist and the man of science.

It is peculiarly the mark of our age to have produced a race of articulate and artistic specialists who are able to convert the intricate material of the laboratory or the observatory into food for the imagination.　Thanks to the efforts of Eddington, Jeans, and Whitehead, we are all now, or may be, amateur metaphysicians, physicists, and astronomers.　Science may despise our superficiality, but a significant movement of ideas has been generated, and a new racial consciousness is in process of development. The repercussions of this process must infallibly convey a shock to the more sensitive creative minds, but a period of absorption and assimilation is evidently necessary, and as yet we are too near the source to adjust our minds to the new world outlook.

It is in respect of this larger vision that our modernity has failed. Our distrust of edification has made us afraid of high seriousness. For the moment we prefer to be amusedly annoyed. But in fairness to ourselves we might suggest that there is merit in a frankness that is so unbesmirched by hypocrisy; and looking back to the century that has gone we cannot relish a public opinion whose worship of decency involved its victims in so large a sacrifice of freedom. We may not think profoundly, but we are at least permitted to write or say what we think.

More than seventy years ago Mill told us in his *Liberty* that any author who outraged the conventional beliefs of his day signed his own sentence of outlawry. There was something earnest and well-mannered in his protest, and this tradition of good behavior in controversy was maintained by his successors, T. H. Huxley and John Morley. These were all effective pioneers, but somewhat too respectable in tone and decorous in argument to be characteristically modern in our sense of the term. The time was to come when the sensibilities of the public were to be more rudely shocked, and when the young author to secure a hearing required merely to capitalize his impudence. To assail accepted standards, in Mill's day an act of courage entailing martyrdom, was now to become the readiest highway to success.

Who was the *enfant terrible* who first abandoned gloves and fought with his bare hands? We are at a far enough remove in time to say with assurance that it was Samuel

Butler, though he died before he saw the full effect of the blows he delivered. While he lived he could only solace himself with the sardonic consciousness of what the world was missing in failing to appreciate him.

Presently Archer launched Ibsen on English readers. Nietzsche followed, and Shaw began to explode his juvenile fire-crackers. He assured the world that they were veritable bombs, and we have gone on believing him. In any event ideas were in for a thorough house-cleaning, and all the ornaments on our mental shelves were dusted, smashed, or turned upside down. We began to think they looked just as well in their inverted state. This was in the "naughty nineties," when respectability was going out of fashion, with Wilde, Dowson, Symons, and *The Yellow Book* as preferred substitutes.

We soon got serious enough in another way when Wells and Galsworthy essayed to show us where to plant our footsteps; but in spite of them and Shaw, reformatory zeal is not the hall mark of the modern spirit. However, these men I have named are sufficient moderns in a fatherly way, and if one wished to design a family tree the filiation would be clear enough. Grandparents—Butler and Ibsen. Parents —Shaw, Wells, Bennett, Galsworthy, Conrad, and the Russians. For precocious younger brothers or sisters we might name E. M. Forster, Norman Douglas, May Sinclair, J. D. Beresford, Somerset Maugham, and James Stephens; and for irresponsible sons or daughters who might conceivably repudiate their parentage we might suggest D. H. Lawrence, Aldous Huxley, Virginia Woolf, Wyndham Lewis, Rebecca West, the Sitwells, Stella Benson, Katherine Mansfield, Dorothy Richardson, and James Joyce. They are a lively lot, but where they will steer the apple-cart or where upset it is not yet evident. There are some grandchildren whose voices have not yet quite broken, but who manage to sing in tune. David Garnett, Margaret Kennedy, Gerhardi and Evelyn Waugh are the most vocal of these, but on a big stage they are relatively unregarded figures.

Where does America stand in this category?

In Canada only one novelist, Miss Mazo de la Roche, has established herself internationally, but in her work, deft and adequate as it is, there is nothing aggressively modern. Morley Callaghan is more defiantly experimental, and is definitely and promisingly of the new movement. The United States can claim in Hawthorne and Henry James two world authors, neither of whom was eager to break with the traditions of form and matter which he had inherited. They were finely tempered spirits, and had little in common with the vehemence and stridency of the writers who at present dominate the field. These are for the most part an angry group, with too little of the milk of human kindness, and with too self-conscious a desire to plant their satiric barb. They are the matadores of the western world, and as they slash and hack and hew the pent-up Puritanic beast, the crowded tiers applaud.

What new code will emerge from this onslaught upon established creeds, traditions, and habits of life we must leave to the future to determine. Old writers and young writers who wear the badge of modernity whether in Europe or America are alike concerned with a reorganization of values. Wells and Galsworthy want a different world but a better, and they are at some pains to draw up a programme of reform. The youngsters are for the most part careless of substitutions. They despise the old, find the present a good world to laugh at or expose, but evince no eagerness to invent one that will be proof against disillusionment. The older men said: "We made the muddle, let us cure it." The younger men deny responsibility and despair of a remedy. What happened to them chiefly was the war, and by the variation in the point of view we can measure the distance that divides the spectator from the participant. For a decade or two the novel will continue to dance on ruins. At the moment high seriousness is out of fashion.

What opinions can we hazard for the future? Is human nature in such rapid process of change that social contacts will bear henceforth a totally altered character, and will our individual problems shift their base, and burden us with complications and perplexities compared with which our present confusion is a clear and simple story? And, co-operating with the shifting of the point of view, is the prevailing boldness of technical experiment destined to alter the process of novel writing in so revolutionary a degree as to make traditional formulas a mere academic curiosity?

Human nature is of tough and enduring substance, and must remain fundamentally the same through the countless centuries that lie ahead of us. Laughter, tears, joy, despair, faith and doubt, love and death, will accompany life through all the coming ages, and we shall laugh or weep at substantially the same things. But each age must still find its shifting accommodation to surface changes. Temporary dislocations will occur, and the race and the individual must establish themselves upon a new equilibrium. Finality is never reached, and we must perpetually satisfy ourselves with approximations to a perfection which can never be achieved.

Yet despite the rooted steadfastness of human nature, the surface variations are often cataclysmic. At the moment the more sensitively minded of the population are acutely and violently aware of seismic disturbances that seem destined to cleave a gulf between the new and old. Props that sustained us in the past have been rudely knocked away. Religious faith has been undermined, and there is scarcely an ideal that preserves its power to stimulate our actions or modify our thought. In this process of social and individual adjustment the serious novel must bear its part, for there is no form of literary expression so competent to reach life at so many different points. There you may get the wise or the foolish answer to the riddle of human destiny.

Mr. Wells is a monstrously clever fellow, and his industry is almost unparalleled. The combination should have meant much for fiction, but the results have been comparatively disappointing. He started with an equipment that was, save for one important particular, complete. He had a rich and racy faculty of observation, a sufficient penetration into character especially upon its comic side, and he was master of a style without subtlety or magnificence it is true, but which for the purposes of fiction was thoroughly workman-like and effective. What the fairy godmother left out of the gift bag was the conviction that the writing of novels is an art, and not a mere lucky accident. At first he was content to be merely ingenious, and delighted the readers of the last generation with the comicalities of Kipps or the fantastic possibilities of time machines and chemical compounds that produced the most diverting results. We discovered in him a small-scale Dickens and a Jules Verne grown witty and modernized. His ambition soon took a larger scope, and *The Fortnightly Review* opened its pages to his vision of a reconstructed world. He became energetically and angrily didactic, but unfortunately he was not satisfied to confine himself to the manner of expression proper to the social reformer. He wearied of pamphleteering, but stinted nothing of his revolutionary ardor, and with the instinct of the propagandist sought out a form that would provide his ideas with the widest circulation. His choice fell upon fiction where already he had shown some proficiency, and the world accepted him as a novelist who had something to say. To this point Mr. Wells cannot be a subject of adverse criticism. There is happily such a thing as intellectual fiction, and it is astonishing how many ideas the novel can absorb and survive. His own early books are proof of this, and down to the days at least of *The New Machiavelli* Mr. Wells was as competent as any novelist could be who sought to combine new ideas with the old manner. But he did ultimately crack, as the saying is, and if we read him now it is not with any hope of artistic satisfaction in the process. He is merely the victim of his own ideas: he is no longer a public entertainer.

It is difficult to mark the exact spot where degeneration begins. By the time anyway when *The World of William Clissold* was written he had ceased to be a novelist. Partly his perverse idea of the purpose of fiction is to blame, and partly his uncontrolled verbosity. We might be saved a multitude of unnecessary novels if a limitation were imposed upon the use of secretaries. In the days of his obscurity Mr. Wells presumably wrote by hand or painfully thumped a type-machine. In any event he was compelled to go slow enough to realize the value of word economy. He gives one the impression now of dictating Napoleon-wise to six secretaries, and the results confirm the supposition. In *William Clissold* there is a section called the Open Conspiracy, and in that section there is this paragraph: "I think now I have made plain what I mean by Open Conspiracy. It is the simplification by concentration into larger organizations of the material life of the whole human community in an atmosphere of unlimited candour.

It is explanation and invitation to every intelligent human being to understand and assist. It is the abandonment of all reservation in the economic working of the world. It is the establishment of the economic world state by the deliberate invitation, explicit discussion, and co-operation of the men most interested in economic organization, men chosen by their work, called to it by a natural disposition and aptitude for it, fully aware of its importance and working with the support of an increasing general understanding."

This chapter opened with a quotation from Richardson which may be more antiquated, but which certainly is more entertaining. Richardson had recognized at least the necessity of dramatizing his material. Mr. Wells is merely improvising with obvious earnestness from a platform.

Mr. Wells has written many books in the third person where the "I" of the story is the omniscient novelist. But his favorite form is the loose and all inclusive autobiographic method where the "I" is generally a young politician or scientist who has had a penurious but imaginative childhood, a wholly unsatisfactory schooling, and has either proceeded to one of the antiquated universities on a scholarship, or has gone direct into a South Kensington laboratory. He usually marries, but meets some one whom he likes better than his wife, and this produces the angry complications of the story.

In *The New Machiavelli*, one of his ablest books, "I" is such a politician whose career is ultimately sacrificed to the wasteful proprieties of a hypocritical age. Its advantage over *William Clissold* derives from its superior dramatic quality. Especially is the alienation from Margaret dexterously and candidly and sympathetically presented, as also the corresponding attachment to the woman who supplants her. It is because of this dramatic quality and because for once Mr. Wells is conscious of the technical difficulties of his plan that this book is in an artistic way more successful than usual.

"The most impossible of all autobiographies," he writes "is an intellectual autobiography. I have thrown together in the crudest way the elements of the problem I struggled with, but I can give no record of the subtle details; I can tell nothing of the long vacillations between protean values, the talks and re-talks, the meditations, the bleak lucidities of sleepless nights."

He does after all manage to give us enough of these, and we get a sufficient picture of Remington's mind, for half the book is made up of the Wells-Remington view of constituted things. But Remington's person, if not his personal quality, remains in shadow, and when he is thinking things out he impresses us more as a highly intelligent recording secretary than as a character in a book. His outward-looking eyes limn a few unforgetable figures like the Baileys, but in this objective sense the book might have been made more competent. That is the price we must pay for its highly intellectualized direction.

Chapter XXII

FRENCH REALISM

Gissing, Moore, and Bennett

A novel is simply a collection of experiments. (Hippolyte Taine on Stendhal.)

It may have been remarked that we have fared a long way on our journey through the novel without the aid of certain time-worn labels dear to the heart of the literary historian. We must make now a grudging concession to necessity and seek to discover if any virtue resides in the terms romantic and realistic as applied to English fiction.

Many reasons justify our abstention. The terms are vague, and their connotation variable from generation to generation. A novelist like Balzac or Flaubert whom we label realist or naturalist is in certain aspects of his work disconcertingly romantic, and a romantic like Hugo has a capacity for amassing realistic detail that the most documentary novelist might envy. And finally, our English writers are not prone like the French to formulate doctrines, and to govern their art by the set prescriptions of a school. Idealistic and realistic tendencies are abundantly evident throughout our literature, but nothing is gained by dubbing Fielding, George Eliot, or the Brontës romantic or the reverse.

George Moore and Bennett, however, compel us to the examination of a doctrine into which their long experience of France initiated them. More than any of their predecessors or contemporaries they were men of coteries, and their talent in its initial efforts at least was controlled in its direction by the theories they had imbibed. In Bennett's case the accommodation was easy, but for Moore, the temperamental romantic, realism was a strait jacket which he wore with evident discomfort and then discarded. The man it fitted was George Gissing whose incentive came not from theory but from his own temperament.

There are many tedious ways of expounding a doctrine, but since we are not bound by any compulsion of thoroughness let us choose the amusing approach to the subject that we find in the literary correspondence of Flaubert and George Sand. This does not cover all the aspects of realism,—its concern for physiology, its documentary exactitude, or its pessimism, but it does state with fullness Flaubert's zest for impersonality, and gives also the appropriate idealistic comment of the other partner in the argument.

"I experience an invincible repugnance in setting on paper anything of my own heart; I even find that a novelist has no right to express his opinion on anything. Has God ever expressed his opinion? . . . The first comer is more interesting than Gustave Flaubert, because he is more general, and consequently more typical."—Flaubert.

"Put nothing of one's heart in what one writes? As for me it seems that one can put nothing else there. Can one separate one's mind from one's heart? Is it something different? Can a being so divide himself? Finally, not to give oneself entirely in one's work seems to me as impossible as to weep with anything but one's eyes, or to think with anything but one's brain."—Sand.

"Not to intervene! I think that great art must be scientific and impersonal. You must by an effort of mind transport yourself into your characters, and not draw them into your own orbit."—Flaubert.

[230]

"But to hide your opinion on the characters you draw, and leave the reader in consequence uncertain as to the opinion he must entertain of them, is to wish not to be understood, and from that moment the reader leaves you. What the reader wants above all is to penetrate our thought, and that is what you refuse him with disdain."—Sand.

"As for expressing my opinion on the people I introduce, no, a thousand times no! I do not recognize my right to do so. If the reader does not draw from a book the morality which should be found there he is either an imbecile, or the book is false from the point of view of exactitude. For, from the moment that a thing is true it is good. Obscene books are immoral only if they lack truth."—Flaubert.

Flaubert's argument has prevailed to this extent that the too manifest intrusion of the author's personality is looked upon now as a misdemeanor. His passionate concern for the balanced phrase and the appropriate word did not have a like fortune with his realistic following. With regard to fullness of documentation he came to realize that the successive laboring of a subject was inconsistent with its beautiful presentation, and when beauty clashed with exactitude his mind was clear where the sacrifice should be made. It was the man who ransacked libraries for *Salammbô* and consulted 1500 volumes for *Bouvard et Pécuchet* who could heretically write: "I regard as very secondary the technical, detailed, local information, in short the historical and exact aspect of things. I am seeking above all beauty, and in that my companions are only moderately interested."

George Moore

It was evidently then not from Flaubert that Moore derived the calculated and unremitting drabness of *The*

Mummer's Wife and *Esther Waters*. George Eliot's praise of plain people he may have inattentively read, but her idealization of the commonplace could only have irritated his sense of fact. Balzac, who was one of the gods of his literary Pantheon, may have given him a hint that simple types were good æsthetic prey, but we rather suspect a source that he has never mentioned, and hazard the supposition that he stole a graft from the graceful but poison-dropping tree that the Goncourts so confidently planted. The pathological fury with which he pursues Mrs. Ede to her drunkard's grave is a disciple's reproduction of their clinical obsessions.

Zola, as critic or creator, has never had much influence in England. In their extreme form his theories failed to take root even in his own country, and the defection of five disciples, with of course its accompanying manifesto was evidence of their failing power. In formulating these once famous theories Zola made no claim to originality. His modest pretension was to chain art to the chariot of science, and if literature now marches on an independent path we must partly thank his abortive attempt to effect the unholy alliance. So long as he followed the lead of Taine his efforts were not without their fruit. When naïvely he sought to make art a subordinate province of science, and selected Claude Bernard's *Study of Experimental Medicine* as his textbook, his mission was at an end. From Taine he got his determinism with its resultant pessimism. "Whether facts are physical or moral matters not, they have always causes. There are causes for ambition, for courage, for truth, as for digestion, muscular movement, animal heat. Vice and virtue are products like vitriol and sugar." Here is Zola's version of this idea with a Claude Bernard tincture: "When it has been proved that the human body is a machine whose wheels can be manipu-

lated at the will of the experimenter, we must pass on-
wards to the emotional and intellectual acts of man. . . .
We have experimental chemistry and physics; we shall
have experimental physiology; later still the experimental
novel. That is a progression which imposes itself, and the
last stage of which it is easy to perceive even today. All
holds together. It was necessary to proceed from the determinism of dead matter to arrive at the determinism of
living bodies; and since men of science, like Claude Bernard, now demonstrate that fixed laws govern the human body, we may announce without fear of decep-
tion the hour when the laws of thought and emotion
will be formulated in their turn. A like determinism
must regulate the stone on the highway and the mind
of man."

Taine's determinism, and with it Zola's, goes so far as
to proclaim the inevitability of the literary product. It is
extruded of necessity from circumstance, and an author is
less responsible for his masterpiece than the race to which
he belongs, the *milieu* in which he lives, and the moment
of time in which his lot is cast. A work of art is therefore
an automatic birth. Diligence would seem to be the only
prerequisite. The writer himself is strictly conditioned by
circumstance, and it is his duty to discover in the characters he fashions the same shaping causes. Let him above
all document himself thoroughly in the environment in
which they move and success is a foregone conclusion.
Can we not see an army of novelists notebook in hand
stalking their prey? Fineness of notation is the last thing
required. "What I wish to study," said Zola, "is tempera-
ments and not characters," and he became as Lemaître
described him "the brutal and sad poet of blind instincts,
gross passions, carnal loves, of the low and repugnant
parts of human nature." He was something more and

better than that, but our immediate need is served if a background has been however rudely sketched in for the books we shall now consider.

A Mummer's Wife appeared in 1884, and is, for what it is worth, a gift from France. The realistic formula is conscientiously carried out, and George Moore has succeeded in abstracting from the book all the interesting and characteristic elements of his personality,—his elfishness, his impudence, and the acrid poetry through which these qualities are strained. What is left is a humorless gift of observation which for readers who are satisfied with the reflection that "life is just like that" confers a cheerless charm on the story. Like Emma Bovary the heroine, God save the mark, is bored with her life, with her querulous sick husband and her railing mother-in-law, and as with Emma the sentimental romanticism of her nature craves some issue of escape. This is afforded by the opportune arrival of a lodger, Mr. Lennox, the manager of a provincial operatic company on tour in the pottery towns. A seduction follows, an elopement, ultimately a divorce and marriage, and always the small Bohemian excitements of the peripatetic stage. Kate's voice earns her small triumphs but jealousy plagues her, and drink and ill-temper achieve her ruin. If the book has a thesis it is in conformity with the realistic superstition of the irresistible pressure of environment, and it was perhaps to correct that superstition that ten years later Moore wrote *Esther Waters* which seeks to prove precisely the opposite thing. Esther is a servant girl virtuous though erring, who suffers incredibly but resists with equal strength. The atmosphere of the servant's hall, the stable and the race-track is substituted for the atmosphere of the stage, and in both cases Moore was able to authenticate the detail from his own experience. His report then has a freshness denied to the realist who

[234]

laboriously accumulates his local color, and it is only his detailed analysis of disease that has this second-hand effect.

GEORGE GISSING

Let us for the moment leave the resolutely acquired drabness of Moore, and turn to Gissing whose low tones are more natural and certainly more sincere. If disinterestedness is an essential feature of realism he will not count for significance in the movement. Too much of his own harsh and narrow experience went into the making of his books to permit the spirit of critical detachment which Moore consciously imposed upon himself as an experiment in artistic discipline. Than Gissing no English novelist has ever been more passionately autobiographic, and none more angrily zealous in setting forth the case against life. He had a positive genius for discomfort, and had no power like his master Dickens to relate himself acquiescingly or humorously to the varied spectacle of the world. It is a failure undoubtedly of animal spirits, and none of his novels reflects even a tinge of the gravely tempered joy that dubiously shines through the *Ryecroft Papers*. There is no such lift in the horizon in the two characteristic books we shall briefly examine.

New Grub Street is of the year 1891, and if not his undisputed masterpiece it is more competent in a technical sense than anything he has done. He is content here to set forth the facts, bitterly and complainingly it is true, but without the explanatory amplifications that usually beset him. His subject is literary failure, and if his treatment has some of the distortion incidental to satire it is certainly not warped by any sentimental appeal to our sympathies. The book does not necessarily compel us to believe that all genius is neglected and that the opportunistic timeserver always arrives. It does not compel us to believe that wives and children are inevitably an encumbrance whom the literary aspirant must shun. If these are inferences that the reader takes from Gissing's presentation it is rather his limited insight than the author's distortion that is to blame. We are given an important fraction of the truth, and I cannot see how the purposes either of truth or art would have been better served if Jasper Milvain had met disaster, if Amy had been a more compliant wife, if Reardon under her tender ministrations had forged through to success, and his friend Biffen had fascinated his public with *Mr. Bailey, Grocer*. Sentiment has its brief innings when Reardon dies in Amy's arms, but there is ironic compensation in the fact that at the close of the book she is reposing in the arms of Jasper Milvain. It is a novel of marked intellectual power and rich in characterization. It was Thomas Seccombe's opinion that "He never wrote with such a virile pen: phrase after phrase bites and snaps with a singular crispness and energy; material used before is now brought to a finer literary issue. It is by far the most tenacious of Gissing's novels."

Born in Exile followed in 1892, Gissing being subservient to the Grub Street necessity of a novel a year. A grim book it is of course, but in a less pleasant because less artistic way than its predecessor. In *The New Grub Street* we see a recognizable infusion of himself in Reardon and in Whelpdale's American experience, and many of his less desirable qualities get into the person of Godwin Peak in the later story. At least we may say that Gissing's resentment of poverty is there in full measure, but translated into a type of dishonest snobbishness from which we hope that he was free. Peak is an æsthetic intellectual whose aspirations are frustrated by his conditions. So far the parallelism is evident and acceptable. The ugly twist that the book takes is Peak's deliberate betrayal of his own nature.

[236]

An avowed sceptic he discovers an opportunity of marrying a girl of social position and wealth, and to gain her love he follows her to Exeter, and ingratiates himself with her father by studying for Holy Orders. It required more than Gissing's ability to recover from so false a situation, and the nervelessness of the dialogue is an indication of his failure. This is a specimen of Peak's conversation with Mr. Warricombe: "Christianity is an organism of such vital energy that it perforce assimilates whatever is good and true in the culture of each successive age. To understand this is to learn that we must depend rather on *constructive*, than on *defensive*, apology. That is to say, we must draw evidence of our faith from its latent capacities, its unsuspected affinities, its previsions, its adaptability, comprehensiveness, sympathy, adequacy to human needs."

Here is a conversation with the daughter Sidwell whom he is supposed to love: " 'A liberal mind is revolted by the triumphal procession that roars perpetually through the city highways. With myriad voices the city bellows its brutal scorn of everything but material advantage. There every humanizing influence is contemptuously disregarded. I know, of course, that the trader may have his quiet home where art and science and humanity are the first considerations; but the *mass* of traders, corporate and victorious, crush all such things beneath their heels. Take your stand (or try to do so) anywhere near the Exchange; the hustling and jolting to which you are exposed represents the very spirit of the life about you. Whatever is gentle and kindly and meditative must here go to the wall—trampled, spattered, ridiculed. Here the average man has it all his own way—a gross utilitarian power.' 'Yes, I can see that,' Sidwell replied thoughtfully." What else could the poor girl say?

Equally unsatisfactory are the many author's explanations of situation and character which belong to the discarded lumber of letters (i.e. Part IV, Ch. II), and in every respect the book shows a falling away from many of its predecessors. Our conclusion must be that Gissing's grasp of technique was insecure, and that his success was more an affair of mood and theme than of design. As for the realism of his books we may leave that matter in the air. His tendency with occasional lapses is anti-sentimental and ironic, and his preference is for somber themes. That is the extent of a realism which had in it no hint of theory or discipleship. How far these prevailed with Arnold Bennett we may now determine.

ARNOLD BENNETT

In that frivolous book the *Truth about an Author* Bennett tells the story of his literary apprenticeship with a characteristic blend of modesty and self-assurance. Tenacity of purpose of course we discover in the record, and endless zest for work even in the days when journalistic success was the height of his aspiration. When assurance of creative power came with the acceptance of a story by *The Yellow Book* his equipment would not seem to the casual glance promising; but with the full result before us we can realize how calculated this equipment was to produce the original quality we associate with his name. No writer of our day is more essentially English by temperamental bias and choice of theme, yet we learn to our surprise that until he was launched on his career he had no consciousness whatever of the tradition of English fiction. Before he had read a word of Scott, Jane Austen, Dickens, Thackeray, or George Eliot he was deeply versed in Balzac, Flaubert, the Goncourts, de Maupassant, and Turgénev. We may say, therefore, that never did a novelist so national in his quality come to his work more free from national pre-possessions. The only English novelist who influenced him in his formative period was Samuel Butler, and that influence was less upon his art than upon his point of view. Technically, therefore, his ancestry was French. His life abroad confirmed this process, and this emancipated Provincial of the Five Towns returned to walk the London streets in clothes of Parisian cut. Our question is now whether they fitted him well.

This compels a brief return to the realistic programme with which our chapter opened. We indicated there the documentary zest of the French practitioners, and their sometimes too labored desire to "condition" their characters by an exact notation of their environment. Bennett shares their zeal, but so long as he wrote from the fullness of his own experience there is no obvious laboring of the detail. It is sufficient, exact, and significant, and this holds true not only of his masterly Five Town studies, but of such a book as *Riceyman Steps* where the scene is transferred to a London suburb. There are signs towards the last that he was coming to the end of his material, for in *The Imperial Palace* he was compelled to get up his subject, and compile a dossier of the facts he wished to use.

He was never a convert to the animalism of the later French naturalists, but a certain cautious freedom he learned from them and a relaxation at least of the severer standards of decorum which our Victorian novelists assumed, whenever men and women were gathered together or met in solitary places. If a thing required to be said no superstitious taboos deterred him, but amorous passion always seemed to him a trifle ridiculous, and he preferred to view it at a humorous remove.

Bennett began as a devotee of Flaubert's "Mot juste," though the cadenced phrase was never with him an obsession. Yet his style despite his 500,000 words a year has few of the slovenly devices we associate with the haste of journalism. He is consistently a good writer with a recognition of his natural limitations. When, for example, he is descriptive it is witty effectiveness rather than pictorial fervor that we shall discover. He proclaims his passion for beauty,—his power to see it "even where it is not," but his sense of the poetical was curiously warped, and in a measure commercialized. There is a sensible dearth of green grass, streams, and flowers and sunsets in his work, and it is no exaggeration to say that the funnels of an Atlantic liner or a factory chimney moved him more profoundly than the vision of a hill or a tree. In the region of compositional beauty he is more nearly Flaubertian, for he has no lack of engineering skill, and plans his structure with masterly precision. His story marches not with the mechanical progression of a plot, but by its own indwelling motive power. In other words, he was a born novelist, and to call him old-fashioned by our present standards is perhaps no severe disparagement.

Flaubert and de Maupassant insisted that fiction should be in the fullest possible degree self-sustaining. Narration is a privilege that must be accorded to an author, but he is not justified in commenting on the drama he sets in motion. Bennett approves this discipline and rarely swerves from it. In a characteristic book like *Riceyman Steps* we find the barest minimum of direct author's comment. Once in describing the delightful Elsie he fails to restrain himself: "No egotism in those features! No instinct to fight for her rights and to get all that she could out of the universe! No apprehension of injustice! No resentment against injustice! No glimmer of realization that she was the salt of the earth!" Comments like the following are excessively rare: "Few people save certain bodily sufferers and certain

victims of frustration know the infernal, everlasting perseverance of which pain, physical or mental, is capable."
"Probably in human activity there is no such thing as a single motive." His distrust of edification is constant, and his philosophy is confined to the presentation of the concrete instance from which the reader may draw his own inference. He rarely generalizes therefore in the manner of George Eliot or even Balzac, and his more discreet type of intervention will be found generally to connect itself with the special case. Dr. Raste—still in the same novel—finds that after a year the procrastinating Henry has a copy of Shakespeare that he wanted. " 'I could have sold it,' said Henry, 'but the truth is I've been keeping it for you. I felt sure you'd be looking in one of these days. I meant to drop you a postcard to say I'd found it, but somehow,—'

"All this was true. For at least ten months Mr. Earlforward had intended to drop the postcard and had never dropped it. Yet his conviction that one day he would drop it had remained fresh and strong throughout the period."

This paragraph has more in it than Mr. Earlforward's reflections and less than ordinary editorial comment. It is not a gross intrusion of the author's personality, but rather the author putting the case before us more clearly than Earlforward would have been able to do in his own words.

There remains the question of "drabness," a matter we have discussed already in connection with Moore and Gissing. In Moore we discovered a purely æsthetic drabness. So Dégas had painted and so Moore would essay to write. Having produced two of the most systematic realistic novels of English origin, he continued to produce himself, and it is this communicative and subjective Moore who will live. Gissing was much less systematic and theoretic, and his books took their hue from the circumstances of a dreary life and the promptings of an unhappy disposition. He wrote from resentment. Not merely the conditions which he describes but the characters also who are their product, are set before us with the purpose of generating in us some fraction of the annoyance that went to their creation. Bennett's atmosphere is no less gray, but we can breathe with relish an air that has passed so joyously through his lungs. The difference between the two writers is not wholly temperamental, for if Bennett had not made an early escape from drabness we suspect that it would have weighed as heavily on his spirit. The emancipated man can view in a mood of humorous detachment conditions which continuance would have made unendurable, and he can paint them too with more revealing truth than when he was their slave. There is a retrospective tenderness then in Bennett's rendering of simple life, and he moves almost into the region of poetry in his evocation of a past of which he was once a part. His people are almost pathetically simple. Their creator knows their limitations, but he has mastered a device peculiarly his own whereby their narrow activities gain significance. His effect is obtained by a continual contrast of what we might call the "outside" and the "inside" views of a person's motives, actions, and character. We get a double-angled truth from this dual vision. There is the working of the individual's own mind, and the reflections of some adjacent mind with as a further control the subtly-concealed co-operation of the author's mentality. One illustration, again from *Riceyman Steps*, will suffice: "Dr. Raste, or anybody else, looking down at the couple beneath Violet's splendid eiderdown, would have seen merely a middle-aged man and a middle-aged woman with haggard faces worn by illness, fatigue, privations, and fear. But Henry did not picture himself and Violet thus; nor Violet herself and Henry. Henry did not feel middle-aged. He did not feel himself to be any particular age. His interest in life and in his own existence had not diminished during this enormous length of time which had elapsed since he first came into Riceyman Steps as a young man. In his heart he felt no older than on that first night."

Henry James and Mrs. Woolf fail to discover significance in Bennett. James grants him what he calls "saturation," which means an abundant sense of life and the fullest factual possession of his material. But he only squeezes a juicy and capacious orange, and this is never to be considered an intellectual operation. Mrs. Woolf too finds him overburdened with detail laboriously accumulated, wittily conveyed, but not intelligently applied. We admit Bennett's worship of facts for their own sake, but even if he does not organize them profoundly he has a faculty of making them come alive. But he is in his own mild way a philosopher, for he realizes that "however dull and prosaic a man may appear to others, however tedious his life may seem, to himself his life is always exciting, amazing, and he himself a daily miracle."

The present writer has by prudent intention refrained from absolute judgments, and a similar commendable prudence has caused him to abstain from estimating too precisely the relative merits of the authors he has treated. May I be permitted here to break through this too scientific reserve, and indulge in harmless prophesy? If another incarnation brings me back to earth two hundred years hence, I shall promptly ask my bookseller for *The Old Wives' Tale*. He will not have it in his front window, but he will have it on his shelves; and as he hands it to me he will say: "What grand novels those old Edwardians wrote."

CHAPTER XXIII

AMERICAN REALISM, SEX, AND THEODORE DREISER

With Theodore Dreiser the American novel foreswears fealty to the English tradition. The emancipation is not complete, but the intention is evident. There had been a hint of subserviency in the old time allegiance, but now this vanishes and a new Declaration of Independence is proclaimed. A desire to express America to herself had long been cherished, but this had been combined with a recognition of the superior value of the English product. With the new century this admission of the necessary inferiority of America's effort was definitely more faint, and the ambition of self-expression correspondingly stronger; but as yet there was no sufficient body of literature to substantiate the claim of independence. Thirty years have passed and within that space of a generation a new literature has come into being, which the unbiassed foreign critic must recognize as characteristically national, and which from the point of view of art he cannot afford to neglect.

In this movement Dreiser has played an important part. As a thinker, and here he has pretensions on which we must not set too high a value, he is in England's debt, for Darwin and Herbert Spencer were his intellectual parents; but for his literary affiliations we must look elsewhere. In the expurgated realism of Howells he saw nothing to emulate. Stephen Crane and Frank Norris were evidently more to his liking, but sometime before the projection of his business epics, *The Financier* and *The Titan*, he must have saturated himself in Balzac and Zola, and it was they who supplied both frame and canvas for his picture.

The French critic Lemaître, had probably never seen Dreiser's name in print, but he had nevertheless a remarkable insight into his talent. The essay to which I refer will be found in volume one of *Les Contemporains*. He first questions the general realistic pretension of presenting the facts of life without distortion or emphasis. It is true "That the works which interest us most to-day issue from the observation of men as they are, possessed of bodies, and living in conditions which exert an influence upon them. But it is true also that the artist in order to transport his models to the novel or the stage is compelled to select, to retain of reality only the expressive aspects, and organize them to bring into relief the dominant quality either of a milieu or a character."

I may here give away my secret and say that Lemaître's concern is not with Dreiser but with Emile Zola. The parallelism is sufficiently complete to justify a continuance of his statement.

"He appears to us more and more as the brutal and sad poet of blind instincts, gross passions, carnal loves, and of the low and repellant parts of human nature. What interests him in man is above all the animal, and in each human type the particular animal that this type envelopes. It is this that he loves to show, and it is the rest that he eliminates in distinction from the practice of the idealistic novelist. Eugène Delacroix said that the human face by a bold simplification of its features, by the exaggeration of some and the reduction of others, might be reduced to the face of a beast: it is in this fashion that Zola simplifies his souls."

Commenting on the constant physiological basis of

Zola's analysis Lemaître has this to say of one of his rare virtuous women: "If she has to struggle for a moment it is against a physiological influence, and it is not her will that triumphs but her health. Thus by the suppression of free will, by the elimination of the old basis of classical psychology which consisted essentially in the struggle of will and passion, Zola succeeds in constructing figures of an imposing and gross beauty, grandiose and truncated images of elementary forces—evil and deadly like the plague, or good and beneficent like the sun and spring. The result is that all fineness of psychology disappears. Zola's greatest effort succeeds only in painting for us the uncontested progress of a fixed idea, a mania or a vice. Unchangeable or always borne in the same direction, such are his characters. . . .

"But with whatever life it may be, even incomplete and discrowned, he makes them live; he has that most important of all gifts. And not merely the main figures, but on the second plane the smallest heads take life under the gross fingers of this moulder of beasts. They live at small cost doubtless, generally by virtue of an indication that is grossly and energetically particular; but they live, each apart and all together. For he knows also how to animate his groups, and set masses in movement."

The tragic direction of all this is obvious. "Never perhaps has the pessimistic obsession been carried to such excess." At his outset he found some satisfaction in physical love and its works "but now it seems that he has hatred and terror for all that flesh with which he is obsessed. He seeks to vilify it; he lingers in the depths of the human beast, in the play of the forces of the blood and nerves wherever they can deal out their insults to human pride. He ferrets into and displays the secret misfeatures of the flesh and its evil manifestations. He multiplies about adultery the circumstances that degrade it, and reduces love to a tyrannic need and an impure function. Of woman he sees only the mysterious stains of her sex. In man he sees the brute, in love the physical union, in maternity the accouchement. . . . Bestiality and imbecility are then in Zola's eyes the basis of humanity. . . . If the impression is sad it is powerful. I pay my compliments to those fine and delicate spirits for whom measure, decency, and correctness are to such an extent the whole of a writer that even after the *Assommoir* and the *Joie de Vivre* they hold Zola in small esteem, and send him back to school because he has not flattered humanity, and perhaps does not always write perfectly. I must not resent so distinguished a judgment. Let them refuse all the rest to M. Zola, can one deny him creative power, restricted if you will but prodigious within its limits? Protest as I may, even these brutalities, I know not how, impose upon me by their number, and these indecencies by their mass. . . . One of the virtues of M. Zola is an indefatigable and patient vigor. He has a piercing vision for concrete things, all the externals of life, and has this special gift to render what he sees: namely the ability to retain and accumulate a greater quantity of detail than any other describer of the same school; and this he does coldly, tranquilly, without weariness or disgust, and giving to everything the same crisp projection, so that the unity of each picture consists not as with the classics in the subordination of the sparse details to the whole, but if I may say so, in their interminable monochrome effect. . . . M. Zola has never been an impeccable writer, nor very sure of his pen. In his early books he took more pains, but since *Nana* he has conceived a contempt for style, and writes more swiftly and at large without concerning himself too much with the details of the phrase. But in both periods it is not difficult

[247]

to discover sufficiently shocking faults particularly offensive to people accustomed to the classics, to university people and old professors who know their language well. . . . Yes, all that is true, and I am very sorry. But it is far from being universally true. And since in these novels everything is planned on a large scale, intended to be viewed as a whole and from a distance, we must not quibble about phrases, but take it as it was written in great morsels and blocks and judge the value of the style by the total effect of the picture. We will recognize that an aggregation of phrases which are not all irreproachable ends nevertheless by giving us a vast and seizing vision of objects, and that this magnifying style, without fine shading and sometimes without precision, is eminently fitted by its monotonous exaggerations and its multiplied emphasis to render with power the vast scope of concrete things."

I make no excuse for this long transcription. It is surely one of the curiosities of criticism that an article written upon one author should have so exact a bearing upon the form and matter of another author whose originality we do not propose to challenge. Mr. Dreiser's literary affinities require no further exposition, and but little qualification or addition is necessary to establish the complete picture of the man and his work. But before we examine one of his typical books we may make Mr. Dreiser our text for a brief excursus on a subject that his novels, like Zola's before them, have brought into prominence. The subject is the sex motive in fiction.

This should be, but is not, a pleasant topic to treat, and for this the novelists rather than the subject are responsible. The liberation from tension has caused such a recoil of the spring, and the whole mechanism is in a state of such violent vibration as to breed confusion in the mind and rob it of the judicial poise that makes investigation profitable. We can be sure at least of our historic facts. Defoe at the outset dealt with disreputable situations with common-sense deliberation. Fielding's frankness is of the same order, a touch of irony and comic detachment being the differentiating feature of his art. Molly and Jenny and Lady Bellaston are incidents that disturb Jones only as they affect his central passion. Where this is concerned he is respectability incarnate, and his love for Sophia runs true to the code of his day. Sterne again takes the light-hearted and humorous view of love. Mr. Saintsbury resents his "sniggering indecency." The phrase is not deserved. His was never the method of the frontal attack. He prefers always the circuitous approach to his subject; and it pleased him to think of love as a forbidden region round whose outskirts he might range. Frankness of statement repelled him, and to denounce him as suggestive is to misinterpret the order of his imagination. It was only along the path of suggestion that it could operate. Smollett's coarseness we concede, but it has little to do with the passion of love.

Had the capacity to delineate the deeper emotions of the heart been vouchsafed to Scott his importance would never have been challenged. Without it his reputation stood so high that the novelists of three generations practiced his discretion. The result was that fiction must find its energies elsewhere, and though there is much marrying and giving in marriage, discreet seductions, and artfully concealed adulteries, for the better part of a century we had a literature without passion. A sign of the times was Thackeray's plaintive preface to *Pendennis*. Some feminine readers had fallen away from him for the book's indecency! "Since the author of *Tom Jones* was buried, no writer of fiction among us has been permitted to depict to his utmost power a *man*. We must drape him and give him a certain conventional simper. Society will not tolerate the Natural in our art."

The French meanwhile were robbing us of our ascendancy, and it was mainly the authors conversant with their practice who began to restore it. We were timid enough at first. George Meredith is supposed to have led the way, but there is nothing peculiarly outspoken even in his boldest book *One of Our Conquerors*. Hardy created a scandal which we find it difficult to understand with *Tess of the D'Urbervilles* and *Jude the Obscure*, and there was much chatter about Elinor Glyn's futile *Three Weeks*. These books were of the early nineties, and since then the deluge is on us. America's lingering Puritanism compelled even a later start. Stephen Crane was probably the earliest offender in 1891 with *Maggie, A Girl of the Streets*, and Dreiser nine years later earned a publisher's ban with *Sister Carrie*.

We have incontestably won our freedom, but the completeness of the victory is in doubt. Let us apply uninspired common-sense to one of the most difficult problems of our day. There is no need to question the potency of the sex impulse, nor any particular reason to deplore the intelligent application of this strong emotion to the purpose of fiction. In our natural lives we feel it necessary to place some curb upon the wildness of its movement. This is not a discipline imposed by the conventions only but by civilization itself. Is fiction well advised to release this control, and to permit one human energy among many to possess itself entirely of the field? That surely would be leaving too many important things out of the picture, for nothing can equal the usurping power of passion when the barriers are down. If our desire is for proportion there is something to be said in favor of intelligent restraint. Again, if it is a question of values, we will set as high an estimate as you please on love. But is it love or sheer carnality that we are usually presented with? So far does this last alternative prevail that we are compelled to identify two things that may be united, but which usually stand apart. Love is by nature expansive only in hidden ways. Its highest expression is a secret thing, and now it is brought out into the market place. There is surely some illogicality in flaunting it so extravagantly. I have no desire to accuse our better writers of pornographic intentions. Most of them are too savagely serious for that; but in spite of themselves they seek to convert the reader into a species of peeping-Tom for whom the secrets of the boudoir provide a vicarious excitation. May I close a subject which tends to grow unpleasant by an assertion that may be challenged? It is my personal opinion that the two men of greatest intellectual power who have permitted sex to invade their writings are James Joyce and D. H. Lawrence. All genius is supposed to be abnormal, but in them abnormality is carried to its extremest limit with the result that it loses all representative value. They represent themselves, but how many besides? The question is surely pertinent.

Stuart Sherman's arraignment of Dreiser is on the dual grounds of morality and art. He treads in the footsteps of Lemaître, acquiescing in the blame and eliminating the praise. The abnegation of free-will above all distresses him, and in the matter of style he ranges himself with that fastidious class whom the French critic touches with such delightful irony—the people accustomed to the classics, university people, and old professors who know their language well. He fails to note the rude vigor and the evocative power as he had failed to appreciate the courage and relentlessness of the delineation. In all these respects Lemaître who had never read Dreiser understood him better than the man who hated him.

A close examination would doubtless reveal many minor differences between Dreiser and Zola, but in a general way they are sufficiently identical. Where Zola gains by comparison is in the superior energy of his imagination. His work is rich in symbols. Human beings and things inanimate achieve an intensity that expands the individual into the type and gives to lifeless objects unwonted dominance, —as if, endowed with will and purpose, they were conscious partners in the designs of fate. It is an imaginative quality that he shared with Victor Hugo, but of this species of hallucination Dreiser's more literal mind is free. It leaves him the more unembarrassed for his strictly realistic task.

Dreiser's purpose in *The Genius* is to present the life-career of an artist who springs from commonplace surroundings, has early struggles to establish himself, succeeds, fails, and partially recovers. His vicissitudes throughout are bound up in his relations with a succession of women. A brusque summary will illustrate for the young practitioner of fiction the methods of construction according to the realistic formula. Properly fashioned one realistic novel will differ from another mainly by the names of persons and localities. There need be no plot, but the incidents will march with obvious consecutiveness, and the story will be organized as patiently and methodically as a mason builds a wall. It would seem that this particular type had reached the limit of its development, but it will perpetually recur.

Here then are the bare bones of the book. A typical middle-western family described, father, mother, two daughters, and Eugene Witla, the son. Rudimentary psychology of the latter, artistic, but admires girls—"was mad about them." Stella appears—some dialogue scenes to indicate her attractiveness. This more obvious to Eugene than to the reader. Newspaper experience: "I say Witla why don't you go to Chicago?" Goes accordingly. City described through his sensations. Hard work, storing stoves, house-runner for real estate office, driver for a laundry. Hearty interest indicated for Margaret Duff, a laundry hand. Collector for a furniture company. Art ambition grows. Night classes at art institute and progress. Warm affection for Ruby Kenny, a model. This worth developing. Visits his family, meets Angela Blue and vaguely feels he might wish to marry her. She is five years his senior. Newspaper illustrator in Chicago. Affection for Ruby Kenny persists. Various scenes described. Angela pays visit to Chicago, but knows nothing of Ruby. "She came again in early November and before Christmas and Eugene was fast becoming lost in the meshes of her hair. Although he met Ruby in November and took up a tentative relation on a less spiritual basis—as he would have said at the time—he nevertheless held his acquaintanceship with Angela in the background as the superior and more significant thing. She was purer than Ruby; there was in her certainly a deeper vein of feeling, as expressed in her thoughts and music. . . . Why should he part with her, or even let her know anything of this other world that he touched? He did not think he ought to." (Mr. Sherman failed to note this sense of moral obligation in Eugene.) Much more in this vein on the Angela-Ruby complication. Suddenly determines to go to New York, not to escape from this dilemma which barely exists for him, but to satisfy his art ambition. So Ruby is deserted, and one heart-broken letter from her (later discovered by the married Angela) ends the situation. Impressions of New York (description). Gets work as illustrator. Visits

Angela Blue's family and likes them. Upsets Angela greatly by insisting on premarital rights. Studies life in New York. Women multiply, more intellectual and artistic than before, especially Christina an opera singer. Liaison with her described. Meanwhile Angela waits afar. At long last marries. Eugene has a very successful exhibition of his paintings. To Paris with Angela. More realistic pictures but less success. Health breaks down, medical reason supplied. Peddles pictures. Down and out. Work as laborer for railroad. Angela goes home. Strenuous love affair with married daughter of landlady. This discovered by mother and Angela on her return. Eugene by now very cold with Angela. Climbs back to health and prosperity as art director for large concerns. Ultimately $25,000 a year in New York. The most vehement affair of his life with the eighteen-year-old Suzanne Dale. Fierce conflict with Mrs. Dale and his own wife. Almost a third of the story occupied with this episode. Loses his position. Suzanne affair frustrated by her mother's energy. Angela dies in childbirth (fully described) and we leave Eugene with his daughter, again an artist of note, but as interested as ever in the other sex with only an increase of caution.

I make no excuse for the baldness of this survey. For a book where words counted for more than mere statement it would be an impertinence. It serves here to exhibit the now antiquated pattern Dreiser repeats from one novel to the next. With his sincerity, his courage, his heavy-paced impressiveness acknowledged, we turn to two writers about whose artistry there can be no question.

Chapter XXIV

TWO ANTI-REALISTS*

Willa Cather and Cabell

WILLA CATHER

The chapter title does not imply that Miss Willa Cather is not often piercingly true and searchingly direct. It means simply that she does not write according to the formula of novelists who call themselves and are called realists. This formula the two preceding chapters have sufficiently illustrated, and we are now free to consider fiction as a representation of life upon a pattern evolved from the theme itself and from the otherwise untrammeled inclination of the artist. There is no reason why such writers should not respond to the appeal of the actual, and it may happen indeed that they have the better of the argument if truth to the facts of human nature is the goal. For man is an inconsequent animal, and to exhibit him as the mere child of circumstance is to ignore the elements of his humanity to which he most passionately clings.

It is fortunate that we cannot attach Miss Cather to any particular school, and if she shares qualities in common with other writers no discipleship is involved.

Her books tend more and more to be chronicles and pictures, and she makes her appeal to readers who still delight in the almost forgotten art of narration, and who value the power of words to evoke an image. Description therefore is not an idle accessory but of the essence of her

---

*Passages quoted by permission of Alfred A. Knopf, Inc., and Robert M. McBride & Co., New York.

art, and so vivid is her visual sense, so wingedly light her energy of phrase, that familiarity with the scene would confirm but could not intensify the truth and beauty of her presentation.

Illustrations of her skill might be taken almost at random. In that most perfect of her books *Death Comes for the Archbishop*, Latour is lost in the thirsty Rio Grande desert:

"When he realized that he was astray, his canteen was already empty and his horses seemed too exhausted to retrace their steps. He had persevered in this sandy track, which grew ever fainter, reasoning that it must lead somewhere.

"All at once Father Latour thought he felt a change in the body of his mare. She lifted her head for the first time in a long while, and seemed to redistribute her weight upon her legs. The pack mule behaved in a similar manner, and both quickened their pace. Was it possible they scented water?

"Nearly an hour went by, and then, winding between two hills that were like all the hundreds they had passed, the two beasts whinnied simultaneously. Below them, in the midst of that wavy ocean of sand, was a green thread of verdure and a running stream. This ribbon in the desert seemed no wider than a man could throw a stone,—and it was greener than anything Latour had ever seen, even in his own greenest corner of the Old World. But for the quivering of the hide on his mare's neck and shoulders, he might have thought this a vision, a delusion of thirst."

It is not difficult to discover the subtle touches by which this description is humanized and dramatized.

One of the Bishop's many problems was Padre Martinez. Here is the graphic portrait seen through the Bishop's eyes. "Father Latour had had polite correspondence with Martinez, but had met him only once, on that memorable occasion when the Padre had ridden up from Taos to strengthen the Santa Fe clergy in their refusal to recognize the new Bishop. But he could see him as if that were only yesterday,—the priest of Taos was not a man one would early forget. One could not have passed him on the street without feeling his great physical force and his imperious will. Not much taller than the Bishop in reality, he gave the impression of being an enormous man. His broad high shoulders were like a bull buffalo's, his big head was set defiantly on a thick neck, and the full-cheeked, richly-coloured, egg-shaped Spanish face—how vividly the Bishop remembered that face! It was so unusual that he would be glad to see it again; a high, narrow fore-head, brilliant yellow eyes set deep in strong arches, and full, florid cheeks,—not blank areas of smooth flesh, as in Anglo-Saxon faces, but full of muscular activity, as quick to change with feeling as any of his features. His mouth was the very assertion of violent, uncurbed passions and tyrannical self-will; the full lips thrust out and taut, like the flesh of animals distended by fear or desire."

Miss Cather has told us how this inspired chronicle was born: "My book was a conjunction of the general and the particular, like most works of the imagination. I had all my life wanted to do something in the style of legend, which is absolutely the reverse of dramatic treatment. Since I first saw the Puvis de Chavannes frescoes of the life of Sainte Geneviève in my student days, I have wished that I could try something a little like that in prose; some-thing without accent, with none of the artificial elements of composition. In the golden legend the martyrdoms of the Saints are no more dwelt upon than are the trivial incidents of their lives; it is as though all human expe-riences, measured against one supreme spiritual experience, were of about the same importance. The essence of such writing is not to hold the note, not to use an incident for all there is in it—but to touch and pass on. I felt that such writing would be a kind of discipline in these days when the situation is made to count for so much in writing. . . . In this kind of writing the mood is the thing . . . what I got from Father Machebeuf's letters was the mood, the spirit in which they accepted the accidents and hardships of a desert country, the joyful energy that kept them going. To attempt to convey this hardihood of spirit one must use language a little stiff, a little formal, one must not be afraid of the old trite phraseology of the frontier. Some of those time-worn phrases I used as the note from the piano by which the violinist tunes his instrument. . . . I did not sit down to write the book until the feeling of it had so teased me that I could not get on with other things. The writing of it took only a few months, because the book had all been lived many times before it was written, and the happy mood in which I began it never paled. It was like going back and playing the early composers after a surfeit of modern music."

It is to be wished that more novelists might give so revealing an account of themselves! By way of supplement not much is needed. The colors are perhaps too vivid to bear comparison with the delicate wash of Chavanne's frescoes, and the pictures have sometimes the boldness and sharpness of an etched vignette. The characters too are more definitely individualized,—a whole memorable gallery of them so vivid that one marvels at the seemingly effortless skill which produced them.

Father Latour and Vaillant are the central figures, and their portraiture emerges from the narrative with no apparent intercession by the author. Of external comment there is nothing, and for the ordinary resource of analysis in aid of characterization she substitutes the mood of revery. Father Latour perpetually recovers in dream the memories of his youth in far away Auvergne, when he and Vaillant were students in the Clermont Seminary. Vaillant is more sturdily a child of the immediate hour, his olfactory imagination occasionally stirred by the odor of ancient soups. Incident, too, plays its part, and we are indeed insensible if we read the chapter "December Night" and fail to know and love the Bishop better at its close. It reminds us of similar episodes in *Les Misérables*, but its pathos is less theatrical and with no conscious appeal to the reader's response.

Some of the episodes of the book are designed less to illustrate character than to play their part in the general atmospheric effect, and without exception they make their contribution. "The Legend of Fray Baltazar" is such a detached episode, and of all the digressions in modern literature it is surely one of the most entertaining. Its sufficient justification is the narrative energy it develops. Its illustrative value is all sheer gain.

So much cannot be said of the Tom Outland digression in an inferior novel *The Professor's House*. The anecdote within the anecdote is a device of hers which she constrains us to accept in many of her books. In this case all action is suspended for nearly a hundred pages, and the effort of accommodation is made with difficulty. We have familiarized ourselves with a Professor St. Peter whose mind has been centered for many years on his historical writings and only secondarily on his family. We watch the growing detachment from wife and children, but see no decrease in his scholarly ambitions. So wrapped up in his work is he that he continues to write in his old bare room with its one dim window, its gas stove, and its dressmaker's forms, when his family have moved into comfort across the way. This is all amusing enough, and we share his relief when they all go abroad and leave him with his garden and his work. We are prepared for a rupture, but not for the dislocation that the author too fancifully provides. It was as if she had felt constrained to justify the Outland digression in terms of the Professor's character. She therefore cancels almost everything we have learned about him, develops the Outland story to disproportionate length, and constrains us to believe that its primitivism has led St. Peter back to his own primitive boyhood. His intervening life is a meaningless blank. "What he had not known was that, at a given time, that first nature could return to a man, unchanged by all the pursuits and passions and experiences of his life, untouched even by the tastes and intellectual activities which have been strong enough to give him distinction among his fellows and to have made for him, as they say, 'a name in the world!' Perhaps this reversion did not often occur, but he knew it had happened to him. He did not regret his life, but he was indifferent to it. It seemed to him like the life of another person."

This is a very different thing from the debt which many artists owe to the revived impressions of childhood and youth, and which Miss Cather has emphatically acknowledged. "I think that most of the basic material a writer works with is acquired before the age of fifteen. That's the important period: when one is not writing. Those years determine whether one's work will be poor or rich."

This statement may need some qualification, but at least it presupposes a continuity and unity that the Professor's psychology does not present.

Miss Cather is on surer ground in a later book *Shadows on the Rock*. Here we find all or nearly all that we have come to associate with her name. The familiar signs are a sensitive use of words and a musically cadenced phrase, a free indulgence in description, a substitution of revery for analysis, and a multiplication of anecdote to satisfy her own narrative impulse and supply the reader with added lines and colors for the enrichment of her picture. There are of course no sex complications, and she avoids the dramatic crises which the historical novelist invents if he cannot discover. It is history in undress uniform and not on parade, and of the great figures that we encounter, Laval and Frontenac, she chooses to give us an intimate rather than an imposing picture. It was remotely the method of Scott who eased himself of responsibility by making the subordinate figures provide the story. But Scott's story was always an exciting one with all the attributes of the conventional plot; and his great figures cast a heavier shadow on his pages.

Miss Cather from the days of *O Pioneers* has always sought to strike her roots in the primitive bed-rock of life. Primitivism gloriously sustained her in *Death Comes for the Archbishop* and played her false in *The Professor's House.* Adventure, uncouth scenery, savage races furnish her material, and the rites and practices of the most ancient Christian church are a constant stimulus to an imagination that finds no generative virtue in the laxer discipline of her own faith. If there is a committee on propaganda in the Catholic Church they should translate the books of this Protestant writer for distribution through the world.

JAMES BRANCH CABELL

Mr. Cabell is a happy accident in American literature. He has no ancestors, he will have no successors, but his importance is unquestioned. Uniqueness is not necessarily a virtue, but here is an author untouched by all the modes of the current hour who imposes himself upon us by the quality of his imagination, by the force and consistency of his dominant conception, by the persistent if monotonous charm of his style, and by the incisiveness of his thought. It is in this last respect only that he is recognizably modern, if by that term we imply irony and wit applied to the criticism of established things, and a sense of the ultimate futility of our human destiny. Revolting from the discipline of life he fashions a dream world, phantasmagoric and unreal to outward seeming, but where the wings of his imagination find a resisting and sustaining air. But as in all aërial flights danger lurks in the landing, so in Mr. Cabell's forced returns to earth his dream-chariot lies as often as not an undistinguishable wreck. He has rarely made a safe and scientific descent. At the end of the journey Jurgen finds Dame Lisa darning his socks, and Kennaston's talisman of dreams is no more than the broken half of the cover of his wife's pot of complexion cream. The equation between illusion and reality is wittily worked out but never satisfactorily solved, for with Mr. Cabell the actual is the illusory, and only dreams are true.

Mr. Cabell is systematic to the point of intricacy in the organization of his score of books. We have a handful of short stories, a critical prologue and an epilogue, four domestic novels, and five major books concerned with the Manuel Saga. Let us first get what help we may from the criticism.

Beyond Life is an all-night monologue by the author's friend Charteris. The theme is romance as an escape from reality, or perhaps rather as the revelation of a higher reality. We have noted the stages of the novel's advance from the impossible, through the possible, to the probable. In the last stages we are willing to concede the heightening effect that comes from artistic selection and concentration. Yet normal reality is the point of departure and the constant touchstone. But Charteris-Cabell will not have it so. "There has rarely been any ill-advised attempt to depict life as it seems in the living of it, or to crystallize the vague notions and feeble sensations with which human beings, actually, muddle through to an epitaph; if only because all sensible persons, obscurely aware that this routine is far from what it ought to be, have always preferred to deny its existence. . . . For, as has been said before an inveterate Sophocles notes clearly that veracity is the one unpardonable sin, not merely against art, but against human welfare. . . . Humanity would seem at an early period to have wrenched comfort from prefiguring man as the hero of the cosmic romance. For it was unpleasantly apparent that man did not excel in physical strength, as set against the other creatures of a planet whereon may be encountered tigers and elephants. . . . But to acknowledge such disconcerting facts would never do. . . . Among the countless internecine animals that roamed earth, puissant with claw and fang and sinew, an ape reft of his tail, and grown rusty at climbing, was the most formidable, and in the end would triumph. . . . And so to-day, as always, we delight to hear about invincible men and women of unearthly loveliness—corrected and considerably augmented versions of our family circle—performing feats illimitably beyond our modest powers. And so to-day no one upon the preferable side of Bedlam wishes to be reminded of what we are in actuality, even were it possible, by any disastrous miracle, ever to dispel the mist which romance has evoked about all human doings."

The argument is specious—more plausible than convincing—and we accept it only as the sincere opinion of a man who has strayed from some mythopœic age for the entertainment of our dusty modern world. If documentary realism is to relax its grip upon the novel, the process will be effected by agencies which will recognize facts without prostitution, and which with all the latitude of sceptical inquiry will still save something for the spirit of wonder and the poetry of life.

The epilogue *Straws and Prayer-Books* is a personal statement which, coming some years later, is a vindication of things written rather than an apology for things to be. The author is his own law, he writes for his own diversion, and communication with a public is the last thing that should concern him. This is defensible doctrine, and if the self-revelation is clear enough the public will not complain though it may entertain some reserve of surprise that publication should proceed from such aloofness. We are glad that there is to be no preaching and relieved at the absention from moral reform. He is still refractory as of old to the discipline of life as we ordinarily live it. "Item, with human life as a whole I have no grave concern, and I am beguiled by no notion of 'depicting' it. My concern is solely with myself. I have no theory of what we call 'life's' cause or object; nor can I detect in material existence any general trend. The stars and the continents, the mountains and these flustering hordes of men, every mole-hill and the diligent dancing of gnat swarms,—all appears to blend in a vagrant and very prettily tinted and generally amusing stream by which I too am swept onward. If but for my dignity's sake, I prefer to conceal my knowledge of this fact.

"Item, there is upon me a resistless hunger to escape from use and wont. . . .

"Item, I really must, in the teeth of all solicitation, refuse to plagiarize anything from what people call 'nature' and 'real life.' My playing, which I term my art, has no concern with things which, in any case, are too ill-managed to merit imitation."

Such then is the man, so far as personal confession can express him. Let us turn now to the superior revelation of the books, and chiefly of those by which he will be remembered. My choice is personal, for I have not space to argue the question of relative merit.

Of his four domestic novels *The Cream of the Jest* is the most entertaining. Felix Kennaston is a Lichfield writer of our day,—for Lichfield read Richmond, Virginia, and for Kennaston if you will, Cabell. It is a story with the "dreaming true" device of *Peter Ibbetson*, for Kennaston's daily life concerns him infinitely less than his nightly excursions with that Ettare whom Hovendile loved when Manuel her father ruled Poictesme. But in its pages we traverse more than seven centuries, for some of the scenes revived relate to the earlier childhood of the world. We are present for example at the burning of the library at Alexandria, and once with Kennaston we stand by the couch of Tiberius Cæsar as he lay ill at Capreæ. We may note that despite his professed contempt for physical circumstance Mr. Cabell is more in debt to historic fact than Mrs. Woolf who in her *Orlando* is satisfied with the recovery of purely imaginary scenes.

The Poictesme series has five books devoted to it, with an appended smaller effort *The Way of Eckben*, in which Mr. Cabell announces the close of his career as artist. But artists' farewells are rarely final, and we may hope that some impulse will break his resolution. Congreve was one of his literary enthusiasms, and he was silent for the last twenty-eight years of a not long life. Congreve had not exhausted the theme of gallantry, but having given it the most complete expression of which he was capable was content not to repeat himself. Mr. Cabell may be mindful of this precedent, in which case we may regret but must respect his silence. He has astonishing inventiveness, but it has always been exercised in one direction. It is doubtful if it could be renewed in another.

Its fruits are a new country and a new mythology, and if not a new philosophy, yet one that is blended of elements that have rarely been conjoined. A trifle over-feminized we may decide his world to be, and a permanent weakness in the books is a lack of penetration into the workings of the feminine mind. Like one of his own characters he never seems to know what is going on in the "small shining heads of women." But they plentifully abound, and there is always pleasant mischief where they are.

Jurgen is incontestably the finest of the series. *The High Place* with its mixture of *diablerie* and sentiment is as certainly the weakest. *Figures of Earth* where Manuel founds his Kingdom of Poictesme I know only by report. *Domnei* is the book of chivalric love, and we might urge that it is a trifle monotonous in its loveliness. The nearest rival to *Jurgen* is *The Silver Stallion*, a book that is subtly witty and cryptically wise, and the full effect of which can be gained only by relating its marvels to our own world of cause and effect. Mr. Cabell therefore, despite all his protestations to the contrary here submits himself, however unwillingly and evasively, to the discipline of life. The fellowship of the Silver Stallion was another Round Table under the leadership of Manuel. When he miraculously disappears and his apotheosis begins the ten lords of the Silver Stallion go severally in search of him, and carry his gospel through the world. It is of their adventures that the book is made. Selection is difficult, but one remembers with vividness the chapters that give the account of the Demiurgy of Donander, or Kerin's search for truth in the Well of Ogde, and the manner of his return to the wife who had pushed him over the curb.

Such unity as it has *The Silver Stallion* derives from the

Messiah myth, its dominant theme. The continuity of *Jurgen* is strung along the character and adventures of the titular hero, who is in some of his aspects a composite of Faust and Peer Gynt. It is in the class of these two fantasies that Mr. Cabell's later creation falls, and if the American Peer Gynt has less wide report than his Scandinavian cousin it is not through lack of inventive faculty in the author. Mr. Cabell has written nothing defter or more delightful, and his imagination has never played more freely on his theme. Our comparison must base itself on ultimate human value, and Mr. Cabell will not accept the pedantic conclusion to which this discussion has led. His most successful book, *Jurgen*, is also his most human book, but its most convinced admirer must admit that Ibsen's masterpiece encloses a larger tract of life, and is more readily translated into terms of our normal experience.

Chapter XXV

THE WAY OF IRONY AND SATIRE *

Maugham, Douglas, Huxley, Lewis

Somerset Maugham

A question of form concerns us here, but it is literary ethics rather than technique that I propose to discuss. Notorious examples of contemporary personal references will occur to every reader of Mr. Somerset Maugham and Mr. Aldous Huxley. With no harsh intention we may inquire what has been the practice of novelists of the past with respect to the presentation in their books of living celebrities or of the illustrious dead. We may omit from our inquiry the unsatiric portrait. Beauchamp as Admiral Maxse or Stevenson masquerading as Woodseer need not detain us. No process of libel or action of assault and battery could result from such kindly transformations, which also are so remote as to be unrecognizable. Let us fasten our attention rather on instances where malice playful or venomous has been manifested.

Fielding's Square and Thwackum had probably their living undistinguished originals, Smollett not seldom vented his private spites in venomous caricatures, and we know that Sterne eased a cherished grudge in the person of Dr. Slop. But so far as I am aware we must wait for Dickens before we reach in the succeeding century the sort of thing we are in search of. Disraeli's novels of course were stuffed with portraits, but they were only politicians. In *Bleak House* two living celebrities are pre-

* Passages quoted by permission of Doubleday, Doran & Company, Inc., and Harcourt, Brace and Company, Inc., New York.

sented to us in the characters of Boythorn and Harold
Skimpole. Landor greeted his portrait with gusts of leonine laughter. Leigh Hunt received the more stinging
travesty of his dilettante æstheticism and his shiftlessness
with less equanimity. But there was more humor than
savagery in the caricature, and it is these qualities that
find their reversal in modern practice. Mr. Wells in *The
New Machiavelli* is still more humorous than savage in his
most recognizable portrait of the Baileys, and Lord Balfour
as Evesham is a generous and genial creation. Mr. Somerset
Maugham and Mr. Aldous Huxley have swerved away
from their habitual feline urbanity to give us a series of
portraits as savage as those of Pope or Dryden in their
most venomous mood. Beyond indicating this as a new
phase of modern fiction it is not obvious that the critic
has any valid license for comment. He may consider the
procedure an offense against good taste, but it is surely a
matter for private accommodation rather than a question
of art. The offended individual has always recourse to the
courts of law, and if he fears that a libel action will proclaim the fact that he recognizes himself in the portrait
he still has two arms with fists at the end of them and
the author has a negotiable face.

Mr. Maugham has specialized also in another kind of
literary portrait, which is a variation of the fictional
biography that Maurois and Ludwig have made fashionable. The variation is in the direction of a quite unromantic frankness with full reservation claimed for a manipulation of facts to suit the purpose of the story. Gauguin
lies obviously at the basis of *The Moon and Sixpence*, and
Thomas Hardy quite as obviously, though the author has
denied it, is the central figure of *Cakes and Ale*.

Gauguin's *Noa-Noa* is not properly to be considered the
basis of *The Moon and Sixpence*. It is a beautiful little idyll

of savagery, as sincere and natural as Herman Melville's not dissimilar narratives, and definitely more tender than Maugham's quite ruthless characterization. Maugham's foundation was rather the known facts of a remarkable career which he felt entitled to manipulate in the interests of his story provided that there was no falsification of the main conception. The Maurois tradition cannot avail itself of such imaginative freedom.

Without too much circumstantiality I will set down the events of Gauguin's life so that we may recognize the extent of deviation in the derived narrative. The author's main concern is not to reproduce the facts but to give a true picture of an extraordinary mind and temperament, of a man with no training in art who in mid-career abandoned his family and his profession because he was under compulsion to paint. There is not only a powerful psychological attraction in the theme, but it illustrates also the supremely selfish yet also self-sacrificing elements that ally themselves with creative genius. As Gauguin displayed it in the midst of incredible suffering and poverty, creative genius is egotism in its most developed form, repellent, inevitable, unlovable, yet wholly indispensable.

The facts upon which this theme is embroidered are briefly these:

Gauguin was born in Paris in 1848. When he was three years old his father took his family to South America and died *en route*. At seven he was taken back to France by his mother, and at seventeen he shipped before the mast for a second voyage to the southern seas. This sailor life lasted for three years until his guardian placed him in a financial firm in Paris. Here he continued for eleven years in complete prosperity and apparent contentment. He married a Danish woman in 1873. His interest in art at this time was of the most superficial kind, but from the time of his meeting Pissarro about 1875 it grew more serious. Occasional pictures were produced, and in 1883 he severed his lucrative business connections for the sake of art. It was not until 1885 that he left his wife.

Years of harsh destitution and passionate painting followed, with probably as little desire as prospect of recognition. The lure of the tropics drew him to Martinique. After a year he returned to France—now in Paris, now Brittany with a band of followers, now in Arles with Van Gogh. In 1891 he made his first voyage to Tahiti, and of this visit *Noa-Noa* is the invaluable record: "I commence to think simply, to have little hatred for my neighbour, even, it may be to love him. I have all the delights of a free animal and human existence. I escape the factitious, I enter into nature with the certainty of a to-morrow like to-day, as free and as beautiful; peace descends upon me, I develope normally, and I have no more vain cares." It was here that he took his girl wife Tahoura, but the idyll closed with his return to France in August, 1893. In 1895 he was back in Tahiti and civilization saw him no more. Illness and destitution pursue him now. In 1901, he moved on to the Marquesas. In 1903 he died there, painting until his hand was too weak to hold the brush.

We are not often so possessed of the material from which an author constructs his work, and the young practitioner or intelligent student of fiction can derive from the resulting book some knowledge of the mechanism that went to its making. Concentration and foreshortening are as necessary as in Shakespeare's adaptations of Plutarch or Holinshed. Substitutions of equivalent facts and inventions of congruous facts will occur. Strickland will be an English stock-broker instead of an operator on the Parisian Bourse. He will abandon his wife with more startling suddenness than the facts warrant; and the whole Stroeve episode will be invented from sufficiently adequate suggestion to exhibit at once his callous brutality and his frenzied devotion to art. We know of Gauguin's early contacts with the tropics, first as a child, then as a sailor. This gives a motivation for his Tahiti decision that the book lacks, and his return to France and ultimate migration to the Marquesas are, for purposes of unity, disregarded. Another minor matter may be mentioned. Gauguin had been painting in a desultory way for eight years before he abandoned his profession, and for ten years before he deserted his wife. Here is the different version of the story:

" 'Then what in God's name have you left her for?'

" 'I want to paint.'

"I looked at him for a long time. I did not understand. I thought he was mad. It must be remembered that I was very young, and I looked upon him as a middle-aged man. I forgot everything but my own amazement.

" 'But you're forty.'

" 'That's what made me think it was high time to begin.'

" 'Have you ever painted?'

" 'I rather wanted to be a painter when I was a boy, but my father made me go into business because he said there was no money in art. I began to paint a bit a year ago. For the last year I've been going to some classes at night.'

" '————Can you paint?'

" 'Not yet but I shall. That's why I've come over here. I couldn't get what I wanted in London. Perhaps I can here.'

" 'Do you think it's likely that a man will do any good when he starts at your age? Most men begin painting at eighteen.'

" 'I can learn quicker than I could when I was eighteen.'

" 'What makes you think you have any talent?'

"He did not answer for a minute. His gaze rested on the passing throng, but I do not think he saw it. His answer was no answer.

"'I've got to paint.'"

Mr. Maugham has adopted the first personal point of view as he was later to do in *Cakes and Ale*. But it is the autobiographical method with a difference, for the unnamed narrator whom I shall designate as Somerset is not in the least concerned with giving us the circumstances of his own life. He is wholly concerned with solving a psychological puzzle, and in the end he admits himself and leaves the reader baffled. The only virtue he claims is intelligent comment and utter veracity. He has all Defoe's eagerness to vouch for the circumstantial truth of his narrative to the point even of disclaiming his report as fiction. "If I were writing a novel rather than narrating such facts as I know of a curious personality, I should have invented much to account for this change of heart" (i.e. Strickland's sudden determination to be a painter). The comment I have said is throughout intelligent, but from fear of pedantry there is no attempt made save in the most general terms to indicate the characteristics of Gauguin's art. The book is emphatically not a treatise on painting.

Young Somerset aged twenty-three and a budding writer meets Strickland the stock-broker in London, and accepts his wife's report that he has no intellectual or artistic interests. The sudden flight occurs, and Somerset accepts the mission of hunting up the fugitive in Paris and bringing him to a realization of the enormity of his act. The supposition is that he has run away with a typist. His efforts are ineffectual. Five years later he is in Paris again, and through the medium of his friend Dirk Stroeve makes contact with Strickland. At this point it is all excellent dramatic fiction culminating in the seduction of Mrs.

Stroeve and her death. What Somerset has not witnessed he learns from Dirk, but he takes the author's license of expanding and dramatizing the account. Strickland's dominating callousness never fails of its emphasis. Mrs. Stroeve has committed suicide, and Somerset is seeking to probe the motives that led Strickland to seduce her and to cast her off:

"'But why did you want to take her away with you?' I asked.

"'I didn't,' he answered frowning.

"'When she said she was coming I was nearly as surprised as Stroeve. I told her when I'd had enough of her she'd have to go, and she said she'd risk that.' He paused a little. 'She had a wonderful body, and I wanted to paint a nude. When I'd finished my picture I took no more interest in her.'

"'And she loved you with all her heart.'

"He sprang to his feet and walked up and down the small room.

"'I don't want love. I haven't time for it. It's weakness. I am a man, and sometimes I want a woman. When I've satisfied my passion I'm ready for other things. I can't overcome my desire, but I hate it; it imprisons my spirit; I look forward to the time when I shall be free from all desire and give myself without hindrance to my work. Because women can do nothing except love, they've given it a ridiculous importance. They want to persuade us that it's the whole of life. It's an insignificant part. I know lust. That's normal and healthy. Love is a disease. Women are the instruments of my pleasure; I have no patience with their claim to be helpmates, partners, companions.'"

A week later Somerset hears that Strickland had gone to Marseilles. He never saw him again.

And now, in consequence, the technique of the book

must change, and the method of Conrad is invoked to carry it to its conclusion.

Fifteen years later Somerset goes to Tahiti, which is nine years after Strickland's death. He meets Captain Nichols, he meets the Jewish trader Cohen, he meets Captain Brunot, Mrs. Johnson, and Dr. de Coutras, and by their reports presented with dramatic vividness the remainder of the story is pieced out.

When he returns to England Somerset finds Mrs. Strickland and her son busy at their pious task of apotheosis.

I cannot dwell at such length on *Cakes and Ale*, not because it is a lesser book, but because the method and the manner are substantially the same. It is an older, wiser, but I fear not kindlier Somerset who tells the story. He manifests less willingness to admit the significance of genius. Gauguin's greatness he conceded. The supposititious Hardy is merely reaping the benefit of his great age. The British public always demands some grand old man of letters for its worship, and Wordsworth and Tennyson and Hardy supplied the need. It relishes either the pathos of youthful genius and an early death, or is imposed upon by the dignity of years. Driffield prevailed merely by endurance. He was a good craftsman, and a wholesome modest human being whose solemn wink to his young friend revealed his estimate of his own importance. On Driffield's death the very recognizable Alroy Kear had been engaged by the widow to write a consecrated life of her great husband. He seeks to interest Somerset in this pious enterprise, for Somerset as a boy had known Driffield before fame had come to him, and that rather disreputable first wife of his, Rosie, about whom in Roy's opinion the least said the better. Somerset does not accept the commission, but *Cakes and Ale* is mainly his own rendering of these early days. The constant inweaving of the

past with the present is one of the many technical virtues
of the book. Its general thesis has disturbed some sensitive
readers. It is not quite a sufficient defense for Mr. Maugham
to say that he was not representing Hardy. Driffield had
been a sailor and Hardy was a constant landsman. Driffield wrote no poetry, and Hardy's main intellectual contribution was through his verse. And though he was
twice married his first wife presumably bore no resemblance
to the immortal Rosie. These distinctions only constitute
a further deviation from fact than he permitted himself
with Gauguin. The derivation of the portrait is equally
unmistakable; and while we need not share the consternation of the more squeamish readers, we must admit that
the choice of an apparent Hardy for a hero was unfortunate.
It is not that we fear the truth but that the truth is not
told. The "debunking" biography has a current vogue.
Hardy needed no deflation, and Mr. Maugham has emphasized his naturalness to the full. We have no quarrel
with that, but why in the interests of naturalness sacrifice
every vestige of dignity, and why these too superficial
reservations on the score of his greatness?

It is a brilliant but uncomfortable book.

NORMAN DOUGLAS

Mr. Maugham, Mr. Douglas, and Mr. Huxley are so
clearly of the same intellectual family that the play of
individual difference between them is more difficult to
indicate than the qualities that bind them together. Ur-
bane, ironic, sophisticated, witty—the epithets might be
multiplied that mark their identity. If Norman Douglas
falls below the other pair in creative energy he is not their
inferior in brilliance, and he has the merit of formulating
a method which at least influenced the later Maugham and
dominated the commencing Huxley.

South Wind therefore has a significance that goes beyond its intrinsic merits. It was published in 1917, and almost year by year it has been reprinted. There are four editions in the single year, 1924. *Crome Yellow* appeared in 1921, and it is inconceivable that its tone and movement would have been quite the same without its predecessor. This can be said without any hint of slavish dependence or discipleship.

What then has Mr. Douglas done? He has satisfied himself with a reduced canvas and an exiguous story. Jane Austen was content to work upon "two or three families in a village." Mr. Douglas is not more ambitious. There is no family life in his books,—instead he chooses a dozen individuals whom chance has thrown together on an imaginary island, Nepenthe, off the Mediterranean African coast. Two of these he endows with the root qualities of eloquence, namely a curious and precise knowledge and the power to generalize from particulars. Mr. Keith and Count Caloveglia might readily change places with Mr. Cardan and Mr. Calamy, or any other pair of Mr. Huxley's fashioning. In the notation of their characters there is perhaps a sharper accent, for he is not quite so much at the mercy of his own brilliance as the younger writer. His urbanity too is more constant, and he is free from the rancor that envenoms both Mr. Maugham's rendering of Alroy Kear and Mr. Huxley's presentation of Burlap. In all of them we find the same caressingly sinister tone, and the same atmosphere of moral deliquescence. No physical reason is assigned by the others for the weakening of the moral fiber. We may blame the war, the progress of science, or the decay of religion. The result is the same. In *South Wind* it is the moist sirocco that works the havoc among the Anglo-Saxon colony, and even the sturdy Russians, the White Cows, are victims of the prevailing lassitude.

Mr. Heard, the erstwhile saintly Bishop of Bampopo, is not immune from the contagion, and he develops a spirit of accommodation of which he had not suspected himself capable. Actions that once would have filled him with horror he views with equanimity, and he is quite willing to condone if not to approve his cousin's summary method of ridding herself of an obnoxious husband. He enjoys drinking Mr. Keith's excellent wine rather than Mr. Parker's poisoned whisky, but this is merely a palate preference and not a moral choice. Mr. Heard is the only person who is capable of a critical reaction, and we have seen him to be an unsatisfactory reagent. The author of course will not help us, and it is useless to go to the others for a moral judgment. We rely momentarily on that noble figure Count Caloveglia whose eloquent defense of beauty seems to proceed from such an unsullied passion. Alas! Mr. van Koppen sails away with the satisfaction of knowing that he has been duped, and without begrudging Caloveglia's daughter her handsome dowry. We are reminded of Charles Lamb's similar satisfaction in being duped, and that he would not willingly have been without the idea of so "specious an old rogue."

The very considerable charm of this book is evidently not dependent on the virtue of its individual characters, and it is doubtful whether a more extended analysis would capture its secret. Some of the value comes from the writing which is easily and gracefully incisive, and still more from the author's power to create a picture in the mind. If we have not felt deeply we have at least seen.

Aldous Huxley

Three members of this chapter group are as interested in ideas as they are in fiction, and from this limited point of view Mr. Huxley is the most stimulating. From of

old thinking people have been herded into two classes,—
they are either Platonists or Aristotelians. The eclectic
Mr. Huxley escapes this classification, and his case suggests
a new formula. In this revised distribution we must give
our preference either to the how or what of thinking.
The "What You Thinkers" seek rest in positive statements,
absolute results, organized and tidy systems. They are the
supporters of dogma and authorized convention, the foes
of diversity and doubt. The "How You Thinkers" are not
necessarily confirmed sceptics, but they assuredly are more
determined individualists than the others, less swayed by
the dominance of fixed opinions, and supremely concerned
with the untrammeled play of their intellectual faculties.
Life is a perpetual flux and change, and such stabilization
of values as they demand finds for them its closest approximation in the integrity of the intellectual process.

Mr. Huxley is then something more and less than a
novelist. Indeed it may be our duty to show how poor a
novelist he can on occasion be, but if we succeed in that
we shall deal no unrecoverable blow to his reputation.
He will continue to "bombinate," and we shall continue
to read him.

In *Point Counter Point* he put forth his maximum of effort
and reached his maximum of power. For a consideration
of the books which preceded I shall avail myself of portions of a most interesting unpublished analysis by a
former student of mine, Mr. Earle Birney. A brief word
may here be said concerning his latest book *Brave New
World*.

It is a Utopia of the remote future, but we must not
imagine that Mr. Huxley commits himself with enthusiasm
to his own inventions. Herein he refreshingly differs from
the ordinary Utopian novelist who projects his image of a
perfected world with complete self-satisfaction. His con-

cern is rather with the dangers of an unregulated scientific advance which is bringing Utopias perilously within the range of possibility. The stabilized and mechanized world of his satiric picture is not an incentive but a warning.

On a reduced scale Mr. Huxley might be described as the Voltaire of this modern age. The Frenchman's levity, irony, scepticism, his multifarious knowledge and his awareness of scientific and philosophical advance are also his by virtue of an affinity of temperament and by the legitimate process of intellectual descent. He is a spiritual child of Voltaire but with one grave omission in the heredity, for there is nothing in his brilliant combination of qualities that corresponds with the great Frenchman's untiring warfare against oppression. Voltaire was able to fuse his sceptical irony with humanitarian ardor. In Huxley the first element is active at the expense of the latter, and *Brave New World* is interesting mainly because it manifests, if ever so faintly, a dawning concern for the future of the race. We may describe it not inaccurately as a *conte philosophique* in the Voltairian manner.

Mr. Huxley's first novel, *Crome Yellow* (1921) presents a typical set down for the summer months at an ordinary English country house. Most of the group have sufficient means to be relieved from work, and are therefore at liberty to pursue a life of brilliant talk and animal behavior. But though their intellects have accepted the modern belief in unbelief, their emotional natures are less blasé, still desiring order, romance, purpose. The conflict fills them with a sense of vague dissatisfaction, made all the more vexatious because inescapable. The lesser lights seek stability by isolating themselves in hobbies, as does Wimbush, or in cults, as does Priscilla. The more uncompromising, as Denis and Mary, remain to the end of the book in a state of ingenuous restlessness which cannot be dispelled even by the most assiduous cultivation and expression of the ego.

The people in *Those Barren Leaves* (1925) are in the same condition. Here are the disenchanted ones again, a little more affluent perhaps, spending September at an Italian villa—some of them even a little more clever and experienced. Again, a few lesser minds, as those of Falx and Mary Thriplow, manage to secure some grubby satisfaction from the unenvied pursuit of their own little fads and hypocrisies. Others make muddled compromises with life, but with less success. Lilian Aldwinkle "believes in passion, passionately," but the creed fails to satisfy when age removes her power to attract worshippers. The unadulterated moderns, the Calamys and the Chelifers, go about in discontent, perpetually doing what they don't want to do simply because they don't know what they want to do, and never will. They argue to pass the time, never to persuade, and make love to stave off boredom. They have a grudge against the Tree of Life for growing in such sterile soil, and in their preoccupation with this grudge they increase the general infertility by remaining barren leaves themselves. Even in the literal sense of the phrase, only two, and they the least typical of the group, Irene and Hovenden, give promise of quickening "the ancient root of life."

Antic Hay (1923) deals with the Londoners in London. Again the theme concerns the *post-bellum* artists and dilettanti, those who, like Galsworthy's Michael Mont have "a feeling that Progress has been found out." Unlike him, however, they have declared in consequence for entire freedom from social aim or moral obligation, only to find emancipation turn to *ennui*. Gumbril, the central character, slides deliberately into aimlessness when the book opens, and he and his set are thenceforward pictured seeking for bizarre experiences and occupations in the futile effort to get on good terms with life. They lead each other an endless dance, an antique "hay," whose complex gyrations have lost all meaning and much of their power to exhilarate. Like Edward the Third's entertainers, they too dance with goat feet, for sex has lost its sanctity and now provides only the least unsatisfying distraction. The somewhat obscure title is therefore apt enough, and suggests the central theme of the book.

In structure the three books hold sufficiently together.

The plot of *Antic Hay* is of the slightest, sufficient merely to illustrate the theme. Young Gumbril, possessed of a modest income and a desire to avoid responsibility, quits his ushership and proceeds to "graze upon the lawns" with his Bohemian friends. With them he discusses, brilliantly but with complete inconsequence, art, religion, sex, and life with theories for enduring it. He makes various experiments in passion, and in this part of his antic dance complicates the motions of his partners. Throughout, he, like Denis and Calamy and Chelifer, does not know what he wants to do nor why he does what he is doing. He sells a whimsical patent for pneumatic trousers; and when boredom has, for the time at least, quenched his curiosity about life, he seeks temporary escape in a continental business trip for the promotion of his patent,—and the book stops.

It is to be noticed that Mr. Huxley is up-to-date in his method of plot construction. He does not ignore narrative, but he gives his story an air of reality by making it slight and loosely connected, as are the events in most people's lives. He dispenses with the technique of the professed novelist; there is no heightening, climax, final suspense, or catastrophe. The situation between Shearwater and his wife may be cleverly complicated, but the knot is tied merely for the fun of it, and left unloosened. The end, too, is carefully untheatrical, carefully devoid even of the sense of inevitability. What slight plot exists is told for the most part directly, though previous events are generally revived indirectly. Thus, incidents in the past life of Gumbril Junior, and of Myra Viveash are made known through their streams of consciousness. In *Those Barren Leaves* the past of Francis Chelifer is indicated by the artificially indirect method of recording his autobiography.

In this last named book many of Chelifer's confessions must be classified, however, as somewhat pointless digression. Much of the past revived has no bearing on the present action, and often does not even offer us information on the characters concerned in it. The whole account of the "Rabbit Fancier's Gazette" seems to be inserted solely to introduce "rabear" into the English language. In other passages of this book poems and stray verses are dragged in without reason or effect. In all these novels the narrative suffers repeated interruption from vagaries which neither advance action, reveal character, nor illustrate theme. In *Crome Yellow* the progress of the story is twice delayed while the author inserts two excellent short stories disguised as extracts from the "History." They are gems in the fantastic style, but they have nothing to do with *Crome Yellow*, and certainly could not have been written by Wimbush. A twentieth-century morality is thrust into *Antic Hay*, and though it does show what might faintly interest the jaded Londoner, it is really in the story, I suspect, because Mr. Huxley had written it, and found this the most opportune device by which to have it published. Similarly conversations are stretched beyond their natural length in order that the novelist may have his say, with comfortable indirectness, upon architecture or etymology, or display his ability to parody

American advertising. Characters are introduced, as the assistant at the Albemarle galleries, simply to provide humor, and are dismissed again without an attempt to connect them with the action or the theme. Comedy, variety, surprise, are certainly achieved, but proportion, form, and economy are sacrificed. A Jamesian would not approve the substitution.

Mr. Huxley has not been credited with the ability to create large-scale characters, though about his success in satiric portraiture there can be no dispute. Generally he pursues the current method of allowing the characters to reveal themselves through a selected record of their thoughts. Gumbril, as the pivotal character, begins the story with his reflections in chapel; we are at the outset presented with his mental outlook. Further revelations are made easy by this predisposition to self-analysis; and he, and Myra, and Coleman also to some extent, are interested in other people's psychology as befits "intellectuals." Frequent analyses of one character by another are thus motivated, and indirect comment made natural. Author's comment is in *Antic Hay* and *Crome Yellow* nonexistent, unless the direct descriptions of face and dress, in which the physically ludicrous and character-betraying are seized upon and exaggerated, might be construed as a form of author's intervention. But at least there is occasional co-operation of the writer's mentality, for criticism supposedly arising in Gumbril's mind becomes so thinly disguised, so slightly shaded by the Gumbril screen, that it might be identical with the author's. In *Those Barren Leaves* Mr. Huxley seems definitely to abandon a consistent indirectness, and Lord Hovenden's mental peculiarities are often described and criticized by the author at first hand.

Mr. Huxley's characters reveal themselves by speech and deed too; and a rather striking feature of his technique

[284]

is his care to vary the different methods of delineation in quick succession. Casimir Lypiatt (surely Keats's friend Haydon revived) is introduced first through Gumbril's thoughts, then by his own thundering conversation, supplemented by a straightforward physical description, itself character-revealing. Running hand in hand with this is suggestion through physical contrast in the person of the butlerish Albemarle. Then quickly we enter Lypiatt's consciousness, and are cleverly made aware of his habit of self-intoxication. Author's statement of facts follows, phrased to be critically insinuative; then conversation which dramatizes the traits already suggested. Finally there is clear criticism out of Gumbril's mind. The variety and veracity of these methods help to make the portraits definite and three-dimensioned, while the author keeps well in the distance.

Nevertheless, such methods do not always with Mr. Huxley insure the creation of a human character, and only the principals in each of his books have a satisfying fidelity to life. Denis, Gumbril, Calamy, and Chelifer are human beings, but I think they owe their life, literally, to the presence of the author within them. They represent progressive stages in the development of Aldous Huxley. Mr. Wells, in his note to *William Clissold*, asserts that self-projection on the part of an author is inescapable if a living character is fully to be presented; details, of course, will be altered. I think, at any rate, that this holds true for the novels under discussion. Mr. Huxley may not be as essentially timid and impressionable as Gumbril, but he surely possesses such qualities to a great extent, else he could not have represented them with such a precise and complete illusion of life.

And Mr. Huxley has surely acted and reacted at some time or other, much as did Gumbril Junior. The latter's thinking is always heterodox, undisciplined by any moral code; he plays with ideas freely and whimsically. Always he strives to be dispassionate, but can succeed only as does the earwig, by living below passion. He finds it an uncomfortable descent; he is confronted with things that will not fit into his insect world: memories of his mother and of the English countryside; Mozart's twelfth sonata and the enchantment of Emily, so strangely chaste; his father's genuine unselfishness towards Porteous; starlight. But you cannot profit by the discovery; write it down in books and the next morning you read to laugh; so there you are, even an earwig's life is uncomfortable. In this bewilderment of thought in conflict with emotion lies the comical secret about Gumbril: he is so profoundly ingenuous, in spite of everything. Naïvety is fundamental in his character, and gives him a "temporary earnestness" even in speech. It makes him appear nervous and lacking in willpower—"the weak, silent man," Myra calls him—and it creates an absurd gap between his theory and his practice. Only with a false beard can he nerve himself to satisfy his amorous desires. He extends more credit to other people's ideas than his own, and falls into the plagiarizing ways of the caterpillar. He is very human; and his inferiority complex is treated with ironical sympathy as well as with scientific understanding.

But the other characters, as I have intimated, do not impress one as being so roundly and distinctly human; though they are at least life-like. For Mr. Huxley can describe physical idiosyncrasies with such humorous imagination that the reader is convinced that the people behind the clothes and features are human beings, whether they act humanly or not. Shearwater and Lypiatt and Rosie are really "types," and by that I mean they have been carefully put together from certain definite characteristics

selected by the author to illustrate a common human failing, not a single human being. They are representatives,
the products of technique working mechanically for a
purpose. Shearwater is the stock "physiologue," embedded
in science, just as Falx is the stock labor leader, absorbed
in the people's plight. Shearwater's "place" in the scheme
of the book is apparent when Myra unwillingly casts her
spell over him. Passion enters and Science flies out of the
window; Shearwater only escapes by jumping out after his
first Goddess, at the risk of his neck and the sure abandonment of his peace. And the moral of that is: even single-
minded Science offers no secure haven from modern unrest.
Huxley, behind the scenes, shows us that even his scientific
puppet has also to dance.

Lypiatt, again, is the example of the Incurable Actor.
He has the physical appearance of a genius and has contracted the habit of pretending that he has the Leonardo
inspiration as well. Since he has browbeaten himself into
belief in his own powers, he escapes for a time the disillusionment which envelops Myra and Gumbril. But
eventually he is compelled to face his own worthlessness
and we leave him contemplating suicide, though still more
likely to make bad literature out of the idea than to per-
form the act. He might be one of a hundred second-rate
artists in London, and just because of that he could not
be any particular one of them. He is a habit of mind to
be satirized, not a human being to be studied.

Mercaptan is the image of the literary poseur; he is one
of the few who can manage, with no aims and no illusions,
to remain satisfied. He is happy so long as he may be permitted to lead his own delicate and delicious existence in the
most civilized of all possible worlds. On the whole, Mercaptan finds the antique hay all the more delightful because
so meaningless. He too, then, is a type of the second-rate

artist and the capripede; he is one of the dancers and he fur-
nishes an excuse for satire and for brilliant and rambling
talk. And yet Huxley has described his Mercaptan, too,
with such vividness that we hesitate to label him a puppet.
He suggests fascinating human values, if he does not suggest
a human being.

Nevertheless, I would be inclined to pronounce Mr. Huxley's characterization, except in the case of his principal
personages, a throw-back to the method of Dickens, or
perhaps even of Chaucer, rather than a continuation in the
art of Henry James. His method is not necessarily to be
censured on that account. The sustained entertainment
which each of his novels offers, goes to prove that he
has judged his own powers rightly, and has used them
to the best advantage. Whether a technique subordinated to the uses of comedy is less to be praised than
one subordinated to the purposes of realism is of course
an alternative upon which only personal taste can pronounce.

It is of interest to note that Huxley employs the "tag"
device, which Dickens found so useful. Each personage
has a little physical peculiarity of which the reader is
constantly reminded. Mercaptan has his "alas, too snout-
like nose" which is always coming into notice, to the
cheapening of its owner's epicureanism. In *Crome Yellow*
the presence of Mary Bracegirdle is inseparable from the
"serious moon-like innocence of her face." It is an old
trick to secure farce; the reader is not allowed to sym-
pathize. It is a part of Mr. Huxley's literary pose that
his characters must never appear in any other garb than
the sock, no matter how earnestly they themselves clamor
for buskins. Shearwater's futile and peace-destroying passion for Myra might easily be presented with pathos, but
can also be made absurd. The author creates and regularly

renews the latter impression: "and Shearwater revolved within the walls of his great round head his agonizing thoughts of Mrs. Viveash."

Coleman is a comic figure in his own right. He is the swaggering Rabelaisian, with a magnificent command of blasphemy. As a character he is, of course, too good, too bad, if you like, too perfectly bizarre for daily life; he, also, is a buffo, created to round out Mr. Huxley's burletta. Physically he is vivid and human, socially he is by no means a class representative, but intellectually he is there to represent a phase of ultra-modern *savoir vivre*. In his case, it is that particular phase which finds cause for peals of diabolic laughter in the spectacle of the "exquisitely, and piercingly and deliciously vile."

Myra Viveash, too, though clear-cut and full-fashioned, is not intended to be a human being. She is given none of the complexity, nothing of that mixture of definite and indefinite traits which gives Fleur Forsyte, for example, such rich and individual life. All the humanity has been pruned out of Myra, until she remains nothing but a highly artistic conception of modern aimlessness. She represents all the women who have experienced and lost taste for everything. The one definite pleasure she had found in life, a genuine and sustained passion for Tony, had been destroyed by the war. The experience had left her with the suspicion that there might be other lasting consolations for life, if only she could find them. The suspicion prevents her from finding comfort in a stoical endurance of lassitude, and forces her into a haphazard and fruitless search for the old thrills. But we must not commit the sin of sympathizing. Mr. Huxley interposes: "Her voice, as she spoke, seemed always on the point of expiring, as though each word were the last, uttered faintly and breakingly from a death-bed"; "Her eyes had a formidable capacity for looking and expressing nothing"; and always she smiles "that queer downward-turning smile which gave to her face, through its mask of laughter, a peculiar expression of agony." These vivid peculiarities of voice, eye, and smile are recalled again and again, and with each fresh reminder, the reader is lifted, gently but firmly, up to the standing-ground of the amused spectator. Once planted there, he will not cry out because the players are too perfect to be human.

Since the majority of the characters are not strictly human beings, they do not appear convincing when regarded as a group. And this is rather a pity, for it is always a considerable satisfaction to the reader if he can feel that he is regarding a real slice of life. Mr. Huxley was no doubt recalling people and doings in the Wheel Group when he invented the Gumbril set, with their spectacular and stormy meetings in Soho restaurants. But the Sitwells and Aldous Huxley hobnobbed for literary creation. What possible attractions brought Lypiatt and Mercaptan to lunch together, and what is Shearwater doing in such company? Fidelity to life is unnecessarily lost by an omission to make the "set" one which would group itself.

Rich as these books are, and I have not exhausted yet their wit or their wisdom, they fall short not only of the power of *Point Counter Point*, but are also measurably inferior in their architecture. Little is motivated and nothing concluded, and their laughing scepticism is uncorrected by any hint of seriousness. They lack even the savagery that may be born of deep convictions when suaver solutions fail. In this book he has changed all that. We have of course the same bravura passages of talk, but they come from the heart of a strong situation or at least relate themselves inevitably to the speaker. Cardan, Chelifer, and Calamy are interchangeable units in spite of surface differences. But in *Point Counter Point* even between Philip Quarles and Mark Rampion who are the author's divided ego, there can be no substitution, and sharper discriminations separate the remaining characters. His description too has lost none of its sparkle and incisiveness. "Few things," he had told us in *Those Barren Leaves*, "are more profoundly boring and unprofitable than literary descriptions. For the writer, it is true, there is a certain amusement to be derived from the hunt for apt expressive words. Carried away by the excitement of the chase he dashes on, regardless of the poor readers who follow toilsomely through his stiff and clayey pages like the runners at the tail of a hunt, seeing nothing of the fun."

The reader would gladly grant him a wider license than his severe prescriptions of economy will permit.

It is however in the more expert organization of his theme and in the deeper intellectual significance of its reference that we discover the book's superior quality.

How then we ask ourselves, is it shaped? Philip Quarles gives us a hint of the author's intention, for he knew, if he could not achieve, the kind of novel he wished to write. The musical title gives us our direction, for one of Quarles's note-book jottings develops the idea of the musicalization of fiction with modulations not merely from one key to another, but from mood to mood. "A theme is stated, then developed, pushed out of shape, imperceptibly deformed, until, though still recognizably the same, it has become quite different. In sets of variations the process is carried a step further. Those incredible Diabelli variations, for example. The whole range of thought and feeling, yet all in organic relation to a ridiculous little waltz tune. Get this into a novel. How? The abrupt transitions are easy enough. All you need is a sufficiency of characters and parallel contrapuntal plots. While Jones is murdering a wife Smith is wheeling the perambulator in the park. You alternate the themes. More interesting, the modulations and variations are also more difficult. A novelist modulates by reduplicating situations and characters. He shows several people falling in love, or dying, or praying in different ways—dissimilars solving the same problem. Or *vice versa*, similar people confronted with dissimilar problems. In this way you can modulate through all the aspects of your theme, you can write variations in any number of different moods."

Though the *tempo* is rapid in this book, we are moved but slowly onward in time, barely more than the two or three weeks required to bring Quarles and his wife home from India—the short space only that is required to ripen and frustrate a few liaisons. Like Virginia Woolf and Joyce he is more concerned with giving an effect of simultaneity, though even to this device he refuses to be rigorously bound. Once indeed he dips far back to revive Rampion's past, and then proceeds again with his blocks of juxtaposed narrative.

Quarles and Rampion I have called his alter-egos. In Quarles he presents under a veil as his own weakness the tendency to over-intellectualize, a danger subtly analyzed not only in this book but in the Pascal essay of *Do What You Will*. Rampion represents the fortification of intellect not by the restraining will but by the liberating sensations and instincts, and what he seeks to achieve is the "equilibrium of balanced excesses." All the other characters of the book range themselves within the scope of these extremes, but Quarles and Rampion are the most studied examples. His types throughout never fail of vitality, are never mere abstract illustrations of an abstract principle. The reckless Lucy Tantamount, the degenerate Spandrill, the veering Walter Bidlake are unmistakable human beings, and the fatuously brilliant Burlap still walks the streets of London.

SINCLAIR LEWIS

Four unregarded novels led up to the explosion of Mr. Sinclair Lewis's *Main Street* in 1922. Within two years there were thirty-one reprintings and 390,000 copies sold. We all recall the excited interest it aroused. Despite its many reprintings it does not survive a rereading,—a test to which every important novel must submit. It is a book indeed of a quite incredible dullness and filled with ghastly people. This last characteristic is presumably a part of the satiric intention, and we may let it pass. Its dullness is another matter. It does not derive from an incomplete knowledge of his material, but rather from an imperfect control of what he too abundantly possessed. Stuart Sherman found in it a beauty comparable to that which we relish in *Emma Bovary*. The comparison is inept, for in Flaubert the deft and delicate phrasing is merged in the larger compositional beauty which constitutes his work a masterpiece for permanent reference whatever technical changes the novel hereafter may undergo.

As one of a series it has more importance than its individual value would warrant. Its deadly iteration is embedded in its theme—the small-scale study of an overgrown prairie village where the poverty of incident announces itself perforce in a monotony of repetition and the feebleness of thought in conversation of a quite masterly banality. The very ruthlessness of the book breeds a suspicion in our minds that the analysis of *Main Street* lacks truth by reason of the systematic omission of all redeeming factors. It was certainly not thus that Willa Cather read her pioneering west, and her partisanship does not strike us as a sentimentalized perversion of the facts. When we pass from Gopher Prairie to Zenith we graduate into a larger world which is more imposing only by its grosser material emphasis. It has bigger and better and more numerous bathrooms, the flivver has yielded to the touring car and the limousine, soda water fountains have multiplied, and the mass instincts of democracy satisfy themselves with get-together organizations, boosters' clubs, and other loud-voiced mediums of self-glorification. The serpent had entered into the smaller paradise of Gopher Prairie, but Carol is such a foolish little rebel that her protest carries no weight. In the complacent world of Zenith the rebels are back-ground figures. Babbitt has his momentary lapse into revolt, but this was a psychological error, for the world at large has accepted his name as the perfect symbol of unintelligent and enthusiastic acquiescence in things as they are.

It was the book *Babbitt* that probably earned Sinclair Lewis the Nobel prize. Its publication in 1922 marked, if we may borrow his own term, the zenith of his fame. He survived the immense popularity of *Main Street* by producing an admittedly finer and equally successful work. The awarding of the Nobel prize is a searching test of a reputation, and many critics affirm a progressive declension of power since *Babbitt* was produced. Almost all novelists, let Hardy and Meredith suffice as examples, show disconcerting dips from their heights of power. Mr. Lewis has never again made so resounding a report through the world, but this does not necessarily bespeak a diminution of skill. Something depends on the theme, and it is too much to expect that more than twice in a life-time an author could discover a subject so congenial to his powers. *Elmer Gantry* was spoiled by bad temper. The distinguished master of satire who wrote it forgot that the world's great examples of the *genre* are the fruits of anger controlled. In *Arrowsmith* his target is still American civilization, but here for the first time he was in unfamiliar country and accepted a guiding hand. The laboratory material, painfully acquired and not wholly mastered, makes the book difficult reading for the layman, and for the specialist insufficient. One advance is to be registered, for three characters, Martin, his wife Leora, and Dr. Gottlieb are sympathetically presented, but wholly without sentimental emphasis. *Mantrap* is an inadequate picture of the Canadian wilderness. Mr. Lewis was probably too tired to travel far. But read it as a travesty of all primitive idealisms and you will be amused. There remains *Dodsworth*, all but his latest effort, and I would hazard the statement that in this book there is every promise of a future major development. There are still arrows in his quiver. Perhaps the shining targets are not so numerous.

It is with the manner of the making of this book and of *Babbitt* that we shall now concern ourselves after we have disposed of a few general questions that arise from his attitude towards life and art.

The present generation of American novelists has made us sceptical of the hundred per cent American. There is perceptible inconsequence in this adverse bias. The concerted revolt against derived traditions which has given such impetus to American fiction presupposes, or at least should imply, a sense of American self-sufficiency. "We want no imposition of effete old world standards," was the rallying cry that stimulated Sinclair Lewis and a score of others to their creative work. "Let English and French writers concern themselves with their own conditions. It is for us to express America to herself, and not look through borrowed lenses." As a rallying cry the results have proved it good, for never before has the reputation of American authors stood so high throughout the world. Yet if we want a deviation from fixed standards of composition we go to Joyce, or Virginia Woolf, or Dorothy Richardson rather than to Sinclair Lewis or Hergesheimer. The only American innovators are those who are aware of these models, if partial exception be not made in favor of Dos Passos and Ernest Hemingway.

We concede the abundant and praiseworthy exploitation of American material, but here, too, a faint inconsequence is to be noted which peculiarly concerns the work of Mr. Sinclair Lewis. There is a passage in *Dodsworth* which deserves to be quoted at length. Professor Brant has been giving a conversational lecture, and a brilliant one, on the virtues of Europeanism. Dodsworth comes less convincingly to the defense of his own country:

"What most Europeans think of America! Because we were a pioneer nation, mostly busy with farming and cod-fishing and chewing tobacco, a hundred years ago, Europe thinks we still are. The pictures of Americans in your comic papers indicate to me that Europe sees all Americans as either money-lenders who lie awake nights thinking of how they can cheat Europe, or farmers who want to spit tobacco on the Cathedral of St. Mark, or gunmen murdering Chicagoans in their beds. My guess is that it all comes from the tradition that Europeans started a hundred years ago. Here a few weeks back, when we were in Vienna, I picked up *Martin Chuzzlewit*, and waded through it. Funny, mind you, his picture of America a hundred years ago. But he shows a bunch of people along the Ohio River and in New York who were too lazy to scratch, who were ignorant as Hottentots and killed each other with revolvers whenever they felt like it, with no recourse. In fact, every American that Dickens shows in the book is a homicidal idiot, except one—and he wanted to live abroad! Well! You can't tell me that a degenerate bunch like that could have taken the very river-bottom swamps that Dickens describes, and in three generations have turned 'em into the prosperous cement-paved powerful country that they are to-day! Yet Europe goes on reading hack authors who still steal their ideas from *Martin Chuzzlewit* and saying, 'There, I told you so.' Say do you realize that at the time Dickens described the Middlewest—my own part of the country—as entirely composed of human wet rags, a fellow named Abe Lincoln and another named Grant were living there; and not more than maybe ten years later, a boy called William Dean Howells (I heard him lecture once at Yale, and I notice that they still read his book about Venice *in* Venice) had been born. Perhaps some European observers to-day are missing a few Lincolns and Howells!

"The kind of pride that you describe, Professor, as belonging to the real aristocratic Europeans, is fine—I'm all for it. And I want to see just that kind of pride in America. Maybe we've gone too fast to get it. But as I wander around Europe, I find a whale of a lot of Americans who are going slow and quiet, and who are thinking—and not all of 'em artists and professors, by a long shot, but retired business men. We are getting a tradition that—Good Lord! You said you'd been lecturing. I'm afraid I have, too!"

That is the note of vibrant Americanism. But where else in Lewis will you find it? Here and there perhaps in *Arrowsmith*. The rest is undiluted vitriol with America the victim.

It is not our business here to adjudicate on the relative greatness of Mr. Sinclair Lewis and his friendly rival in popular favor, Mr. Theodore Dreiser. Of neither can it be said that he has made any notable contribution to the technical advance of fiction. Dreiser is the more formula-ridden of the two, and in an impressively conscientious way altogether heavier in the exposition of his material.

[297]

Lewis's realism is of a lighter and more flexible type, more dartingly satiric, and more humorous. Before he became a Mencken crusader he must have read diligently in the pages of Wells and Dickens. In the mere matter of construction there is no need to dwell upon his work at any length.

When we have said that *Babbitt* is clearly organized we have said almost enough. The first hundred pages give us a Babbitt day rendered in closest detail. The remaining three hundred move us onward through an indeterminate year or so of time. We meet the sleeping Babbitt first at dawn: "His large head was pink, his brown hair thin and dry. His face was babyish in slumber, despite his wrinkles and the red spectacle-dents on the slopes of his nose. He was not fat but he was exceedingly well fed; his cheeks were pale, and the unroughened hand which lay helpless on the khaki-colored blanket was slightly puffy. He seemed prosperous, extremely married and unromantic; and altogether unromantic appeared this sleeping-porch, which looked on one sizable elm, two respectable grass-plots, a cement driveway, and a corrugated iron garage."

We dress with Babbitt, and share the Kippsian complications of the wet bath towels and elusive safety blades. We meet his wife in her bedroom, and breakfast with them *en famille*. The children are not attractive even to their parents. He starts the cold engine, fills with gas, and then having parked with clumsy dexterity the realtor's fascinating office day begins. What need to follow further? As a sociological phenomenon Babbitt is complete. The European reader is satisfied that he is inhabiting the mind and sharing the physical activities of the complete American. Analysis is rudimentary, for the ecstasy that emanates from this brain is not profoundly contemplative. But all the other notations are there, and even the phonetic speech transcriptions, so initially baffling to the foreigner, are significant brush-strokes of the finished picture. It is doubtful if Europe can offer so sinister a study of conditions whose every detail can be faithfully referred to its original source. The American reader can offset these conclusions by the larger synthesis his own experience provides. He knows how many Babbitts there are in the land, and that he is not of the number.

Is *Dodsworth*, we ask, a safer foreign guide? Less bounded in space, and more diversified in type, does this book give us therefore a more proportioned version of the truth?

From a native viewpoint the answer cannot be satisfactory. Sam Dodsworth is presented as a wholly sympathetic figure, a man of creative executive capacity moving in a world of relatively large affairs. He is by no means a caricature of "big business," and it is now in terms of this naturalness and inherent decency, and not by relation to the fatuousness of the lesser Babbitt, that a continent's civilization is to be measured. An adverse judgment is here to be rated as a considered opinion, and we come to the anomalous conclusion that this rebel of the new America, Sinclair Lèwis, stands in the matter of culture where Henry James had stood before. Indeed, if the comparison is to be pushed to an extreme he is much less generous to his fellow-countrymen, while equally loyal to the virtues of the older world.

As a fable *Dodsworth* is the best thing that Mr. Sinclair Lewis has contrived. Essentially modern in tone it is still an old-fashioned story of a growing estrangement between husband and wife whose complications we follow with thoroughly old-fashioned interest. In vitality it is not inferior to the best English novels of the period. If it falls short in point of brilliance let us remember Dodsworth's reluctant admission that while Americans may be garrulous they have not yet learned how to talk about things that matter. Sam certainly had not mastered the art of easy urbanity. When he returned from Europe Tub Pearson met him on the threshold, grinning.

"'Well, you fat little runt!' said Sam, which meant, 'My dear old friend, I am enchanted to see you!' And Tub gave answer, 'You big stiff, so they couldn't stand you in Yurrup any more, eh? So you had to sneak back here, eh? You big bum!'"

And they adjourned for a drink and to discuss the eighteenth amendment.

Chapter XXVI

PSYCHO-ANALYSIS AND JAMES JOYCE

We, of the older generation, have outlived too many literary revolutions to be disturbed by any clamorous contemporary reputation. Mr. Joyce's *Ulysses* has been more than ten years before the world, and by assailants and defenders alike it is still described as the most revolutionary single book that the century has produced. The defenders may have been excessive in eulogy, but they have at least justified themselves by better books or articles than have the attacking side. Mr. Shane Leslie's discussion of *Ulysses* in *The Quarterly Review* for October, 1922, is a model of argumentative weakness. The man who did not like Dr. Fell rested his case on a temperamental disharmony, and did not think it necessary to give reasons for his lack of appreciation. Mr. Gerald Gould has written frequently with discernment on his chosen theme of current fiction. But *Ulysses* disturbs his vision: "a book almost exactly like the London Telephone Directory in size and weight, and only slightly less monotonous in style." The ineptitudes on the other side are less glaring. A book of encyclopedic knowledge and dark symbolism like *Ulysses* demands commentative analysis. The author refuses to give us any help, but interpreters like Larbaud in France, Curtius in Germany, Fehr in German Switzerland, Gilbert in England, and Gorman in America seem to be telling the truth not too laboriously, and Edmund Wilson's recent *Axel's Castle*, again from America, is a triumph of sane and penetrating criticism.

I confess that I do not accept with equal zest the less

authoritative commendations from other hands of the still unfinished *Work in Progress*. A limit must be set to the labor we are willing to bestow even upon a masterpiece, and until light breaks upon our darkness we shall be content to think that even this labor bestowed would be in vain.

For *Ulysses* a generative power has been claimed above that of any book of modern times. Evidences of its influence are sufficiently manifest. Virginia Woolf, Thomas Wolfe, Nathan Asch, Conrad Aiken, John dos Passos, Rex Stout, Waldo Frank, William Faulkner and Döblin, the German author of *Alexanderplatz*, reflect it, but always with reservations and modifications that preserve their individuality. The only logical continuator of Joyce is Joyce himself. In *Ulysses* he had apparently produced all that the method was capable of creating. In *Work in Progress* his obsessions, not too securely controlled in *Ulysses*, have mastered him. What was obscure but full of meaning has now become unintelligible, and, since we must flatter our own intelligence, meaningless. We submitted to the waking unconscious with sufficiently good grace. The sleeping unconscious is a region into which even genius cannot penetrate, and we must remember that Joyce here essays to take us deep below the level of our dreams. Could we make such a journey we should crave a clear mapping of the route. Mr. Joyce has exhausted all the resources of Dadaism, Expressionism falsely so-called, and *Sur-réalisme* to render his report even more obscure than his heroically impossible subject demanded.

Four sufficiently orthodox and therefore simple books preceded *Ulysses*. His verse volume *Chamber Music* (1907) has none of the obvious marks of his developed talent. Miss Rebecca West is relieved to find the poetry of meager value, for it keeps the author of *Ulysses* within the limits of ordinary mortality. Its imitativeness is its only mark of originality, for instead of writing in the vein of the Irish Renaissance, he is content to reproduce the music of the Jacobean lyric. *Exiles* (1918) is a clear-cut psychological drama on Ibsenite lines. *Dubliners* (1914) had a chequered history. Mr. Joyce informs us that it was written in 1904. In 1906 it was accepted by Grant Richards. A passage deemed offensive to the reigning King stood in the way of publication. After Edward's death negotiations went on with Messrs. Maunsel of Dublin. Many more changes were insisted on, and litigation threatened. The book was ultimately set up, but the printer refused to hand over the copies, broke up the type, and burned the edition. Joyce secured the only copy. Two years later Grant Richards brought out the book in London. Like Synge's refractory *Playboy of the Western World* (1907) the earlier *Dubliners*, and even before publication, was an energetic storm-center in its place of origin. Synge had given fantastic expansion to qualities deep-rooted in the Irish temperament. It was Joyce's offense that he told the same kind of truths without emphasis. By the time that the book ultimately appeared the Irish had learned to accommodate themselves better to the type of criticism it conveyed, and its acceptance was so favorable that Joyce might readily have been tempted to become the Irish Tchekov. In its manner there is nothing to suggest his actual future development beyond the capacity it displays of relentless realistic observation, and after all the realism of *Ulysses* is sporadic. *The Portrait of the Artist as a Young Man* (1916) is a more genuine forerunner of *Ulysses*, but with the latter's technical mannerisms still only in germ. It is obviously autobiographical, and brings the Dædalus of the later book from childhood, through youth, to early manhood.

The legend on the final page of *Ulysses* is *Trieste-Zurich-Paris*, 1914–1921. It was published in full in 1922. The only other author in England for whom a claim of priority might be advanced in the application of psycho-analytic methods to literary uses is Dorothy Richardson. Her Pilgrimage series began with *Pointed Roofs* in 1915. Joyce has never acknowledged any debt to her, but in conversation with M. Valéry Larbaud he said that he got his hint from *Les Lauriers Sont Coupés* of Edouard Dujardin, which dates back as far as 1887. For remoter sources we may go to the great confessional books of earlier centuries, to Montaigne, Pepys, and Rousseau, who mined as deep and as freely in their inner natures as their external methods would permit, and to the author of *Tristram Shandy* who still more closely resembles Joyce in the darting allusiveness of his thought and the quaint baggage of learning he carried in his mind. Something too of Swift's intransigence had passed into his blood. Like Miss Dorothy Richardson he must also have been independently influenced by the new emphasis which science has set upon the subconscious element in human nature. Dujardin's book was more genuinely initiative, though it had to wait nearly thirty years before its hint was taken.

It is a gentle book with a delicate poetic quality that masks its cynicism. Like Joyce's *Dubliners* it is a study in futility. The hero loves an actress, lavishes gifts upon her, but when he is on the point of realizing his desire, she sends him home to bed with a gracious appointment for another *rendez-vous* which he fails to keep.

The internal monologue is sometimes obvious enough, and by relation to the practice of Dujardin's successors it suffers from the defect, if such we must call it, of being always clear. M. Prince is in a restaurant dining alone. His thoughts dwell upon a couple at an adjoining table. His food comes in. "Here is the soup, the smoking soup; be careful that the waiter does not splash me. No; let us

[304]

eat. This soup is too hot; let us try again—not bad. I lunched rather late, and I am not at all hungry. But one must dine. Finished, the soup. That woman has looked this way again" etc. We must admit that we have not yet reached a very mysterious region of the mind. It becomes more poetic when later in the evening he dresses to visit the woman of his desire, and more particularly when he is day-dreaming, or rather night-dreaming, by his open window. But there is a lot of fussy reflection on opening his door, hunting for the matches, lighting the candle. If he sees his table he says "why there's the table. If I want to cross the room I must walk round it." The pitfalls of a later day are here: the frequent lack of significance in the items, and the welter of heterogeneous matter that surges into the mind when intellectual control is absent.

George Eliot, Meredith, and James had made new inroads into the intricacies of character by an extended application of the method of analysis. This process we have already discussed at sufficient length in the introductory pages. To the super-analysts of a later day it seemed too artificial and ineffective as an approach to reality. After all it was visibly author's work. What is now desired is an effect of immediacy, with no disturbing control between the process and its registration. It is a search for the absolute zero of experience, and like that scientific quest it is doomed to failure. Stark reality will never reveal itself, for experimentation introduces the disturbing factor. No one today disputes the importance of the unconscious, but many will deny its ascendancy. It cried for exploration, but there was no need for it to usurp control, and such adverse comment as we are inclined to make is in the interests of proportion and consequently of truth. As Miss Drew in *The Modern Novel* has wittily said these people give the Unconscious a fountain pen and bid it write. If that were only true we should have confidence in the result. But it *is* the author who holds the pen.

The plain reader does not feel competent to constitute himself a judge of the validity of the old-time analysis. We concede the author a certain power of divination, and if he gives a clear and consistent report of the mind-processes and hidden motives of his figures we are content. We accept this as a valuable aid to characterization, though we may grow impatient at its effect in slowing up the narrative movement of the story. The new type analysis of the uncontrolled flickering of the mind is another matter. It is obviously a far more difficult task for the author, but we do not feel the necessity of being trained psychologists to gauge the truth. We merely look in our own minds and say "is that the way I think when I am not think-ing?" Surely we may do without the textbooks here. Mr. Bloom is luckily a very average man, and save for the wild grotesqueness of the brothel scene he is living a very average day. The incidents which mark it are few, and are significant only for the larger meanings arbitrarily imposed upon them by the author. Yet these chance happenings occasion cerebral activities in this commonplace mind for which our own experience can furnish no parallel. Between the loose flowing reflections of Dædalus and Bloom, with little aid from external action, hundreds of pages of large quarto size are eked out. If truth is the aim the book is out of scale, and artifice for artifice there would not seem to be much to choose between the old analysis and the new. I am not suggesting that the Joycean method is lawless. It *is* the author as I have said who holds the fountain pen; but if there is not superior control there is at least more discrimination in the Henry Jamesian way. The principle of selection is more obviously applied. But the test of ultimate value is the comparative virtue of either method to produce a living result. Whatever the faults of *Ulysses* may be it pullulates with life, and Leopold Bloom is such a triumph of characterization as modern fiction can scarcely match. Revolted often, bewildered continually, we end by being fascinated, and that is a pragmatic test from which there is no escape.

This book so bristles with general problems that when we arrive at the text we shall not have space to treat it. And even some of the preliminary problems must be abruptly met and answered. The book's morality for example. It is probably the most obscene book, in a conventional sense, that has been written in modern times. Only one other man of genius, D. H. Lawrence, has approached Joyce in his utter scorn of reticence. Lawrence deliberately addressed himself to revolutionizing the established views upon sex-relationship, and utter frankness was essential to his argument. Pornography is indefensible because it is superficial. Lawrence is simply loyal to his own idea which is profound, and his work must be his own sufficient defense. All that needs be said is that he has interposed a temperamental barrier between himself and the timid reader, and has cheapened himself for the multitude of readers who seek in literature only a vivid intensification of their own erotic desires. Joyce had no mission for revolutionizing sex. For him it is merely an inescapable fact of life, and aiming at totality he could not afford to disregard it. Whether he was moral or immoral did not in the least concern him. We may argue with conviction that books should reflect the decencies and restrictions that civilized human beings have imposed upon themselves, or we may argue quite as convincingly that books should disregard the politeness that masks the truth. Joyce taxes our liberalism to the utmost. He gives us not only sex, but the perversions of sex, and is animalistically frank on matters where questions of male or female do not obtain. The lyrical climax is reached in that prodigious and preposterous final section where Mrs. Bloom, the all too fleshly symbol of Mother Earth, soliloquizes herself to sleep. As self-revelation nothing could be more complete, and even a sinister beauty emerges from her somnambulistic utterance. But symbolically it is at fault, for not the fertility but only the carnality of the Earth Mother is evoked. And we did not require to reach these concluding pages to realize that in one important aspect this ambitious book falls short of totality. It is a novel where lust abounds but where love is conspicuously absent.

We come now to the book's difficulties which are rewarding and excessive. Such of them as inhere in the rendering of associational processes we may illustrate by any one of a thousand passages that might be chosen. Bloom, as less intellectual and learned than Dædalus, will naturally be easier to follow, but go with him into a chemist's to buy a face lotion and a cake of soap and see where you are landed. With both Bloom and Dædalus difficulties arise from the author's attempt to present different levels of awareness, the conscious and the unconscious shuttlewise interweaving their strands; and even below the threshold our submerged intelligence has its stratifications. Exposition is compelled to be linear, and the time sequence of words is incompetent to render the simultaneity of processes which seem to occur on superimposed planes. Incoherence, broken ejaculations, bewilderingly swift transitions are but a symbolic attempt to render what is fundamentally inexpressible. As if this courageously futile effort did not precipitate sufficient confusion sometimes the subconscious dramatizes itself until we are not certain whether or not we are assisting at an actual scene. Stephen is walking on the Dublin Strand, remorse-stricken by memories of his dead mother. Might it not be a gracious act to call on her brother, Uncle Richie, and Aunt Sara?

"I pull the wheezy bell of their shuttered cottage: and wait. They take me for a dun, peer out from a coign of vantage.

—It's Stephen, sir.

—Let him in. Let Stephen in.

A bolt drawn back and Walter welcomes me.

—We thought you were someone else.

In his broad bed Uncle Richie, pillowed and blanketed, extends over the hillock of his knees a sturdy forearm. Clean chested. He has washed the upper moiety.

—Morrow, nephew.

He lays aside the lapboard whereon he drafts his bill of costs for the eyes of Master Goff and Master Shapland Tandy, filing consents and common searches and a writ of *Duces Tecum.* A bogoak frame over his bald head: Wilde's *Requiescat.* The drone of his misleading whistle brings Walter back.

—Yes, sir?

—Malt for Richie and Stephen, tell mother. Where is she?

—Bathing Crissie, sir.

Papa's little bedpal. Lump of love.

—No, Uncle Richie. . . .

—Call me Richie. Damn your lithia water. It lowers. Whusky!

—Uncle Richie, really. . . .

—Sit down or by the law. Harry I'll knock you down.

Walter squints vainly for a chair.

—He has nothing to sit down on, sir.

—He has nowhere put toit, you mug. Bring in our Chippendale chair. Would you like a bite of something?

None of your damned lawdeedaw airs here; the rich of a rasher fried with herring? Sure? So much the better. We have nothing in the house but backache pills.

All erta

He drones bars of Ferrando's *aria di sortita.*—The grandest number, Stephen, in the whole opera. Listen.

His tuneful whistle sounds again, finely shaded, with rushes of the air, his fists bigdrumming on his padded knees."

This is a literary hoax. Circumstantial as it seems the scene is a figment of Stephen's brain. We are therefore asked to concede not only the inconsequences of revery, but the plausibility of a built-up dialogued drama which never occurred.

The next sentence gives the hoax away. "This wind is sweeter."

Stephen continues to trudge along the shore. His mind wanders to the priest he might have been—"Cousin Stephen, you will never be a saint. Isle of saints. You were awfully holy, weren't you? You prayed to the Blessed Virgin that you might not have a red nose."

There follows a paragraph of the vivid realism that punctuates the pages of *Ulysses* at too rare intervals: "The grainy sand had gone from under his feet. His boots trod again a damp crackling mast, razor shells, squeaking pebbles, that on the unnumbered pebbles beats, [Stephen's Shakespearean obsession asserts itself] wood sieved by the shipworm, lost Armada. Unwholesome sandflats waited to suck his treading soles, breathing upward sewage breath. He coasted them, walking warily. A porter bottle stood up, stogged to its waist, in the cakey sand dough. A sentinel: isle of dreadful thirst. Broken hoops on the shore; at the land a maze of dark cunning nets; farther away chalk scrawled backdoors and on the higher beach

[310]

a dryingline with two crucified shirts. Ringsend: wigwams of brown steersmen and master mariners. Human shells.

"He halted. I have passed the way to Aunt Sara's. Am I not going there? Seems not. No-one about. He turned northeast and crossed the firmer sand towards the Pigeon house."

So we may safely conclude that Stephen did not visit his Aunt Sara and his Uncle Richie.

Parenthetically be it said that some of the difficulties are merely verbal and are stark misprints. In the midst of our other troubles we hardly notice these. Can we not amend "by the law. Harry" into "by the Lord Harry"? and something equally trifling is amiss with "put toit"— perhaps it should read "to put it," who knows? I admit that I am quoting from the uncorrected first edition.

We come now to the more spacious difficulties of the book which lie partly in the structure, and partly in the themes treated. Mr. Gerald Gould's flippant analogy of the London Telephone Directory, the size, the weight, and the monotony,—is an echo of the unwary criticism that dismisses *Ulysses* as a formless chaos. Read attentively the book reveals itself as unique not only in the complexity of the design, but in the orderly care with which this design is unfolded. If over-elaboration is a vice this book lies open to condemnation. Balzac, Flaubert, James, our accredited masters of composition, have given us books which we thought to be articulated to the ultimate degree. We have felt that they were even too finished in their careful calculation of effects, in the harmony and balance of their divisions, in their distribution of weight and emphasis. Compared with Joyce they are children of ingenuity, but none the less we are not constrained to deem them inferior artists. It seems to me that Joyce has had recourse to an excessive tightness of treatment to counteract the excessive

[311]

looseness of his material. Without a binding framework everything would have slipped out of his picture. He makes exacting claims upon our patience that no other writer has ventured to make, and it is certain that no living reader understands the book in its entirety.

Ulysses, as the title suggests, is organized upon a basis of ingenious parallelism with the *Odyssey*. It certainly gains more than it loses by the device. Our scholarly vanity is always appealed to by an element of allusiveness in literature. Many of the references in *Ulysses* are so recondite that they escape our attention, but we all know the *Odyssey*. If some of the correspondences that lie outside of the Homeric field are masked beyond recognition this confusion does not apply to the main parallel. Liberties of course are taken. The link between Telemachus and Stephen Dædalus is of the slightest. They are both searching for a father, and there the resemblance ends. Stephen's intellectual affinities, if we must search a mythical analogue, are with the soaring Greek who gave him his name. Bloom again is a very imperfect Ulysses, and the contacts are mainly comic. Mrs. Bloom is certainly not Penelope; we cannot conceive her as warding off her suitors, and her web was certainly never unwoven. Buck Mulligan as Antinous, Mr. Deasy as Nestor are somewhat artificially connected. An example of how the heroic proportions of the original are keyed down to the pathetic-comic level can be found among some of the other minor characters. Athene, who disguised as Mentor rouses Telemachus to activity, is represented by the old milk-woman who comes into the Martello tower in the opening episode. Athene has been addressing the Gods on Odysseus's behalf: "She spake and bound beneath her feet her lovely golden sandals, that wax not old, and bare her alike over the wet sea and over the limitless land, swift as the breath of the wind. And she seized her doughty spear, shod with sharp bronze, weighty and huge and strong, wherewith she quells the ranks of heroes with whomsoever she is wroth, the daughter of the mighty sire. Then from the heights of Olympus she came glancing down, and she stood in the land of Ithaca, at the entry of the gate of Odysseus, on the threshold of the courtyard, holding in her hand the spear of bronze, in the semblance of a stranger, Mentes the captain of the Taphians." So Homer, and now Joyce, in a passage that is deliberately lowered, yet not without its poetry: "—How much, sir? asked the old woman.

—A quart, Stephen said.

"He watched her pour into the measure and thence into the jug rich white milk, not hers. Old shrunken paps. She poured again a measure-full and a tilly. Old and secret she had entered from a morning world, may be a messenger. She praised the goodness of the milk, pouring it out. Crouching by a patient cow at daybreak in the lush field, a witch on her toadstool, her wrinkled fingers quick at the squirting dugs. They lowed about her whom they knew, dewsilky cattle. Silk of the kine and poor old woman, names given her in old times. A wandering crone, lowly form of an immortal serving her conqueror and her gay betrayer, their common cuckquean, a messenger from the secret morning. To serve or to upbraid, whether he could not tell: but scorned to beg her favour." In the transformation scene in the brothel she is Old Gummy Granny— a very unYeatsian symbol of Ireland:

Old Gummy Granny in sugarloaf hat appears seated on a toadstool, the death flower of the potato blight on her breast.
Stephen
"Aha! I know you, gammer! Hamlet, revenge! The old sow that eats her farrow!"

[313]

Old Gummy Granny

(*Rocking to and fro.*) "Ireland's sweetheart, the King of Spain's daughter, alanna. Strangers in my house, bad manners to them!" (*She keens with banshee woe.*) "Ochone! Ochone! Silk of the kine!" (*She wails.*) "You met with poor old Ireland and how does she stand?" A fierce brawl ensues, an epitome *in Excelsis* of all the brawls the Dublin streets have ever known, and Gummy Granny thrusts a dagger towards Stephen's hand—"Remove him acushla" (i.e. stab the British soldier). "At 8.35 A.M. you will be in heaven and Ireland will be free.—"

One of the most spirited adventures of Odysseus was with Polypheme, the one-eyed Cyclops. In this the hero's original indiscretion had to be redeemed by cunning. The blinded giant makes reprisal by hurling the peak of a great hill after the retreating ship. How will Joyce match the grandiosity of this gesture? It would hardly be correct to say that there is a toning down in his reproduction. The comic exuberance of the whole episode is the raciest example of sustained realism in the book, and even an effect of gigantism is secured in the big talk and fearsome aspect of The Citizen. "So we turned into Barney Kiernan's and there sure enough was the citizen up in the corner having a great confab with himself and that bloody mangy mongrel, Garryowen, and he waiting for what the sky would drop in the way of drink. . . . The figure seated on a large boulder at the foot of a round tower was that of a broadshouldered deepchested stronglimbed frankeyed redhaired freely freckled shaggybearded widemouthed largenosed longheaded deepvoiced barekneed brawnyhanded hairylegged ruddyfaced, sinewyarmed hero. From shoulder to shoulder he measured several ells and his rocklike mountainous knees were covered as was likewise the rest of his body wherever visible, with a strong growth of tawny prickly hair in hue and toughness similar to the mountain gorse. The widewinged nostrils from which bristles of the same tawny hue projected were of such capaciousness that within their cavernous obscurity the fieldlark might easily have lodged her nest. The eyes in which a tear and a smile strove ever for the mastery were of the dimensions of a goodsized cauliflower. A powerful current of warm breath issued at regular intervals from the profound cavity of his mouth, while in rhythmic resonance the loud strong hale reverberations of his formidable heart thundered rumblingly, causing the ground, the summit of the lofty tower and the still loftier walls of the cave to vibrate and tremble."

A most endearing personality for the mild-spoken Bloom to encounter! I have not space to enumerate the many touches that reproduce the spirit of the original,—the prevailing anonymity (even the drinks are not given a name), the repeated allusions to blindness, the savage hatred of the foreigner, the multiplied tree references on the mere hint of Homer's description of the pines and oaks and poplars that encircle the cave. Mr. Joyce's systematic labor here and throughout is unresting. Nothing corresponds to the blinding of the giant, beyond the suggestion that the Sinn-Fein citizen is blind drunk, and for the hurling of the mountain-side after the escaping hero he substitutes the heaving of an empty Jacob's biscuit box.

"—Gob, the devil wouldn't stop him till he got hold of the bloody tin anyhow and out with him and little Alf hanging on to his elbow and he shouting like a stuck pig, as good as any bloody play in the Queen's royal theatre.

—Where is he till I murder him?

And Ned and J. G. paralysed with the laughing.

—Bloody wars, says I, I'll be in for the last Gospel.

[315]

But as luck would have it the jarvey got the nag's head round the other way and off with him.

—Hold on, citizen, says Joe. Stop!

Begob he drew his hand and made a swipe and let fly. Mercy of God the sun was in his eyes or he'd have left him for dead. Gob, he near sent it into the county Longford. The bloody nag took fright and the old mongrel after the car like bloody hell, and all the populace shouting and laughing and the old tin box clattering along the street."

The multiplied bloodys are to be explained by the fact that here, and here only in the book, the narrative is put in the mouth of an unnamed frequenter of Barney Kiernan's saloon.

The episode closes with a burlesque description of the earthquake that followed the heaving of the tin.

Superficially *Ulysses* may be described as an account of the thought life and the incidental life of Stephen Dædalus and Leopold Bloom in Dublin during a space of twenty hours from June 16, 1904 at 8 A.M. to June 18 at 4 A.M. Simultaneous happenings concerning other characters— notably Mrs. Bloom—are from time to time introduced.

There is a systematic distribution of episodes, which as we have seen run roughly parallel with the action of the Odyssey; and these episodes are subordinated to a larger three-fold group division. The first part has three episodes covering the movements of Dædalus between 8 A.M. and noon, and these episodes bear the names Telemachus, Nestor, Proteus. Part two is mainly concerned with Bloom, but before it is completed he has made contact with Dædalus. It covers the time from 8 in the morning until past midnight of the following day. The episodes are Calypso, The Lotus-Eaters, Hades, Æolus, The Lestrygonians, Scylla and Charybdis, The Wandering Rocks, The

Sirens, The Cyclops, Nausicaa, The Oxen of the Sun, and Circe. In the third part Bloom and Stephen have emerged from the Brothel. They stop first in a cabman's shelter—Eumæus—reach Bloom's house—Ithaca—, and this brings us to the eighteenth and final episode of the book—Penelope—where Mrs. Bloom ruminates for forty-two royal quarto pages without a full stop or comma.

Such is the outer frame of the book. True to his mediæval habit of thought Mr. Joyce has given a still more precise elaboration of each episode. That of Æolus, the windy god, will serve as an example. The Scene is the Newspaper. The Hour is noon. The bodily organ associated with the presentation is the Lungs. The presiding art is Rhetoric, the prevailing color is Red, the Symbol is Editor, and the technique is Enthymemic.

To many this may appear fussy and unnecessary. Since the list varies with each episode the author has gone to infinite trouble to differentiate his material. It is presumably then in the interests of variety that he has introduced these devices. Flaubert and James worked for a polished surface, evenness of tone, and a harmony of total effect. Though their method of attack may vary from book to book their general manner always resembles itself. Rhetorically no book ever written is so multifarious as *Ulysses*. It was one of the Goncourts who said we could never write the books we wanted. In Joyce every phrase is deliberate. This is the book he intended to write, and its wildest extravagances are calculated. The reference just made to the presiding motives for each episode is evidence of this fact. The results are sometimes of dubious value, but it is not wise for us to reject them prematurely. At first the Homeric application of the Oxen of the Sun episode is not obvious, and the succession of parodies may seem to us merely an ingenious literary exercise. But the contact is not so re-

mote as would appear. In Homer the Oxen are a symbol
of fertility. Our scene is a maternity hospital. The parodies
serve the purpose, somewhat too obscurely we admit, of
representing the development of the embryo, and there are
many casual references in the text to prenatal conditions
which only the medically competent can appreciate. An
apparently meaningless reference to the headless sardines
swimming in oil has its quite definite significance. When
the sacred kine have been slain and Odysseus and his men
have left the triangular island:—"In that same hour Zeus
thundered and cast his bolt upon the ship, and she reeled
all over being stricken by the bolt of Zeus, and was filled
with sulphur." The profane talk of the young medicos
which had so shocked Ulysses Bloom has a like ending:
"A black crack of noise in the street here, alack, bawled
back. Loud on left, Thor thundered: in anger awful the
hammerhurler. And Master Lynch bade him have a care
to flout and witwanton as the god self was angered for his
hell-prate and paganry. And he that had erst challenged
to be so doughty waxed pale as they might all and shrank
together and his pitch that was before so haught uplift
was now of a sudden quite plucked down and his heart
shook within the cage of his breast as he tasted the rumour
of that storm."

There are more things to keep us alert than the Homeric
parallelisms, and our enforced adaptation to the abrupt
changes of style from section to section. Some of the difficulties seem trifling, while others lead us into deep places.
There is a silly potato and an equally futile cake of soap
that keep repeating in Bloom's consciousness, and tags
and ends of phrases recur like "Met Him Pike Hoses,"
which is Mrs. Bloom's phonetic version of metempsychosis.
These are some of the milder humors of the book, which
we need not take too seriously. The reach and range of

Stephen's reflections demand much more careful watching. They lead us a merry dance over fields of mediæval metaphysics and advanced modern speculation. Everything from Aristotle and Thomas Aquinas to Freud and Einstein is there in random snatches and fugitive implication, reflected through a Hamlet personality with its mingled melancholy and fierceness. A right understanding is to be had only in the light of Joyce's own life and the spiritual autobiography he gave us in the *Portrait of the Artist*. For the appreciation of *Ulysses* this book is indispensable.

There we have the background of broken family life, the religious and political controversies on which Irish youth is fed, the severe scholastic training, the impregnation with Catholic doctrine, and the resolute and defiant sundering of intellectual fetters. He gains his liberty but he is not free, for the mere act of revolt is powerless to eradicate tendencies and habits of thought so deeply rooted in his nature. In spite of himself Joyce remains to the end a Catholic thinker.

Chapter XXVII

THE STREAM OF CONSCIOUSNESS*

Dorothy Richardson, Virginia Woolf

DOROTHY RICHARDSON

Instead of the rude gauntlet of Joyce, Miss Dorothy Richardson flicks a delicate glove in the face of the reading public. She lacks the Irishman's fierce creative energy, his versatility and variety, yet in the ten volumes of her *Pilgrimage* she has built up a work of consecutive and developing power which will represent to the future a positive contribution to the technical evolution of fiction. With a score of other women writers in England and America she challenges the old superstition that her sex is incompetent to produce anything save the raw material of the human race.

It must be admitted that statistically the facts run counter to woman's creative capacity either in the fine arts or the abstract sciences. Havelock Ellis in his *Study of British Genius* discovered in the pages of the *Dictionary of National Biography* 975 men and 55 women who might be designated eminent,—a damaging proportion of eighteen to one. Mrs. Cora Sutton Castle in her *Statistical Study of Eminent Women* went further afield. After a survey of numerous encyclopædias and biographical dictionaries she reached the conclusion that "it is a sad commentary on the sex that from the dawn of history to the present day less than 1,000 women have accomplished anything that

---

* Passages quoted by permission of Gerald Duckworth & Co., Ltd., London, and Harcourt, Brace and Company, Inc., New York.

history has recorded as worth while. . . . It has been as
sovereigns, politicians, mothers and mistresses that women
have acquired the greatest distinction."

Eminence is a relative word, and a confrontation of
Mary Somerville, who represents science on Ellis's list,
with men even of the second or third order might readily
induce the too hasty conclusion that there is a radical and
permanent difference in the mental caliber of the two sexes.
In the fine arts of music, painting, and sculpture the results
would be the same, despite the fact that music and painting
have been for two centuries more essential elements in the
preliminary education of women than of men. No picture
by a woman hangs on the walls of the world. Cooking
and hair-dressing have always lain within the peculiar
province of women, but here again the creative artists are
men, and until the recent rise to eminence of Chanel,
Schiaperelli, and Bruyère the same statement would have
applied to the dressmaker's art. In dancing and acting
women have been pre-eminent for a hundred years, but
that concession cannot serve as a salve to feminine vanity.
Their remarkable recent work in fiction, and their only
less remarkable advance in poetry are the sole foundations
on which we can build hopes for their creative future.
In fiction, so far at least as England and America are concerned, they challenge comparison in merit and production
with their masculine rivals. One cannot mention Joanna
Baillie with Shakespeare, but we are permitted to think
that Jane Austen is a finer writer than Scott. No woman
has yet grown to the stature of Tolstoy, Dostoevsky, or
Balzac, but it would be rash to prophesy what the future
may hold in store.

Let us reject at once the myth of women's mental inferiority, and rest our conclusions rather on difference of
opportunity, and on a possible difference in quality. It

would be a clear gain to humanity if we could assert this last distinction, but our current physiology gives us insufficient grounds for a sure hypothesis. It speaks in terms of genes and chromosomes. It gives the male child the chromosome X of the mother, and the female child two chromosomes X, one from either parent. Here is a basis of difference if we knew what it meant. Havelock Ellis holds the view that genius is a recessive abnormality, and that the males of the race possess a greater variability than the females. While this may lead to a greater range of physical abnormalities, it has no obvious bearing upon the functions of the brain in precipitating thought. And the emotional argument is equally inapplicable. If sensitiveness and receptivity are part of the creative process women would seem at large to hold an initial artistic advantage were it not for the fact that the male artist possesses in the highest degree these typically feminine qualities. In a crude way we can discern the obvious physical disabilities under which the normal woman suffers, and which militate against prolonged and arduous mental labor, but even that argument fails us when we think of the constitutional weakness of many of our men of genius. A long educational experience of both sexes does not permit me to infer the mental inferiority of either. The farthest I would be inclined to go in that direction would be to admit the man's greater capacity for abstract thinking. The intuitive flash women have, but their lack of power to prolong it might conceivably explain man's creative superiority in music and in the plastic arts where they incline to the abstract side.

We have been proceeding down an alley insufficiently lighted and momentarily blind. Should we turn in another direction there is almost no aspect of woman's apparent creative inferiority that cannot be explained in terms of her social and economic subjection. In some countries she has achieved a partial emancipation. She has still imperfectly adapted herself to her new freedom, but the results of a few decades have been astonishing. It is not fair to say that her work is marked by any sense of her own inferiority, but she is still fighting mad, and only when she has emerged from the polemical stage will she reveal the full reach of her capacity.

Miss Richardson is still too near the struggle, and the queer blending of resentment and acquiescence in her work is proof that she has not reached the serenity that may co-exist either with comic exuberance or tragic intensity. But the struggle for reconciliation is philosophically and profoundly there, and even were her books not remarkable for the forthright naturalness of a highly original method the spiritual effort they embody would keep them alive.

Much, of course, that you would look for in the ordinary novel, you will seek in vain. There is no consecutive and concerted story, and no selection of incident for the core of climax it may contain. Whatever happens derives its value from the mere fact of Miriam Henderson's awareness and interest. Many will find this dull, and will refuse the surrender or even the co-operation of their own minds. To a less prejudiced or hostile view the general effect is on the contrary sufficiently exciting, although from book to book we note a variation of intensity and therefore of interest. But even when our interest slackens we are conscious that we are receiving something that has never been given so adequately before. Jane Austen wrote books from the feminine point of view, but she has never essayed to give us the unimpeded outpourings of the feminine consciousness. Miss Richardson has admittedly achieved a less brilliant surface, but she has explored a deeper mine; and if any truth lies in our affirmation not only of a circumstantial difference in the lot of men and women but of a qualitative distinction as well in their mental equipment, the value of her experiment both humanly and æsthetically is incontestable.

Few writers in our literature have found a method in their first novel and maintained it to their last. The statement holds true at least for the two Richardsons, who show no traces of the groping experimentation which marks the work of so many masters of the craft. We are never sure what Virginia Woolf will give us. With Dorothy Richardson we always know what to expect. The effects she aimed at she could evidently achieve in only one way, and she wards off monotony by brilliance and brevity of statement. Each novel of the ten is a compact and self-sufficient whole, yet each contributes to the totality of the result. At the close we realize that she has placed us in fuller possession of a feminine mind and temperament than any other author of her day. More clamorous reputations have invaded our ears, but Dorothy Richardson will continue to sound.

She begins quietly with *Pointed Roofs* where Miriam Henderson at eighteen is resident mistress in a German school. Already we feel that she is a perceptive mind, but her reactions to experience are still elementary as befits her undeveloped state. In these earlier books there is less dipping into the "stream of consciousness" than we find as the series advances. Miriam is always the reflecting center, but she is more objectively presented than later. It is not until we reach *Honeycomb* that there is an occasional passage from "she" to "I." Dialogue is brisk and constant, and serves as an effective aid to characterization. In the complete absence of analysis of other minds this is essential to firm portrayal. In *Pointed Roofs* Fräulein Pfaff is the only established character. As individuals multiply in her growing world they acquire a sharper identity, and it will be worth our while when we reach them to discover, if we can, the secret of their life.

In *Backwater* Miriam is with the Pernes in a North London school. The only contact that survives is with the Brooms with whom many subsequent holidays are spent. A young Jew named Max who had touched her girlish imagination is dead, and her mother is ill. Her mind is beginning to move, but she offers it strange nourishment—Ouida, Mrs. Hungerford, Rosa Nouchette Cary. But its unaided operations have begun to reveal the mystic sensitiveness that grows stronger with the years: "The day's work tired her to death. She must hide somewhere. . . . She would not be wanted. . . . If you were not wanted. . . . If you knew you were not wanted—you ought to get out of the way. Chloroform. Someone had drunk a bottle of carbolic acid. The clock struck ten. Gathering up the newspaper she folded it neatly, put it on the hall table and went slowly upstairs, watching the faint reflection of the half-lowered hall gas upon the polished balustrade. The staircase was cold and airy. Cold rooms and landings stretched up away above her into the darkness. She became aware of a curious buoyancy rising within her. It was so strange that she stood still for a moment on the stair. For a second, life seemed to cease in her and the staircase to be swept from under her feet. . . . 'I'm alive.' . . . It was as if something had struck her, struck right through her impalpable body, sweeping it away, leaving her there shouting silently without it. 'I'm alive. . . . I'm alive.' Then with a thump her heart went on again and her feet carried her body warm and happy and elastic easily on up the solid stairs. She tried once or twice deliberately to bring back the breathless moment standing still on a stair. Each time something of it returned. 'It's me, *me;* this is *me* being alive,' she murmured with a feeling under her like the sudden drop of a lift. But her thoughts distracted her. They were eagerly talking to her declaring that she had had this feeling before."

These moods of mystical absorption and of unanalyzable rapture occur repeatedly and unbidden, and give interesting relief to a character otherwise dominated by its habit of sharp realistic discrimination. A strange feature of these experiences is that the mood of absorption serves only to intensify the subject's sense of individual difference. They are Miriam's passport to immortality—hence joyous, but they maintain her a separate person whose strongest desire is to preserve her individuality. This Michael Shatov ultimately discovered, and if Hypo Wilson succeeded once in breaking down her guard we are free to suspect that the episode will not be a link for the future. There is a hard outer shell in her character which yields to the compulsion of intellect but not of passion.

In *Honeycomb* Miriam is less happy as governess to the Corrie children in the west of England. Her sisters Sarah and Harriett have married, and her mother has died. *The Tunnel* is a book of genuine power with more variety than we have yet encountered. Mrs. Bailey's boarding-house in Tansey Street and the dental office in Wimpole Street abound with life, and there is altogether a great expansion in Miriam's peopled world. The Orlys and Mr. Hancock, the Wilsons, Mag and Jan, Miss Dear and Mr. Taunton are sometimes comically and always convincingly alive. We promised an attempt to discover the secret of their vitality, but when we come to the task it is more difficult than we had supposed. Their speech is always revealing, yet without the aid of the repetitive tags to which even Dickens descended, and without the convulsing episodes on which authors so frequently depend for the most searching of their effects. The author withholds her analytic aid, and also the usual retrospective comment which brings the character fully documented to our gaze. What Miriam cares to tell us of their past we learn, and that is mainly nothing. She meets her people, notes some surface aspect of their appearance, and remembers their talk which she presumably edits when she gets home. That, save for the last item, is what happens in life, and that is Miss Richardson's sufficient formula. She reserves to herself the editor's right of selection and elimination. Dialogue accepts the discipline, the "stream of unconsciousness" tends to reject it, though we note that the waste-paper basket of Miriam's mind is less copious and heterogeneous than Bloom's or Stephen's, and when upset makes a less untidy litter on the floor.

Her notations of place are as sharp and effective as her dialogue. Her revelations of the London of the 'nineties especially are as good examples of realistic impressionism as can be found today. Miriam is quite careless about telling us how she gets from place to place. Her author creator for example does not tell us that in the Easter Holidays she boarded the Great Western for the Wilsons. We merely find ourselves there with her, and if she enjoys the curve of a wave or the contour of a tree we may share her pleasure. As with so many of the women writers of our time her phrasing is deft and true. They have the feminine gift of being instinctively right, and whatever our relative rating of mentality may be, for sheer writing the woman bears away the palm. Dreiser may be more impressive than Willa Cather, but as a manipulator of the President's English he is in the primer class.

Interim is a declension from the high level of *The Tunnel*. We still have Mag and Jan to divert us, but the Canadian doctors are flat, and Miriam's second Jew, Mendizabble, has not much to recommend him. The climax of the series is reached with *Deadlock* and *Revolving Lights* which have all her virtues and none of her defects, unless Miriam's blazing femininity be counted as such. "How awful to have nothing but a man's consciousness" was a fixation in her mind before she had met her third Jew Michael Shatov. To this quaint gentle creature she owed a deeper mental debt than she was willing to acknowledge, and it is the to and fro of their relationship that gives these two books their high significance. She repudiates him in the end not from racial fastidiousness, but because to marry a Jew implied such surrender of her personality as she was not willing to concede. We must admit that Miriam's femininity lacks the quality of tenderness and the capacity for subordination that have hitherto been the distinguishing qualities of her sex. Hers are feminine books if you will, though of an order that has but newly dawned.

Miss Richardson has presumably finished with Miriam. She has not married, she has not died, but she has traversed an arc of life, and the ten books she dominates are sufficiently complete without these somewhat overworked finalities. Other books will follow, and perhaps a married Miriam will give us in them her view of the world. But much as we have enjoyed our accompanied tour with her, we should enjoy still more a less unbroken presentation of reality which might permit us to know her and others in a different way. *The Pilgrimage* has been a unique contribution to our literature, but its indefinite prolongation would be a mistake.

Virginia Woolf

Monotony can never be urged as a vice in Virginia Woolf. She has been able to carry a very sensitive mind into the dangerous purlieus of journalism, and is known even more widely as a publicist than as a novelist. She has brilliantly told us that the woman artist tends to suffer from her militancy. Wisely then she reserves her polemics for her articles, and so tempers anger with wit that she is able to make her most damaging points without the petulance that controversy so frequently engenders. The case for woman as creative artist has never been more effectively presented than in *A Room of One's Own* where she makes us partners in her thought process, and leads us on consentingly from step to step of her argument. We should concede to the woman as to the male novelist the privilege of communicating the imperfections of either sex. A savage emphasis in any direction we resent. Mrs. Woolf's singular fairness and impartiality are never in question, and the only hint of hostile bias is her portrait of Mr. Ramsay in *To the Lighthouse*, and in *Mrs. Dalloway* the portrait of Sir William Bradshaw.

Mrs. Woolf has committed herself in a high journalistic way to many things beside the woman question. It is only from Miss Richardson's practice that we infer her theories of novel writing. She is of the tribe of aloof artists who veil their personal opinions. Mrs. Woolf in *The Common Reader*, *The Hogarth Essays*, and in a series of articles, "Phases of Fiction," contributed to *The Bookman*, has made her views on fiction emphatically clear. She is dissatisfied with the work of the Edwardians, as she calls them, whose acclaimed leaders are Galsworthy, Wells, and Bennett. Their novels are competent, massive, and solidly built with huge blocks of description, narrative and reflection that would seem with their imposing four-square bulwark to leave no crack or crevice for imperfection to creep in. And their defenses are further fortified with all the scientific and sociological resources that modern ingenuity can provide. These are the blazing artillery that bangs from the walls. But in the din and confusion we neither hear nor see the essential things. And Mrs. Woolf, accepting Arnold Bennett's contention that characterization is the basic condition which alone can assure fiction its permanence, approvingly quotes him: "The foundation of good fiction is character-creating and nothing else. . . . Style counts, plot counts; originality of outlook counts. But none of these counts anything like so much as the convincingness of the characters. If the characters are real the novel will have a chance; if they are not oblivion will be their portion." And, continues Mrs. Woolf, "he goes on to draw the conclusion that we have no young novelists of first-rate importance at the present moment, because they are unable to create characters that are real, true and convincing."

With such apparent agreement where does the cleavage occur? Mrs. Woolf's contention is that the Edwardians think of character as something to be weighed and measured. They are complete materialists, and interpret human nature in terms of physical relations and external detail. Their books are imposing rubbish piles where poetry, subtlety, spirituality not only are indiscoverable but find no lodgment. But they have a method which for their purposes is sure and satisfactory. The younger moderns wishing for different effects cannot use their tools. Their experimentation therefore we cannot designate as pure caprice, but as a sincere effort to arrive at an aspect of the truth of the utmost importance, yet which has hitherto been imperfectly expressed. That they fail more often than they succeed is not a valid argument against their effort.

Mrs. Woolf's plea then is for poetry, and her regard for the writers of the past is proportioned to their poetic vision. Jane Austen alone she values on other grounds as a woman of genius who writes in a womanly way. But her heart goes out more spontaneously to the Brontës and to Emily in particular, "because Emily was a greater poet than Charlotte. When Charlotte wrote she said with eloquence and splendour and passion 'I love,' 'I hate,' 'I suffer.' Her experience though more intense, is on a level with our own. But there is no 'I' in *Wuthering Heights*. There are no governesses. There are no employers. There is love, but it is not the love of men and women. Emily was inspired by some more general conception. The impulse which urged her to create was not her own suffering or her own injuries. She looked out upon a world cleft into gigantic disorder and felt within her the power to write it in a book. That gigantic ambition is to be felt throughout the novel—a struggle, half thwarted but of superb conviction, to say something through the mouths of her characters which is not merely 'I love' or 'I hate,' but 'we, the whole human race' and 'you, the eternal powers.' . . . It is this suggestion of power underlying the apparitions of human nature and lifting them up into the presence of greatness that gives the book its huge stature among other novels."

Mrs. Woolf began her career with two novels in the traditional form. *The Voyage Out* is especially masterly, and the reader is not conscious that convention has hampered in any way the free expression of her mind. Rachel, the girl who dies, and Helen Ambrose, must have satisfied Arnold Bennett's exacting character demands, yet theme and treatment alike might be described as rather poetic than realistic. With character-drawing and poetry in such effective combination we might think that a compromise had been reached which would realize Mrs. Woolf's idea for fiction. But she was evidently not content. She wrote another conventional book, *Night and Day*, and then in some of the short stories of *Monday and Tuesday* initiated her campaign of adventurous experiment. In her last book

The Waves poetry has triumphed to the complete discomfiture of character. There are people with human names, tapestry figures that move only when some gust eddies along the wall, but no action unites them, and they bear a confused symbolic relation not with one another but with Life, Time, and Eternity.

The intervening books are more recognizably fiction,—a word whose definition we are willing to strain to the utmost limit provided that we retain even a shadowy action that binds a human group in a relation however shadowy. *Orlando* is fantastic biography, fiction if you will because invented, and entirely fascinating in idea and presentation. *Jacob's Room*, the first of her deviations failed to prove that her abandonment of tradition was justified. That she was more interested in writing this than *The Voyage Out* indicates that matter was in her mind that demanded its own peculiar medium of expression. The book itself is a series of dissolving views, where character takes its chance with the rest. The solidest impression we have of Jacob is the now famous pair of boots which persist when he has departed.

Before turning to the two unmistakable triumphs of her method—*Mrs. Dalloway* and *To the Lighthouse*, we must make free of Mrs. Woolf's own words in her essay on "Modern Fiction." "Admitting the vagueness which afflicts all criticism of novels, let us hazard the opinion that for us at this moment the form of fiction most in vogue more often misses than secures the thing we seek. Whether we call it life or spirit, truth or reality, this, the essential thing, has moved off, or on, and refuses to be contained any longer in such ill-fitting vestments as we provide. Nevertheless, we go on perseveringly, conscientiously, constructing our two and thirty chapters after a design which more and more ceases to resemble the vision in our own minds. So much of the enormous labour of proving the solidity, the likeness to life, of the story is not merely labour thrown away but labour misplaced to the extent of obscuring and blotting out the light of the conception. The writer seems constrained, not by his own free will but by some powerful and unscrupulous tyrant who has him in thrall, to provide a plot, to provide comedy, tragedy, love interest, and an air of probability embalming the whole so impeccable that if all his figures were to come to life they would find themselves dressed down to the last button of their coats in the fashion of the hour. The tyrant is obeyed; the novel is done to a turn. But sometimes, more and more often as time goes by, we suspect a momentary doubt, a spasm of rebellion, as the pages fill themselves in the customary way. Is life like this? Must novels be like this?

"Look within, and life, it seems, is very far from being 'like this.' Examine for a moment an ordinary mind on an ordinary day. The mind receives a myriad impressions—trivial, fantastic, evanescent, or engraved with the sharpness of steel. From all sides they come, an incessant shower of innumerable atoms; and as they fall, as they shape themselves into the life of Monday or Tuesday, the accent falls differently from of old; the moment of importance came not here but there; so that, if a writer were a free man and not a slave, if he could write what he chose, not what he must, if he could base his work upon his own feeling and not upon convention, there would be no plot, no comedy, no tragedy, no love interest or catastrophe in the accepted style, and perhaps not a single button sewn on as the Bond Street tailors would have it. Life is not a series of gig lamps symmetrically arranged; life is a luminous halo, a semi-transparent envelope surrounding us from the beginning of consciousness to the end. Is it not the task of the novel-

ist to convey this varying, this unknown and uncircum-
scribed spirit, whatever aberration or complexity it may
display, with as little mixture of the alien and external as
possible? We are not pleading merely for courage and
sincerity; we are suggesting that the proper stuff for fiction
is a little other than custom would have us believe it."

This is clever but partisan argument, and Mrs. Woolf is
creating a bogey where perhaps none exists. Tradition
has a capacious maw but it devours only the feeble. The
strong will find it many-sinewed and flexibly jointed,—
an altogether spirited yet accommodating mount if they
deign to ride it. She rode it well and firmly at her first
trial. It went through its paces to perfection, and would
have been quite willing to take any jump she put it to.
But though it was in its prime and had never misbehaved
she sent it to the knacker yard, and began to break in an
altogether untried and unruly colt. Excellent rider though
she is, she was unplaced with *Jacob's Room*. With no addition of weight she ran a filly, *Mrs. Dalloway*, in the next
race and was placed against heavy odds. Two seasons later,
with a neuter horse, *To the Lighthouse*, she ran a most spirited
race, and many of her admirers, though the judges were
against her, still maintain that she won by a neck. With
The Waves she withdrew from regular racing.

Wordsworth's assertion is not to be disputed that every
original author must create the taste by which he is ap-
preciated. He was compelled to wait a few generations for
full recognition, and Wordsworth is a major writer who
cannot be considered very revolutionary in his assault upon
tradition. Mrs. Woolf is definitely not a major, and her
deviation from convention is much more drastic. Whatever posterity may do for her, the present penalty she
pays for her courage and sincerity is a much more limited
audience than her talent deserves. Her doom is the coterie,

her reward a satisfied conscience. It would be folly to blame her open-eyed choice. In a large way the novel profits by intelligent experiment, and speaking in terms of her own activity it is probable that by her innovations she reached results that could not have been otherwise achieved.

Her main quest is for poetry and subtlety, and for a presentation of incident in closer consonance with reality than the exigencies of artificial plot-making permit. By her admission Emily Brontë was a poet, and Hardy, and Conrad were poets. We could readily extend her list by including Meredith, James, and Lawrence; and in no instance are we aware that poetic expression was hampered by the normal methods they accepted. I admit that poetry —we need not think in terms of verse making—implies many things. Beyond everything is implied the power to conceive of life poetically, and here the named authors are not of like significance. But in the illuminating flash of their phrase, in its sudden flowering into the metaphor that reveals tracts of meaning that lie beyond the scope of pedestrian prose, they are akin. And Mrs. Woolf is of their tribe on the expressional side of poetry at least.

Her gift of figurative speech would have suffered no impediment with the acceptance of the accustomed habit of fiction. But if we read her mind aright there were certain subtleties of poetry that could not so accommodate themselves. Poetry and prose considered from the aspect where they most diverge, and are therefore most characteristic, proceed from essentially different types of thinking. Prose thought is purposive, poetic thought is associational. There is much of the developed child in the poet. The darting inconsequence of the child's mind is a delight to its elders, though its operations need not have the profound significance that Wordsworth ascribed to them.

[335]

The poet's associational tracts are equally alive. One thing as readily suggests another, but years "have brought the philosophic mind," and experience gives his most daring transitions their weight of significance. In the intervals of creation he has wrestled with life's problems like ordinary men. He has done much hard thinking, yet in the mood of creation we do not get the logical steps of this intellectual operation, but its fine flowering rather, the rich precipitation of accumulated experience. If we seek the real reason for Mrs. Woolf's rejection of consecutive fiction it was that she desired to record, as a poet might, the movement of the mind in revery. And the poetic results in her two best books are incontestable.

It would not be fair to her to suggest an uncontrolled disorder in their structure. *Mrs. Dalloway* and *To the Lighthouse*, despite their apparent dislocation are firmly fashioned. *Mrs. Dalloway* has the twofold unity of one day in London with Big Ben to chime off the hours. Comparison with Joyce's Dublin day is inevitable, but that has larger implications and deserves more nearly to be considered a day in the life of the race. In each book an effort is made to express simultaneity. Mrs. Woolf takes two chance episodes—a royal motor blocked in the Bond Street traffic, and an aëroplane writing smoke letters in the sky. Multitudes share these experiences, and an attempt is made to note the simultaneous reactions of a number of people. Joyce's treatment of the same idea in his chapter, "The Wandering Rocks," is more interesting and entertaining. This attempt to render a cross section of life is constant with Dos Passos, and can be found too in Huxley's *Point Counter Point*. Older novelists used a slower clock, and there is something pauseful in the way they turn the wheels of time or stay their deliberate revolution to deal with events happening simultaneously. An electrical nota-

tion now copes with time's swift spinning. Transitions
are sudden, and the return to progressive narrative is un-
prepared and sometimes non-existent.

But with all the stream-of-consciousness writers simultaneous time is less important than past time. They prefer
to forget the temporal prison that confines us, and to assert
the mind's contempt of the tenses. Past, present, and
future are poetry's natural home. The less visionary poetic
novelist does not by inclination inhabit the future, but
memory is perpetually at her task of evocation. Remove
the past from *Mrs. Dalloway* and the book would dwindle.
Vagrant memories voyage backwards at the slightest hint,
and though inconsecutiveness has been imputed to her as
a fault she really errs in the direction of a too close articu-
lation of experience past. When we resurrect in memory
it is an image that is evoked and the shadow of a mood.
The supplying of consecutive words is gratuitous aid from
the novelist which Mrs. Woolf supplies but Joyce refuses
to render. *To the Lighthouse* is a more satisfying book, for
the past is in the story. We actually experience it, and
then as the years pass we have the excitement and the pity
of recapturing it. With what eerie tenderness do we not
accompany the callous charwomen through the deserted
rooms where once we lived! We were with Mrs. Ramsay
when she soothed the little James to sleep and hung her
shawl over the terrifying boar's head. Mrs. Bast and
Mrs. McNab speculate about the head and the shawl in
their cleaning, but we know their secret who shared in
the act. And now Mrs. Ramsay is long years dead, and
what does it all mean? This, Lily Briscoe wonders too,
and we share that wonder as we have shared her experience. The book is a little masterpiece, for seldom have
so much poetry, speculation, and character been compressed within so little space.

Chapter XXVIII

FOUR AMERICAN WRITERS *

Anderson, Hemingway, Dos Passos, Faulkner

Three of these writers have given us their measure—a satisfying measure we admit it to be. The fourth and youngest, Faulkner, has already revealed more creative energy than any of his contemporaries, but the time has not yet arrived to cast his horoscope. He is still intelligently but violently experimenting. There is much crashing in the underbrush, but he is hewing out a recognizable path. Where it will lead him is the debatable question. His full strength he has put out only in one book *The Sound and the Fury*, and its almost incredible difficulty is not an initial recommendation. The ordinary intelligent reader does not relish such apparent contemptuous treatment from an author. But with the difficulties overcome we are inclined to admit that they may have been necessary to the plan, and that a simple approach would have deprived the book of the impressiveness it gains from its very complexity. While we admit the virtue of clarity we are not prepared to insist that a profound treatment of life shall reveal itself at a glance. The others do not strike so deep to the root of things. In Anderson and Hemingway difficulties do not exist, and in Dos Passos they are unnecessary and irritating.

Anderson's superior age, though he was late in starting, marks him out as an ancestor. I cannot detect his traces in

* Passages quoted by permission of The Viking Press, Scribner's Sons, Harrison Smith, and Robert Haas, Inc., New York.

Dos Passos, but his impress is evident on the early Hemingway, and Faulkner confesses gratitude if not discipleship in his dedication of the *Sartoris* volume. He is not yet a spent force, but his influence has been absorbed. He has given no evidence that he can produce anything upon a massive scale, but no American writer of the second rank has been so stimulating. His effect has been greater than his achievement. How far Hemingway's inspired animalism will lead him the future will show. No one living is more skilled than he in rendering the surface impacts of sensation, but he is rather like the French atheist who doubts his own doubting. His callousness perhaps conceals a reformatory intention. The puzzling thing about him is that in his most successful novel *A Farewell to Arms* he should have tinctured his natural irony with sentiment, and should have made free concession to the romantic impulses he was wont to treat with such scant courtesy. He deals with love as a serious thing, and satisfies his realistic conscience with a Cæsarean operation. Dos Passos has written three books in the manner announced by *Manhattan Transfer*. The two last are in sequence. He will be compelled to write a third in continuation of *1919*. It will be a powerful survey of a world in ruins, for he is a man of genius with burning social convictions. But a further continuation of his method would be a grave artistic blunder. When he shows flexibility we shall concede his title to distinction. His awkward change of manner within the covers of a single book is not the sort of flexibility we have in mind.

Strong individualities defy group classification, but some resemblances amidst differences emerge when we examine how these men write, what they write, and how they plan—their style, their matter, and their structure.

With regard to subject matter the authorities stand

in some need of correction. Much has been said of the ferment of revolt which launched the present movement, and which expressed itself in the rejection of traditional discipline and in contemptuous reaction against the Puritanic code. We grant the truth of this, though tradition and perhaps even Puritanism are harder to throw off than some young people imagine. But there is another contention of more dubious truth, and I will state the case as Mr. Carl Van Doren gives it in his *Contemporary American Novelists*. The passage is from the chapter named "The Revolt from the Village: Edgar Lee Masters"; "The newest style in American fiction dates from the appearance, in 1915, of *Spoon River Anthology*, though it required five years for the influence of that book to pass thoroughly over from poetry to prose. For nearly half a century native literature had been faithful to the cult of the village, celebrating its delicate merits with sentimental affection and with unwearied interest digging into odd corners of the country for persons and incidents illustrative of the essential goodness and heroism which, so the doctrine ran, lie beneath unexciting surfaces. Certain critical dispositions, aware of agrarian discontent or given to a preference for cities, might now and then lay disrespectful hands upon the life of the farm; and even these generally hesitated to touch the village, sacred since Goldsmith in spite of Crabbe, sacred since Washington Irving in spite of E. W. Howe." This may be reinforced by reference to Mr. Lewisohn's similar statement in *Expression in America;* "Of capital importance for the future was E. W. Howe's *The Story of a Country Town*. For in it we have the first strong note of that long and bitter revolt from the American village, wholly stripped of its pseudo-pastoral and sentimental trimmings, which was to culminate many years later in the works of Edgar Lee Masters and Sherwood Anderson."

Sweet Auburn is dead beyond resurrection. Indeed it never existed, but in the realistic tenderness and poetry of Anderson's "Winesburg" I see nothing of the contemptuous anger so authoritatively implied. Hemingway is wholly urban and cosmopolitan. Yet as his characters move from one city bar to another we get charming glimpses of an alcohol-tinted landscape. But he is not village-conscious, and this applies still more to the restless and wholly unpoetic Dos Passos. On the storm-lashed surface of Faulkner there are pools of quiet, and there is nothing in his psychology to prevent in the process of his manifold experimentation some future idyllic and wholly tender presentation of village life.

In the craft of words they are all competent and interesting. When Arnold Bennett announced Faulkner as "The coming man" he said that he wrote "generally like an angel." We are glad of the "generally," for his forcefulness betrays him often into over-emphasis. There is a too perpetual straining for similitudes, since everything is not of necessity like something else. Fertility in image-creating power is a virtue too rare in modern writing to merit condemnation, and an ultimate pruning of excess will some day permit us to expunge Arnold Bennett's "generally." We suspect that he does not always know the meaning of the long words he uses, and there are mannerisms in his constructions that irritate us by their frequency: "and pretty soon there were gulls looking *like* they had pink and yellow feathers, slanting and wheeling around—and it was *like* there was a street in a city." A mannerism confined to *As I Lay Dying* may be noted without comment. It is so constantly and confidently employed that it must rest on some obscure artistic reason which is not readily apparent. The ordinary habit in dialogue is to represent the speakers with variations in the phrase announcing them. To every speech in this book is attached the bald statement, "he said," "I said," or "he says," "I says."

Like most good writers of our day Mr. Faulkner conceals himself within his book. The compositional law of that strange novel, *As I Lay Dying*, is that each chapter reveals the consciousness of one particular character. Vardaman is the child of the family: "It is dark. I can hear woods, silence: I know them. But not living sounds, not even him." Up to this point it is a child thinking. But in a moment we are miles away from the child's consciousness: "It is as though the dark were resolving him out of his integrity, into an unrelated scattering of components —snuffings and stampings; smells of cooling flesh and ammoniac hair; an illusion of a co-ordinated whole of splotched hide and strong bones which, detached and secret and familiar, an *is* different from my *is*"—etc. This is rather a compositional, than a stylistic flaw. When the ordinary analyst reads a mind we are often conscious of the author's presence. The psycho-analyst more rarely intrudes. An excuse for the old-time author's intervention was that it gave him an opportunity to express himself apart from the story. It was a dangerous expedient which only good writing could condone. Such deviations are extremely rare in Faulkner, but there is a passage in Part IV of *Sartoris* where the author stops his story to write a long paragraph on the mule. It is a fine specimen of undramatic writing, and he would be a captious critic who would wish it away.

Mr. Anderson's style is less varied and angular, and on the whole less powerful. It has none of the errors incident to strain, for I suppose he was the first American writer to cultivate the device of under-statement. It is a manner that lends itself to parody and to unskillful imitation. It may lead towards the inarticulateness of Gertrude Stein or the vividness of Hemingway. With its originator, though it has now become a shade too conscious, it has been an effective medium of expression giving him control of quite novel dramatic and poetic effects. One could dip at random in his works and find a representative specimen. As characteristic as anything in his novels is a passage from *A Story Teller's Story* where he describes a crisis in his life. In the middle of a successful career, in the act even of dictating a letter, Anderson decides to be a writer and walks out of the factory door, more or less as the fictitious Bruce Dudley was later to walk away from his wife. The episode is told with a casual simplicity that dangerously verges upon, but always escapes, bathos.

"It was a trying moment for me. There was the woman, my secretary, now looking at me. What did she represent? What did she not represent? Would I dare be honest with her? It was quite apparent to me I would not. I had got to my feet and we stood looking at each other. 'It is now or never,' I said to myself, and I remember that I kept smiling. I had stopped dictating to her in the midst of a sentence. 'The goods about which you have inquired are the best of their kind made in the——'

"I stood and she sat and we were looking at each other intently. 'What's the matter?' she asked. She was an intelligent woman, more intelligent I am sure than myself, just because she was a woman and good, while I have never been good, do not know how to be good. Could I explain all to her? The words of an explanation marched through my mind: 'My dear young woman, it is all very silly but I have decided to no longer concern myself with this buying and selling. It may be all right for others but for me it is poison. There is the factory. You may have it if it please you. It is of little value I dare say. Perhaps it is money ahead and then again it may well be it is money behind. I am uncertain about it all and now I am going away. Now, at this moment, with the letter I have been dictating, with the very sentence you have been writing left unfinished, I am going out that door and never come back. What am I going to do? Well now, that I don't know. I am going to wander about. I am going to sit with people, listen to words, tell tales of people, what they are thinking, what they are feeling. The devil! It may even be I am going forth in search of myself.' . . .

"Whether at the moment I merely became shrewd and crafty or whether I really became temporarily insane I shall never quite know. What I did was to step very close to the woman and looking directly into her eyes I laughed gayly. Others besides herself would, I knew, hear the words I was now speaking. I looked at my feet. 'I have been wading in a long river and my feet are wet,' I said.

"Again I laughed and I walked lightly toward the door and out of a long and tangled phase of my life, out of the door of buying and selling, out of the door of affairs.

"'They want me to be a "nut," will love to think of me as a "nut," and why not? It may just be that's what I am,' I thought gayly and at the same time turned and said a final confusing sentence to the woman who now stared at me in speechless amazement. 'My feet are cold wet and heavy from long wading in a river. Now I shall walk on dry land,' I said, and as I passed out at the door a delicious thought came. 'Oh, you little tricky words, you are my brothers. It is you, not myself, have lifted me over this threshold. It is you have dared give me a hand. For the rest of my life I will be a servant to you,' I whispered to myself as I went along a spur of railroad track, over a bridge, out of a town and out of that phase of my life."

Hemingway wears his master's clothes with a difference.

In dialogue he is more effective. Low-pitched though it is, it vibrates with strange intensity, and carries a surprisingly large proportion of the weight of the story. In the inter-spaces mannerisms creep in, and the simplicity of Anderson disintegrates into a loosely articulate continuity that a paragraph from *A Farewell to Arms* will exemplify:

"They were fighting in the Carpathians. I did not want to go there anyway. It might be good though. I could go to Spain if there was no war. The sun was going down and the day was cooling off. After supper I would go and see Catherine Barkley. I wished she were here now. I wished I were in Milan with her. I would like to eat at the Cova and then walk down the Via Manzoni in the hot evening and cross over and turn off along the canal and go to the hotel with Catherine Barkley. Maybe she would. Maybe she would pretend that I was her boy that was killed and we would go in the front door and the porter would take off his cap and I would stop at the con-cierge's desk and ask for the key and she would stand by the elevator and then we would get in the elevator and it would go up very slowly clicking at all the floors and then our floor and the boy would open the door and stand there and she would step out and we would walk down the hall and I would put the key in the door and open it and go in and then take down the telephone and ask them to send a bottle of *capri bianca* in a silver bucket full of ice and you would hear the ice against the pail coming down the corridor and the boy would knock and I would say leave it outside the door please. Because we would not wear any clothes because it was so hot and the window open and the swallows flying over the roofs of the houses and when it was dark afterward and you went to the win-dow very small bats hunting over the houses and close down over the trees and we would drink the capri and the door locked and it hot and only a sheet and the whole night and we would both love each other all night in the hot night in Milan. That was how it ought to be. I would eat quickly and go and see Catherine Barkley."

Dos Passos has nothing of this slovenly continuousness in his writing. But there is a staccato aspect of Hemingway's style that he can reproduce with an even more biting realistic effect. He is more penurious in dialogue, and in his characteristic latest books resorts largely to biographical narrative where the need of clear statement fights down all tendency to oddity. These aberrations from the regular are amply provided for in the cryptic *Camera Eye* interludes of the *42nd. Parallel* and *1919*. He is a brilliant and ambitious writer, but whether it is from his total lack of poetry, or from his desire to crowd too many aspects of life within the compass of one book his novels lack harmony, are difficult to remember, and do not repay rereading.

Mr. Sherwood Anderson is a comparatively mild rebel for whom dissatisfaction with things as they are is mainly, if not merely, an incentive to self-expression. In *Marching Men* he made his only contribution to the social revolutionary idea. By inclination he is an individualist who thinks that every man must work out his own salvation. He realized, and rightly we think, that his own lot was to be a teller of tales rather than a maker of garments, or whatever his factory produced. He therefore turned the lock in the door, and confronted the world as a manufacturer of words. To the end of his career he has been creating people of crude strength, adversaries of circumstance who win no battles but never acknowledge defeat. He has constituted himself the poet of a shirt-sleeve civilization with none of the amenities of life to compensate its rigors, and whose inarticulate heroes have none of the satisfactions which even the distressed artist enjoys. He excels in the short sketch; the larger canvas confuses him, for he has never envisaged life as a coherent whole. His best long work is in the books where the trembling mirage of the past supplies the theme. *Tar* is reminiscential, poetic, and therefore successful. *Dark Laughter* is far from being a great novel, but in its light way it is as interesting a technical experiment as America has produced. All the usual props of fiction are discarded. Narrative is restricted to the irreducible minimum, and dialogue, whose main virtue is normally to produce the impact of the present moment, is almost all "recovered." There are many fragments of remembered conversation that drift through the minds of the characters, but dialogue contemporaneous with the action of the story is extremely rare and most exiguous when found. For example, when Grey returns from the parade after Bruce had left his wife's room he is allowed to utter the monosyllable "well." Or again when Aline makes him face her and Bruce in the garden she is allowed a full sentence: " 'The child I am expecting is not your child, Fred.' Fred said nothing. What was to be said?" A two-line speech from his wife follows shortly. "And now words had come to Fred. How humiliating! He was pleading with her. 'It's all wrong. Don't go Aline! Stay here! Give me time! Give me a chance! Don't go!' "

Despite the elimination of all the usual expository material of the novelist the book is crystal clear, and substantially not so thin as many novels fashioned in the conventional mold.

William Faulkner has more to tell us about life, but he demands also much more of our attention. It requires not only a strong stomach, but a strong head to read him. He has been so short a time upon the stage that a few words upon his literary career will be justified, and an examination of his most difficult book *The Sound and the Fury* not superfluous.

There is a mathematical formula known as "Trial by Error." Faulkner is applying this process to fiction, and if he is fortunate enough to benefit by his mistakes he bids fair to be America's greatest novelist. He is best known by *Sanctuary* which is not a satisfactory, hardly even a representative, example of his work. If a novelist encounters horror by the way we shall not ask him to step aside, but the calculated manufacture of superfluous horrors is another matter. In other books Faulkner is sufficiently grim, but there the tragic material is not imported but inheres in the theme. My recommendation to a reader who might wish to measure Faulkner with other writers of traditional fiction would be to read his first spirited novel *Soldier's Pay*, or the more massively constructed *Sartoris* where he consents to use the customary devices for securing local color and achieving character. But more essential to an understanding of the man are the two experimental books *As I Lay Dying* and *The Sound and the Fury*. The last is barred from adequate recognition by its almost insuperable difficulty; the beauty of the first is concealed by the premeditated monotony of the treatment, and jeopardized by the crude horror of its theme. A simple-witted family loads the dead body of the wife and mother on a rickety wagon and for nine days trundles the putrefying corpse to its distant burial. What happens on the journey is presented by the members of this queer *cortège* in turn.

Some travelers enjoy a voyage throughout, however rough the weather. Some are sea-sick all the way, while others recover from their qualms sufficiently to find tonic restoration in the journey. Let this lame apologue suffice in lieu of an exposition of this strange and original book.

Can a poem, a drama, or a novel be deep without being difficult? A mathematical or philosophical treatise is shallow if too readily understood. Is a work of art to be governed by another law, and must hard thinking here and penetrating vision always issue in complete clarity of expression? If that is true one of the most significant novels of our time is an artistic failure. It is because I feel that *The Sound and the Fury* is on the contrary an artistic triumph, a book not only of profound human value but of deft and intricate architecture, that I contest the general soundness of the theory.

A first reading of this book is a baffling experience, and because the novelist is careless of his explanations the commentator must supply them. The story is of a southern family in decay. Three members of the family have charge of the first three books. The fourth is author's narrative. Book I is called *April Seventh, 1928*, and its presiding mind is Benjy, the 33-year-old idiot,—an ambitious challenge this to the stream-of-consciousness novelist! Here are the opening paragraphs:

"Through the fence, between the curling flower spaces, I could see them hitting. They were coming toward where the flag was and I went along the fence. Luster was hunting in the grass by the flower tree. They took the flag out, and they were hitting Then they put the flag back and they went to the table, and he hit and the other hit. Then they went on, and I went along the fence. Luster came away from the flower tree and we went along the fence and they stopped and we stopped and I looked through the fence while Luster was hunting in the grass.

" 'Here, caddie.' He hit. They went away across the pasture. I held to the fence and watched them going away.

" 'Listen at you, now.' Luster said. 'Ain't you something, thirty three years old, going on that way. After I done went all the way to town to buy you that cake. Hush up that moaning. Ain't you going to help me find that quarter so I can go to the show tonight?' "

Luster, the best nigger boy in fiction, is Benjy's guardian.

As we read on we encounter italics, by which generally, but unfortunately not always, are indicated the pictures from his childhood that float into the imbecile's mind. His elder sister Caddy had been the friend of his childhood, (we discover in a later book that she has just paid a furtive visit to her old home) and this describes his passion for haunting the edge of the golf links. He hears the players call "caddie." It is obvious that a first reading will not give us all the hints that bind up the past, but by degrees we piece together the full story. There are three brothers,— Quentin the oldest, and Jason younger than Benjy. The sister Caddy has been wayward. A marriage has been patched up with Herbert, a young banker who promises to give Jason employment. But when Caddy has an illegitimate child he turns her away, her old home is closed to her, and she becomes a prosperous kept woman with all a mother's solicitude for her child who has been given her brother Quentin's name. There is confusion of identity that might well have been avoided. On page 28, the Quentin who had hitherto been "he" the brother, becomes "she," the child of Caddy. It takes all our alertness to discover whether we are in the year 1928, or 1910 or even earlier.

With these difficulties solved the first book holds well together. The second book is the book of Quentin, and takes us back to the year 1910. He is at Harvard, where he had been ambitiously sent at the cost of the sale of some property of Benjy's. He has determined to commit suicide, urged to the act by the thought of Caddy's disgrace. So we are dealing here also with an unhinged mind, and some of the difficulties refuse to resolve themselves. The unpunctuated pages in Joyce's manner are singularly unilluminating.

Book III is Jason's, now since his father's death, the head of the family. It is eighteen years after Quentin's suicide, and one day earlier than the so fluctuating date that controls Benjy's book. There is consummate self-revelation here of a crafty and criminal consciousness. His mean tyranny and harshness shine through the pages, and Dilsey has some justification for her assertion that it was his harshness that drove the girl Quentin to a duplication of her mother's reckless behavior. It is plain sailing from here to the end. The last book as I have said is author's narrative, and is superb in quality throughout. It is largely Dilsey's book, but all the characters we know drift into it whether actually or by reference. The date is April Eighth, 1928.

Our confidence is established at the outset, and how well the author has availed himself of his narrative privilege is clear even from the opening paragraphs where he is describing Dilsey, the negro cook, emerging from her cabin to take up her duties of the day. Indeed, so masterly throughout is his command of traditional methods that we are permitted to wonder why he so fiercely assailed them in the earlier books of the story. The results are significant enough to reconcile us, and he has achieved an accumulative effect which straightforward narrative could not have secured. Our perspective of vision is enlarged and sharpened, the characters are inwardly and outwardly revealed, and the tragic reach of his conception is presented to us with an impressiveness that no other book of recent years has attained.

Chapter XXIX

OMISSIONS AND CONCLUSIONS:

CHIEFLY LAWRENCE*

My conscience is at rest concerning the many omissions of notable names from this survey. If it pricks me at all it is for failure to treat Trollope and Borrow in the last century and D. H. Lawrence in this. The last omission explains itself from the fact that after the turn of the century I have dealt mainly with experimentalists in form, and here Lawrence is not a prevailing example. But his sheer importance on other grounds compels me to more than a passing mention of his brilliant and significant work. The romancers and adventure writers I must regretfully leave unexplored, though I am mindful of the many pleasant and profitable hours they have yielded me. If I were to write a chapter entitled "Delightful Novels" it would argue the case for relaxation in all sincerity. A philosophical colleague of mine told me the other day of his struggles with a book of William Faulkner's. To find relief and lucidity he turned not as he might have done to Stevenson, Hewlett, or Don Byrne but to a graduate thesis on Professor Whitehead. The instance might readily be multiplied.

There is nothing to puzzle us in the mere text of a Lawrence book. His presentation is straightforward, his language clear; our difficulty arises from the profound strangeness of the experiences he seeks to communicate. No novels of our day have been so strikingly self-revealing.

* Passages quoted by permission of the Viking Press, New York.

[352]

To understand the books, therefore, we must understand the man, and for us who have not known him in the flesh the task of building him up from his books is fascinatingly difficult. His friends have not given us much assistance. Mr. Aldous Huxley's introduction to the *Letters* is helpful to the extent that it is a sympathetic interpretation by a man of intellect of a man of intuition. It is not the interpretation of a kindred spirit; but we value it because of its revelation of the essential lovableness of a man who bears the reputation of all the unsocial virtues—intractability, irascible aloofness, and hatred of his kind. The Middleton Murry study reduces his friend to a pathological case, and the hint of malignancy that goes with its cleverness constructs a picture of the man that appears hopelessly misleading. The text supports him, but we refuse to believe that genius of this caliber can be explained in terms of a Freudian complex. The Huxley comment is sufficiently explicit: "In *Son of Woman*, Mr. Middleton Murry has written at great length about Lawrence—but about a Lawrence whom you would never suspect, from reading that curious essay in destructive hagiography, of being an artist."

We fall back then perforce upon the wonderful *Letters*, and upon the many passages in the novels where Lawrence is giving dramatic expression to his fundamental beliefs. Even then we shall not pretend to understand him, and this not by reason of any lapse of clarity in the utterance, but by virtue of the disconcerting strangeness of those beliefs. With all a prophet's ardor he combines the prophet's fanatical determination to renovate life from its foundations. The sociological writers of our day may be revolutionary radicals. But they aim at a reconstruction merely of the framework of society. Lawrence strikes deep to the root of things. Monstrously wrong he may be, but burningly sincere he certainly is, and from beginning to end of his career surprisingly consistent with himself. Dedicating himself to the search for the undiscoverable God, he is sensitive as no other writer of our age to the tides of darkness and the tides of light that flow in the recesses of being.

Let us begin by glancing at an aspect of his talent that is not difficult to understand, but which is none the less uncanny in its power. We have dwelt upon the descriptive virtues of a few of our writers with primacy of value bestowed on Hardy. Lawrence I would assert to be still more remarkable. In Hardy we have a relatively restricted range of localized description. Lawrence traverses the world, and wherever he goes evokes the spirit of place, and with an even subtler magic and suggestiveness of phrase. The animate and inanimate world were his province. Poems and prose alike confirm Huxley's statement: "He seemed to know, by personal experience, what it was like to be a tree or a daisy or a breaking wave or even the mysterious moon itself. He could get inside the skin of an animal and tell you in the most convincing detail how it felt and how, dimly, inhumanly, it thought." The aloofness of the Australian landscape, the hard brilliancy of the Mexican, enter into the texture of *Kangaroo* and *The Plumed Serpent*, and infect the characters they present. During the war the Lawrences lived in Cornwall by the sea. He writes to Mr. J. D. Beresford, the novelist who had lent them the house:

"It is quite true what you say: the shore is absolutely primeval: those heavy, black rocks, like solid darkness and the heavy water like a sort of first twilight breaking against them, and not changing them. It is really like the first craggy breaking of dawn in the world, a sense of the primeval darkness just behind, before the Creation. That is a very great and comforting thing to feel, I think: after all this whirlwind of dust and grit and dirty paper of a modern Europe. I love to see those terrifying rocks, like solid lumps of the original darkness, quite impregnable: and then the ponderous, cold light of the sea foaming up: it is marvellous. It is not sunlight. Sunlight is really firelight. The cold light of the heavy sea is really the eternal light washing against the eternal darkness, a terrific abstraction, far beyond all life, which is merely of the sun, warm. And it does one's soul good to escape from the ugly triviality of life into this clash of two infinities one upon the other, cold and eternal."

Angry and embittered as he often was, and struggling often for the very breath of life, we realize from what depths of being Lawrence drew his restoration. Moods sometimes also came upon him when he desired to sever all the links that bound him to humanity, when even to hate seemed no longer desirable and love was a burden.

"These days Somers, too, was filled with fury. As for loving mankind, or having a fire of love in his heart, it was all rot. He felt almost fierily cold. He liked the sea, the pale sea of green glass that fell in such cold foam. Ice-fiery, fish-burning. He went out on to the low flat rocks at low tide, skirting the deep pock-holes that were full of brilliantly clear water and delicately-coloured shells and tiny, crimson anemones. Strangely sea-scooped sharp sea-bitter rock-floor, all wet and sea-savage. And standing at the edge looking at the waves rather terrifying rolling at him, where he stood low and exposed, far out from the sand banks, and as he watched the gannets gleaming white, then falling with a splash like white sky-arrows into the waves, he wished as he had never wished before that he could be cold, as sea-things are cold, and murderously fierce. To have oneself exultantly ice-cold, not one spark of this

[355]

wretched warm flesh left, and to have all the terrific icy energy of a fish. To surge with that cold exultance and passion of a sea thing! Now he understood the yearning in the seal-woman's croon, as she went back to the sea, leaving her husband and her children of warm flesh. No more cloying warmth. No more of this horrible stuffy heat of human beings. To be an isolated swift fish in the big seas, that are bigger than the earth; fierce with cold, cold life, in the watery twilight before sympathy was created to clog us."—*Kangaroo*.

There is no mistaking this anti-social mood that so often possessed him. Too many passages support it, too many of the circumstances of his life justify it, that it should be denied. But the yearning for communion is also there. There is no desire to abnegate his humanity, and his profoundest dissatisfaction with himself is when he fails to find his way in the maze of human relationships—the passionate relationship of the blood or the vertebral relationship of the instinctive life. "What ails me," he wrote to a friend, "is the absolute frustration of my primeval societal instinct. . . . I think societal instinct much deeper than the sex instinct—and societal repression much more devastating. There is no repression of the sexual individual comparable to the repression of the societal man in me, by the individual ego, my own and everybody else's. I am weary even of my own individuality, and simply nauseated by other people's."

Mr. Middleton Murry confuses the issue by stating that Lawrence's creative work was motivated throughout by his own sex frustration. We must grant a disharmony, but it is not that. It rests rather in the general condition of our modern civilization, and it is a race solution that he craves. He was clear-sighted enough to know that he was doomed to defeat, and this explains the vehemence of his anger. Lawrence did not belong to the accepting tribe.

We have moved too far away from primitive impulses, and our substitution of mind for instinct is not justified by any inherent rightness in our thinking. One more quotation, and the last of any length, will make this clear:

"My great religion," he wrote to his friend Collings, "is a belief in the blood, the flesh, as being wiser than the intellect. We can go wrong in our minds. But what our blood feels and believes and says, is always true. The intellect is only a bit and a bridle. What do I care about knowledge? All I want is to answer to my blood, direct, without fribbling intervention of mind, or moral, or whatnot. I conceive a man's body as a kind of flame, like a candle flame, forever upright and yet flowing: and the intellect is just the light that is shed on to the things around—which is really mind—but with the mystery of the flame forever flowing, coming God knows how from out of practically nowhere, and being *itself*, whatever there is around it that it lights up. We have got so ridiculously mindful, that we never know that we ourselves are anything—we think there are only the objects we shine upon. And there the poor flame goes on burning ignored, to produce this light. And instead of chasing the mystery in the fugitive, half-lighted things outside us, we ought to look at ourselves, and say 'My God, I am myself!' That is why I like to live in Italy. The people are so unconscious. They only feel and want: they don't know. We know too much. No, we only *think* we know such a lot. A flame isn't a flame because it lights up two, or twenty objects on a table. It's a flame because it is itself. And we have forgotten ourselves."

The letter goes breezily forward in a less didactic strain, but here evidently is the root of his incurable restlessness and spiritual discontent. If he cannot find equilibrium within himself what hope is there for a world that is careless of the problem? Always in search of this primeval urge he finds it most unsullied in flower and rock and beast and bird and sea. Man defeats him. Humanity has betrayed its trust. A developed consciousness has bred impurities in our vision. Gleams of the lost Eden shine on him in Cornwall, in Italy, in Mexico, but a fugitive gleam at the best. The mercenary snake has crept into the garden. In the Cornish people "the old race is still revealed, a race which believed in the darkness, in magic, and in the magic transcendency of one man over another, which is fascinating. Also there is left some of the old sensuousness of the darkness and warmth and passionateness of the blood, sudden, incalculable. Whereas they are like insects, gone cold, living only for money, for *dirt*. They are foul in this. They ought all to die."

In Italy it was the same, in Mexico the same. His happiest book was written about the Etruscans; for being dead they could not disturb him, and having no history he could invent one to the color of his own desire.

It is only the unconscious then that holds for Lawrence the pure unsullied core of primitiveness. Sex is our most ancient inheritance, and this we have sought to corrupt by unwarrantable sophistication and indefensible taboos. Its present perverted state was to Lawrence wholly detestable. "I, who loathe sexuality so deeply, am considered a lurid sexuality specialist. *Mi fa male allo stomaco.*" He refused to regard his suppressed novel *Lady Chatterley's Lover* as anything other than a protest against prevailing sex conceptions. "I believe in the phallic consciousness, as against the irritable cerebral consciousness we're afflicted with: and anybody who calls my novel a dirty sexual novel is a liar. It's not even a sexual novel: it's a phallic. Sex is a thing that exists in the head, its reactions are cerebral, and its processes mental. Whereas the phallic reality is warm and spontaneous—"

To the lay reader this is all somewhat confusing, and we cannot see how Lawrence could hope to be understood. We must absolve him from all pornographic intention, but Secretaries of State who banned him and a public hot on the trail of the prohibited book would assuredly misconstrue his purpose. It is a thousand pities, for books of such high quality are rare. Morals are diversely estimated on the score of intention or effect. The Utilitarian would be forced to condemn him on the final ground, the Christian to absolve him on the other. Of the offense against good taste he is guilty with a multitude of quite intentional offenders. But he outruns all his fellows in frankness, demonstrates where they are silent, and particularizes where they suggest.

His novels are all expansions of these ideas. They do not arise from situation or character, nor develop along the lines of any clearly articulated story. Characters indeed in the ordinary sense can scarcely be said to exist. Instead we encounter streams of energy, electrically charged, and unstable as the lightning that follows the path of highest attraction to its goal. Given a man and a woman it is impossible to predict their behavior except that it will ultimately discharge itself in some vehement explosion. *Sons and Lovers* revealed his capacity for orthodox presentation, but within the scope of that book he wearied of consistency and sharpness of outline. Shortly after it was written he wrote to Edward Garnett: "Somehow that which is physic, non-human in humanity is more interesting to me than the old-fashioned human element, which causes one to conceive a character in a certain moral scheme and make him consistent. The certain moral scheme is

[359]

what I object to. In Turgénev, and in Tolstoy, and in Dostoevsky, the moral scheme into which all the characters fit—and it is nearly the same scheme—is, whatever the extraordinariness of the characters themselves, dull, old, dead. . . . You mustn't look in my novel (*The Rainbow*) for the old stable ego of the character. There is another ego, according to whose action the individual is unrecognizable, and passes through, as it were, allotropic states which it needs a deeper sense than any we've been used to exercise to discover are states of the same single radically-unchanged element—Again I say, don't look for the development of the novel to follow the lines of certain characters: the characters fall into the form of some other rhythmic form, as when one draws a fiddle-bow across a fine tray delicately sanded, the sand takes lines unknown."

We must admit that Lawrence's novels lie very loosely within the folds of the old or the later Jamesian tradition. Nor in form do they accommodate themselves more readily to the daring innovations of his younger contemporaries. They are as organic merely as the jet of his vehement purpose will allow them to be. *Sons and Lovers*, *The Rainbow*, *Women in Love*, and *The Plumed Serpent* have a recognizable if wayward structure with sex or religion as dominant theme. These compelling motives are subordinated in *Kangaroo*, and political theorizing does not prove itself such an effective binding cement. It pays the price for being so interestingly autobiographical, for its fine qualities are almost nullified by the looseness of its texture. Somers is of course Lawrence and Harriet as recognizably his wife. The male-female love antagonism is no longer a controlling motive. It is wrested from its central place, and as a work of art the book falls to pieces. An essay chapter "At Sea in Marriage" is thrust into the middle. This is followed by a chapter call "Bits" which consists of excerpts from

Australian comic papers. "Chapter follows chapter, and nothing doing" he guiltily yet defiantly admits. "If you don't like the novel, don't read it. If the pudding doesn't please you, leave it, leave it. I don't mind your saucy plate. I know too well that you can bring an ass to water, etc." In Chapter XVI "A Row in Town," we have another essay contribution from the author on mob and mass psychology, and earlier in the book another chapter "The Night-mare" of more than fifty pages which gives us a valuable, but most unfictional account of Lawrence's experiences in the war.

The careless spontaneity of a man of genius, however passionate his convictions, will not always furnish forth a good novel. We can imagine Lawrence's rejoinder. He was not anxious to write fine novels, but to write great books. He would rather produce a *Moby Dick* than a *Golden Bowl*.

Now that we have reached the summing-up stage I am glad that I have held out no promise of discovering a philosophy of fiction. I rejoiced rather in the idea that fiction was the most flexible of literary forms, and capable of adapting itself with wonderful sensitiveness to the changing demands of successive ages. To find a good subject and to make the most of it is the one unchanging law, provided that this does not imply that all the resources of form have been exhausted. *Tom Jones* is an admirable book, but its virtues would not constrain a novelist with a similar theme to reproduce its method. The technical devices that suit one age are not necessarily adapted to another, and the procedure of our own day will seem quaint and antiquated to our grandchildren.

We are in the midst of a period of intensive renovation in all the creative arts, and the novel reveals its sensitiveness by the peculiar violence of its experimentation. The smoke of battle is too dense to yield a clear horizon, so we cannot find our latitude by any noon-day sun, nor our true direction by any polar star. We must have recourse to an artificial reckoning, and though he is neither noon-day sun nor polar star Henry James will serve our rough and ready purpose. He was not nor ever will be a popular writer, but he will be immortal as a point of reference, a permanent base line on which the geodetic survey of fiction may conveniently rest. He was the first of our novelists to be consistently form-conscious. He established a school. The school no longer flourishes. While it functioned the classes were very orderly and well-mannered, but a rowdy element entered, and in the din and confusion the master's exquisitely modulated voice was scarcely heard. But the refractory pupils owe more than they will admit to his presence and precept.

Leaving parable for matter of fact, what briefly did James in theory and practice strive to do? In the first place he proposed effective models of construction, and these were not the prophetic and violent Russians, but the Gallicized Turgénev, Balzac, and with reservations Flaubert. From their example he developed his own compositional theories which all converged on making the story a self-supporting unit. The author must disappear, and the point of view whether single or multiple must be so adjusted that the reader has immediate access to the theme. Infinite care must be exercised to exclude all heterogeneous material, for the novel must have unity of tone and a suave consistency of surface. The narrative, pictorial, and dialogue elements must be adjusted to the nicest proportions, and everywhere the effort must be made to work with dramatic intention. He strongly disliked the "seated mass of information" which bulks so large in the ordinary novel.

He stressed the progressive revelation of character, and talked somewhat obscurely perhaps of the virtues of indirect presentation, "that magnificent and masterly *indirectness* which means the only dramatic straightness and intensity." The old-time artificial plot was discarded in favor of pattern. There must be a minimum sufficiency of story, but the narrative movement must proceed by its own momentum, and always from the central situation. Incidents, like characters, must never be intrusive. Analysis is an effective instrument of characterization, but it must be a continuous and coherent presentation of unspoken thought. The process is not naturally dramatic, therefore it should be made as inward as possible. Above all the author should refrain from analytic comment on his own account quite as rigorously as he refrains from explicit moral judgments. The sentimental exhortations of Richardson and Dickens vanish as completely as the commentative embroidery of Eliot, Thackeray, or Meredith.

The novel with James would seem to have been effectively launched—a trim craft with polished brass and silken sails to catch the lightest airs. But it was evidently not fitted for stormy seas. Back into the ship-yards it accordingly went, and a vessel of cruder design took the water. The timbers creaked and groaned, foul smoke poured out of the funnels, and the wild crew spat upon the deck. The navigator's name is not securely known. Some call him Joyce, and others aver that a woman captain named Woolf is on the bridge. But the vessel she sails rides the waves very lightly, and is bound for another port which forever changes its name.

In any event the writing men of the new century have been making havoc with the Jamesian tradition. They found him I think too neat and tidy for their purpose, and above all too scrupulously polite, too much "in the forms" as James himself would say. In the preceding sketches I have not indicated the full extent of the deviations. Some of them I think are merely literary stunts which will have no chance of survival. And whatever the rebels may say James started something that will continue. Let us admit that his subject matter is too quintessential for an age so tragically tested as our own. There is nothing to show that his procedure would not adapt itself to cruder and harsher conditions. Indeed my contention is true that many of the innovators are much closer to him than they think, as a glance at the items I have specified above will prove. The quarrel one might have with some of them is that they are a shade too conscious of their form. Mr. Rex Stout is not perhaps an important example, but he produces a full-length novel (*How Like a God*) evolved while its central character is climbing a flight of stairs. And the technical devices of a Dos Passos to secure what is called the "breadth-wise" cutting of the slice are no less extraordinary, and perhaps no less certainly wasted. At least I cannot imagine the establishment of a Dos Passos tradition. What is common to many of them, and this one does not find in James, is the development of associational thinking issuing for the most part from morbidly abnormal minds which are subject to no directive control from themselves nor from the creating author. When the possibilities of this device are exhausted it will not entirely pass away, but will lose its dominance. Books then will not be so lopsided as they are at present. Signs of a reaction are already evident in the interesting work of Hemingway and Morley Callaghan. They are possibly moving too far in the other direction, for analysis of the new type or the old is absent from their pages, and analysis with all the difficulties it entails is a proved value in fiction.

APPENDIX

BIBLIOGRAPHY

The following bibliography was prepared under the direction of Miss Margaret Ray, Assistant-Librarian of Victoria University, University of Toronto. The arrangement is as follows:

(1) A general reference list of books on the English novel, with publisher and date of publication.

(2) A series of bibliographies of the thirty-eight authors given most extensive treatment in the text.

The individual bibliographies are arranged as follows:

(a) A brief biography of the author.

(b) A chronological list of the novels and (except in the case of authors like James where a complete list would occupy too much space) the short stories, with date of publication.

(c) A recommended edition (i.e. a standard edition) with date of publication, following (in parentheses) the individual work.

(d) A chronological list of the author's works other than fiction which throw light upon the author's methods of fiction-writing, followed by a recommended edition.

(e) A selected list of commentaries on the author (1) in book form, (2) in periodicals.

Students making an intensive study of a specific author should consult, in addition to the individual bibliography, the general reference list for further material on the subject of their study.

Additional material on the technique of fiction and on special aspects of it may be found in the section *Working Suggestions*, which follows this bibliography.

General surveys of literature such as *The Cambridge History of English Literature*, *A History of English Literature* by Legouis and Cazamian, and *A Survey of English Literature* by Oliver Elton, are available for consultation on all reference shelves, and have, therefore, not been listed.

Appendix

A Bibliography of the English Novel

Adams, S. H., Austin, Mary, and others. The Novel of To-morrow and the Scope of Fiction, by Twelve American Novelists. Bobbs-Merrill, 1922.

Baker, Ernest. A History of the English Novel. The Age of Romance; from the Beginnings to the Renaissance. Witherby, 1924.

Baker, Ernest. A History of the English Novel. The Elizabethan Age and After. Witherby, 1929.

Baker, Ernest. A History of the English Novel. Later Romances and the Establishment of Realism. Witherby, 1929.

Baldwin, Charles C. Men Who Make Our Novels. Dodd, 1924.

Beach, Joseph. The Outlook for American Prose. University of Chicago Press, 1926.

Beach, Joseph. The Twentieth Century Novel; Studies in Technique. Century, 1932.

Besant, Sir Walter, and James, Henry. The Art of Fiction. DeWolfe, 1911.

Brewster, Dorothy, and Burrell, Angus. Dead Reckonings in Fiction. Longmans, 1924.

Bullett, Gerald. Modern English Fiction; a Personal View. Jenkins, 1929.

Burton, Richard. Masters of the English Novel; a Study of Principles and Personalities. Holt, 1909.

Canby, H. S. American Estimates. Harcourt, 1929.

Chevalley, Abel. The Modern English Novel; Translated by Ben Ray Redman. Knopf, 1925.

Collins, Norman. The Facts of Fiction. Gollancz, 1932.

Cooper, Frederic. Some American Story Tellers. Holt, 1911.

Cooper, Frederic. Some English Story Tellers; a Book of the Younger Novelists. Holt, 1912.

Cross, W. L. The Development of the English Novel. Macmillan, 1899.

Cunliffe, J. W. English Literature during the Last Half-Century. Macmillan, 1923.

Dawson, William. Makers of English Fiction. Revell, 1905.

Drew, Elizabeth. The Modern Novel; Some Aspects of Contemporary Fiction. Harcourt, 1926.

Follett, Helen, and Follett, Wilson. Some Modern Novelists; Appreciations and Estimates. Holt, 1918.

Follett, Wilson. The Modern Novel; a Study of the Purpose and the Meaning of Fiction. Knopf, 1918.

Ford, Ford Madox. The English Novel; from the Earliest Days to the Death of Joseph Conrad. Lippincott, 1929.

Forster, Edward Morgan. Aspects of the Novel. Harcourt, 1927.

George, Walter Lionel. A Novelist on Novels. Collins, 1918.

Gordon, George, pseud. See Baldwin, Charles C.

Gould, Gerald. The English Novel of To-day. Dial Press, 1925.

Grabo, Carl. The Technique of the Novel. Scribner, 1928.

Greig, John. Scheherazade; or, The Future of the English Novel, [by John Carruthers (pseud.)]. Dutton, 1928.

Hall, Ernest. The Satirical Element in the American Novel. University of Pennsylvania, 1922.

Hamilton, Clayton. A Manual of the Art of Fiction, Prepared for the Use of Schools and Colleges; with an Introduction by Brander Matthews. Doubleday, 1918.

Horne, Charles. The Technique of the Novel. Harper, 1908.

Hueffer, Ford Madox. See Ford, Ford Madox.

James, Henry. Notes on Novelists, with Some Other Notes. Scribner, 1914.

Johnson, Richard Brimley. Some Contemporary Novelists: Men. L. Parsons, 1922.

Johnson, Richard Brimley. Some Contemporary Novelists: Women. L. Parsons, 1920.

Lawrence, D. H. Studies in Classic American Literature. Boni, 1923.

Leavis, Q. D. Fiction and the Reading Public. Chatto, 1932.

Lewisohn, Ludwig. Expression in America. Harper, 1932.

Lovett, Robert, and Hughes, Helen. History of the Novel in England. Houghton, 1932.

Lubbock, Percy. The Craft of Fiction. Scribner, 1921.

Mencken, H. L. A Book of Prefaces. Garden City, 1927.

Michaud, Régis. The American Novel To-day; a Social and Psychological Study. Little, Brown, 1928.

Muir, Edwin. The Structure of the Novel. Harcourt, 1929.

Myers, W. L. The Later Realism; a Study of Characterization in the British Novel. University of Chicago Press, 1927.

Overton, Grant. The Philosophy of Fiction. Appleton, 1928.

Overton, Grant. The Women Who Make Our Novels. Dodd, 1918.

Parrington, Vernon. Main Currents in American Thought; an Interpretation of American Literature from the Beginnings to 1920. 2 vols. Harcourt, 1927.

Perry, Bliss. A Study of Prose Fiction. Houghton, 1920.

Phelps, William Lyon. The Advance of the English Novel. Dodd, 1916.

Phelps, William Lyon. Essays on Modern Novelists. Macmillan, 1918.

Priestley, J. B. The English Novel. Benn, 1927.

Raleigh, Sir Walter. The English Novel; Being a Short Sketch of its History from the Earliest Times to the Appearance of Waverley. Murray, 1903.

Rickword, Edgell, ed. Scrutinies, vol. 2. Wishart, 1931.

Saintsbury, George. The English Novel. Dutton, 1913.

Tompkins, J. M. S. The Popular Novel in England, 1770–1800. Macmillan, 1933.

Valentine, Allan C. The English Novel. Oxford, 1927.

Van Doren, Carl. The American Novel. Macmillan, 1921.

Van Doren, Carl. Contemporary American Novelists, 1900–1920. Macmillan, 1922.

Vines, Sherard. Movements in Modern English Poetry and Prose. Oxford, 1927.

Walker, Hugh. The Literature of the Victorian Era. Macmillan, 1910.

Weygandt, Cornelius. A Century of the English Novel. Century, 1925.

Wharton, Edith. The Writing of Fiction. Scribner, 1925.

Wheeler, Harold. Contemporary Novels and Novelists: A List of References to Biographical and Critical Material. University of Missouri, 1921.

Williams, Harold. Two Centuries of the English Novel. Smith, Elder, 1911.

ANDERSON, SHERWOOD

Born in Camden, Ohio, in 1876. His father was, as described by his son, a "lovable, improvident fellow, colorful, no-account, who should have been a novelist himself." He moved from place to place in Ohio, and Sherwood's education was very irregular, as he went to work at the age of twelve years to help provide for the family—working in factories chiefly. At the age of seventeen he went to Chicago and drifted from job to job for four years. Served in the Spanish-American War. He became manager of a paint factory in Ohio, but walked out one day and never went back. He returned to Chicago and secured a position in an advertising agency. He met Theodore Dreiser and other writers of "the Chicago group." He wrote *Windy McPherson's Son,* which was eventually published in 1916. Another novel was written during this time while Anderson was recovering from a nervous breakdown in the Ozark Mountains, but he became so disgusted with it that he threw the manuscript out of the train window in his return to Chicago. *Marching Men,* a novel on factory conditions, was published in 1917. A book of verse, *Mid-American Chants,* followed in 1918. By this time his work had received a great deal of attention, although much of the comment was unfavorable. He went abroad in 1921, and on his return lived in New Orleans for a year with William Faulkner. Later he bought a property in Marion, Virginia, where he has since lived, occupying himself with the writing of novels and the editing of two newspapers, one Republican and the other Democratic. He has been married three times. *Dark Laughter,* published in 1925, is considered his best novel.

BIBLIOGRAPHY

Novels

Windy McPherson's Son. 1916. (Viking Press, 1921)
Marching Men. 1917. (Viking Press, 1917)
Poor White. 1920. (Modern Library, 1926)
Many Marriages. 1923. (Viking Press, 1923)
Dark Laughter. 1925. (Boni & Liveright, 1925)
Tar; A Midwest Childhood. 1926. (Boni & Liveright, 1926)
Beyond Desire. 1932. (Liveright, 1932)

Short Stories

Winesburg, Ohio. 1919. (Viking Press, 1919)
The Triumph of the Egg. 1921. (Viking Press, 1921)
Horses and Men. 1923. (Viking Press, 1923)
Alice, and The Lost Novel. 1929. (Mathews, 1929)

Miscellaneous Works

A Story-Teller's Story. [Autobiography] 1924. (Viking Press, 1924)
The Modern Writer. 1925. (Lantern Press, 1925)
Sherwood Anderson's Notebook. 1926. (Boni & Liveright, 1926)
Hello Towns. 1929. (Liveright, 1929)
Perhaps Women. 1931. (Liveright, 1931)

Studies and Reviews

BOOKS

Boynton, Percy.	More Contemporary Americans.
Calverton, V. F.	The Newer Spirit: A Sociological Criticism of Literature.
Canby, H. S.	Definitions. Second Series.
Chase, C. B.	Sherwood Anderson.
Collins, Joseph.	Taking the Literary Pulse.
Drake, W. A. (ed.)	American Criticism.
Fagin, N. B.	Phenomenon of Sherwood Anderson.
Farrar, John (ed.)	The Literary Spotlight.
Garnett, Edward.	Friday Nights.
Hackett, Francis.	Horizons.
Hansen, H.	Midwest Portraits; a Book of Memories and Friendships.
Hind, C. L.	Authors and I.
Karsner, David.	Sixteen Authors to One.
Mais, S. P. B.	Some Modern Authors.
Rosenfeld, P.	Port of New York.
Sherman, S. P.	Critical Woodcuts.
Spratling, W. P.	Sherwood Anderson and Other Famous Creoles.
West, Rebecca.	Strange Necessity.
Whipple, T. K.	Spokesmen: Modern Writers and American Life.
Wickham, H.	The Impuritans.

PERIODICALS

American Collector   5: 157 (1928).
Bookman   75: 642 (1932).
Catholic World   130: 129 (1929).
English Journal   16: 271 (1927).

Bibliography

Letters 1: 23 (1928).
Nation 135: 432 (1932).
New Republic 54: 399 (1928); 73: 168 (1932).
New Statesman 30: 330 (1927).
North American Review 224: 140 (1927).
Saturday Review of Literature 9: 305 (1932).
Sewanee Review 37: 159 (1929).
Southwestern Bulletin (Memphis) September, 1929.
World Tomorrow 15: 525 (1932).

AUSTEN, JANE

Born December 16th, 1775, at Steventon, Hampshire, where her father was rector. Her mother, Cassandra, was the daughter of Reverend T. Leigh, and niece of Theophilus Leigh, for fifty years master of Balliol. Jane was the youngest of seven children. She spent the first twenty-five years of her life at Steventon and occasionally took part in private theatricals. She learned French, a little Italian, and was remarkably dexterous with the needle. She read standard literature, was familiar with the *Spectator*, and minutely acquainted with the work of Richardson. In 1801, the family moved to Bath, where the father died; in 1805 they moved to Southampton, and in 1809 to Chawton. There Jane lived until her death in 1817. She was buried at Winchester in the center of the north aisle of Winchester Cathedral. Her first novel, *Pride and Prejudice*, was written in 1797, but was not published until 1813. Her second novel, *Sense and Sensibility*, which was written in 1798, was published two years before her first novel. *Northanger Abbey* and *Persuasion* both appeared posthumously, in the year following her death.

BIBLIOGRAPHY

Novels

Sense and Sensibility. 1811. (Everyman's Library, Dutton, 1906)
Pride and Prejudice. 1813. (Everyman's Library, Dutton)
Mansfield Park. 1814. (Everyman's Library, Dutton)
Emma. 1816. (Everyman's Library, Dutton)
Northanger Abbey. 1818. (Everyman's Library, Dutton)
Persuasion. 1818. (Everyman's Library, Dutton)

Miscellaneous Works

Love and Friendship. (Stokes, 1922)

The Watsons. [Completed by S. Oulton] (Appleton, 1923)

Plan of a Novel. (Oxford, 1926) [350 copies printed. From the originals now in the Pierpont Morgan library and the British Museum]

Letters to her sister Cassandra and Others. 2 vols. Ed. by R. W. Chapman. (Clarendon Press, 1932)

Volume the First. [Reprinted from a manuscript in the Bodleian Library] (Clarendon Press, 1933)

Studies and Reviews

BOOKS

Adams, O. S.	Story of Jane Austen's Life.
Alden, R. M. (ed.)	Critical Essays of the Early Nineteenth Century.
Apperson, G. L.	Jane Austen Dictionary.
Bailey, J. C.	Introductions to Jane Austen.
Bald, M. A.	Women Writers of the Nineteenth Century.
Bradley, A. C.	Miscellany.
Canby, H. S.	Emma and Mr. Knightley: A Critical Essay.
Chesterton, G. K.	Uses of Diversity.
English Association.	Essays and Studies. Vol. 2.
Johnson, R. Brimley.	Jane Austen.
	Women Novelists.
Johnson, R. Brimley (ed.)	Famous Reviews.
Keynes, G.	Jane Austen: A Bibliography.
Leigh, J. E. A.	Memoir of Jane Austen.
Leigh, W. A., and R. A. A.	Jane Austen, Her Life and Letters. A Family Record.
Lynd, Robert.	Old and New Masters.
Mais, S. P. B.	Books and Their Writers.
Phelps, W. L.	Essays on Books.
Priestley, J. B.	English Comic Characters.
Ralli, A. J.	Critiques.
Rhydderch, David.	Jane Austen: Her Life and Art.
Royal Society of Literature.	Essays by Divers Hands. New Series, vols. 7, 8, 10.

Bibliography

Smith, Goldwin.	Life of Jane Austen.
Squire, J. C.	Life and Letters of Jane Austen.
Summers, A. J.	Essays in Petto.
Thomson, C. L.	Jane Austen. A Survey. (Contains a complete bibliography)
Villard, L.	Jane Austen. Sa Vie et Son Œuvre. Annales de l'Université de Lyon.
Walkley, A. B.	More Prejudice.
	Still More Prejudice.
West, Rebecca.	Preface to *Northanger Abbey*. (Travellers' Library)
Wordsworth, E.	Essays Old and New.

PERIODICALS

Bulletin of the John Rylands Library, Manchester 12: 314 (1928).
Cornhill Magazine 65: 24 (1928); 69: 435 (1928); 70: 435 (1931).
English Association, Pamphlet No. 68 (1927).
Fortnightly Review 37: 262 (1885).
Fraser's Magazine 61: 30 (1860).
National Review 46: 507 (1931).
Nineteenth Century 102: 125 (1927).
Quarterly Review 14: 188 (1815); 24: 352 (1821).
Times Literary Supplement Aug. 25: 565 (1927).
Yale Review 17: 380 (1928).

BENNETT, (ENOCH) ARNOLD

Born in 1867, in North Staffordshire, near the Five Towns which he made so famous, the son of a solicitor. Educated in Newcastle Middle School and the University of London. Read law in his father's office and began his literary career as a free-lance journalist on a local newspaper, *The Staffordshire Sentinel*. Abandoned law in 1893 to become assistant editor of *Woman;* succeeded to editorship in December, 1896; resigned in 1900 to devote himself to writing. In the same year he married a Frenchwoman, and lived in France until 1908. His first novel, *A Man from the North*, had appeared in 1898, but his masterpiece, *Old Wives' Tale*, did not come out until 1908, and reflects the influence of his years in France. He has produced a great many novels, the best of which deal with the Five Towns, and a number of which are merely pot-boilers. Besides these he has written plays, short stories, and articles. He died in 1931.

Bibliography

Novels

A Man from the North. 1898. (Methuen, 1930)
The Grand Babylon Hotel. 1902. (Chatto, 1932)
Anna of the Five Towns. 1902. (Methuen, 1929)
Leonora. 1903. (Chatto, 1932)
A Great Man. 1904. (o.p.)
Sacred and Profane Love: A Novel in Three Episodes. 1905. (Chatto, 1932) [Revised Ed. The Book of Carlotta. 1911] (Doran, 1911)
Whom God Hath Joined. 1906. (Ward, Lock, 1932)
The Ghost: A Fantasia on Modern Themes. 1907. (Jarrolds, 1929)
Buried Alive: A Tale of These Days. 1908. (Doubleday, 1931)
The Old Wives' Tale. 1908. (Modern Library, 1931)
The Glimpse: An Adventure of the Soul. 1909. (o.p.)
Helen with the High Hand: An Idyllic Diversion. 1910. (Nelson, 1928)
Clayhanger. 1910. (Doubleday, 1931)
The Card: A Story of Adventure in the Five Towns. 1911. [American ed. Denry the Audacious] (Doran, 1911)
Hilda Lessways. 1911. (Doran, 1924)
The Regent: A Five Towns Story of Adventure in London. 1913. (Methuen, 1929)
The Old Adam. 1913. (Doran, 1913)
The Price of Love. 1914. (o.p.)
These Twain. 1915. (Doran, 1915)
The Lion's Share. 1916. (Cassell, 1927)
The Pretty Lady. 1918. (Cassell, 1932)
The Roll Call. 1919. (Hutchinson, 1929)
Lilian. 1922. (Cassell, 1930)
Mr. Prohack. 1922. (Ward, Lock, 1931)

Bibliography

Riceyman Steps. 1923. (Cassell, 1928)
Elsie and the Child. A Tale of Riceyman Steps. 1924. (Cassell, 1924)
Lord Raingo. 1926. (Cassell, 1928)
The Loot of Cities. 1927. (Nelson, 1927)
The Gates of Wrath: A Melodrama. 1927. (Methuen, 1927)
The Strange Vanguard. 1928. (Cassell, 1930)
Accident. 1929. (Doubleday, 1929)
Imperial Palace. 1930. (Doubleday, 1930)

Short Stories

Tales of the Five Towns. 1905. (Chatto, 1930)
The Grim Smile of the Five Towns. 1907. (Chatto, 1930)
The Matador of the Five Towns. 1912. (Doran, 1912)
The Woman Who Stole Everything, and Other Stories. 1927. (Cassell, 1929)
Teresa of Watling Street. 1931. (Ward, Lock, 1931)
The Night Visitor, and Other Stories. 1931. (Doubleday, 1931)
Stroke of Luck; and Dream of Destiny. An Unfinished Novel. 1932. (Doubleday, 1932) [English ed. Dream of Destiny (an Unfinished Novel), and Venus Rising From the Sea]

Miscellaneous Works

(To be studied in connection with the novels.)

The Truth About an Author. 1903. (Methuen, 1928)
How to Become an Author. 1903. (o.p.)
Literary Taste: How to Form It. 1909. (Doran, 1909)
The Author's Craft. 1915. (o.p.)
Journal. [Edited by Newman Flower] 3 vols. Vols. 1–2, 1932; vol. 3, 1933. (Viking Press, 1932–1933)

Studies and Reviews

BOOKS

Bennett, M.	My Arnold Bennett.
Cooper, F. T.	Some English Story Tellers; a Book of the Greater Novelists.
Cross, W. L.	Four Contemporary Novelists.

Darton, F. J. H.	Arnold Bennett.
Hind, C. L.	Authors and I.
Priestley, J. B.	Figures in Modern Literature.
Scott, Dixon.	Men of Letters.
Sherman, S. P.	On Contemporary Literature.
Smith, P.	A. B.
Wells, G. H.	The Problem of Arnold Bennett.
West, Geoffrey, pseud.	See Wells, G. H.
West, Rebecca.	Arnold Bennett Himself.

PERIODICALS

Current Literature 50: 553 (1911).
English Review 39: 140 (1924).
Harper's Magazine 122: 633 (1911); 124: 638 (1912).
Life and Letters 6: 413 (1931).
Literary Review May 14th, 1927.
Living Age 269: 131 (1911); 291: 251, 771 (1916); 324: 691 (1925).
London Mercury 9: 394 (1924).
Nation 101: 741 (1915); 102: 133 (1916); 117: 717 (1923).
National Review 46: 702 (1931)
New Republic 25: 203 (1921); 48: 272 (1926); 66: 194 (1931).
New Statesman 22: 148 (1923); 28: 18 (1926).
Nouvelle Revue Française May, 1931.
Revue de France July 1, 1931.
Saturday Review 141: 231 (1926); 142: 446 (1926).
Saturday Review of Literature 8: 106 (1931).
Spectator 137: 593 (1926).
Yale Review 18: 302 (1929).

BRONTË, CHARLOTTE AND EMILY

Charlotte, Emily, Branwell, and Anne Brontë were the children of an Irish clergyman, perpetual curate of Thornton, later of Haworth, in Yorkshire. Charlotte was born in 1816, Emily in 1818. In 1824, Charlotte and Emily spent one year at a school for clergymen's daughters at Cowan's Bridge, afterwards described in *Jane Eyre*. The remainder of their education was received mainly at home, with the exception of the year that Charlotte spent at Roehead School near Leeds. In 1836 Charlotte got a position as governess at Roehead School in order to pay for her brother Branwell's education, taking Emily with her as a pupil, but she was obliged to relinquish the position in 1838, owing to ill-health. Both Charlotte and Emily wrote a great deal during their youth, and in 1836 Charlotte sent some poems to Southey, who declined them. Charlotte was employed as a governess in private homes over a period of several years, in the course of which she refused two proposals of marriage. She and Emily decided to start a private school, and early in 1842 went to Brussels to Monsieur Héger's school to gain teaching experience. They returned in October of the same year, but Charlotte went back to M. Héger's school as instructress. The fruit of this experience on the continent was Charlotte's *Villette* and *The Professor*. In 1846, Charlotte, Emily, and Anne published a small volume of their collected verse, under the pseudonym of Currer, Ellis, and Acton Bell, but the poems received little notice. In 1847, *The Professor* was rejected, but *Jane Eyre* (written during a period of sadness occasioned by her brother's disgrace, her father's blindness, and her sisters' illness) received immediate success. Emily's novel, *Wuthering Heights*, was published in 1847. Emily's health had been declining, and she died in 1848. She had a mysterious, enigmatical character, and possessed a real poetic gift. *Shirley* is an idealized picture of Emily. In 1849 Charlotte visited her publisher in London, and was introduced to Thackeray. In 1850 she made a trip to the English Lakes with Mrs. Gaskell, Matthew Arnold, and Miss Martineau. In June, 1854, she married her father's curate, Arthur Bell Nicholls. In less than a year she died of an illness following childbirth.

BIBLIOGRAPHY

Novels

CHARLOTTE BRONTË [CURRER BELL, pseud.]
Jane Eyre. 1847. (Everyman's Library, Dutton)
Shirley. 1849. (Everyman's Library, Dutton)
Villette. 1853. (Everyman's Library, Dutton)
The Professor. 1857. (Everyman's Library, Dutton)
Emma. [A fragment] 1860. (Cornhill Magazine, April, 1860)

EMILY BRONTË

Wuthering Heights. 1847. (Everyman's Library, Dutton)

Studies and Reviews

BOOKS

Adams, W. H.	Women of Fashion and Representative Women in Letters and Society. Celebrated Englishwomen of the Victorian Era.
Bayne, Peter.	Essays in Biography and Criticism. Two Great Englishwomen: Mrs. Browning and Charlotte Brontë.
Bennett, J. O.	Much Loved Books.
Benson, E. F.	Charlotte Brontë.
Birrell, A.	Life of Charlotte Brontë.
Bradley, C. F.	The Brontës, and Other Essays.
Brontë Society.	Publications
Clarke, Isabel C.	Haworth Parsonage. A Picture of the Brontë Family.
Clutton-Brock, A.	Essays on Books.
Dimnet, A.	The Brontë Sisters.
English Association.	Essays and Studies. Vols. 5, 14.
Ferguson, R.	The Brontës Went to Woolworth's. Charlotte Brontë.
Fulcher, P. M. (ed.)	Foundations of English Style.
Gaskell, Mrs. E.	Life of Charlotte Brontë.
Gosse, Sir Edmund.	The Challenge of the Brontës.
Harrison, Frederic.	Charlotte Brontë's Place in Literature.
Holloway, L. C.	Charlotte Brontë.
Holroyd, A.	Currer Bell.
Kenton, Edna.	A Forgotten Creator of Ghosts, Joseph Sheridan Le Fanu, Possible Inspirer of the Brontës.
Kingsley, W. W.	Views on Vexed Questions.
Langbridge, R. G.	Charlotte Brontë: A Psychological Study.
Martineau, H.	Biographical Sketches.
Mathews, T. S.	The Brontës: A Study.
Ralli, A. J.	Critiques.

Bibliography

Reid, T. Wemyss.   Charlotte Brontë. A Monograph.
Robinson, A. M. F.   Emily Brontë. (Eminent Women Series.)
     Grands Écrivains d'autre-Manche.
Romieu, E., and G.   Three Virgins of Haworth.
Saintsbury, George.   Three Mid-Century Novelists.
Selden, Camille, pseud.   L'Esprit des Femmes de notre Temps.
Shorter, Clement.   The Brontës' Life and Letters.
     Charlotte Brontë and Her Circle.
     Charlotte Brontë and Her Sisters.
Sinclair, May.   The Three Brontës.
Skelton, Sir John.   Essays in History and Biography.
Smith, G. G.   Poets and Novelists.
Spens, Janet.   Charlotte Brontë.
Stephen, Sir Leslie.   Hours in a Library.
Sugden, K. A. R.   A Short History of the Brontës.
Swinburne, A. C.   A Note on Charlotte Brontë.
Symons, Arthur.   Stories of the Victorian Writers.
Walker, Mrs. J. R.   Dramatis Personæ.
Ward, Mary.   Charlotte Brontë's Feminine Characters
     —a Revolt against Some Victorian
     Ideals. Univ. of Pittsburgh Bulletin,
     No. 28.
Willcocks, M. P.   Between the Old World and the New.
Wilson, Romer.   All Alone: The Life and Private History
     of Emily Jane Brontë.
Woolf, Virginia.   The Common Reader.
Wright, W.   The Brontës in Ireland.

PERIODICALS

Atlantic Monthly   60: 705 (1887).
Bookman   10: 163 (1896).
Cornhill Magazine   1: 485 (1860).
Fortnightly Review   100: 524 (1913).
Forum   19: 29 (1889).
Fraser's Magazine   36: 690 (1847);   51: 527 (1885).
Living Age   24: 481 (1850);   34: 417 (1852);   54: 680 (1857);
   130: 801 (1896);   199: 59 (1893);   219: 276 (1898);   220: 377
   (1899);   269: 515 (1911).
Nation   135: 286 (1932).
Nineteenth Century   103: 133 (1928);   108: 533 (1930).

North American Review   67: 354 (1848),   196: 714 (1912).
Publications of the Modern Language Association of America
43: 494 (1928).
Quarterly Review   84: 153 (1848).
Queen's Quarterly   39: 414 (1932).
Revue des Deux Mondes   24: 470 (1849);   40: 714 (1849).
Saturday Review of Literature   9: 217 (1932).
Virginia Quarterly Review   January, 1929.

CABELL, JAMES BRANCH

Born at Richmond, Virginia, on April 14th, 1879, of an old
Southern family.   After attending private school he entered
William and Mary College.   He was an instructor there in Latin
and Greek from 1896 to 1898 and was graduated with very high
honors in 1898.   He was engaged in newspaper work for two
years, and spent the eight succeeding years in the writing of
books and short stories.   He worked in the coal mines of West
Virginia from 1911 to 1913.   He became interested in genealogical
and historical research, and was appointed Genealogist of the
Virginia chapter of the Sons of the Revolution, and subsequently
has held several other offices as genealogist or historian of various
clubs and organizations.   He married Priscilla Bradley in 1913.
His first book, *The Eagle's Shadow*, was published in 1904.   Most
of his novels belong to an allegorical series known as the *Biography
of Manuel*, which relates the history of an imaginary mediæval
country, Poictesme, and the adventures of Count Manuel and
his line of descendants.   Although a number of books had appeared before *Jurgen* was published in 1919, it was the suppression
of this book which gave Cabell national recognition.   In addition
to his novels and short stories he has written poetry, essays,
works on genealogy, and one play.   His book of essays, *Beyond
Life*, explains his philosophy of life and art.

BIBLIOGRAPHY

Novels

The Eagle's Shadow. 1904. (McBride, 1923)
The Cords of Vanity. 1909. (McBride, 1920)
The Soul of Melicent. 1913. [See Domnei]

Bibliography

The Rivet in Grandfather's Neck. 1915. (McBride, 1922)
The Cream of the Jest. 1917. (McBride, 1921)
Jurgen. 1919. (McBride, 1919)
Domnei. A Comedy of Woman Worship. 1920. [Revised edition of The Soul of Melicent] (McBride, 1920)
Figures of Earth. 1921. (McBride, 1921)
The High Place. 1923. (McBride, 1923)
The Silver Stallion. 1926. (McBride, 1926)
Something About Eve. 1927. (McBride, 1927)
The White Robe. 1928. (McBride, 1928)
The Way of Ecben. 1929. (McBride, 1929)

Short Stories

The Line of Love. 1905. (McBride, 1921)
Gallantry. 1907. (McBride, 1922)
Chivalry. 1909. (McBride, 1921)
The Certain Hour. 1916. (McBride, 1916)
The Music from Behind the Moon. 1926. (McBride, 1932)

Studies and Reviews

BOOKS

Boyd, Ernest.	Portraits, Real and Imaginary.
Boynton, Percy.	Some Contemporary Americans.
Bregenzer, B. M., and Loveman, S. (eds.)	Round-Table in Poictesme: A Symposium.
Brussell, I. R.	Bibliography of the Writings of James Branch Cabell.
Clark, E.	Innocence Abroad.
De Casseres, B.	Forty Immortals.
Farrar, John.	The Literary Spotlight
Holt, Guy.	A Bibliography of the Writings of J. B. Cabell.
Karsner, David.	Sixteen Authors to One.
Macy, J. A. (ed.)	Between Dawn and Sunrise: Selections from Cabell's Writings.
McNeill, W. A.	Cabellian Harmonics
Mencken, H. L.	James Branch Cabell.
Starrett, V.	Buried Cæsars.

Appendix

Van Doren, Carl.   James Branch Cabell.
Walpole, Hugh.   The Art of James Branch Cabell.
Wickham, H.   The Impuritans.
Williams, Blanche C. Our Short-Story Writers.

PERIODICALS

American Mercury   1: 504 (1924);   13: 38, 251 (1928).
Athenæum   2: 1339 (1919).
Bookman   52: 200 (1920);   66: 211 (1927);   68: 335 (1928).
Catholic World   129: 459 (1929).
Commonweal   1: 355 (1925).
Current Opinion   78: 340 (1925).
Dial   64: 392 (1918);   66: 225 (1919);   76: 363 (1924).
Freeman   3: 186 (1921).
Letters   1: 6 (1928);   2: 6 (1929).
Literary Review   1: 3 (1921);   4: 3 (1924).
Nation   111: 343 (1920);   112: 914 (1921);   113: 664 (1921);
    115: 377 (1922);   119: 470 (1924);   122: 559 (1926);   125:
    386 (1927);   130: 17 (1930);   136: 409 (1933).
New Republic   26: 187 (1921);   38: 157 (1924);   41: 151
    (1924);   53: 52 (1927);   61: 201 (1930).
Outlook   153: 348 (1930).
Saturday Review   38: 278 (1930);   39: 485 (1931).
Saturday Review of Literature   2: 769 (1926);   4: 249 (1927);
    6: 1108 (1930).
Sewanee Review   37: 193 (1929).
Virginia Quarterly Review   5: 336 (1929).

CATHER, WILLA

Born near Winchester, Virginia, December 7th, 1876, of English ancestry. At the age of eight moved to a ranch in Nebraska,
where she came into contact with Scandinavians, Bohemians,
Germans, Russians, and French. She received her elementary
education at home; read English and Latin classics. She attended
high school in Red Cloud, Nebraska, and completed her education at the University of Nebraska in 1895. Later she moved to
Pittsburgh and was appointed dramatic critic of *The Daily Leader*.
She relinquished that position in 1901 and became head of the
English department of Allegheny High School. Was managing

[384]

Bibliography

editor of *McClure's Magazine* from 1908 to 1912. She traveled extensively abroad and in the southwestern United States. Since leaving *McClure's* she has written a number of novels and short stories, each of which has added to her literary reputation. In 1922 she won the Pulitzer Prize with her novel, *One of Ours*. Her books have been translated into French, Bohemian, and Swedish. She has written one volume of poetry, *April Twilights* (1903). She is unmarried.

BIBLIOGRAPHY

Novels

The Bohemian Girl. 1912. (o.p.)
Alexander's Bridge. 1912. (Houghton, 1922)
O Pioneers! 1913. (Houghton, 1913)
The Song of the Lark. 1915. (Houghton, 1915)
My Antonia. 1918. (Houghton, 1926)
One of Ours. 1922. (Knopf, 1922)
The Professor's House. 1925. (Knopf, 1925)
My Mortal Enemy. 1926. (Knopf, 1926)
Death Comes for the Archbishop. 1927. (Knopf, 1927)
Shadows on the Rock. 1931. (Knopf, 1931)

Short Stories

The Troll Garden. 1905. (o.p.)
Youth and the Bright Medusa. 1920. (Knopf, 1925)
Obscure Destinies. 1932. (Knopf, 1932)

Studies and Reviews

BOOKS

Beaty, J. O., and others (eds.)	Facts and Ideas.
Boynton, Percy.	Some Contemporary Americans.
Canby, H. S.	Definitions. Second Series.
Cockayne, C. A. (ed.)	Modern Essays of Various Types.
Collins, Joseph.	Taking the Literary Pulse.
Gay, R. M. (ed.)	Fact, Fancy and Opinion.
Gruening, E. H. (ed.)	These United States. Second Series.
McCullough, B. W., and Burgum, E. B. (eds.)	Book of Modern Essays.

[385]

Morley, C. D. (comp.)	Modern Essays. Second Series.
Overton, G. M.	Women Who Make Our Novels.
Rankin, T. E., and others (eds.)	Further Adventures in Essay Reading.
Rapin, R.	Willa Cather.
Sergeant, E. S.	Fire Under the Andes.
Sherman, S. P.	Critical Woodcuts.
Squire, J. C., and others (eds.)	Contemporary American Authors.
Van Dyke, H.	The Man Behind the Book.
West, Rebecca.	Strange Necessity.
Whipple, T. K.	Spokesmen: Modern Writers and American Life.
Witham, R. A. (comp.)	Essays of To-day; Informal and Formal.

PERIODICALS

American Collector   6: 67 (1928).
Anglia Beiblatt   39: 215 (1928).
Bookman   74: 134 (1931).
Catholic World   135: 641 (1932).
Century   110: 309 (1925).
Commonweal   13: 464 (1931).
English Journal   13: 373 (1924).
Englische Studien   63: 323 (1929).
Figaro   May 16, 1930.
Forum   76: 559 (1926).
Independent   119: 283 (1927).
Literary Review   4: 331 (1923).
London Mercury   13: 516 (1926).
Nation   117: 236 (1923);   135: 563 (1932).
New Republic   30: sup. 5 (1922);   43: 91 (1925);   67: 345 (1932).
North American Review   219: 641 (1924).
Saturday Review of Literature   8: 216 (1931).
Sewanee Review   37: 221 (1929).
Virginia Quarterly Review   7: 585 (1931).
World Review   3: 140 (1926).
Yale Review   N.S. 21: viii (1931).

Bibliography

CONRAD, JOSEPH

Josef Konrad Korzeniowski was born in the Ukraine in 1857, the son of a Polish family of patriots and exiles. He spent his childhood in Cracow, and received a good education, learning to speak and write French fluently. His first acquaintance with English Literature was made through Polish translations of Shakespeare and Dickens. The novels of Marryat, Cooper, and Victor Hugo inspired him with a romantic love for the sea, and at the age of seventeen he went to Marseilles and for two years served on French ships in the Mediterranean and along the South American coast. In 1878 he became an able seaman on a British coasting vessel, and two years later he sailed as third mate on a clipper ship bound for Sydney. By 1884 he had become a master in the British merchant service and a British subject. He acquired a working knowledge of the English language between 1878 and 1880. He began his first novel, *Almayer's Folly*, in 1889 during a period of ill-health occasioned by a Congo fever. When published in 1895 it was recognized as an original note in English fiction. Soon after his emergence as a writer he gave up the sea, married an Englishwoman and went to live in Kent. He was not sufficiently established as a novelist to live by his writing, so a Civil List pension was secured for him and was relinquished when the sales of his books gave him a sufficient income. In the following twenty-five years he wrote more than twenty novels, nearly all dealing with some aspect of sea-faring life or the scenes of his voyages, several plays, travel sketches, essays, and reminiscences. *The Nigger of the Narcissus* (1897), *Lord Jim* (1900) and *Nostromo* (1904), are considered his most outstanding novels. He died on August 3rd, 1924, leaving unfinished an historical tale which was published in the following year under the title, *Suspense*. A volume of essays also was published posthumously in 1926.

BIBLIOGRAPHY

Novels

Almayer's Folly: A Story of an Eastern River. 1895. (Doubleday, 1915)
An Outcast of the Islands. 1896. (Doubleday, 1920)
The Nigger of the Narcissus: A Tale of the Sea. 1897. (Doubleday, 1921)

Lord Jim: A Tale. 1900. (Doubleday, 1922)
The Inheritors: An Extravagant Story. 1901. (Dent, 1924)
Romance: A Novel. 1903. (Dent, 1924)
Nostromo: A Tale of the Seaboard. 1904. (Doubleday, 1921)
The Secret Agent: A Simple Tale. 1907. (Doubleday, 1907)
Under Western Eyes. 1911. (Doubleday, 1926)
Chance: A Tale in Two Parts. 1913. (Doubleday, 1913)
Victory: An Island Tale. 1915. (Doubleday, 1915)
The Shadow-Line: A Confession. 1917. (Doubleday, 1917)
The Arrow of Gold. 1919. (Doubleday, 1920)
The Rescue: A Romance of the Shallows. 1920. (Doubleday, 1920)
The Rover. 1923. (Doubleday, 1923)
The Nature of a Crime. 1924. (Duckworth, 1924)
Suspense. 1925. (Doubleday, 1925)

Short Stories

Tales of Unrest. 1898. (Doubleday, 1916)
Youth: A Narrative and Two Other Stories. 1902. (Doubleday, 1920)
Typhoon and Other Stories. 1903. (Doubleday, 1926)
A Set of Six. 1908. (Doubleday, 1915)
'Twixt Land and Sea: Tales. 1912. (Doubleday, 1912)
Within the Tides: Tales. 1915. (Doubleday, 1916)
Tales of Hearsay. 1925. (Doubleday, 1925)

Miscellaneous Works

Some Reminiscences. 1912 (American ed. A Personal Record).
Notes on Life and Letters. 1921.
Last Essays. 1926.

Studies and Reviews

BOOKS

Bancroft, W. W.	Joseph Conrad: His Philosophy of Life.
Bridges, H. J.	The God of Fundamentalism.
Canby, H. S.	Definitions. Series One.
Conrad, Jessie.	Joseph Conrad as I Knew Him.
Cross, W. L.	Four Contemporary Novelists.
Cunningham-Graham, R. B.	Inveni Portam, Joseph Conrad.

Curle, R.   Last Twelve Years of Joseph Conrad.
Cushwa, F. W.   Introduction to Conrad.
Doubleday, Nelson.   Approach to Conrad.
English Association.   Essays and Studies. Vol. 6.
Fernandez, R.   Messages.
Ford, Ford Madox.   Joseph Conrad.
Freeman, John.   The Moderns.
Galsworthy, John.   Castles in Spain and Other Screeds.
Garnett, Edward.   Friday Nights.
     Letters from Conrad: 1895–1924.
Heydrick, B. A. (ed.)   Familiar Essays of To-day.
Huneker, J. G.   Ivory Apes and Peacocks.
Jean-Aubrey, G.   Joseph Conrad, Life and Letters.
Kellett, E. F.   Reconsiderations.
Lynd, Robert.   Books and Authors.
Macy, J. A.   Critical Game.
McFee, W.   Harbours of Memory.
     Swallowing the Anchor.
Mégroz, R. L.   Joseph Conrad's Mind and Method.
Mencken, H. L.   A Book of Prefaces.
     Selected Prejudices.
     Prejudices. Fifth Series.
Morf, G.   The Polish Heritage of Joseph Conrad.
Morley, C. D. (comp.)   Modern Essays. Second Series.
Muir, Edwin.   Latitudes.
O'Flaherty, Liam.   Joseph Conrad. An Appreciation.
Overton, G. M.   Authors of the Day.
Pence, R. W. (ed.)   Essays by Present-day Writers.
Price, A. J.   Appreciation of Joseph Conrad.
Safroni-Middleton, A.   Tropic Shadows.
Schelling, F. E.   Appraisements and Asperities.
Shackelford, L. B., and
  Gass, F. P. (eds.)   Essays of our Day.
Squire, J. C.   Life and Letters.
Stauffer, R. M.   Joseph Conrad.
Symons, Arthur.   Notes on Joseph Conrad with Some
     Unpublished Letters.
Walpole, Hugh.   Joseph Conrad.
Walpole, V.   Conrad's Method: Some Formal As-
     pects.

Waugh, Alec.	Tradition and Change.
Wise, T. J.	A Bibliography of the Writings of Joseph Conrad (1895–1920).
Woolf, L. S.	Essays on Literature.
Woolf, Virginia.	The Common Reader.
	Second Common Reader.

PERIODICALS

Adelphi 2: 354 (1924).

American Mercury 1: 253 (1924); 4: 505 (1925); 23: 251 (1931).

Atlantic Monthly 119: 223 (1917); 149: 233 (1932); 149: 403 (1932).

Bookman 38: 476 (1914); 39: 662 (1914); 40: 99 (1914); 53: 102 (1921); 56: 402 (1922); 74: 648 (1932).

Catholic World 92: 796 (1911); 109: 163 (1919); 119: 799 (1924).

Century 115: 385 (1928).

Contemporary Review 125: 54 (1924).

Criticism 3: 6 (1924).

Current Opinion 77: 630 (1924).

Dial 61: 172 (1916); 66: 638 (1919); 69: 169 (1920).

Edinburgh Review 231: 318 (1920); 241: 126 (1925).

Englische Studien 51: 391 (1918).

Fortnightly Review 89: 627 (1908); 132: 534 (1929).

Forum 53: 579 (1915).

Hibbert Journal 23: 141 (1924).

Living Age 236: 120 (1903); 276: 264 (1913); 302: 792 (1919); 304: 101 (1920); 309: 221 (1921); 320: 512 (1924); 322: 551 (1924); 324: 622 (1925); 328: 308 (1926); 328: 637 (1926); 340: 537 (1931).

London Mercury 9: 319 (1923); 9: 502 (1924).

Nation 98: 395 (1914); 107: 510 (1918); 119: 179 (1924); 120: 45 (1925).

New Criticism 4: 782 (1926).

New Republic 16: 109 (1918); 19: 56 (1919); 27: 25 (1921).

New Statesman 12: 375 (1918); 13: 590 (1919).

Nineteenth Century 107: 103 (1930).

North American Review 178: 842 (1904); 200: 270 (1914); 208: 439 (1918).

Bibliography

Scribner's Magazine   77: 3 (1925);   90: 379 (1931).
Yale Review   14: 295 (1925);   18: 699 (1929).

DEFOE, DANIEL

Born in 1660 or 1661 in the parish of St. Giles, Cripplegate. His parents were Nonconformists and Defoe received his education accordingly at a Noncomformist institution, qualifying in philosophy and theology for the ministry. He did not enter the church, however, but went into business about 1685. After about seven years his business career ended in bankruptcy, and although he became engaged in another business enterprise he devoted his energies largely to political pamphleteering. At first he was a strong Whig as witnessed by his obscure rôle in the Monmouth Rebellion and his conspicuous rôle in William III's reception. He supported William warmly in his political pamphlets, and after William's death in 1702 attacked the High Church party. He was imprisoned at Newgate for his ironical pamphlet, *The Shortest Way with Dissenters.* It is apparent that he married about 1702, but precisely when and whom are not definitely known. In 1704 he established the *Review,* which he edited until its suppression in 1713; following this he became connected with Lord Oxford's *Mercator.* Defoe's career in fiction began with *The Storm* in 1704, and *Mrs. Veal's Ghost* in 1706, but it was not until 1719 that *Robinson Crusoe* appeared. This was followed by a six-year period of fiction writing, during which *Moll Flanders* and *Roxana* were published. Political pamphlets, poems, and fictitious accounts are the substance of his writings. He died in 1731.

BIBLIOGRAPHY

Novels *

Robinson Crusoe. 1719. (Everyman's Library, Dutton, 1906)
The Dumb Philosopher. 1719.
The King of Pirates. 1719.
Duncan Campbell. 1720.
Memoirs of a Cavalier. 1720. (Constable, 1926)
Captain Singleton. 1720. (Everyman's Library, Dutton, 1906)

* The best collection for working purposes of Defoe's works is The Shakespeare Head Edition of the Novels and Selected Writings of Daniel Defoe. In fourteen volumes. (Blackwell, 1928.)

Moll Flanders. 1722. (Modern Library, 1926)
Journal of the Plague Year. 1722. (Everyman's Library, Dutton, 1908)
Colonel Jacque. 1722.
The Fortunate Mistress, or Roxana. 1724.
A New Voyage Around the World. 1725.

Short Stories *

History of the Great Storm. 1704.
Mrs. Veal's Ghost. 1706.
Duncan Campbell. 1720.
Mr. Campbell's Pacquet. 1720.
Cartouche. 1722.
Highland Rogue (Rob Roy). 1723.
Murders at Calais. 1724.
Jonathan Wild. 1725.
John Gow. 1725.
The Friendly Damon. 1726.
Mere Nature Delineated. 1726.
† Life and Adventures of Mrs. Christian Davies commonly called Mother Ross. [Soldiers' Tales] (McBride, 1929)

Studies and Reviews

BOOKS

Cather, Willa.	Introduction to *The Fortunate Mistress*. (Borzoi Classics)
Chadwick, W.	Life and Times of Daniel De Foe.
Davies, W. H.	Introduction and biographical note to *Moll Flanders*. (Abbey Classics)
Dawson, W.	Makers of English Fiction.
Dibelius, Wilhelm.	Englische Romankunst.
Dottin, Paul.	The Life and Strange and Surprising Adventures of Daniel De Foe. [Translated from the French by Louise Ragan]
Follett, W.	Introduction to *The Life of Jonathan Wild*. (Borzoi Classics)

* The best collection for working purposes of Defoe's works is The Shakespeare Head Edition of the Novels and Selected Writings of Daniel Defoe. In fourteen volumes. (Blackwell, 1928.)
† Defoe is supposedly the author of this work.

Bibliography

Forster, John.	Historical and Biographical Essays.
Gildon, C.	Robinson Crusoe Examined and Criticized.
Gückel, W., and Günther, E.	Daniel Defoes und Swifts Belesenheit und literarische Kritik.
Hazlitt, W.	*Defoe's Works*, with a Memoir of His Life and Writing.
Hearnshaw, F. J. C. (ed.)	The Social and Political Ideas of Some English Thinkers of the Augustan Age.
Horten, M.	Studien über die Sprache Defoes.
Hubbard, L. L.	The Narrative of the El-ho Sjouke Gabbes by Hendrik Smeeks.
Hutchins, H. C.	Robinson Crusoe and its Printing.
Jackson, H. E.	Robinson Crusoe: Social Engineer.
Minto, W.	Daniel Defoe.
Nicholson, W.	The Historical Sources of Defoe's Journal of the Plague Year.
Pastor, A.	The Idea of Robinson Crusoe.
Quiller-Couch, Sir A. T.	Adventures in Criticism.
Roorda, G.	Realism in Daniel De Foe's Narrative of Adventure.
Scott, Sir Walter.	Miscellaneous Prose Works.
Secord, A. W.	Studies in the Narrative Method of Defoe.
Stephen, Sir Leslie	Hours in a Library.
Trent, W. P.	Daniel Defoe.
Ullrich, H.	Defoes Robinson Crusoe. Die Geschichte eines Weltbuches.
Van Doren, Carl.	Introduction to *Moll Flanders*. (Borzoi Classics)
Wilson, Walter	Life of Daniel Defoe. 3 vols.
Wright, T.	Life of Daniel Defoe.

PERIODICALS

American Mercury   19: xii (1930).
Anglia Beiblatt   36: 133 (1925);   37: 134 (1926).
Annales Politiques et Littéraires   82: 74 (1924).

Blackwood's Magazine   217: 503 (1925).
Contemporary Review   115: 664 (1919).
Current Opinion   65: 393 (1918);   67: 177 (1919).
Deutscher Litztag   3: 2142 (1926).
Deutscher Rundschau   54: 47 (1928);   214: 47 (1928).
Englische Studien   54: 367 (1920);   55: 231 (1921);   56: 281 (1922);   57: 136, 309, 315, 316 (1923);   59: 452, 457 (1925); 63: 120 (1929).
English Journal   16: 31, 359 (1927).
English Studies   8: 189 (1926);   13: 75 (1931).
Freeman   5: 514 (1922).
Germanisch-romanische Monatsschrift   17: 458 (1930).
Holborn Review   67: 37 (1925).
Journal of Applied Psychology   7: 195 (1923).
Journal of English and Germanic Philology   19: 94 (1920); 22: 302 (1923);   25: 132 (1926);   28: 443 (1929);   29: 451 (1930);   30: 55 (1931).
Literatur, Die   28: 556 (1926).
Living Age   315: 776 (1922).
London Mercury   22: 140, 227 (1930).
Mercure de France   November 15, 1922;   January 1, 1924.
Modern Language Notes   39: 235 (1924);   42: 121 (1927); 22: 378 (1929);   45: 479 (1930).
Modern Language Review   20: 109 (1925).
Nation (London)   33: 363 (1923).
Nation and Athenæum   38: 19,   642 (1924);   39: 14,   419 (1925);   41: 5, 147 (1927).
New Statesman   13: 190 (1919);   21: 330 (1923).
Notes and Queries   8: 348 (1921);   147: 291 (1924);   149: 467 (1925).
Outlook   123: 202 (1919).
Publications of the Modern Language Association   36: 509 (1921).
Queen's Quarterly   38: 89 (1931).
Revue Politique et Littéraire   58: 442 (1920).
Saturday Review   143: 198 (1927).
Saturday Review of Literature   2: 339 (1925);   6: 769 (1930); 7: 296 (1930).
Times Literary Supplement   April 23: 313 (1931).
University of California Chronicle   25: 175.

Bibliography

DICKENS, CHARLES

Born at Sandport, Portsea, February 7th, 1812, of humble parentage. Academic education limited by family finances. He began his literary career as a reporter, and first won distinction while serving on the *Morning Chronicle* in 1835. As early as 1833 he had begun to write for periodicals. In 1836 he married Catherine Hogarth, and ten children were born of this union. In April of the same year, the first of *Pickwick Papers* appeared, later to be incorporated as his first novel. *Oliver Twist* followed in 1838. The remainder of his life he devoted entirely to writing. He traveled widely on the Continent from 1844 to 1856, and visited America in 1842 and in 1867. He was much interested in theatricals and wrote both plays and poems. His death was hastened by the fatigue and excitement of giving a great many public readings of his works. He died on June 9th, 1870, and was buried in Westminster Abbey.

BIBLIOGRAPHY

Novels *

Pickwick Papers. 1837.
Oliver Twist. 1838.
Nicholas Nickleby. 1839.
Master Humphrey's Clock. 1840.
Old Curiosity Shop. 1840.
Barnaby Rudge. 1840.
A Christmas Carol. 1843.
Martin Chuzzlewit. 1844.
The Chimes. 1844.
The Cricket on the Hearth. 1845.
The Battle of Life. 1846.
Dombey and Son. 1848.
The Haunted Man, and the Ghosts' Bargain. 1848.
David Copperfield. 1850.
Bleak House. 1853.
Hard Times. 1854.
Little Dorrit. 1857.
A Tale of Two Cities. 1859.

* The most convenient edition is the Uniform Edition, 20 volumes. (Macmillan.)

Edwin Drood. 1870.
Great Expectations. 1861.
Our Mutual Friend. 1865.

Short Stories

[These are too numerous to list in a brief bibliography. They may be consulted in *Christmas Stories, Reprinted Pieces and the Lazy Town of Two Idle Apprentices,* and *Sketches by Boz* (Uniform Edition, Macmillan).]

Studies and Reviews

BOOKS

Bagehot, W.	Literary Studies, Vol. 2.
Barnes, A. W.	Dickens Guide.
Boyd, E. A.	Literary Blasphemies.
Brewer, L. A.	Leigh Hunt and Charles Dickens.
Chancellor, E. B.	Dickens and His Times.
Charles, E.	Some Dickens Women.
Chesterton, G. K.	Appreciations and Criticism of the Works of Charles Dickens.
	Come To Think of It.
	Uses of Diversity.
Clark, C.	Dickens and Democracy and Other Studies.
Clutton-Brock, A.	Essays on Books.
Cor, R.	Un romancier de la vertu et un peintre du vice: Ch. Dickens et M. Proust.
Crothers, S. M.	Humanly Speaking.
Dexter, W.	Some Rogues and Vagabonds of Dickens.
	The Story of the Life of the World's Favourite Author.
Dibelius, Wilhelm.	Charles Dickens.
Dickens, Sir Henry F.	Memories of My Father.
Elison, O.	Charles Dickens, Novelist.
Forster, John.	Life of Charles Dickens.
Fraser, C. L.	Characters of Dickens.
Galsworthy, John.	Castles in Spain and Other Screeds.

Bibliography

Gissing, George.	Charles Dickens. Critical Studies of the Works of Charles Dickens.
Harrison, Frederic.	Dickens' Place in Literature.
Hayward, A. L.	Dickens Encyclopædia.
Holdworth, W. S.	Charles Dickens as a Legal Historian.
Jeans, S.	Charles Dickens.
Kent, W.	Dickens and Religion.
Lang, Andrew.	Essays in Little.
Ley, J. W.	Dickens Circle.
Marzials, Sir F. T.	Life of Charles Dickens.
McCullough, B. W., and Burgum, E. B. (eds.)	Book of Modern Essays.
Moses, B.	Charles Dickens and His Girl Heroines.
Murry, J. M.	Pencillings.
Pagan, A. M.	Charles Dickens and Some Others.
Phelps, W. L.	Essays on Books.
Philip, A. J.	A Dickens Dictionary and a Dictionary of Dickens' Originals.
Phillips, W. C.	Dickens, Reade, and Collins: Sensation Novelists.
Pierce, G. A.	Dickens Dictionary.
Procter, W. C.	Christian Teaching in the Novels of Charles Dickens.
Quiller-Couch, Sir A. T.	Charles Dickens and Other Victorians.
Roberts, C. E. B.	This Side Idolatry (fictionized biography).
Sawyer, C. J., and Darton, F. J. H.	Dickens and Barabbas.
Shore, W. T.	Charles Dickens.
Sitwell, O.	Dickens.
Stonehouse, J.	Green Leaves.
Straus, R.	Charles Dickens.
Swinburne, A. C.	Charles Dickens.
Thomson, C. J.	Bibliography of the Writings of Charles Dickens.
Van Amerongen, J. B.	The Actor in Dickens.

[397]

Van Dyke, H.	Companionable Books.
Wagenknecht, E. C.	Charles Dickens the Man.
Ward, A. W.	Dickens. (Men of Letters Series)
Whipple, E. P.	Charles Dickens.
Willcocks, M. P.	Between the Old World and the New.
Zweig, S.	Three Masters.

PERIODICALS

Argosy 40: 282.
Blackwood's Magazine 77: 451; 109: 673.
Catholic World 123: 395 (1926).
Century Magazine 83: 322 (1912).
Christian Examiner 32: 15.
Connoisseur 81: 231 (1928).
Contemporary Review 10: 203; 128: 82 (1925); 135: 331 (1929).
Cornhill Magazine 58: 118.
Critic 8: 301.
Current Literature 52: 341 (1912).
Dial 71: 537 (1921); 74: 1 (1923).
Dublin Review 68: 315; 141: 285 (1907).
Edinburgh Review 68: 75.
English Review 10: 257.
Fortnightly Review 38: 762; 70: 944; 88: 269 (1907).
Forum 81: 54 (1929).
Fraser's Magazine 21: 381; 82: 130.
Living Age 234: 449 (1902); 246: 791 (1905); 250: 819 (1906); 269: 118 (1911); 272: 800 (1912); 276: 229 (1913); 288: 417 (1916); 293: 308, 735 (1917); 297: 502 (1918); 304: 778 (1920); 312: 480 (1922); 316: 38 (1923); 320: 374 (1924).
London Quarterly Review 35: 265; 117: 29 (1912).
Nation 10: 380; 35: 57.
National Review 7: 458.
Nineteenth Century 54: 765 (1903).
North American Review 69: 383; 77: 409; 195: 381 (1912).
North British Review 4: 165; 7: 61; 15: 57.
Saturday Review 146: 291 (1928).
Scottish Review 3: 125.

Bibliography

Scribner's Magazine   51: 656 (1912);   85: 395 (1929).
Spectator   69: 950;   106: 313 (1911).
Westminster Review   82: 414.
Yale Review   N.S. 2: 142 (1912).

DOS PASSOS, JOHN

Born on January 14th, 1896, in Chicago. Received his A.B. degree *cum laude* from Harvard in 1916 and since then has lived in Chicago, New York, Washington, London, Brussels, Madrid, and Paris. During the Great War he served with the Ambulance Service from 1917 until July, 1919. After the war he married Miss Kate Smith of Chicago. He has developed recently a strong social consciousness, and was arrested during the Sacco-Vanzetti demonstrations and incarcerated in a cell with Michael Gold, editor of the *New Masses*. Dos Passos is a frequent contributor to the *New Masses* and other radical journals. His first novel, *One Man's Initiation*, was published when he was twenty-one. His war novel, *Three Soldiers*, presenting the experiences of privates in the United States army roused violent discussion. *Manhattan Transfer* (1925) and *The 42nd Parallel* (1930) are his best known novels. In addition to his six novels he has written poetry, plays, essays, travel sketches, and a sociological study, and has translated Blaise Cendrars' *Panama*.

BIBLIOGRAPHY

Novels

One Man's Initiation. 1917. (o.p.)
Three Soldiers. 1921. (Garden City, 1929)
Streets of Night. 1923. (o.p.)
Manhattan Transfer. 1925. (Harper, 1925)
The 42nd Parallel. 1930. (Harper, 1930)
1919. 1932. (Harcourt, 1932)

Studies and Reviews

BOOKS

Baldwin, Charles C.   Men Who Make Our Novels.
Beach, J. W.   The Twentieth Century Novel.
Boynton, Percy.   Some Contemporary Novelists: The Personal Equation in Literature.

Collins, Joseph.   Taking the Literary Pulse.
Lewis, Sinclair.   John Dos Passos' *Manhattan Transfer.*

PERIODICALS

Bookman   54: 393 (1921);   71: 210 (1930);   75: 32 (1932).
Calendar of Modern Letters   4: 70 (1927).
Commonweal   16: 55 (1932).
Dial   71: 606 (1921);   72: 640 (1922).
Forum   87: iv (1932).
Freeman   4: 282 (1921).
Independent   107: 16, 97 (1921).
Living Age   343: 178 (1932).
London Mercury   5: 319 (1922).
Nation   113: 480 (1921);   130: 298 (1930);   134: 344 (1932).
Nation and Athenæum   30: 148 (1921);   48: 170 (1930).
New Republic   28: 162 (1921);   31: 366 (1922);   51: 52
    (1927);   58: 256 (1929);   62: 157 (1930);   67: 157 (1931);
    70: 303 (1932).
New Statesman and Nation   3: 770 (1932).
Saturday Review of Literature   2: 361 (1925);   3: 677 (1927);
    8: 600 (1932).
Spectator   145; 422 (1930);   148: 910 (1932).

DOUGLAS, NORMAN

Born in 1868 in Austria, of Scottish ancestry.   He began the study of music at the age of twelve.   At the age of twenty-four he secured a post in the diplomatic service, which he held for twelve years, during which period he visited many countries and learned several languages.   He became interested in the study of zoölogy, geology, and archæology, and went to the island of Capri to live, where he continued his investigations and wrote treatises on them.   His articles were published in *The Zoölogist* between the years 1886 and 1895.   In 1901 came his first attempt at creative writing with *Unprofessional Tales*, which were published under the pseudonym "Normyx."   In 1911 *Siren Land*, a travel book on Greece, was published, but attracted little attention.   *South Wind*, his first novel, was published in 1917.   It established his reputation as a writer, although it brought him little financial gain.   Since then he has published four novels.

Bibliography

In 1930 he published *Goodbye to Western Culture*, which presents a scathing indictment of European and especially British culture. He has written several books of travel, essays, scientific sketches, and critical articles, in addition to his novels and tales.

BIBLIOGRAPHY

Novels

South Wind. 1917. (Modern Library, 1925)
They Went. 1920. (Dodd, 1926)
Alone. 1921. (Chatto, 1932)
In the Beginning. 1928. (Day, 1928)
Three of Them. 1930. (Chatto, 1930)

Short Stories

Unprofessional Tales. 1901. (o.p.)
Nerinda. 1929. (Day, 1929)

Miscellaneous Works

Looking Back; an Autobiographical Excursion. (Harcourt, 1933)

Studies and Reviews

BOOKS

Beach, J. W.	The Twentieth Century Novel.
Lynd, Robert.	Books and Authors.
Mais, S. P. B.	Books and Their Writers.
McDonald, E. D.	Bibliography of the Writings of Norman Douglas.
Scarborough, Dorothy.	Introduction to *South Wind*. (Modern Readers' Series, Macmillan, 1929)
Tomlinson, H. M.	Norman Douglas.
Van Doren, Carl.	Introduction to *South Wind*. (Limited Editions Club, 1932)

PERIODICALS

Adelphi   1: 627 (1924).
Bookman   53: 249 (1921);   66: 42 (1927);   67: 578 (1928).
Books   [New York Herald-Tribune]   May 20, 1928.
Dial   65: 117 (1918);   70: 580 (1921).
London Mercury   3: 114 (1920).

Nation 93: 61 (1911); 101: 632 (1915).
Nation and Athenæum 28: 167 (1920); 43: 795 (1928).
New Republic 55: 76 (1928); 60: 183 (1929).
New Statesman 9: 306 (1917); 22: 122 (1923).
Outlook 153: 111 (1929).
Saturday Review 111: 651 (1911); 136: 404 (1923); 146: 365 (1928).
Saturday Review of Literature 4: 495 (1928).
Spectator 141: 340 (1928).

DREISER, THEODORE

Born in 1871 at Terre Haute, Indiana, of German ancestry. He was educated in the public schools of Warsaw, Indiana, and at the University of Indiana. He began his literary career as a newspaper reporter on the *Chicago Globe* in 1892. He was editor of *Every Month*, a literary and musical magazine, from 1895 to 1898. 'In 1898 he married, but has since been divorced. His first novel, *Sister Carrie*, was published in 1900. He held various editorial positions on the *Century*, *Cosmopolitan*, and other popular magazines, and in 1907 became editor-in-chief of the Butterick Publications. Since 1910 he has devoted his time exclusively to writing. Several of his novels were banned immediately after publication because of their frankness on sex matters. In 1925 *An American Tragedy* was published and received greater public recognition than any of his other novels. In 1927 he made an official visit to Russia, and published his impressions in the following year in his book, *Dreiser Looks at Russia*. In addition to his novels he has written poetry, plays, essays, and books of description and travel, as well as an autobiography. In 1932 his sociological study, *Tragic America*, was published.

BIBLIOGRAPHY

Novels

Sister Carrie. 1900. (Boni & Liveright, 1921)
Jennie Gerhardt. 1911. (Boni & Liveright, 1923)
The Financier. 1912. (Boni & Liveright, 1927)
The Titan. 1912. (Boni & Liveright, 1923)
The "Genius." 1915. (Boni & Liveright, 1923)
An American Tragedy. 1925. (Boni & Liveright, 1926)

Bibliography

Short Stories

Free, and Other Stories. 1918. (Modern Library, 1924)
Twelve Men. 1919. (Boni & Liveright, 1919)
Chains. 1927. (Boni & Liveright, 1927)
A Gallery of Women. 2 vols. 1928. (Boni & Liveright, 1929)

Miscellaneous Works

A Book about Myself [autobiography]. 1922. (Boni & Liveright, 1922)
Dawn; A History of Myself. 1931. (Liveright, 1931)

Studies and Reviews

BOOKS

Anderson, Sherwood.	Horses and Men.
Auerbach, J. S.	Essays and Miscellanies. Vol. 3.
Bennett, Arnold.	Savour of Life.
Bourne, R. S.	History of a Literary Radical.
Boyd, Ernest.	Portraits.
Boynton, Percy.	Some Contemporary Americans.
Drake, W. A.	American Criticism.
Dudley, D.	Forgotten Frontiers; Dreiser and the Land of the Free.
Duffus, R. L.	American Criticism.
Foerster, Norman (ed.)	Humanism and America.
Hastings, W. T. (ed.)	Contemporary Essays.
Hazard, L. L.	The Frontier in American Literature.
Karsner, D.	Sixteen Authors to One.
Mallory, H. S. (ed.)	Backgrounds of Book Reviewing.
McDonald, Edward D.	Bibliography of the Writings of Theodore Dreiser. (1928)
Mencken, H. L.	Book of Prefaces.
	Prejudices, Second Series.
Munson, G. B.	Destinations.
Rascoe, Burton.	Theodore Dreiser.
Sherman, S. P.	Main Stream.
	On Contemporary Literature.
Squire, J. C.	Contemporary American Authors.
Whipple, T. K.	Spokesmen: Modern Writers and American Life.

[403]

PERIODICALS

Catholic World   132: 1 (1930).
Commonweal   12: 626 (1930).
Dial   62: 343, 507 (1917);   80: 331 (1926).
Forum   81: 65 (1929).
Living Age   331: 43 (1926);   339: 375 (1930).
Mentor   18: 38 (1930).
Nation   101: 648 (1915);   122: 152 (1926);   132: 613 (1931).
New Republic   46: 113 (1926).
North American Review   207: 902 (1918).
Saturday Review   142: 522 (1926).
Saturday Review of Literature   2: 475 (1925);   7: 875 (1931).
Spectator   118: 139 (1917).

ELIOT, GEORGE, Pseud. [Mary Ann Evans]

Born at Arbury farm, Chilvers Coton, Warwickshire, England, November, 1819. Educated at boarding schools until the age of seventeen, when her mother died and she took complete charge of her father's house. In 1851 became assistant editor of the *Westminster Review*. In 1854 she entered into a connection with George Henry Lewes which she always regarded as a marriage, although it had not legal sanction. Her first novel, *Scenes of Clerical Life*, appeared in 1858. Her greatest success came with the publication of *Adam Bede* in 1859. She studied in Florence, Italy, in preparation for *Romola*, which appeared as a serial in the *Cornhill Magazine* from July, 1862, to August, 1863. In addition to her novels she wrote some poems, translations, and essays. She wrote no more after Lewes's death in 1878. In May, 1880, she married J. W. Cross, and died in December, 1880.

BIBLIOGRAPHY

Novels

Scenes of Clerical Life. 1858. (Everyman's Library, Dutton, 1910)
Adam Bede. 1859. (Everyman's Library, Dutton, 1906)
The Mill on the Floss. 1860. (Everyman's Library, Dutton, 1908)
Silas Marner. 1861. (Everyman's Library, Dutton, 1907)
Romola. 1863. (Everyman's Library, Dutton, 1909)

Bibliography

Felix Holt. 1866. (Everyman's Library, Dutton, 1909)
The Spanish Gypsy. 1868. (Houghton, 1906)
Middlemarch. 1872. (Macmillan, 1926)
Daniel Deronda. 1876. (Home Library, 1901)

Studies and Reviews

BOOKS

Bassett, J. J.	The Purpose in George Eliot's Art.
Berle, L. W.	George Eliot and Thomas Hardy.
Blind, M.	George Eliot.
Bonnell, H. H.	Charlotte Brontë, George Eliot, Jane Austen. Studies in Their Work.
Bridges, H. J.	As I Was Saying.
Browning, O.	Life of George Eliot.
Cooke, G. W.	George Eliot.
Cournos, J.	Modern Plutarch.
Cross, J. W. (ed.)	Life of George Eliot.
Dannhäuser, P.	Die Dorfschilderung bei George Eliot und ihren Vorgängern.
Deakin, M. H.	Early Life of George Eliot.
Fremantle, A.	George Eliot.
Gosse, Sir Edmund.	Aspects and Impressions.
Haldane, E.	George Eliot and Her Times.
Hind, C. L.	More Authors and I.
Hutton, R. H.	Essays.
	Modern Guides of English Thought.
Jacob, J.	George Eliot.
James, Henry.	Notes and Reviews.
	Partial Portraits.
Lösch, O.	Das Naturgefühl bei George Eliot und Thomas Hardy.
May, J. L.	George Eliot: A Study.
Morley, J. M.	Critical Miscellanies.
Myers, F. W. H.	Essays.
Paterson, A.	George Eliot's Family.
Pfeiffer, S.	George Eliots Beziehungen zu Deutschland.
Pond, E. J.	Les idées morales et religieuses de George Eliot.
Romieu, E., and G.	The Life of George Eliot.

[405]

Simon-Baumann, L.	Die Darstellung der Charaktere in George Eliots Romanen.
Stephen, Sir Leslie.	George Eliot.
Toyoda, M.	Studies in the Mental Development of George Eliot.
Van Dyke, H.	Companionable Books.
Willcocks, M. P.	Between the Old World and the New.
Woolf, Virginia.	The Common Reader.

PERIODICALS

Atlantic Monthly   18: 479 (1866);   136: 659 (1925).
Blackwood's Magazine   133: 524 (1883).
Century   23: 57 (1881);   104: 642 (1922).
Contemporary Review   116: 600 (1919).
Cornhill Magazine   43: 152 (1917).
Dial   1: 181 (1880).
Fortnightly Review   112: 883 (1919).
Independent   108: 263 (1922).
Living Age   58: 274 (1858);   115: 100 (1872);   142: 123 (1879);   148: 318, 381, 608, 651, 664, 731 (1881);   155: 211 (1882);   164: 638 (1885);   302: 595 (1919);   303: 416, 704 (1919).
Nation   31: 456 (1880);   32: 201 (1881);   109: 683 (1919).
National Review   1: 260 (1883);   11: 191 (1888).
North American Review   210: 837 (1919).
Outlook   58: 62 (1926).
Quarterly Review   108: 469 (1860).
Saturday Review of Literature   2: 97 (1925);   3: 777 (1927).
Spectator   58: 151 (1886).
Studies in Philology   27: 25 (1930).
Westminster Review   110: 105 (1878);   124: 161 (1885).
Yale Review   N.S. 9: 256 (1920).

FAULKNER, WILLIAM

Born in Ripley, Mississippi, in October, 1897, the descendant of distinguished Southern ancestors including governors, generals, and at least one author. He attended the University of Mississippi for two years, leaving when the Great War broke out, to join the Canadian Flying Corps. He was severely wounded in a plane

Bibliography

crash and was promoted to the rank of Lieutenant. At the end of the war he spent several months tramping through Europe. Returning to the United States he went to New Orleans, where he shared an apartment with Sherwood Anderson. He began to devote all his time to writing, occasionally having to resort to manual labor to eke out a livelihood. His first publication was a volume of poems, *The Marble Faun*, which appeared in 1924. While engaged in the writing of his first novel, *Soldier's Pay*, which was published in 1926, he contributed a number of sketches to the Sunday edition of the *Times-Picayune*. In 1929 he married Estelle Oldham Franklin. *The Sound and the Fury*, published in 1929, startled his critics and confused many readers, since part of the story is recorded by the idiot son of the Southern family whose retrogression is the theme of the novel. *As I Lay Dying* (1930), *Sanctuary* (1931), and *Light in August* (1932) also deal with abnormal and perverted Southerners.

BIBLIOGRAPHY

Novels

Soldier's Pay. 1926. (Boni & Liveright, 1926)
Mosquitoes. 1927. (Boni & Liveright, 1927)
Sartoris. 1929. (Harcourt, 1929)
The Sound and the Fury. 1929. (Cape and Harrison Smith, 1929)
As I Lay Dying. 1930. (Cape, 1930)
Sanctuary. 1931. (Chatto, 1933)
Light in August. 1932. (Smith, Haas, 1932)

Short Stories

These 13. 1931. (Cape, 1931)

Studies and Reviews

BOOKS

Scott, E.   On William Faulkner's *The Sound and the Fury*.

PERIODICALS

American Mercury   25: 24 (1932).
Bookman   74: 17, 411 (1932);   75: 736 (1932).
Commonweal   17: 139 (1930).
Forum   86: 10 (1931);   88: 6 (1932).

Nation   133: 491 (1931);   135: 402 (1932).
New Republic   51: 236 (1927);   68: 271 (1931);   72: 300 (1932).
North American Review   235: 66 (1933).
Outlook   151: 311 (1929);   153: 268 (1929).
Saturday Review of Literature   3: 933 (1927);   6: 601 (1929); 8: 201 (1931);   9: 153 (1932).

FIELDING, HENRY

Born at Sharpham Park, near Glastonbury, Somerset, on April 22nd, 1707, son of Lieutenant Edmund Fielding, a grandson of the Earl of Desmond. Up to the time of his mother's death he was educated by a clergyman; afterwards he went to Eton. He began to write plays and his first comedy, *Love in Several Masques*, was produced at Drury Lane in 1728. He took a course of studies at Leyden University soon after. Continuing as a playwright, his two most successful attempts were *The Author's Farce* (1730) and *Tom Thumb* (1730). In 1734 he married Charlotte Craddock of Salisbury. In 1736 he became manager of the Haymarket Theatre and met with pronounced success, but, failing to secure the Lord Chamberlain's license, was obliged to abandon his career as a theatrical producer in 1737. He began the study of law in the same year, and during this period did a considerable amount of literary work. In 1740 he was called to the bar. He traveled the Western Circuit and attended the Wiltshire sessions. He still wrote at intervals and is credited with the authorship of the famous *Apology for the Life of Mrs. Shamela Andrews* (1741), a parody of Richardson's *Pamela*, although his authorship of this has never been proven. His first novel, *Joseph Andrews* (1742), was intended to ridicule Richardson's *Pamela*, but the element of parody fell into the background as Fielding's interest in his theme grew. He next published three volumes of *Miscellanies* (1743), consisting partially of essays and verse, but containing also the *History of the Life of the Late Mr. Jonathan Wild, the Great*. Meanwhile his wife had died of fever, and in 1747 he married his wife's maid. In the following year he was made a principal justice of the peace for Middlesex and Westminster. His most famous novel, *Tom Jones; or, the History of a Foundling*, was published in the same year. While engaged in his literary work he was also taking his duties as a magistrate seriously and published an *Enquiry into the Causes of the Late Increase of Robbers* in 1751. In 1752 *Amelia* appeared. His strenuous labors caused a physical breakdown and he was compelled to abandon his legal work. He started on a voyage to Lisbon early in 1754, and died in August, 1754, two months after he reached Lisbon. His pamphlet, *Journal of a Voyage to Lisbon*, was published posthumously.

BIBLIOGRAPHY

Novels

The History of the Adventures of Joseph Andrews. 1742. (Everyman's Library, Dutton)
The Life of the Late Mr. Jonathan Wild, the Great. 1743. (Greenberg, 1926)
The History of Tom Jones, a Foundling. 1749. (Everyman's Library, Dutton)
Amelia. 1752. (Everyman's Library, Dutton)

Studies and Reviews

BOOKS

Banerji, H. K.	Henry Fielding, Playwright, Journalist and Master of the Art of Fiction. His Life and Works.
Binz-Winiger, E.	Erziehungsfragen in den Romanen von Richardson, Fielding, etc.
Bissell, F. O.	Fielding's Theory of the Novel.
Blanchard, F. T.	The Novels of Fielding.
	Fielding the Novelist.
Cross, W. L.	The History of Henry Fielding.
	Introduction to *The History of Tom Jones*. (Knopf, 1924).
De Castro, J. Paul.	Fielding's Invocation to Fame.
Digeon, A.	The Novels of Fielding.
Dobson, Austin.	Henry Fielding. (English Men of Letters Series)
	Henry Fielding, a Memoir.
Farnelli, G.	Henry Fielding e la sua epoca.
Godden, G. M.	Henry Fielding: A Memoir.
Green, Emanuel.	Henry Fielding, his Works. An Independent Criticism.

Hazlitt, W.	Lectures on English Comic Writers.
Lawrence, Frederick.	Life of Henry Fielding.
Macy, J. A.	Introduction to *The History of Tom Jones*. (Brentano)
Murphy, Arthur.	Life and Genius of Fielding.
Radtke, Bruno.	Henry Fielding als Kritiker.
Roscoe, Thomas.	Introduction to The Works of Fielding, Smollet and Swift.
Saintsbury, George.	Introduction to *Complete Novels of Henry Fielding*. (Bigelow, Brown, 1928) Introduction to *Complete Works of Henry Fielding*. 12 volumes. (Macmillan) Introduction to *The History of Joseph Andrews*. (Dutton, 1912)
Scott, Sir Walter.	Life of Henry Fielding.
Stephen, Sir Leslie.	Biographical Essay in 1882 Edition of *Works*.
Thackeray, W. M.	English Humourists of the Eighteenth Century.
Thornbury, E. M.	Henry Fielding's Theory of the Comic Prose Epic.

PERIODICALS

Athenæum 2: 304 (1883).
Blackwood's Magazine 181: 550 (1907).
Bookman 42: 389 (1915); 48: 20 (1918).
Century Magazine 110: 115 (1925).
Edinburgh Review 243: 336 (1926).
Fortnightly Review 87: 620 (1907).
Living Age 47: 769 (1855); 121: 643 (1874); 133: 3 (1877); 229: 793 (1901).
Modern Language Notes 42: 32, 165 (1927).
North American Review 68: 41 (1849).
Notes and Queries 156: 342 (1929).
Quarterly Review 34: 349 (1826); 98: 100 (1855); 103: 66 (1858); 163: 34 (1886).
Saturday Review of Literature 1: 905 (1925).
South Atlantic Quarterly 8: 222 (1909).
Yale Review 8: 107 (1918).

Bibliography

GALSWORTHY, JOHN

Born in 1867, at Coombe in Surrey, of an old Devonshire family. Educated at Harrow and New College, Oxford, where he was graduated with an honor degree in law. He was called to the Bar in 1890, but after practicing for a short time he gave it up and began extended travels. He framed the material which he had gathered into stories and published them under the name of "John Sinjohn." It was on one of his sea trips that he made the acquaintance of the then unknown Joseph Conrad, and encouraged him to devote himself to writing. Galsworthy's first novel, *Jocelyn*, was published in 1898. The first suggestion of the *Forsyte Saga* novels appeared in 1901, under the title *Salvation of a Forsyte*. Since that date he has written a number of novels, culminating in the *Forsyte Saga*, as well as essays and sketches, and a large group of plays. In 1918 he refused a knighthood. In 1929 the Order of Merit was bestowed on him and in 1932 he received the Nobel Prize. He died on January 31st, 1933.

BIBLIOGRAPHY

Novels

Jocelyn. 1898. (Duckworth, 1899)
Villa Rubein. 1900. (Scribner, 1916)
A Man of Devon. 1901. (o.p.)
The Island Pharisees. 1904. (Scribner, 1926)
The Man of Property. 1906. (Scribner, 1925)
The Country House. 1907. (Scribner, 1926)
Fraternity. 1909. (Scribner, 1926)
The Patrician. 1911. (Scribner, 1918)
The Dark Flower. 1913. (Scribner, 1927)
The Freelands. 1915. (Scribner, 1915)
Beyond. 1917. (Scribner, 1927)
Saint's Progress. 1919. (Scribner, 1919)
In Chancery. 1920. (Scribner, 1920)
Awakening. 1920. (Scribner, 1920)
To Let. 1921. (Scribner, 1921)
The Forsyte Saga. 1922. (Scribner, 1922)
(Containing *The Man of Property*, *Indian Summer of a Forsyte*, *In Chancery*, *Awakening*, and *To Let*)
The White Monkey. 1924. (Scribner, 1924)

The Silver Spoon. 1926. (Scribner, 1926)
Swan Song. 1928. (Scribner, 1928)
Maid in Waiting. 1931. (Scribner, 1931)
Flowering Wilderness. 1932. (Scribner, 1932)
One More River. 1933. (Published posthumously, Scribner, 1933)

Short Stories

From the Four Winds. 1897. (Unwin, 1897)
A Motley. 1910. (Scribner, 1910)
The Little Man and Other Satires. 1915. (Scribner, 1915)
Five Tales. 1918. (Scribner, 1918)
The Burning Spear. 1919. (Scribner, 1919)
Captures. 1923. (Scribner, 1923)
Abracadabra. 1924. (Scribner, 1924)
Caravan. 1925. (Scribner, 1925)
    (Containing *Salvation of a Forsyte*, first written in 1901)
Two Forsyte Interludes. 1927. (Scribner, 1927)
    (Containing *Silent Wooing* and *Passers By*)
On Forsyte 'Change. 1930. (Scribner, 1930)

Studies and Reviews

BOOKS

Conrad, Joseph	Last Essays.
Cooper, F. T.	Some English Story Tellers.
Cross, W. L.	Four Contemporary Novelists.
	English Association, Essays and Studies. Vol. 4.
Ervine, St. J.	Some Impressions of My Elders.
Harris, Frank	Contemporary Portraits, Third Series.
Hind, C. L.	Authors and I.
Kaye-Smith, S.	John Galsworthy.
Mais, S. P. B.	Some Modern Authors.
Marrot, H. V.	Bibliography of the Works of John Galsworthy. (1928)
Phelps, W. L.	The Advance of the English Novel.
Schalit, L.	John Galsworthy.
Skemp, A. R.	See English Association.
Waugh, Alec.	Tradition and Change.

Bibliography

PERIODICALS

American Mercury 5: 375 (1925).
Dial 59: 201 (1915).
Edinburgh Review 241: 271 (1925).
Living Age 264: 607 (1910); 331: 90 (1926).
London Mercury 8: 393 (1923).
Nation 89: 520 (1909); 98: 582 (1914).
New Republic 48: 25 (1926).
New Statesman 19: 265 (1922).
North American Review 202: 889 (1915); 215: 255 (1922).
Saturday Review 142: 200 (1926).
Spectator 137: 314 (1926).
Yale Review N.S. 14: 126 (1924).

GISSING, GEORGE ROBERT

Born at Wakefield, England, on November 22nd, 1857. Educated at the Quaker Boarding School of Alderly Edge, and at Owens College, Manchester, where he distinguished himself by his extreme sensitivity and aloofness no less than by academic success. Following a breakdown from overwork, and an affair which severed his connection with the College, he traveled for five years in the United States, where, though absolutely penniless, he married. In 1877 he returned to Europe, spending a year and a half at Jena reading philosophy and writing his first novel, *Workers in the Dawn*, which appeared in England in 1880. He managed to live on a meager tutorship, scorning journalism, and regarding himself as a social outlaw. His next novels, *The Unclassed*, *Demos*, and *Thyrza*, are based on the degrading effects of poverty on character. After a visit to the lands of classical antiquity, financed by the proceeds from his first success, *Demos*, he published *The Nether World* (1889), a study in slow starvation, and *New Grub Street* (1891), a description of his impressions of the United States, which are among his best works. His income increasing, he was able to live outside of London, marry a second time on the death of his first wife, and, in 1897, to revisit Italy, after which he wrote *By the Ionian Sea*. His health failing, he moved to Paris, and then to St. Jean de Luz, where he died on December 28th, 1903, leaving his unfinished historical novel, *Veranilda*, a romance, *Will Warburton*, and collections of short stories to be published posthumously. His works consist of his

[413]

many novels (the best known of which, *The Private Papers of Henry Ryecroft*, was published the year of his death), several volumes of short stories, critical works on Charles Dickens, and an unpublished collection of letters to members of his family.

BIBLIOGRAPHY

Novels

Workers in the Dawn. 1880. (Rudge, 1930)
The Unclassed. 1884. (Benn, 1930)
Demos. 1886. (Nash, 1930)
Isabel Clarendon. 1886. (o.p.)
Thyrza. 1887. (Nash, 1930)
A Life's Morning. 1888. (Nash, 1930)
The Nether World. 1889. (Nash, 1930)
The Emancipated. 1890. (o.p.)
New Grub Street. 1891. (Modern Library, 1926)
Born in Exile. 1892. (o.p.)
Denzil Quarrier. 1892. (o.p.)
The Odd Women. 1893. (Sidgwick, 1911)
In the Year of Jubilee. 1894. (o.p.)
Eve's Ransom. 1895. (Benn's Essex Library, 1929)
The Paying Guest. 1895. (o.p.)
Sleeping Fires. 1895. (Unwin, 1927)
The Whirlpool. 1897. (o.p.)
The Town Traveller. 1898. (Methuen, 1927)
The Crown of Life. 1889. (Methuen, 1927)
Our Friend the Charlatan. 1901. (o.p.)
The Private Papers of Henry Ryecroft. 1903. (Dutton, 1927)
Veranilda. 1904. (Oxford, 1929)
Will Warburton: A Romance of Real Life. 1905. (Dutton, 1905)

Short Stories

Human Odds and Ends. 1897. (Sidgwick, 1911)
*Brownie. (Columbia University Press, 1931)
House of Cobwebs, and Other Stories. 1906. (Constable, 1931)
*Short Stories of Today and Yesterday. (Harrap, 1929)

* Originally published in periodicals.

Bibliography

*Sins of the Fathers and Other Tales. (Covici, 1924)
*A Victim of Circumstances. (Houghton, 1927)

Miscellaneous Works

Introduction to *The Rochester Edition of Charles Dickens*. 1903.
Critical Studies of the Works of Charles Dickens [with an Introduction and Bibliography of Gissing by Temple Scott]. (Greenberg, 1924)
Letters to Members of his Family, Collected and Arranged by A. and E. Gissing, with a Preface by his Son. (Constable, 1931)

Studies and Reviews

BOOKS

Cazamian, M. L.	Roman et Idées en Angleterre.
Clodd, E.	Memories.
Cunliffe, J. W.	English Literature during the Last Half Century.
Harrison, Frederic.	Introduction to *Veranilda*.
Miles, H.	George Gissing; a Critical Study.
More, P. E.	Shelburne Essays, Fifth Series.
Roberts, M. (ed.)	The Private Life of Henry Maitland.
Rotter, A.	Frank Swinnerton und Georg Gissing.
Seccombe, T.	Introduction to *The House of Cobwebs*. (1906)
Swinnerton, F. A.	George Gissing.
Yates, M.	George Gissing.

PERIODICALS

Blackwood's Magazine   225: 653 (1929).
Bookman   63: 683 (1926);   72: 309 (1927);   76: 9 (1929).
Contemporary Review   128: 82 (1925).
Independent   118: 391 (1927).
Living Age   315: 361 (1922).
Nation   40: 722 (1927).
New Republic   50: 49 (1927).
New Statesman   33: 12 (1929).
Nineteenth Century   40: 453 (1906);   102: 417 (1927).
North American Review   216: 364, 691 (1922).

*Originally published in periodicals.

[415]

Appendix

Owens College Union Magazine   January, 1904.
Saturday Review of Literature   3: 821, 980 (1927);   4: 26 (1927).

HARDY, THOMAS

Born in Dorsetshire on June 2nd, 1840, of Jersey descent. He was educated at local schools until 1854 and afterwards privately, and in 1856 was articled to an ecclesiastical architect. In 1859 he began to write poems and essays, but in 1861 he was compelled to apply himself more closely to architecture, sketching and measuring a number of old Dorset churches with a view to their restoration. In 1862 he became assistant to Sir Arthur Blomfield, a London architect. In 1863 he won the medal of the Royal Institute of British Architects for an essay on *Coloured Brick and Terra-cotta Architecture*, and in the same year won the prize of the Architectural Association for design. In 1865 his first short story was published in *Chambers' Journal* and during the next three years he wrote a number of poems. In 1867 he wrote a story and submitted it to Chapman and Hall. George Meredith read the manuscript and advised Hardy not to publish it but to write another story with more plot. Acting on Meredith's advice he wrote *Desperate Remedies*, which was published in 1871. In the following year *Under the Greenwood Tree* was published. In 1874 he married Emma Lavinia Gifford. His first popular success was made by *Far from the Madding Crowd* (1874), which had previously appeared anonymously in the *Cornhill Magazine*. *The Return of the Native* (1878) and *Tess of the D'Urbervilles* (1891) are his most famous novels. The Order of Merit was conferred on him in 1910, and in his later years he received increasing recognition, not only as a novelist, but as a poet, until he was recognized as the sovereign of English letters. His epic-drama, *The Dynasts*, was produced in part at the Kingsway Theatre, London, during the early years of the Great War, and again at Oxford in 1920. From 1909 until his death Hardy wrote nothing but lyrical poetry. Five volumes of poetry were published between 1910 and 1925. His latest collection of poems, *Winter Words*, was published posthumously. Hardy's first wife died in 1912, and in 1914 he married Florence Emily Dugdale, a writer of children's books and a contributor to periodicals. He died on January 12th, 1928, and while his ashes were buried in Westminster Abbey, his heart was buried in the parish churchyard of his native Wessex.

BIBLIOGRAPHY

Novels

Desperate Remedies: A Novel. 1871. (Harper, 1896)
Under the Greenwood Tree. 1872. (Harper, 1896)
A Pair of Blue Eyes: A Novel. 1873. (Harper, 1895)
Far from the Madding Crowd. 1874. (Harper, 1895)
The Hand of Ethelberta: A Comedy. 1876. (Harper, 1895)
The Return of the Native. 1878. (Harper, 1895)
The Trumpet-Major. 1880. (Harper, 1895)
A Laodicean; or The Castle of the De Stancys. 1882. (Harper, 1921)
Two on a Tower. 1882. (Harper, 1895)
The Mayor of Casterbridge: The Life and Death of a Man of Character. 1886. (Harper, 1922)
The Woodlanders. 1887. (Harper, 1904)
Tess of the D'Urbervilles. 1891. (Harper, 1921)
Jude the Obscure. 1895. (Harper, 1923)
The Well-Beloved: A Sketch of Temperament. 1897. (Harper, 1920)
The Poor Man and the Lady. (Not published)

Short Stories

Wessex Tales: Strange, Lively and Commonplace. 1888. (Harper, 1901)
A Group of Noble Dames. 1891. (Harper, 1919)
Life's Little Ironies, A Set of Tales. 1894. (Harper, 1921)
A Changed Man, The Waiting Supper, and Other Tales, Concluding with The Romantic Adventures of a Milkmaid. 1913. (Harper, 1913)

Studie and Reviews

BOOKS

Abercrombie, L.	Thomas Hardy.
Archer, W.	Real Conversations.
Beach, J. W.	Technique of Thomas Hardy.
Berle, L. W.	George Eliot and Thomas Hardy.
Boyd, Ernest.	Literary Blasphemies.
Braybrooke, P.	Thomas Hardy and His Philosophy.

Brennecke, E.	Life of Thomas Hardy.
	Thomas Hardy's Universe.
Canby, H. S.	American Estimates.
	Definitions. Series One.
Chase, M. E.	Thomas Hardy, From Serial to Novels.
Chew, S. C.	Thomas Hardy, Poet and Novelist.
Child, H. H.	Thomas Hardy.
Collins, V. H.	Talks with Thomas Hardy at Max Gate.
De Casseres, B.	Forty Immortals.
Dobrée, B.	The Lamp and the Lute.
Duffin, H. C.	Thomas Hardy.
English Association.	Pamphlet No. 71. (See Fowler, J. H.)
Exideuil, P. d'.	The Human Pair in the Work of Hardy.
Firor, R. A.	Folkways in Thomas Hardy.
Fitch, C. H.	Modern English Books of Power.
Fowler, J. H.	Novels of Thomas Hardy.
Freeman, John.	The Moderns.
Garwood, Helen.	Thomas Hardy, an Illustration of Schopenhauer.
Gorman, H. S.	Procession of Masts.
Hardy, Florence E.	The Early Life of Thomas Hardy, 1840–1891.
	The Later Years of Thomas Hardy, 1892–1928.
Harper, C. G.	The Hardy Country.
	Spirit of Delight.
Harris, Frank.	Latest Contemporary Portraits.
Hedgecock, F. A.	Thomas Hardy, Penseur et Artiste.
Hind, C. L.	Authors and I.
Hopkins, R. T.	Thomas Hardy's Dorset.
Johnson, L. P.	Art of Thomas Hardy.
Lea, H.	Thomas Hardy's Wessex.
Lynd, Robert.	Old and New Masters
Macy, J. A.	Critical Game.
Massingham, H. J., and Massingham, H. (eds.)	Great Victorians.

Bibliography

McDonald, A.   Thomas Hardy.
McDowall, A. S   Thomas Hardy, A Critical Study.
Murry, J. M.   Wrap Me Up in My Aubusson Carpet.
Newton, A. E.   Thomas Hardy, Novelist or Poet?
Powys, J. C.   Visions and Revisions.
Powys, L.   Thirteen Worthies.
Ralli, A. J.   Critiques.
Reilly, J. J.   Dear Prue's Husband.
Sime, J. G.   Thomas Hardy of the Wessex Novels.
Smith, L. W., and others (eds.)   Ventures in Contemporary Reading.
Strong, A. T.   Four Studies.
Tomlinson, H. M.   Thomas Hardy.
Utter, R. P.   Pearls and Pepper.
West, Rebecca.   Two Kinds of Memory.
Willcocks, M. P.   Between the Old World and the New.
Woolf, Virginia.   The Second Common Reader.
Van Dyke, H.   The Man Behind the Book.

PERIODICALS

Academy   55: 251 (1898).
Atlantic Monthly   98: 354 (1906);   120: 359 (1917).
Blackwood's Magazine   193: 823 (1913).
Bookman   64: 720 (1927);   67: 134 (1928).
Catholic World   126: 121 (1928);   128: 407 (1929).
Century   109: 418 (1925).
Contemporary Review   56: 57 (1889).
Current History   27: 829 (1928).
Dial   86: 150 (1929).
Edinburgh Review   215: 93 (1912).
English Association   Pamphlet No. 69.
Fortnightly Review   107: 464 (1917);   129: 205 (1928).
Forum   71: 783 (1924);   79: 436 (1928).
Literary Review   4: 801 (1924).
Living Age   240: 507   (1904);   296: 202   (1918);   302: 175 (1919);   313: 52 (1922);   318: 516 (1923);   324: 303 (1925); 325: 98 (1925).

London Quarterly Review   91: 223 (1899).
Nation   118: 38 (1924).
New Republic   12: 47 (1917);   23: 22 (1920);   25: 190 (1921);
38: 77 (1924);   54: 71 (1928).
Nineteenth Century   77: 644 (1915).
North American Review   194: 96 (1911);   199: 120 (1914);
201: 423 (1915);   220: 330 (1924).
Quarterly Review   199: 499 (1904);   210: 193 (1909);   253:
313 (1929).
Saturday Review   128: 459 (1919).
Saturday Review of Literature   1: 808 (1925);   3: 576 (1927).
Yale Review   13: 322 (1924);   15: 515 (1926);   20: 175
(1930).

HAWTHORNE, NATHANIEL

Born in Salem, Massachusetts, on July 4th, 1804, of New England stock. As a result of an accident at the age of nine, he was educated privately in early life. He entered Bowdoin College in 1821, in the same class with Longfellow. He was graduated in 1825 and determined upon literature as a profession. His first efforts were unsuccessful. *Fanshawe*, his earliest book, was published anonymously in 1828. In 1836 he edited the *American Magazine of Useful and Entertaining Knowledge*. He married Sophia Peabody on July 9th, 1842. His first long novel, *The Scarlet Letter*, was published in 1850, and was received with enthusiasm. In 1853 he was appointed to the Consulship of Liverpool, and spent four years in England. Finding this position a hindrance to his literary career, he resigned in 1857, and spent the next year in Italy. He returned to America in 1860. While traveling for his health, he died at Plymouth, New Hampshire, on May 18th, 1864. His works consist of novels, short stories, tales for children, sketches of life and travel, and some miscellaneous pieces of a biographical or descriptive character.

BIBLIOGRAPHY

Novels

Fanshawe. 1828. (o.p.)
The Scarlet Letter. 1850. (Everyman's Library, Dutton, 1907)

Bibliography

The House of the Seven Gables. 1851. (Everyman's Library, Dutton, 1907)

The Blithedale Romance. 1852. (Everyman's Library, Dutton, 1912)

The Marble Faun, or The Romance of Monte Beni. 1860. (Everyman's Library, Dutton, 1910)

Septimius Felton. 1872. (Little Classic Edition, 1928)

The Dolliver Romance. 1876. (Riverside Edition, 1928)

Doctor Grimshawe's Secret. 1883. (Riverside Edition, 1928)

Short Stories

Twice Told Tales. 1837. (Everyman's Library, Dutton, 1911)

Mosses From an Old Manse. 1846. (Home Library, 1928)

A Wonder Book for Girls and Boys. 1852. (Home Library, 1928)

Tanglewood Tales for Girls and Boys. 1853. (Home Library, 1928)

Studies and Reviews

BOOKS

Arvin, N.	Hawthorne.
Arvin, N. (ed.)	The Heart of Hawthorne's Journals.
Beers, H. A.	Four Americans.
Birrell, A.	Et Cetera.
Bridge, Horatio.	Personal Recollections of Nathaniel Hawthorne.
Browne, N. E.	A Bibliography of Nathaniel Hawthorne.
Brownell, W. C.	American Prose Masters.
Canby, H. S.	Classic Americans.
Carman, Bliss.	Hawthorne.
Chandler, E. L.	A Study of the Sources of the Tales and Romances Written by Nathaniel Hawthorne before 1853.
Conway, M. D.	Life of Nathaniel Hawthorne.
Curl, V.	Pasteboard Masks.
De Casseres, B.	Forty Immortals.
Dhaleine, L.	Nathaniel Hawthorne: sa vie et son œuvre.
Erskine, John.	Leading American Novelists.
Fields, A.	Nathaniel Hawthorne.
Fitch, G. H.	Great Spiritual Writers of America.

Frye, P. H.	Literary Reviews and Criticisms.
Gorman, H. S.	Hawthorne: A Study in Solitude.
Green, Julien.	Un puritain homme de lettres: Nathaniel Hawthorne.
Hawthorne, H.	Romantic Rebel.
Hawthorne, J.	Hawthorne and His Circle.
Howells, W. D.	My Literary Passions.
Hutton, R. H.	Literary Essays.
James, Henry.	Nathaniel Hawthorne.
Lathrop, R.	A Study of Hawthorne.
Lawrence, D. H.	Studies in Classic American Literature.
Mabie, H. W.	Backgrounds of Literature.
Macy, J. A.	The Spirit of American Literature.
Morris, Lloyd.	The Rebellious Puritan: Portrait of Mr. Hawthorne.
Pancoast, Henry S.	An Introduction to American Literature.
Perry, B.	Parkstreet Papers.
Read, H. E.	The Sense of Glory.
Reenan, William.	Hawthorne's "Marble Faun."
Sherman, S. P.	Americans.
Stearn, F. P.	The Life and Genius of Nathaniel Hawthorne.
Stephen, Sir Leslie	Hours in a Library.
Ticknor, Caroline.	Hawthorne and His Publisher.
Ward, A. C.	American Literature, 1880–1930.
Winterich, J. T.	Books and the Man.
Woodberry, G. E.	Literary Memoirs of the Nineteenth Century.
	Nathaniel Hawthorne.

PERIODICALS

American Literature   3: 72 (1931).
Archiv   N.S. 53: 161 (1928).
Bookman   65: 551 (1927);   74: 401 (1931).
English Review   28: 404 (1919).
Hound and Horn   3: 213 (1930).
Living Age   25: 203 (1850); 33: 17 (1852); 34: 327 (1852);
   116: 195 (1873);   231: 720 (1901).
New Republic   54: 399 (1928);   61: 281 (1930).
New Statesman   19: 68 (1922).

Bibliography

North American Review   129: 203 (1879).
Outlook   149: 650 (1928).
Saturday Review of Literature   3: 727, 866, 916 (1927).
Studies in Philology   23: 40 (1926).

HEMINGWAY, ERNEST

Born in Oak Park, Illinois, on July 21st, 1898, the son of a doctor. He was educated in the public schools of Michigan, where he was popular for his prowess as a football player and a boxer. He reported on the *Kansas City Star* for a few months, when he went to France as a volunteer in an American ambulance unit. Later he enlisted in the Italian Arditi, served on the Italian front and was seriously wounded. He received two of the highest military honors from the Italian Government, the *Medaglia d'Argento al Valore Militare* and the *Croce de Guerra*. When he returned to the United States he married and entered newspaper work. The following year he was a reporter on the *Toronto Daily Star*, became its European correspondent, and reported a number of disturbances in the Near East and in Greece, after which he went to Paris as a correspondent for William Hearst's syndicated news. He became a well-known figure in Paris, both for his interest in sport and his literary activities. He was unusually interested in bull-fighting, which interest is reflected in two of his books, *The Sun Also Rises* (1926), and *Death in the Afternoon* (1932), the latter being a study of bull-fighting. His first publication was a volume of stories and poems, *Three Stories and Ten Poems*, published in Paris in 1923. His best-known novel is *A Farewell to Arms* (1929). The volume of his published work is small, but he has had more imitators than almost any other modern writer. He was married for a second time in 1927. He has been living in Florida since his return from Paris.

BIBLIOGRAPHY

Novels

The Sun Also Rises. 1926. (Scribner, 1926)
Torrents of Spring: A Romantic Novel in Honor of the Passing
    of a Great Race. 1926. (Scribner, 1926)
A Farewell to Arms. 1929. (Modern Library, 1932)
Death in the Afternoon. 1932 (Scribner, 1932)

Short Stories

In Our Time. 1925. (Scribner, 1930)
Men Without Women. 1927. (Scribner, 1927)

Studies and Reviews

BOOKS

Beach, J. W.	The Outlook for American Prose.
	The Twentieth Century Novel.
Cohn, L. H.	Bibliography of the Works of Ernest Hemingway.
Ford, Ford Madox.	Introduction to *A Farewell to Arms*. (Modern Library Edition)
Rosenfeld, P.	By Way of Art.
Ward, A. C.	American Literature 1880–1930.
Wilson, Edmund.	Introduction to *In Our Time*. (Scribner, 1930)

PERIODICALS

Bookman   70: 258, 641 (1929).
Calendar of Modern Letters   4: 72 (1927).
Independent   116: 694 (1926);   117: 594 (1926).
Nation   123: 642 (1926);   125: 548 (1927).
New Republic   45: 22 (1925);   48: 101 (1926);   49: 142 (1926);   51: 303 (1927);   53: 102 (1927);   60: 208 (1929).
North American Review   232: 364 (1931).
Saturday Review of Literature   3: 420 (1926);   4: 322 (1927);   6: 231 (1929).

HUXLEY, ALDOUS

Born July 26th, 1894, the third son of Leonard Huxley (eldest son and biographer of the renowned scientist, Thomas Huxley) and Julia Arnold (niece of Matthew Arnold). Attended Eton until he was seventeen when he was forced to leave because of failing eye-sight. When his eyes became better he went to Balliol College, Oxford. In 1919 he joined the editorial staff of *The Athenæum*. That same year he married Maria Nys. He did a great amount of journalistic work including dramatic, musical, and artistic criticism, as well as many reviews of novels and biographical notes. In 1920 he became dramatic critic of the

Bibliography

Westminster Gazette. His first novel, *Crome Yellow*, appeared in 1921. Since then he has been a prolific writer of novels, short stories, essays, and poetry. Of the five novels published to date the best-known is *Point-Counter-Point*, which appeared in 1928. Most of his time is spent in Italy. His latest novel, *Brave New World*, made its appearance in January, 1932.

BIBLIOGRAPHY

Novels

Crome Yellow. 1921. (Phoenix Library, 1930)
Antic Hay. 1923. (Sun Dial Library, 1929)
Those Barren Leaves. 1925. (Phoenix Library, 1930)
Point-Counter-Point. 1928. (Modern Library, 1930)
Brave New World. 1932. (Doubleday, 1932)

Short Stories

Limbo. 1920 (Phoenix Library, 1930)
Mortal Coils. 1922. (Chatto, 1930)
The Little Mexican. 1924. (Chatto, 1930) [American ed. Young Archimedes]
Two or Three Graces. 1926. (Chatto, 1929)
Brief Candles. 1930. (Chatto, 1931)

Studies and Reviews

BOOKS

Adcock, A. St. J.	The Glory That Was Grub Street.
Beach, J. W.	The Twentieth Century Novel.
Collins, Joseph.	Taking the Literary Pulse.
Gould, Gerald.	The English Novel of To-day.
Muir, Edwin.	Transition; Essays on Contemporary Literature.

PERIODICALS

Athenæum   1: 699 (1920).
Canadian Forum   10: 401 (1930).
Current Opinion   68: 830 (1920).
Dial   69: 152 (1920);   72: 630 (1922).
Études   December 20 (1930).
Everyman   16: 255 (1920).

Life and Letters 5: 198 (1930).
Living Age 307: 107 (1920); 332: 158 (1927); 339: 52 (1930).
London Mercury 11: 429 (1925); 15: 391 (1927).
Nation 112: 885 (1921); 114: 349 (1922); 120: 190 (1925); 134: 204 (1932).
New Statesman 19: 156 (1922); 22: 146 (1923).
New Statesman and Nation 3: 172 (1932).
Nouvelles Littéraires July 12, part 1 (1930).
Realist 1: 99 (1929).
Saturday Review 141: 686 (1926); 142: 474 (1926); 153: 152 (1932).
Saturday Review of Literature 5: 637 (1929); 8: 521 (1932).
Spectator 135: 663 (1925); 137: 764 (1926).

JAMES, HENRY

Born in New York City, April, 1843. His youth was spent partly in America, partly in travel on the continent, his education received from tutors, except during brief periods at Geneva, Bonn, and later, Harvard Law School. Debarred by uncertain health from active participation in ordinary life, he found, under the guidance of Charles Eliot Norton and William Dean Howells, an outlet in literature. His first story was published in the *Atlantic Monthly* when he was twenty-one. Throughout an "elegant but fruitful continental vagabondage," centering in Paris and bringing him into contact with Flaubert, Turgénev, Maupassant, Zola, he wrote prolifically, for American publications chiefly, stories, essays critical and discursive, and novels, dealing first as last with the great problem of his own life, the interaction of American and European psychology and environment. His first novel, *Roderick Hudson*, was published in the *Atlantic Monthly*, in 1875. In 1876 James settled in London, later removing to the greater seclusion of Lamb House, Rye. He never married and his close friends in England were Stevenson, Gosse, Sidney Colvin, and A. C. Benson. His attempt at dramatic composition was finally relinquished, an undeniable failure, but the two novels left unfinished at his death testify that James's hand had lost none of its skill. The Great War, which led him to take the step of formally becoming a British subject, a lip service backed by strenuous and valuable work for the Allied cause, ended his creative work and is probably to be blamed for his death in February, 1916. Just two months previously the British Government had paid tribute to his literary distinction by the award of the Order of Merit.

BIBLIOGRAPHY

Novels *

Roderick Hudson. 1876. (Houghton, 1904)
The American. 1877. (Houghton, 1904)
Watch and Ward. 1878. (Macmillan, 1921)
The Europeans. 1878. (Houghton, 1906)
Daisy Miller. 1879
Confidence. 1880. (Houghton, 1906)
Washington Square. 1881. (Harper)
The Portrait of a Lady. 1881. (Macmillan)
The Bostonians. 1886. (Macmillan)
The Princess Casamassima. 1886. (Macmillan)
The Tragic Muse. 1890. (Houghton)
The Other House. 1896. (o.p.)
The Spoils of Poynton. 1897. (Houghton, 1904)
What Maisie Knew. 1897. (Scribner, 1906)
The Awkward Age. 1899. (Harper, 1899)
The Sacred Fount. 1901. (Scribner, 1901)
The Wings of the Dove. 1902. (Scribner, 1902)
The Ambassadors. 1903. (Harper, 1930)
The Golden Bowl. 1904. (Scribner, 1904)
The Outcry. 1911. (Scribner, 1911)
The Ivory Tower. 1917. (Scribner, 1917)
The Sense of the Past. 1917. (Scribner, 1917)

Short Stories

[The novelettes and short stories of Henry James are too numerous to list in a brief bibliography. His most famous short stories *The Turn of the Screw, The Lesson of the Master, The Altar of the Dead*, etc. are available in separate editions. The remainder of his works may be obtained in the collected editions mentioned above.]

* The following collected editions are recommended also:
The Novels and Tales of Henry James. 24v. Scribner, 1907–1909 (Additions vols. 25, 26, 1917).
The Novels and Stories of Henry James. 35v. Macmillan, London, 1921–1923.

Appendix

Miscellaneous Works

French Poets and Novelists. 1878. (Macmillan)
Partial Portraits. 1888. (Macmillan)
Essays in London and Elsewhere. 1893. (Harper)
The Lesson of Balzac and The Question of our Speech. 1905. (Houghton)
A Small Boy and Others. 1913. (Scribner)
Notes of a Son and Brother. 1914. (Macmillan)
Notes on Novelists. 1914. (Scribner)
Letters of Henry James. 2 vols. 1920. (Macmillan)
Notes and Reviews. 1921. (Dunster House)

Studies and Reviews

BOOKS

Beach, J. W.	The Method of Henry James.
Borchers, Lotte.	Frauengestalten und Frauenprobleme bei Henry James.
Bosanquet, Theodora.	Henry James at Work.
Bradford, Gamaliel.	American Portraits.
Brooks, Van Wyck.	The Pilgrimage of Henry James.
Brownell, William C.	American Prose Masters.
Canby, H. S.	Definitions.
Cary, Elizabeth L.	The Novels of Henry James.
Chevalley, Abel.	Le roman anglais de notre temps.
Chislett, W.	Moderns and Near-Moderns.
De Mille, George.	Literary Criticism in America.
Edel, Leon.	The Prefaces of Henry James.
Edgar, Pelham.	Henry James, Man and Author.
Elton, Oliver.	Modern Studies.
Follett, Helen, and Wilson.	Some Modern Novelists.
Freeman, John.	The Moderns.
Garnier, Marie-Reine.	Henry James et La France.
Gosse, Sir Edmund.	Aspects and Impressions.
Grattan, C. H.	The Three Jameses.
Hueffer, Ford Madox.	Henry James.
Hughes, H. L.	Theory and Practice in Henry James.
Kelley, Cornelia P.	Early Development of Henry James.

[428]

Bibliography

Liljegren, S. B.	American and European in the Works of Henry James.
Macy, J. A.	The Spirit of American Literature.
Phillips, Le Roy.	Bibliography of the Writings of Henry James.
Read, Herbert.	The Sense of Glory.
Roberts, Morris.	Henry James's Criticism.
Scott, D.	Henry James.
Sherman, S. P.	On Contemporary Literature.
Van Doren, Carl.	The American Novel.
West, Rebecca.	Henry James.

PERIODICALS

Bookman   43: 219 (1916);   72: 251 (1930);   73: 351 (1931).
Century   3: 24 (1882).
Contemporary Review   101: 69 (1912).
Critic   2: 1 (1883);   34: 338 (1899).
Dial   60: 259 (1916).
Fortnightly Review   116: 458 (1921);   133: 680 (1930).
Forum   55: 551 (1916).
Harvard Monthly   2: 59 (1886).
Living Age   290: 281 (1916);   339: 491 (1931).
Mercure de France   146: 68 (1921).
National Review   1: 257 (1883);   83: 730 (1924).
New Republic   1: 26 (1914);   7: 171 (1916);   50: 112 (1927).
North American Review   176: 125 (1903);   180: 102 (1905).
Poet Lore   39: 117 (1928).
Princeton Review   14: 68 (1884).
Publications of the Modern Language Association   39: 203 (1924);   40: 433 (1925).
Quarterly Review   212: 393 (1910);   226: 60 (1916);   234: 188 (1920).
Queen's Quarterly   39: 65 (1932).
Revue des Deux Mondes   57: 120 (1883).
Yale Review   N.S. 12: 724 (1922);   N.S. 19: 641 (1930).

JOYCE, JAMES

Born in Dublin, February 2nd, 1882, son of John Joyce and Mary Murray. Educated at Clongowes Wood College and Belve-

Appendix

dere College, and at Royal University, Dublin. At school he was quite independent and solitary. His chief studies were the works of Aristotle, Homer, Dante, St. Thomas Aquinas, the Elizabethans, and Ibsen. So interested did he become in Ibsen that he learned Norwegian in order to read him in the original. Joyce knows eighteen foreign languages in all. At nineteen he and another student published a pamphlet entitled *The Day of the Rabblement*, belittling the idea of a National Theatre in Ireland. After graduation he left Ireland to study medicine at the University of Paris, but before long he abandoned this study in order to cultivate his voice for opera singing. The year 1904 marks the beginning of his literary career, for at that time he wrote the stories which compose *Dubliners* and began his first novel. But *Dubliners* did not appear until ten years later and the novel was not completed until the same year. Meanwhile he married Nora Barnacle in 1904 and settled in Trieste, where he taught English. His first publication was *Chamber Music*, a volume of delicate lyrics which have been set to music by various composers. When war broke out Joyce went to Zurich, where he helped to organize the Irish Players, a group of fellow exiles, who gave the first performance of his play, *Exiles*. His first novel, *A Portrait of the Artist as a Young Man*, which appeared in 1916, is largely autobiographical in nature. Stephen Dedalus expounds the æsthetic theories on which *Ulysses* is based. After the war Joyce moved to Paris and has remained there. His second novel, *Ulysses*, is one of the outstanding novels of the twentieth century, though it is banned in Great Britain and the United States. Recurrent attacks of blindness are great obstacles to the continuance of *Work in Progress*, which he himself hardly expects to complete. This work is based on the Italian Vico's theory of the "cycle of history," so that all history, time, and space are telescoped and seen as the present.

BIBLIOGRAPHY

Novels

A Portrait of the Artist as a Young Man. 1916. (Modern Library, 1928)
Ulysses. 1922. (Shakespeare and Co., Paris, 1930) [Suppressed]

[430]

Bibliography

Short Stories

Dubliners. 1914. (Modern Library, 1926)

Anna Livia Plurabelle.

Haveth Childers Everywhere. } Fragments from Work in Progress. 1931. (Faber, 1931)

Tales Told by Shem and Shaun. }

Studies and Reviews

BOOKS

Aldington, Richard.   Literary Studies and Reviews.
Bennett, Arnold.   Things That Have Interested Me. Second Series.
Burgum, E. B. (ed.)   New Criticism.
Canby, H. S.   American Estimates.
Collins, Joseph.   The Doctor Looks at Literature.
Curtius, Ernst.   James Joyce und sein Ulysses.
Duff, C.   James Joyce and the Plain Reader.
Gilbert, S.   James Joyce's Ulysses.
Golding, L.   James Joyce.
Gorman, H. S.   James Joyce: His First Forty Years.
Gould, Gerald.   The English Novel of To-day.
Hackett, Francis.   Horizons.
Huddleston, S.   Articles de Paris.
Huneker, J. G.   Unicorns.
Lovett, R. M.   Preface to Fiction.
Macy, J. A.   Critical Game.
Muir, Edwin.   Transition: Essays on Contemporary Literature.
Orage, A. R.   Readers and Writers.
Rosenfeld, P.   Men Seen.
Shakespeare et Cie, [Paris] (ed.)   Our Examination Round his Factifications for Incamination of *Work in Progress*.
Smith, P. J.   Key to the *Ulysses* of James Joyce.
Squire, J. C.   Books in General.
West, Rebecca.   The Strange Necessity.
Wickham, H.   The Impuritans.
Wilson, E.   Axel's Castle.

[431]

PERIODICALS

Bookman 55: 567 (1922); 59: 518 (1924); 68: 9 (1928); 72: 375 (1930).
Criterion 1: 94 (1922).
Current Opinion 66: 387 (1919); 73: 101 (1922).
Dial 65: 201 (1918); 69: 353 (1920); 75: 480 (1923); 84: 318 (1928).
Egoist 1: 267 (1914); 3: 35 (1916); 4: 21, 64, 74 (1917).
English Review 32: 333 (1921); 35: 538 (1922).
Forum 69: 1174 (1923).
Irish Book Lover 8: 113 (1916).
Life and Letters 2: 273 (1929).
Literary Studies and Reviews, 1931.
Mercure de France June 1, 1922.
Nation 115: 211 (1922); 121: 421 (1925); 132: 634 (1931).
Nation (London) 31: 124 (1922).
Neue Schweizer Rundschau 22: 47, 660 (1929).
New Republic 10: 158 (1917); 31: 164 (1922); 61: 84 (1929); 66: 346 (1931).
New Statesman 9: 40 (1917); 20: 775 (1923); 22: 571 (1924).
Nineteenth Century 113: 491 (1933).
Quarterly Review 238: 219 (1922).

LAWRENCE, DAVID HERBERT

Born on September 11th, 1885, at Eastwood, Nottingham, the son of a coal-miner. He was educated at Nottingham High School and at Nottingham University. He owes much to his mother, an intelligent, rather exceptional woman who had married a man with little education and given to drunkenness. The incompatability of his parents left a deep impression on young Lawrence. After leaving the University he taught for a while in a London school. His first novel, *The White Peacock*, appeared in 1911. Two years later his best-known work, *Sons and Lovers*, was published. In 1914 he married Frieda von Richthofen, a sister of the famous German aviator. Lawrence was rejected for war service on account of ill-health, but because of his wife's nationality he suffered acutely in England during the later years of the war. At the end of the war he traveled extensively in America, in Australia, and in Europe. He lived in Italy for a time owing to increasing ill-health, which was aggravated

Bibliography

by the attitude of the British censors toward his novels. His frank treatment of sex caused several of his books to be suppressed, notably, *The Rainbow* and *Lady Chatterley's Lover*. He was influenced greatly by Freudian psychology, and his own works on this subject, *Psychoanalysis and the Unconscious* and *Fantasia of the Unconscious*, should be read in order to understand his point of view. In addition to his novels and short stories, he has written poetry of a high order, travel sketches, literary criticism, and essays. Two of his novels were published posthumously, *The Virgin and the Gipsy* and *The Man Who Died*. He died on March 2nd, 1930.

BIBLIOGRAPHY

Novels

The White Peacock. 1911. (Secker, 1931)
The Trespasser. 1912. (Secker, 1931)
Sons and Lovers. 1913. (Modern Library, 1923)
The Rainbow. 1915. (Modern Library, 1927)
Women in Love. 1920. (Boni, 1922)
The Lost Girl. 1920. (Boni, 1931)
Aaron's Rod. 1922. (Boni, 1922)
Kangaroo. 1923. (Boni, 1923)
The Boy in the Bush. [With M. L. Skinner] (Boni, 1924)
St. Mawr. 1925. (Knopf, 1925)
The Plumed Serpent. 1926. (Knopf, 1926)
Lady Chatterley's Lover. 1928. (Knopf, 1932)
The Virgin and the Gipsy. 1930. (Knopf, 1930)
The Man Who Died. 1931. (Knopf, 1931; Secker, 1931) [Originally published under the title, The Escaped Cock]

Short Stories

The Prussian Officer, and Other Stories. 1914. (Secker, 1931)
England My England. 1922. (Boni, 1922)
The Ladybird. American ed. The Captain's Doll. 1923. (Boni, 1930)
Glad Ghosts. 1926. (Benn, 1927)
The Woman Who Rode Away, and Other Stories. 1928. (Knopf, 1928)

Rawdon's Roof. 1929. (Mathews and Marrot, 1930)
Love Among the Haystacks and Other Pieces. 1930. (Nonesuch
  Press, 1930)

Miscellaneous Works

Pornography and Obscenity. (Faber and Faber, 1929)
Apropos of Lady Chatterley's Lover. (Secker, 1931)
Letters of D. H. Lawrence, Edited by Aldous Huxley. 1932.
  (Viking Press, 1932)

Studies and Reviews

BOOKS

Aiken, C. P.	Scepticisms.
Aldington, Richard.	D. H. Lawrence.
Arrow, J.	J. C. Squire vs. D. H. Lawrence.
Brett, D.	Lawrence and Brett.
Canby, H. S.	American Estimates.
	Definitions. Series Two.
Carswell, C.	The Savage Pilgrimage.
Carter, F.	D. H. Lawrence and the Body Mystical.
Collins, Joseph.	The Doctor Looks at Literature.
Dobrée, B.	The Lamp and the Lute.
Garnett, Edward.	Friday Nights.
George, W. L.	Literary Chapters.
Goodman, R.	Footnote to Lawrence.
Hughes, G.	Imagism and the Imagists.
Huxley, Aldous.	Music at Night.
Lawrence, A., and	
Gelder, G. S.	The Early Life of D. H. Lawrence.
	Young Lorenzo.
Leavis, F. R.	D. H. Lawrence.
Lucas, F. L.	Authors Dead and Living.
Luhan, M. D.	Lorenzo in Taos.
Macy, J. A.	Critical Game.
McDonald, E. D.	The Writings of D. H. Lawrence (Bibliography).
Muir, Edwin.	Transition: Essays on Contemporary Literature.
Murry, J. M.	Reminiscences of D. H. Lawrence.
	Son of Woman: The Story of D. H. Lawrence.

Bibliography

Nin, A.	D. H. Lawrence; an Unprofessional Study.
Potter, S.	D. H. Lawrence. A First Study.
Rosenfeld, P.	Men Seen.
Seligman, H. J.	D. H. Lawrence: An American Interpretation.
Sherman, S. P.	Critical Woodcuts.
Squire, J. C.	D. H. Lawrence.
Waugh, Alec.	Tradition and Change.
West, Rebecca.	D. H. Lawrence. Ending in Earnest.
Wickham, H.	The Impuritans.

PERIODICALS

Art and Letters 2: 89 (1919).
Athenæum 2: 346, 369 (1915).
Dial 70: 458 (1921); 72: 193 (1922).
Egoist 2: 81 (1915).
Fortnightly Review 132: 500 (1929).
Freeman 1: 451 (1920); 2: 332 (1920).
Life and Letters 4: 303 (1930); 4: 384 (1930).
Literary Review 3: 447 (1922); 4: 143 (1923).
Living Age 341: 533 (1932).
London Mercury 8: 64 (1923); 23: 477 (1931).
Nation 116: 665 (1923); 117: 526 (1923); 130: 320 (1930); 131: 710 (1930).
Nation and Athenæum 31: 655 (1922).
New Republic 27: 329 (1921); 29: 184 (1921); 35: 132 (1923); 36: 236 (1923); 43: 184 (1925); 63: 22 (1930).
New Statesman 19: 388 (1922); 20: 752 (1923); 21: 712 (1923); 25: 285 (1925); 34: 701 (1930).
Saturday Review 149: 514 (1930).
Saturday Review of Literature 1: 319 (1924); 6: 817 (1930); 6: 1130 (1930); 9: 523 (1933).
Spectator 129: 23 (1922); 130: 630 (1923); 133: 364 (1924).

LEWIS, SINCLAIR

Born at Sauk Center, Minnesota, in 1885, of Connecticut stock. He received his A.B. at Yale University in 1907. For a short time he was a disciple of Upton Sinclair and joined his socialist and Utopian colony as janitor. Emma Goldman and other prominent radicals were there at the time. He entered the journalistic field soon after graduation and within a period of ten years was on the staff of magazines in various parts of the United States. He became editor and advertising manager of the George H. Doran Company, but resigned in 1916, to devote his time exclusively to his own writing. His first novel, *Our Mr. Wrenn*, was published in 1914, but did not receive much attention in the literary world. *Main Street*, published in 1921, brought him widespread recognition, and his literary reputation has increased with each subsequent novel. His novels are satires on American life and have won for him the antagonism of large groups of people in the United States whose professions and habits of living he has satirized. He was offered the Pulitzer Prize in 1926, but refused it as a protest against the restrictive terms of the award. In 1930 he was awarded the Nobel Prize in Literature. He has been twice married, first to Grace Livingstone Hegger in 1914, and to Dorothy Thompson, a journalist, in 1928. *Arrowsmith*, his seventh novel, was written during a travel expedition to the Virgin Islands and South America with Doctor Paul de Kruif, the scientist.

BIBLIOGRAPHY
Novels

Our Mr. Wrenn. 1914. (Harcourt, 1923)
The Trail of the Hawk. 1915. (Harcourt, 1923)
The Job. 1917. (Harcourt, 1923)
The Innocents. 1917. (o.p.)
Free Air. 1919. (Harcourt, 1923)
Main Street. 1920. (Harcourt, 1921)
Babbitt. 1922. (Harcourt, 1922)
Arrowsmith. 1924. (Harcourt, 1925)
Mantrap. 1926. (Harcourt, 1926)
Elmer Gantry. 1927. (Harcourt, 1927)
The Man Who Knew Coolidge. 1928. (Harcourt, 1928)
Dodsworth. 1929. (Cape, 1930)
Ann Vickers. 1933. (Doubleday, Doran, 1933)

Studies and Reviews

BOOKS
Boyd, Ernest.   Portraits Real and Imaginary.
Boynton, Percy.   More Contemporary Americans.

Bibliography

Drake, H. A.	American Criticism.
Farrar, John.	The Literary Spotlight.
Harrison, O.	Sinclair Lewis.
Hind, C. L.	More Authors and I.
Karsner, D.	Sixteen Authors To One.
Lippman, W.	Men of Destiny.
Mais, S. P. B.	Some Modern Authors.
McAlpin, E. A.	Old and New Books as Life Teachers.
Michaud, R.	The American Novel of To-day.
Nock, A. J.	Book of Journeymen.
Parrington, V. L.	Sinclair Lewis: Our Own Diogenes.
Sherman, S. P.	The Significance of Sinclair Lewis.
Squire, J. C., and others.	Contemporary American Authors.
Van Doren, Carl.	American and British Literature since 1890. Sinclair Lewis.
Waldman, M.	Contemporary American Authors.
West, Rebecca.	Strange Necessity.
Whipple, T. K.	Spokesmen.
Williams, S. T.	Modern Writers At Work.

PERIODICALS

American Mercury   4: 507 (1925);   10: 506 (1927).

Atlantic Monthly   127 (Supp. 1: 8) (1921).

Bookman   53: 245   (1921);   54: 9   (1921);   72: 453   (1931); 79: 233 (1931).

Bookman (London)   65: 195 (1924);   76: 99 (1929).

Commonweal   5: 577 (1927);   13: 61 (1930).

Dial   78: 515 (1925).

English Journal   16: 251 (1927).

Living Age   325: 429 (1925);   329: 381 (1927).

London Mercury   13: 273 (1926);   19: 658 (1929).

Nation   120: 359 (1925);   122: 546, 672 (1926);   124: 291 (1927);   125: 278 (1927);   127: 81 (1928);   129: 751 (1929); 133: 544 (1930);   136: 125 (1933).

New Republic   10: 234 (1917);   25: 20 (1920);   32: 152 (1922);   42: 3 (1925);   54: 302 (1928);   74: 22 (1933).

New Statesman and Nation   5: 133 (1933).

Nineteenth Century   101: 739 (1927).

North American Review   216: 716 (1922).

Outlook   146: 307 (1927).
Saturday Review   132: 230 (1921);   139: 389 (1925).
Saturday Review of Literature   1: 575 (1925);   3: 637 (1927).
Southwestern Bulletin (Memphis)   pp. 3 ff.   September (1929).
Spectator   129:   928   (1922);   134:   372   (1925);   150:   160 (1933).
University of California Chronicle   30: 417 (1928).

MAUGHAM, W. SOMERSET

William Somerset Maugham was born in 1874 in Paris, where his father was a counselor at the English Embassy. Between the ages of ten and thirteen he lived in England for the first time, as a student in King's School at Canterbury. Subsequently he studied in Germany at the University of Heidelberg. He spent several years at St. Thomas' Hospital in London, graduating with the degrees of M.R.C.S. and L.R.C.P., but he has never practiced medicine. His first novel, *Liza of Lambeth* (1897), centered around the environment in which the hospital was situated and reproduced the slum conditions of Lambeth. In 1902 his first play was produced in Germany. In the same year his novel, *Mrs. Craddock*, appeared and marked the beginning of his literary reputation. In 1907 his play, *Lady Frederick*, was favorably received. His most important novel, *Of Human Bondage*, was published in 1915. Maugham went to Tahiti seeking to discover the secret of the spell of the South Seas, and *The Moon and Sixpence* (1919) was one of the fruits of his travels. His extensive travel resulted in a number of plays and short stories of the Orient. During the World War Maugham served in the Secret Service. *Ashenden, or, The British Agent* (1928), is based on his experiences of that time. *Cakes and Ale* (1930) became a subject of public controversy when critics accused Maugham of having maliciously portrayed two novelists, Thomas Hardy and Hugh Walpole. Maugham married Syrie, the daughter of the famous Dr. Barnardo. They live on the French Riviera. In addition to his novels and short stories he has written about twenty-five plays, and several travel sketches.

BIBLIOGRAPHY

Novels

Liza of Lambeth. 1897. (Doran, 1921)
The Making of a Saint. 1898. (Page, 1922)
The Hero. 1901. (o.p.)
Mrs. Craddock. 1902. (Doubleday, 1928)
The Merry-go-round. 1904. (o.p.)
The Explorer. 1907. (Doran, 1920)
Of Human Bondage. 1915. (Doubleday, Doran, 1928)
The Moon and Sixpence. 1919. (Grosset, 1928)
The Painted Veil. 1925. (Doran, 1925)
The Casuarina Tree. 1926. (Doran, 1926)
Ashenden, or, The British Agent. 1928. (Doubleday, 1928)
Cakes and Ale; or, The Skeleton in the Cupboard, 1930. (Doubleday, Doran, 1930)
Narrow Corner. 1932. (Doubleday, 1932)

Short Stories

Orientations. 1899. (o.p.)
The Trembling of a Leaf: Little Stories of the South Sea Islands. 1921. (Doran, 1921)
Six Stories Written in the First Person Singular. 1931. (Doubleday, 1931)

Studies and Reviews

BOOKS

Adcock, A. St. J.	Gods of Modern Grub Street.
Bason, F. T. (comp.)	Bibliography of the Writings of William Somerset Maugham.
Brewster, D., and Burrell, A.	Adventure or Experience.
Collins, Joseph.	Idling in Italy; Studies of Literature and of Life.
Dottin, Paul.	Somerset Maugham et ses Romans.
Drew, Elizabeth.	The Modern Novel.
Mais, S. P. B.	Some Modern Authors.
Overton, G. M.	Authors of the Day.
Towne, C. H., and others.	Somerset Maugham.

PERIODICALS

Athenæum   1: 302 (1919).

Bookman   74: 336 (1931);   75: 735 (1932).

Calendar of Modern Letters   1: 251 (1925).

Commonweal   17: 719 (1933).

Literary Review   5: 3 (1925).

London Mercury   12: 208 (1925);   16: 85 (1927).

Nation   103: 331 (1916);   109: 227 (1919);   113: 543 (1921);   116: 19 (1923);   133: 576 (1931);   135: 574 (1932);   136: 511 (1933).

New Republic   5: 202 (1915);   21: 57 (1919);   68: 280 (1931).

New Statesman   15: 524 (1920).

New Statesman and Nation   2: 516 (1931).

Outlook   110: 874 (1915).

Saturday Review   135: 54 (1923);   142: 317 (1926);   154: 564 (1932).

Saturday Review of Literature   1: 611 (1925);   8: 40 (1931);   9: 237 (1932).

Spectator   149: 674 (1932).

MELVILLE, HERMAN

Born in New York City in August, 1819. Educated in the Albany Classical School. Shipped as a cabin boy in 1837. Four years later he sailed on a New Bedford whaler, and, dissatisfied, left the ship while harbored in the Marquesas Islands. His experiences among the warlike natives, until his rescue by an Australian whaler, are recorded in his first literary work, *Typee: A Peep at Polynesian Life*, published in 1846. In 1847 he married the daughter of Justice Lemuel Shaw of Massachusetts, and lived in Pittsfield from 1850 to 1863. He then removed to New York, where in 1866 he was appointed to a position in the customs house. In 1885 he retired because of ill-health. All Melville's works, with the exception of a few volumes of poems, deal with life at sea. His masterpiece, *Moby Dick*, is an exciting tale about Mocha Dick, a real whale of history. Another novel, *White Jacket*, led to the abolition of flogging in the United States navy. He died in New York in September, 1891.

BIBLIOGRAPHY

Novels

Typee: A Peep at Polynesian Life. 1846. (Dodd, 1926)
Omoo: A Narrative of Adventures. 1847. (Dodd, 1924)
Mardi: And a Voyage Thither. 1849. (Boni, 1925)
Reburn: His First Voyage. 1849. (Constable, 1929)
White Jacket. 1850. (World's Classics, Oxford, 1924)
Moby Dick or The White Whale. 1851. (Winston, 1931)
Pierre: or The Ambiguities. 1852. (Knopf, 1930)
Israel Potter. 1855. (Vol. 11, Works. Constable, 1923)
The Confidence Man. 1857. (Vol. 12, Works. Constable, 1923)

Short Stories

The Piazza Tales. 1856. (Vol. 10, Works. Constable, 1923)
Billy Budd and Other Prose Pieces. (Vol. 13, Works. Constable, 1923)
The Apple Tree Table and Other Sketches. [Posthumous] (Princeton, 1922)

Studies and Reviews

BOOKS

Birrell, A.   Immortal White Whale.
Boynton, Percy.   More Contemporary Americans.
Brooks, Van Wyck.   Emerson and Others.
Canby, H. S.   Classic Americans.
Cournos, J.   Comparison of Melville with Rimbaud and Doughty.
                           Modern Plutarch.
Drake, W. A. (ed.)   American Criticism.
Freeman, John.   Herman Melville.
Gosse, Sir Edmund.   Silhouettes.
Hind, C. L.   More Authors and I.
Josephson, M.   Portrait of the Artist as American.
Lawrence, D. H.   Studies in Classic American Literature.
Minnigerode, M.   Some Personal Letters of Herman Melville, and a Bibliography.
Morley, C. D.   Modern Essays: Second Series.
Mumford, Lewis.   Herman Melville.
Sadleir, M.   Excursions in Victorian Bibliography.
Stoddard, R. H.   Recollections, Personal and Literary.

Sullivan, J. W. M.   Aspects of Science: Second Series.
Van Doren, Carl.   Lucifer from Nantucket.
Van Vechten, Carl.   Excavations.
Weaver, R. M.   Herman Melville, Mariner and Mystic.

PERIODICALS

American Literature   2: 286 (1930);   3: 72 (1931).
American Mercury   10: 33 (1927);   15: 482 (1929).
Atlantic Monthly   143: 136 (1929).
Century   110: 494 (1925).
Harvard Graduates' Manual   39: 22 (1930).
Publications of the Modern Language Association of America
    June, 43: 502 (1928).
Queen's Quarterly   37: 36 (1930).
Revue anglo-américaine   October   (1927).
Revue des Deux Mondes   May 15 (1849).
Saturday Review of Literature   5: 514 (1928);   5: 945 (1929).

MEREDITH, GEORGE

Born in 1828 at Portsmouth (the Lymport of *Evan Harrington*),
the only child by the marriage in 1824 of Augustus Armstrong
Meredith and Jane Eliza Macnamara. He was educated at St.
Paul's Church school, Southsea, then at a boarding school in the
town, and from early in 1843 until the end of 1844 at the Moravian
School at Neuwied on the Rhine. Apprenticed in 1845 to a
solicitor, but at the age of twenty-one began to contribute poetry
to magazines, and for some years won a scant living by journalism, on the *Daily News* and other London newspapers, and on
the *Ipswich Journal*, for which he wrote leading articles. In
London he was a leader in the group of young philosophical
radicals among whom was John (afterwards Lord) Morley. He
married Mary Ellen Nicolls, widow of a naval lieutenant, in
1849. From 1856 to 1858 he lived in London, doing hackwork
and journalism. He published his first novel, *The Ordeal of Richard
Feverel*, in 1859. His first wife died in 1861 and in 1864 he married
Marie Vulliamy. *The Egoist*, his masterpiece, first appeared in
serial form in *The Glasgow Weekly Herald* in June, 1879, under the
title of *Sir Willoughby Patterne, The Egoist;* in the same year it
was published in three volumes as *The Egoist*. Until 1885, the
year of his second wife's death, his work was not known to the

Bibliography

general public. In 1892, when Tennyson died, he was elected to succeed him as President of The Society of Authors. He received the Vice-presidency of the London Library in 1902, the Order of Merit in 1905, and the gold medal of the Royal Society of Literature. For many years Meredith acted as literary adviser for Messrs. Chapman and Hall, the publishers of his books, and was one of the last of "publishers' readers." His poetry as well as his prose won him a great deal of recognition, especially his book of sonnets, *Modern Love*. He died on May 18th, 1909.

BIBLIOGRAPHY

Novels *

The Ordeal of Richard Feverel. 1859. (Constable, 1922)
Evan Harrington. 1861. (Constable, 1913)
Emilia in England. 1864. Later published as Sandra Belloni.
  1889. (Constable, 1912)
Rhoda Fleming. 1865. (Constable, 1913)
Vittoria. 1867. (Constable, 1913)
The Adventures of Harry Richmond. 1871. (Constable, 1913)
Beauchamp's Career. 1876. (Constable, 1913)
The Egoist. 1879. (Constable, 1922)
The Tragic Comedians. 1880. (Constable, 1911)
Diana of the Crossways. 1885. (Constable, 1915)
One of our Conquerors. 1891. (Constable, 1913)
Lord Ormont and His Aminta. 1894. (Constable, 1912)
The Amazing Marriage. 1895. (Constable, 1914)
Celt and Saxon. 1910. (Constable, 1927)

Short Stories

The Shaving of Shagpat: An Arabian Entertainment. 1855.
  (Constable, 1914)
†Farina: A Legend of Cologne. 1857.
†The House on the Beach. 1877.
†The Case of General Ople and Lady Camper. 1877.
†The Tale of Chloe. 1879.
The Gentleman of Fifty and the Damsel of Nineteen. 1910. (o.p.)

* Works. Special edition. 17v. (Scribner, 1922.)
† These stories have been reprinted and are available in the following collections: Short Stories. Boxhill Edition. (Scribner, 1901.)
The Tale of Chloe and Other Stories. (Constable, 1909.)

Appendix

Miscellaneous Works

An Essay on Comedy. 1897. (Scribner, 1918; Constable, 1927)
Letters. [Collected and edited by his son, W. M. Meredith.] 2v.
(Scribner, 1912)
Letters to Alice Meynell, 1896–1907. (Chaucer Head, 1923)

Studies and Reviews

BOOKS

Bailey, E. J.	The Novels of George Meredith.
Barrie, J. M.	George Meredith.
Beach, J. W.	The Comic Spirit of George Meredith.
Beaty, J. O., and others (eds.)	Facts and Ideas.
Bedford, Herbert.	The Heroines of George Meredith.
Brownell, W. C.	Victorian Prose Masters. Thackeray to Meredith.
Chase, M. E., and Mac-Gregor, M. E. (eds.)	Writing of Informal Essays.
Chesterton, G. K.	Uses of Diversity.
Chislett, W.	George Meredith.
Clutton-Brock, A.	More Essays on Books.
Curle, R. H. P.	Aspects of George Meredith.
Dick, Ernst.	George Meredith. Drei Versuche.
Dixon, N. M.	In the Republic of Letters.
Dowden, E.	New Studies in Literature.
Ellis, S. M.	George Meredith.
Elton, O.	Modern Studies.
Erskine, John.	The Delight of Great Books.
Esdaile, A. J. K.	Bibliography of the Writings in Prose and Verse of George Meredith.
Fernandez, R.	Messages.
Forman, M. B. (ed.)	George Meredith: Some Early Appreciations.
Forman, M. B.	Bibliography of the Writings in Prose and Verse of George Meredith. Meredithiana.

[444]

Bibliography

Gretton, M. S.   The Writings and Life of George Meredith.

Hammerton, J. A.   George Meredith in Anecdote and Criticism.

Harris, Frank.   Contemporary Portraits. First Series.

Henderson, A.   Interpreters of Life and the Modern Spirit.

Henderson, M. S.   George Meredith, Novelist, Poet, Reformer.

Henley, W. E.   Views and Reviews.

Hind, C. L.   Authors and I.

Jerrold, Walter.   George Meredith: An Essay Towards Appreciation.

Le Gallienne, R.   George Meredith: Some Characteristics [which includes a bibliography by John Lane].

Lowes, J. L.   Of Reading Books.

Lynch, H.   George Meredith. A Study.

Meynell, Alice.   Second Person Singular.

Moffat, James.   George Meredith: Introduction to his Novels.

Nevinson, H. W.   Books and Personalities.

Peel, R.   Creed of a Victorian Pagan.

Photiades, C.   George Meredith.

Priestley, J. B.   George Meredith.

Scott, F. W., and Zeitlin, J. (eds.)   Essays Formal and Informal.

Sencourt, R. E.   The Life of George Meredith.

Sherman, S. P.   On Contemporary Literature.

Short, T. S.   On Some Characteristics of George Meredith's Prose-Writing.

Thomson, James.   James Thomson ("B.V.") on George Meredith.

University of Michigan. Department of Rhetoric and Journalism.   Adventures in Essay Reading.

Van Dyke, H.   The Man Behind the Book.

Willcocks, M. P.   Between the Old World and the New.

Witham, R. A. (comp.)   Essays of To-day.
Woolf, Virginia.   The Second Common Reader.

PERIODICALS

Commonweal   5: 360 (1927);   11: 50 (1929).
Contemporary Review   127: 500 (1925);   133: 333 (1928).
Cornhill Magazine   64: 158 (1928).
Die Neueren Sprachen   Vol. 18 (1910–11).
Englische Studien   59, number 1: 17 (1925).
English Journal   11: 140 (1922).
Fortnightly Review   111: 293 (1919);   129: 183 (1928).
Hibbert Journal   14: 613 (1916);   21: 107 (1922).
Journal of English and Germanic Philology   29: 243 (1930).
Living Age   316: 38 (1923);   330: 311 (1926);   334: 638
   (1928).
London Mercury   17: 563 (1928).
Nation (London)   39: 323 (1926).
Nation and Athenæum   42: 713 (1928).
New Republic   60: 355 (1929).
Nineteenth Century   87: 845 (1920).
Revue de Litterature Comparée   3: 463 (1923).
Revue Politique et Littéraire   59: 359 (1921).
Sewanee Review   26: 153 (1918);   31: 346 (1923).
South Atlantic Quarterly   27: 367 (1928).
Spectator   140: 222 (1928).
University of Chicago, Abstracts of Theses, Humanistic Series
   3: 335 (1927).
Yale Review   19: 836 (1930).

MOORE, GEORGE

Born at Moore Hall, County Mayo, Ireland, on February 24th,
1852, eldest son of George Henry Moore, landowner and Member
of Parliament for Mayo.   Educated at Oscott, but was a fitful
student.   In 1870 he went to Paris to study art and joined a group
of French artists which included Manet, Renoir, and Monet, but,
finding that he had little real aptitude for painting, he soon
turned to poetry.   It was not until the late seventies, when he
came under the influence of Zola, that he became interested in
prose-writing.   He returned to London in 1882, did hack journalistic work, and studied prose composition laboriously to prepare

himself for his career. His one definite purpose in life was to liberate English fiction from its "Victorian shackles." His first novel, *A Modern Lover*, was published in 1883, but his first significant work was *A Mummer's Wife*, which appeared in 1885 and showed him a convert to the new French realism and the "philosophical" novel. The great masterpiece of his prime was *Esther Waters*, 1894. Two events of transcending importance in his life were his sojourn in his native country from 1901 to 1910, which "renewed his artistic youth," and his pilgrimage to the Holy Land, made in preparation for the writing of his story of the Christ. In each of his stories of past ages he has "reconstructed a period of history" with perfect authenticity and delicate touch. In addition to his fiction and his story of the Christ (*The Brook Kerith: A Syrian Story*) he has written essays and sketches of Irish scenery and life, criticisms of artists and their work, numerous plays (especially comedies) and a series of autobiographical studies. He died in 1933.

BIBLIOGRAPHY

Novels

A Modern Lover. 1883. (o.p.) [See Lewis Seymour and Some Women]
A Mummer's Wife. 1885. (Heinemann, 1929)
A Drama in Muslin: A Realistic Novel. 1886. (o.p) [See Muslin]
A Mere Accident. 1887. (o.p.) [See Celibates]
Confessions of a Young Man. 1888. (Heinemann, 1928)
Spring Days: A Realistic Novel. 1888. (Uniform edition, Brentano)
Mike Fletcher. 1889. (o.p.)
Vain Fortune. 1890. (o.p.)
Esther Waters. 1894. [Revised, 1920.] (Heinemann, 1929)
Evelyn Innes. 1898. (Benn, 1929)
Sister Teresa. 1901. (Benn, 1929)
The Lake. 1905. (Heinemann, 1928)
Muslin. 1915. [A Drama in Muslin, rewritten] (Heinemann, 1928)
The Brook Kerith: A Syrian Story. 1916. (Macmillan, 1926)
Lewis Seymour and Some Women. 1917. [A Modern Lover, rewritten] (Heinemann, 1928)

Héloise and Abélard. 1921. (Laurie, 1928)
The Pastoral Loves of Daphnis and Chloe. 1926. (Heinemann, The Windmill Library)
Ulick and Soracha. 1926. (Limited Edition, Boni & Liveright)
Aphrodite in Aulis. 1931. (Brentano, 1931)

Short Stories

Celibates. 1895. [Composed of Mildred Lawson; John Norton; A Modern Lover, rewritten; Agnes Lahens] (Brentano, 1915)
The Untilled Field. 1903. (Heinemann, 1931)
In Single Strictness. 1922. o.p. (See Celibate Lives)
A Story-Teller's Holiday. 1924. (Boni & Liveright, 1928)
Celibate Lives. 1927. [One story from The Story-Teller's Holiday and selections from Celibates and In Single Strictness] (Boni and Liveright, 1927)

Miscellaneous Works

Memoirs of my Dead Life. 1905. (Heinemann, 1921)
Hail and Farewell: A Trilogy. Ave, 1911; Salve, 1912; Vale, 1914. (Heinemann, 1925)
Avowals. 1919. (Boni & Liveright, 1928)
Conversations in Ebury Street. 1924. (Heinemann, 1930)

Studies and Reviews

BOOKS

Boyd, Ernest.	Ireland's Literary Renaissance.
Chesterton, G. K.	Heretics.
Freeman, John.	A Portrait of George Moore in a Study of his Work.
Goodwin, Geraint.	Conversations with George Moore.
Gosse, Sir Edmund.	More Books on the Table.
Harris, Frank.	Contemporary Portraits. Second Series.
Hind, C. Lewis.	Authors and I.
Huneker, J. G.	Ivory Apes and Peacocks.
	Pathos of Distance.
	Unicorns.
Littell, Philip.	Books and Things.
Lucas, E. V.	His Fatal Beauty, or, The Moore of Chelsea, A Satire.

Bibliography

Mitchell, S. L.	George Moore.
Murry, J. M.	Wrap Me Up in My Aubusson Carpet.
Quiller-Couch,	
Sir A. T.	Adventures into Criticism.
Sherman, S. P.	On Contemporary Literature.
Squire, J. C.	Books Reviewed.
Williams, I. A.	George Moore, a Biography.
Wolfe, Humbert.	George Moore.

PERIODICALS

Athenæum   2: 150 (1901).
American Mercury   1: 39 (1924);   4: 202 (1925).
Contemporary Review   80: 299 (1901).
Critic   43: 74.
Current Opinion   61: 265   (1916);   68: 98   (1926);   76: 293 (1924).
Dial   69: 448   (1920);   71: 497   (1921);   73: 664   (1922);   75: 341 (1923);   78: 225 (1925);   81: 91, 431 (1926).
English Review   6: 428 (1916);   12: 10 (1912);   16: 167, 350 (1914);   17: 439 (1917);   29: 1489 (1919);   32: 541 (1921); 39: 495 (1924).
Everyman   16: 375 (1920).
Fortnightly Review   110 N.S.: 154 (1921).
Forum   52: 169 (1914).
Independent   53: 2238 (1901);   55: 404 (1913).
Living Age   304: 11   (1920);   305: 353   (1920);   337: 284 (1929).
London Mercury   2: 281   (1920);   3: 673   (1921);   24: 565 (1931).
Nation   76: 420   (1903);   94: 385   (1912);   113: 75   (1921); 132: 416 (1931).
New Critic   4: 368 (1926).
New Republic   37: 98 (1923);   41: 124 (1924).
New Statesman   16: 673   (1921);   19: 518   (1922);   22: 512 (1924);   24: 660 (1925).
North American Review   214: 98 (1921).
Revue des Deux Mondes   17: 917 (1923);   37: 442 (1927).
Saturday Review   141: 425 (1925);   142: 70 (1926);   143: 158 (1927).
Sewanee Review   33: 301 (1925).

Spectator 126: 497 (1921); 129: 342 (1922); 130: 145 (1923); 131: 160 (1923); 132: 413 (1924); 135: 1052 (1925); 137: 382 (1926); 138: 249 (1927); 140: 527 (1928).
Westminster Review   172: 200 (1909).
Yale Review   6: 342 (1917).

RICHARDSON, DOROTHY

Born in England in the late-Victorian era. She lived in a very secluded atmosphere until, at the age of seventeen, she was thrust into the world of affairs to make her own livelihood. Very little is known of her personal life except that she lives in a London suburb and is married to Alan Odle. She was associated with the *Imagist* school of poetry in the prewar years when she began her writing. Her novels are a series of spiritual adventures of a young Englishwoman, Miriam Henderson, as presented through the medium of her own mind. The series is entitled *Pilgrimage*. Her influence on the character of English fiction since her first novel, *Pointed Roofs*, was published in 1915, has been phenomenal. She has virtually established the "stream-of-consciousness" style of writing in England. Her novels are considered to be largely autobiographical in character.

BIBLIOGRAPHY
Novels *

Pointed Roofs. 1915.
Backwater. 1916.
Honeycomb. 1917.
The Tunnel. 1919.
Interim. 1919.
Deadlock. 1921.
Revolving Lights. 1923.
The Trap. 1925.
Oberland. 1927.
Dawn's Left Hand. 1931.

Studies and Reviews

BOOKS

Beach, J. W.   The Twentieth Century Novel.
Collins, Joseph.   The Doctor Looks at Literature.

* The whole series of *Pilgrimage* has been published by Duckworth, London.

Bibliography

Johnson, R. Brimley. Some Contemporary Novelists: Women.
Mais, S. P. B. Books and Their Writers.
Powys, J. C. Dorothy M. Richardson.
Sinclair, May. Introduction to *Pointed Roofs*. (1919 Edition)
Vines, Sherard. Movements in Modern English Poetry and Prose.

PERIODICALS

Adelphi 2: 508 (1924).
Athenæum 1: 140 (1919).
Calendar of Modern Letters 1: 328 (1925).
Current Opinion 66: 387 (1919).
Dial 64: 451 (1918); 67: 442 (1919).
Egoist 5: 57 (1918).
Literary Review 3: 859 (1922).
Living Age 334: 278 (1928).
London Mercury 1: 473 (1919); 8: 208 (1923).
Nation 106: 656 (1918); 109: 720 (1919).
Nation and Athenæum 29: 621 (1921); 42: 284 (1927).
New Republic 20: supp. 14 (1919); 26: 267 (1921); 29: 313 (1921).
Saturday Review 122: 138 (1916); 144: 828 (1927).
Saturday Review of Literature 4: 841 (1928).
Spectator 122: 330 (1919); 126: 403 (1921); 130: 1084 (1923).
Yale Review N.S. 10: 397 (1921).

RICHARDSON, SAMUEL

Born in Derbyshire in 1689, of English parents. His education was slight—he is reported to have attended Christ's Hospital for a short time. He showed signs of talent in boyhood. In 1706 he was apprenticed to John Wilde, stationer, and in 1719 he set up a printing business of his own. He married in 1721 and again in 1731. He became printer of the Journals of the House of Commons, Law-Printer to the King, and Master of the Stationers' Company. His first novel, *Pamela*, appeared in 1740 in the form of letters. Its publication marked the beginning of the modern English novel. Richardson later added two volumes of inferior merit. *Clarissa*, his second and greatest novel, appeared in 1747–1748. It won for him a continental reputation.

Appendix

In 1753 *Sir Charles Grandison,* his last novel, appeared. Many parodies and imitations of his novels appeared soon after the original publications. His novels have been translated into French, Italian, and Spanish, and have been dramatized. He died on July 4th, 1761, and was buried in St. Bride's Church.

BIBLIOGRAPHY

Novels

Pamela, or, Virtue Rewarded. 1740. (Everyman's Library, Dutton)
Clarissa; or, The History of a Young Lady. 1747–1748. (Blackwell, 1930)
Sir Charles Grandison. 1753. (Blackwell, 1931)

Studies and Reviews

BOOKS

Barbauld, Anna L.	Correspondence [of Richardson] to which are Prefixed a Biographical Account of the Author and Observations on His Writings.
Binkley, Harold C.	A Novelist in Letters.
Birrell, A.	Res Judicatæ.
Danielowski, Emma.	Richardsons erster Roman Ertstehungsgeschichte.
Dibelius, Wilhelm.	Englische Romankunst.
Dobson, Austin.	Samuel Richardson.
Dottin, Paul.	Du Nouveau sur Richardson.
	Samuel Richardson.
Downs, B. W.	Richardson.
English Association.	Essays and Studies. Vol. 2.
Hazlitt, W.	Comic Writers.
Henley, W. E.	Views and Reviews. Vol. 1.
Kelly, John.	Pamela's Conduct in High Life.
Krutch, J. W.	Five Masters.
Lang, Andrew.	Letters on Literature.
Masson, David.	British Novelists and Their Styles.
Price, L. M.	Mélanges d'histoire littéraire générale et comparée offerts à Fernand Baldensperger. Vol. 2.

Bibliography

Reade, A. L.	Samuel Richardson and His Family Circle.
Rose, William.	The Republic of Letters.
Schmidt, Erich.	Richardson, Rousseau und Goethe ein Beitrag zur Geschichte des Romans im 18 Jahrhundert.
Scott, Sir Walter.	Miscellaneous Prose Writers. Novelists and Dramatists.
Stephen, Sir Leslie.	Hours in a Library.
Thomson, Clara.	Samuel Richardson.
Traill, H. D.	The New Fiction and Other Essays on Literary Subjects.
Wilcox, F. H.	Prévost's Translation of Richardson's Novels.

PERIODICALS

Athenæum   1: 115 (1900).
Atlantic Monthly   146: 50, 205 (1930).
Dial   45: 75 (1908).
Edinburgh Review   243: 139 (1926).
Englische Studien   49: 220 (1916).
Fortnightly Review   76: 949 (1901).
Germanisch-romanische Monatsschrift   12: 21, 88 (1924).
Journal of English and Germanic Philology   25: 7 (1926).
Living Age   303: 98 (1919).
London Mercury   7: 382 (1923).
Modern Language Notes   37: 314 (1922);   45: 469 (1930).
Modern Language Review   17: 17 (1922).
Modern Philology   16: 495 (1919);   17: 45 (1919);   22: 391 (1925);   28: 423 (1931).
Nation   73: 489 (1901);   93: 120 (1911).
Notes and Queries   11: 181, 224, 263, 303, 342, 383, 425, 465, 506 (1922).
Revue anglo-américaine   August (1928);   February (1929); August (1930).
Revue de Littérature Comparée   4: 590 (1924).
Saturday Review of Literature   5: 832 (1929).
Yale Review   N.S. 19: 181 (1929).

[453]

SCOTT, SIR WALTER

Born on August 15th, 1771, at Edinburgh, of an old Scottish family. He was handicapped from infancy with a lame leg following an illness. His schooling was interrupted frequently during his boyhood, but he had shown an unusual interest in historical and romantic tales from his early childhood, and had begun to collect ballads before the age of ten. As a very young boy he was considered an inimitable story-teller. He attended classes at Edinburgh University in 1783, and in 1788 decided to qualify for an advocate. He was called to the Bar in 1792. In 1797 he married Charlotte Mary Carpenter, daughter of a French refugee, and settled in Edinburgh until he was made assistant to a principal clerk of the quarter sessions in 1806, when he moved to Ashestiel, near Selkirk. He began his literary career with the writing of ballads and longer narrative poems. *The Lay of the Last Minstrel* was published in 1805, and *The Lady of the Lake* in 1810. In 1809 he started a publishing firm which grew out of a printing venture into which he had embarked previously with the Ballantyne brothers, but owing to his generous patronage of minor authors the enterprise was a financial failure, and in 1813 the publishing end of the business was discontinued. Scott was an indefatigable worker, and in addition to his legal work, his interest in the printing firm, and his prolific writing of poetry and historical novels, he did a great deal of editorial work, including an edition of Dryden in eighteen volumes and one of Swift in nineteen volumes. *Waverley*, his first historical novel, was published anonymously in 1814, and within a period of five years eight others of the Waverley series appeared. In 1818 a baronetcy was conferred upon him. He bought the landed estate of Abbotsford, where he built an imitation of a Scotch baronial castle. In 1826 he became bankrupt owing to the failure of his own printing firm and the firm of Constable with which he was closely identified. In 1827 he announced publicly his authorship of the Waverley novels. He died on September 21st, 1832, at Abbotsford.

BIBLIOGRAPHY

Novels

Waverley. 1814. (Everyman's Library, Dutton)
Guy Mannering. 1815. (Everyman's Library, Dutton)

Bibliography

The Antiquary. 1816. (Everyman's Library, Dutton)
Old Mortality; The Black Dwarf. 1816. (Everyman's Library, Dutton)
The Heart of Midlothian. 1818. (Everyman's Library, Dutton)
Rob Roy. 1818. (Everyman's Library, Dutton)
The Bride of Lammermoor. 1819. (Everyman's Library, Dutton)
The Legend of Montrose. 1819. (Everyman's Library, Dutton)
Ivanhoe. 1820. (Everyman's Library, Dutton)
The Monastery. 1820. (Everyman's Library, Dutton)
The Abbot. 1820. (Everyman's Library, Dutton)
Kenilworth. 1821. (Everyman's Library, Dutton)
The Pirate. 1822. (Everyman's Library, Dutton)
The Fortunes of Nigel. 1822. (Everyman's Library, Dutton)
Peveril of the Peak. 1822. (Everyman's Library, Dutton)
Quentin Durward. 1823. (Everyman's Library, Dutton)
St. Ronan's Well. 1824. (Everyman's Library, Dutton)
Redgauntlet. 1824. (Everyman's Library, Dutton)
The Betrothed. 1825. (Everyman's Library, Dutton)
The Talisman. 1825. (Everyman's Library, Dutton)
Woodstock. 1826. (Everyman's Library, Dutton)
The Highland Widow; The Two Drovers; The Surgeon's Daughter. 1827. (Everyman's Library, Dutton)
The Fair Maid of Perth. 1828. (Everyman's Library, Dutton)
Anne of Geierstein. 1829. (Everyman's Library, Dutton)
Count Robert of Paris; Castle Dangerous. 1832. (Everyman's Library, Dutton)

Studies and Reviews

BOOKS

Ball, Margaret.   Sir Walter Scott As a Critic of Literature.
Beers, H. A.   English Romanticism in the Nineteenth Century.
Brandes, G.   Main Currents in Nineteenth Century Literature.
Buchan, John.   Sir Walter Scott.
Burton, R.   Masters of the English Novel.
Carlyle, Thomas.   Critical Essays. Vol. 4.
Carswell, Donald.   Sir Walter; A Four-Part Study in Biography.

Chesterton, G. K.	Varied Types.
Croce, B.	European Literature in the Nineteenth Century.
Crockett, W. S.	Scott Originals; An Account of Notables and Worthies: The Originals of Characters in the Waverley Novels.
Dawson, W. J.	Makers of English Fiction.
Erskine, John.	The Delight of Great Books.
Fairchild, H. N.	Romantic Quest.
Gray, W. F.	Scott Centenary Handbook.
Grierson, Herbert (ed.)	The Letters of Sir Walter Scott.
Grierson, Herbert, and others (eds.)	Sir Walter Scott To-day; Some Retrospective Essays and Studies.
Grierson, Herbert.	Sir Walter Scott; Broadcast Lectures to the Young.
Gwynn, Stephen.	Life of Sir Walter Scott.
Hutton, R. H.	Sir Walter Scott.
James, Henry.	Notes and Reviews.
Ker, W. P.	Collected Essays. Vol. I.
Lang, Andrew.	Sir Walter Scott.
Lockhart, J. G.	Life of Sir Walter Scott.
Patten, J. A.	Sir Walter Scott; A Character Study.
Royal Society of Literature of the United Kingdom.	Essays By Divers Hands. New Series. Vols. 4, 10.
Saintsbury, George.	Essays in English Literature.
Sands, C. N. J.	Sir Walter Scott's Conge.
Seccombe, T., and others.	Scott Centenary Articles.
Sheppard, A. T.	The Art and Practice of Historical Fiction.
Smith, G.	Lectures and Essays.
Van Antwerp, W. C.	Collector's Comment on His First Editions of the Works of Sir Walter Scott.
Woodberry, G. E.	Great Writers.
Worthington, G.	A Bibliography of the Waverley Novels.

Bibliography

Wright, S. F.   Life of Sir Walter Scott.
Wyndham, G.   Essays in Romantic Literature.

PERIODICALS

Atlantic Monthly 46: 313 (1880); 69: 139 (1892); 148: 595 (1931).
Blackwood's Magazine 216: 832 (1924); 219: 265 (1926).
Columbia University Quarterly 17: 40 (1914).
Cornhill 71: 75, 213, 306 (1931).
Current Opinion 65: 188 (1918).
Dial 56: 329 (1914).
Harper's Magazine 46: 142 (1902); 54: 15 (1910).
Journal of English and Germanic Philology 23: 28, 241, 389 (1924).
Living Age 15: 49 (1847); 205: 515 (1895); 236: 684 (1903); 266: 707 (1910); 296: 612 (1917).
Nation 56: 370 (1893).
Nineteenth Century 7: 941 (1880); 96: 531 (1924).
North American Review 1: 403 (1815); 58: 464 (1931).
Publications of the Modern Language Association 45: 1140, 1264 (1930).
Quarterly Review 180: 431 (1895); 213: 33 (1910); 243: 16 (1925).
Queen's Quarterly 37: 335 (1930).
Times Literary Supplement July 7, 1921; Sept. 4, 1924; June 25, 1925; May 27, 1926.

SMOLLETT, TOBIAS

Born in Dalquhurn, Dumbartonshire, in 1721, son of Archibald Smollett, the youngest son of Sir James Smollett of Bonhill. After his father died in 1723, his mother settled in Edinburgh. Tobias received a good education at Dumbarton school. Thwarted in his desire to enter the army, in 1736 he was sent to the University of Glasgow to qualify for the medical profession, and in the same year was apprenticed to a doctor for five years. His taste for satire was exhibited in his play, *The Regicide*, based on Buchanan's description of the death of James I. With this play he sought his fortune in London, but Lyttelton, patron of Thomson and Mallet, would have nothing to do with it. He was saved from starvation by a post as surgeon's mate on a king's ship, and served during the siege of Cartagena in 1741. He married Nancy Lascelles in 1747. Unsuccessful as a surgeon, he began to write fiction. His first novel, *Roderick Random* (1748), was translated into French as the work of Fielding. In 1750 he obtained the degree of M.D. In 1751 *The Adventures of Peregrine Pickle* appeared, and in 1753 *Ferdinand Count Fathom*. Smollett finally gave up medicine for literature and settled in Chelsea. He edited *Don Quixote*, and a literary periodical called *The Critical Review*, organized a *History of England* and *Voyages*, and projected a *Universal History*. In 1760 he contributed *Sir Launcelot Greaves* to the *British Magazine*. He edited the *Briton* until its expiration in 1763, and undertook a translation of Voltaire. Broken in health, he spent two years abroad, which he commemorated in his *Travels* (1766). On his return to London he published *The History and Adventures of an Atom*. He wrote *Humphrey Clinker* near Leghorn in 1770, where he died on September 17th, 1777.

BIBLIOGRAPHY

Novels

The Adventures of Roderick Random. 1748. (Everyman's Library, Dutton)
The Adventures of Peregrine Pickle. 1751. (Everyman's Library, Dutton)
The Adventures of Ferdinand Count Fathom. 1753. (Routledge)
The Adventures of Sir Launcelot Greaves. 1762. (Routledge)
The History and Adventures of an Atom. 2v. 1749. (o.p.)
The Expedition of Humphrey Clinker. 1771. (World's Classics)

Studies and Reviews

BOOKS

Anderson, R.   The Life of Tobias Smollett, with Critical Observations on His Works.
Benjamin, L. S.   Life and Letters of Tobias Smollett.
Buck, H. S.   Smollett as Poet.
Study in Smollett.

Bibliography

Chambers, R.	Smollett; his Life and Selections from his Writings.
Forsyth, William.	Novels and Novelists.
Hannay, D.	Life of Tobias Smollett.
Herbert, D.	Memoir [Preface to *Selected Works of Smollett*, published 1870].
Ireland, Alexander (ed.)	Hazlitt's Selections.
Lang, Andrew.	Adventures Among Books.
Masson, David.	British Novelists and their Styles.
Melville, Lewis (ed.)	Life and Letters of Tobias Smollett.
Noyes, Edward (ed.)	Letters of Tobias Smollett.
Robinson, C. N.	The British Tar in Fact and Fiction.
Saintsbury, George.	Life of Smollett [In 1895 edition of novels].
Smeaton, O.	Tobias Smollett.
Stephen, Sir Leslie.	English Thought in the Eighteenth Century.
Thackeray, W. M.	English Humourists.
Wershoven, F. J.	Smollett et Lesage.
Whitridge, A.	Tobias Smollett.
Wierstra, F. D.	Smollett and Dickens.

PERIODICALS

Atlantic Monthly   3: 693 (1859).
Blackwood's Magazine   167: 697 (1900).
Classical Weekly   23: 9, 17 (1928).
Dial   32: 81 (1902).
Fortnightly Review   129: 210 (1928);   129: 343 (1928).
Macmillan's Magazine   21: 527 (1880).
Modern Language Notes   53: 111 (1928).
Philological Quarterly   7: 368 (1928).
Quarterly Review   103: 66 (1858).

STERNE, LAURENCE

Born at Clonmel, Ireland, on November 24th, 1713, son of Roger Sterne, an English officer. His first ten years were spent in various parts of Ireland and England with his mother and small sister, as they followed his father's regiment from one military station to another. He spent eight years at school at Halifax, in Yorkshire. He was graduated from Jesus College,

Cambridge, in 1736, obtaining his M.A. degree in 1740. He married Elizabeth Lumley in 1741. He entered the church, and in 1743 he held the living of Sutton, near York, as well as the living of Stillington, and was prebendary of York Cathedral. He established a dairy farm in order to increase his income, but his farming experiments were not successful. For more than twenty years (1738–1759) he lived at Sutton, and followed the ordinary pursuits of a rural parson who enjoyed substantial preferment. In 1747 he first appeared in print under his own name when he published a sermon entitled *The Case of Elijah and the Widow Zerephath Consider'd.* His wife became insane in 1758 and was removed to a private asylum, and Sterne in his loneliness began to write *Tristram Shandy.* He was obliged to publish the first two books privately, but they attracted a great deal of attention, and a London publisher offered to print a collected edition of his sermons under the title, *Sermons by Mr. Yorick,* as well as a new edition of *Tristram Shandy.* He continued to write further episodes in the life of "Tristram Shandy," which provoked a great deal of unpleasant comment in England because of their coarseness. In 1762 he became very ill and traveled in southern France and Italy for his health, but returned to England to publish the last volume of *Tristram Shandy,* and the first two volumes of *A Sentimental Journey through France and Italy.* He died in London on March 18th, 1768.

BIBLIOGRAPHY

Novels

The Life and Opinions of Tristram Shandy. 1928. (Everyman's Library, Dutton)
 Volumes I and II. 1759.
 Volumes III and IV. 1761.
 Volumes V and VI. 1762.
 Volumes VII and VIII. 1765.
 Volume IX. 1767.
A Sentimental Journey through France and Italy. 1768. (Oxford.

Miscellaneous Works

Letters of the Late Reverend Laurence Sterne to his Most Intimate Friends with a Fragment in the Manner of Rabelais, to

Bibliography

Which are Prefixed Memoirs of his Life and Family, Written by Himself, Published by his Daughter, Lydia Sterne de Medalle. 1775. (Lane, 1929)
Second Journal to Eliza. [Letters from Yorick to Eliza] 1775. (Lane, 1929)
Twelve Letters to his Friends on Various Occasions, to Which is Added his History of a Warm Watch-Coat, with Explanatory notes. 1775. (Lane, 1929)

Studies and Reviews

BOOKS

Bagehot, W.	Literary Studies.
Benjamin, L. S.	The Life and Letters of Laurence Sterne.
Bennett, J. O.	Much Loved Books.
Bensley, E.	An Alleged Source of *Tristram Shandy*.
Binz-Winiger, E.	Erziehungsfragen in den Romanen.
Birrell, A.	Men, Women and Books.
Cross, W. L.	The Life and Times of Laurence Sterne.
Curtis, L. P.	The Politics of Laurence Sterne.
De Reul, P.	Laurence Sterne.
Dibelius, Wilhelm.	Englische Romankunst.
Elevin, W.	Some Eighteenth Century Men of Letters.
Fitzgerald, P.	Life of Laurence Sterne.
Froe, A. de.	Laurence Sterne and his Novels Studied in the Light of Modern Psychology.
Frye, P. H.	Visions and Chimeras.
Gordon, G. S.	Companionable Books. Series One.
Gosse, Sir Edmund.	More Books on the Table.
	Selected Essays. First Series.
Hewlett, M. H.	Extemporary Essays.
Johnson, R. Brimley (ed.)	The Letters of Laurence Sterne.
Klingemann, G.	Goethes Verhältnis zu Laurence Sterne.
Ludwig, A.	Zu Dickens und Sterne.

Melville, Lewis.	Life and Letters of Laurence Sterne.
Meynell, Alice.	Second Person Singular.
More, P. E.	Shelburne Essays.
Newton, A. E.	Greatest Book in the World.
Orage, A. R.	Readers and Writers.
Pinger, W. R.	Laurence Sterne and Goethe.
Priestley, J. B.	English Comic Characters.
	Introduction to *The Life and Opinions of Tristram Shandy.* (Lane, 1928)
Quiller-Couch, Sir A. T.	Adventures in Criticism.
Read, H. E.	The Sense of Glory.
	Introduction to *A Sentimental Journey through France and Italy.* (Scholartis, 1931)
Saintsbury, George.	Introduction to *A Sentimental Journey,* and *The Journal to Eliza.* (Everyman's Library, Dutton, 1927)
Scherer, Edmond.	Essays on English Literature. [Translated by G. Saintsbury]
Scott, Sir Walter.	Miscellaneous Prose Works.
Sherman, S. P.	Critical Woodcuts.
Sichel, Walter.	Sterne, a Study.
Stapfer, P.	Life of Laurence Sterne.
Traill, H. D.	Sterne.
Weygandt, C.	Tuesdays at Ten.
Woolf, Virginia.	Introduction to *A Sentimental Journey through France and Italy.* (Oxford University Press, 1928)
	The Second Common Reader.
Zweig, S.	Sternstunden der Menschheit.

PERIODICALS

Archiv   156: 235 (1929).
Atlantic Monthly   96: 127 (1905).
Blackwood's Magazine   217: 297 (1925).
Bookman   29: 467 (1909);   30: 253 (1909);   30: 640 (1910);   42: 394 (1915);   58: 10 (1923).
Current Literature   49: 443 (1910).
Dial   53: 51 (1912);   58: 293 (1915).

Bibliography

Edinburgh Review   218: 335 (1913).
English Review   16: 228 (1914).
Fortnightly Review   93: 1137 (1910).
Living   Age   265: 700   (1910);   278: 480   (1913);   280: 121
   (1914);   280: 611 (1914).
Modern Language Notes   42: 321 (1927);   44: 379 (1929).
Modern Philology   14: 217 (1916);   16: 205 (1918).
Nation   89: 346 (1914).
Nation (London)   46: 347 (1929).
North American Review   191: 273 (1910).
Notes and Queries   159: 27, 84 (1930).
Outlook   154: 220 (1930).
Revue de littérature comparée   7: 459 (1927).
Saturday Review of Literature   2: 69 (1926).
Spectator   103: 310 (1909);   111: 904 (1913).
Westminster Review   174: 399 (1910).
Yale Review   N.S. 15: 99 (1925).

THACKERAY, WILLIAM MAKEPEACE

Born at Calcutta, July 18th, 1811. His father and grandfather
were both in East India Company's service. Educated at Charter-
house and Trinity College, Cambridge, but left in 1830 without
a degree. Visited Weimar and Rome, and on his return entered
the Middle Temple. Early in 1833 became contributor to, and
later editor of, the *National Standard*, a short-lived weekly. His
interest in art drew him to Paris in 1834 to study. In 1836 he
married Isabella Shawe, daughter of an Indian colonel.   His
eldest daughter, Lady Ritchie, also wrote novels and edited a
biographical edition of her father's works. He moved to London
in 1837 where he was a regular contributor to the *Times*, *New
Monthly*, and *Fraser's*. His first book, *The Paris Sketch-Book*, appeared in 1840 and was followed by many short stories and
sketches. Thackeray became contributor to *Punch* during its
first year and continued so until 1851. *Vanity Fair*, as did many
of his other works, appeared first in serial form, and its completion in 1848 established his reputation as novelist. Most of his
important novels were written between 1848 and 1854, and during
this period he visited America twice on lecture tours. In 1857
he was unsuccessful in an attempt to enter Parliament as Radical
candidate for Oxford. In 1860 the *Cornhill Magazine* appeared

with Thackeray as editor, and although he resigned two years later he continued as contributor. He died on December 24th, 1863, and was buried at Kensal Green.

BIBLIOGRAPHY

Novels *

Vanity Fair. 1848.
Pendennis. 1850.
Henry Esmond. 1852.
The Newcomes. 1853.
The Virginians. 1859.

Minor Novels, Short Stories, and Sketches *

The Tremendous Adventures of Major Gahagan. 1838–1839.
Snob Papers. 1838–1839.
The Memoirs of Mr. Charles J. Yellowplush. 1841.
The Fitz-Boodle Papers. 1842–1843.
Men's Wives. 1843.
The Memoirs of Barry Lyndon, Esquire. 1844.
A Legend of the Rhine. 1845.
The Christmas Books of Mr. M. A. Titmarsh. 1847–1855.
The History of Samuel Titmarsh. 1849.
The Great Hoggarty Diamond. 1849.
Roundabout Papers. 1860–1863.
Lovel the Widower. 1861.
The Adventures of Philip. 1863.
Denis Duval. 1867.
Catherine. 1867.

Studies and Reviews

BOOKS

Benjamin, L. S. William Makepeace Thackeray.
Bennett, J. O. Much Loved Books.
Berdan (ed.), and
  others. Modern Essays.
Curtis, G. W. Oxford Book of American Essays.

* The best edition of his complete works is the Biographical Edition, with Introductions by Anne Thackeray Ritchie. (Harper, 1899.)

Bibliography

Dark, S.	William Makepeace Thackeray.
Elwin, M.	Thackeray, a Personality.
Johnson, C. P.	The Early Writings of Thackeray.
Johnson, R. Brimley (ed.)	Famous Reviewers.
Lyall, Rt. Hon. Sir A. C.	Studies in Literature and History.
Merivale, H., and Marzials, F. T.	Life of Thackeray.
Payne, W. M. (ed.)	American Literary Criticism.
Quiller-Couch, Sir A. T.	Charles Dickens and Other Victorians.
Rankin, T. E. (ed.), and others.	Further Adventures in Essay Reading.
Ritchie, Lady.	Letters.
Saintsbury, George.	Selected Modern English Essays. Consideration of Thackeray.
Shepherd, R. H.	Bibliography of Thackeray (1880).
Trollope, Anthony.	Life of Thackeray.
Van Dyke, H.	Companionable Books.
Wells, C. W.	Essays in Criticism (California University, Department of English).
Whibley, Charles.	Thackeray (a Critical Commentary).
Willcocks, M. P.	Between the Old World and the New.
Williams, O.	Some Great English Novels.
Winterich, J. F. T.	Books and the Man.

PERIODICALS

Atlantic Monthly   13: 371 (1864).
Blackwood's Magazine   77: 86 (1855).
Chambers's Journal   69: 641 (1892).
Cornhill Magazine   9: 655 (1864);   63: 705 (1927);   64: 83, 210, 362 (1928);   67: 553 (1930).
Forum   18: 376 (1894).
Harper's Magazine   140: 177 (1920).
Living Age   16: 271;   18: 412;   20: 497;   30: 97;   37: 307; 40: 483;   47: 769;   80: 375, 476;   81: 3;   84: 55;   104: 387; 116: 579;   178: 159;   190: 44;   213: 335;   219: 818;   306: 776 (1848–1920).
London Mercury   8: 380 (1923).

London Quarterly Review   22: 375.
Modern Language Notes   35: 31 (1920).
Nineteenth Century   91: 57 (1922).
North American Review   77: 199 (1853).
Saturday Review of Literature   4: 1013 (1928).
Spectator   66: 303 (1890).

WELLS, HERBERT GEORGE

Born at Bromley, Kent, September 21st, 1866. Educated in a
private school at Bromley, and Midhurst Grammar School, until
the age of thirteen years, when he became first a drug salesman,
and later a draper's assistant. He studied privately, and at sixteen,
became assistant master at Midhurst Grammar School. He entered Normal School of Science, South Kensington, on a scholarship, where he received the degree of B.Sc., with first class
honors, in 1888. His first marriage was in 1890. In 1894 he married Amy Catherine Robbins. He taught school until illness
forced him to take up journalism in 1893. Since then he has devoted his whole time to writing. His first novel, *The Time
Machine*, was published in 1895. Besides his realistic and sociological novels and scientific romances, this novelist, essayist, pamphleteer, sociologist, historian, and propagandist has produced
copious non-fiction writings, notably his *Outline of History* in 1920.

BIBLIOGRAPHY

Novels

The Time Machine: An Invention. 1895. (Holt, 1922)
The Wonderful Visit. 1895. (Dutton, 1929)
The Island of Doctor Moreau. 1896. (Doubleday, 1929)
The Wheels of Chance: A Cycling Holiday Adventure. 1896.
   (Macmillan, 1896)
The Invisible Man: A Grotesque Romance. 1897. (Collins, 1931)
Love and Mr. Lewisham. 1900. (Scribner, 1924)
The Sea Lady: A Tissue of Moonshine. 1902. (Benn, 1927)
Kipps: The Story of a Simple Soul. 1905. (Collins, 1931)
Tono-Bungay. 1908. (Collins, 1931)
Ann Veronica. 1909. (Harper, 1909)
The History of Mr. Polly. 1910. (Boni & Liveright, 1931)
The New Machiavelli. 1910. (Collins, 1930)

Bibliography

Marriage. 1912. (Duffield, 1912)
The Passionate Friends. 1913. (Collins, 1931)
The Wife of Sir Isaac Harman. 1914. (Macmillan, 1916)
Bealby: A Holiday. 1915. (Macmillan, 1922)
The Research Magnificent. 1915. (Macmillan, 1915)
Mr. Britling Sees It Through. 1916. (Macmillan, 1917)
The Soul of a Bishop. 1917. (Macmillan, 1917)
Joan and Peter. 1918. (Macmillan, 1919)
The Undying Fire. 1919. (Macmillan, 1919)
The Secret Places of the Heart. 1922. (Macmillan, 1922)
Christina Alberta's Father. 1925. (Macmillan, 1925)
The World of William Clissold. 1926. (Doran, 1926)
Meanwhile. 1927. (Doran, 1927)
Mr. Blettsworthy on Rampole Island. 1928. (Doubleday, 1928)
The King Who Was A King; An Unconventional Novel. 1929.
    (Doubleday, 1929)
The Autocracy of Mr. Parham. 1930. (Doubleday, 1930)
The Bulpington of Blup; Adventures, Poses, Stresses, Conflicts,
    and Disaster in a Contemporary Brain. 1933. (Macmillan,
    1933)

Utopias and Stories of Social Reconstruction

The War of the Worlds. 1898. (Harper, 1922)
When the Sleeper Wakes. 1899. (See The Sleeper Wakes)
The First Man in the Moon. 1901. (Collins, 1931)
The Food of the Gods and How It Came to Earth. 1904. (Scrib-
    ner, 1924)
A Modern Utopia. 1905. (Scribner, 1925)
In the Days of the Comet. 1906. (Scribner, 1924)
The War in the Air. 1908. (Macmillan, 1908)
The Sleeper Wakes. [When the Sleeper Wakes, rewritten] 1911.
    (Collins, 1930)
The World Set Free: A Story of Mankind. 1914. (Collins, 1927)
Men Like Gods. 1923. (Macmillan, 1923)
The Dream. 1924. (Macmillan, 1924)

Studies and Reviews

BOOKS
Braybrooke, P.   Peeps at the Mighty.
                        Some Aspects of H. G. Wells.

Brooks, Van Wyck.	The World of H. G. Wells.
Brown, I. J. C.	H. G. Wells.
Burt, M. S.	Other Side.
Chandler, L. J.	H. G. Wells.
Chesterton, G. K.	Come to Think of It.
	Fancies Versus Fads.
	Mr. H. G. Wells and the Giants.
Crawford, A. H.	The Religion of H. G. Wells, and Other Essays.
Cross, W. L.	Four Contemporary Novelists.
Crozier, J. B.	Last Words on Great Issues.
Drake, W. A. (ed.)	American Criticism. (1926)
Freeman, John.	The Moderns.
Gardiner, A. G.	Pillars of Society.
Guyot, Edouard.	H. G. Wells.
Hackett, Francis.	Horizons: A Book of Criticisms.
Jackson, H.	Romance and Reality.
Kennedy, J. M.	English Literature 1880–1905.
Lacon. (pseud.)	Lectures to Living Authors.
Lynd, Robert.	Books and Authors.
Mencken, H. L.	Prejudices. First Series.
Price, J. S.	The World in the Wellsian Era.
Pritchard, F. H. (ed.)	From Confucius to Mencken.
Scott, Dixon.	Men of Letters.
Scott-James, R. A.	Personality in Literature.
Shanks, Edward.	First Essay in Literature.
Sherman, S. P.	Critical Woodcuts.
	On Contemporary Literature.
Slosson, E. E.	Six Major Prophets.
Wells, G. H.	H. G. Wells.
West, Geoffrey, pseud.	See Wells, G. H.
Williams, Harold.	Modern English Writers.
Wolf, E. C.	H. G. Wells, A Sketch of His Life and Works.

PERIODICALS

Adelphi   1: 56 (1923);   3: 609 (1926).
American Mercury   6: 509 (1925).
Century   94: 831 (1917);   105: 686 (1923);   114: 636 (1927).
Commonweal   4: 644 (1926);   6: 476 (1927).

Bibliography

Current Opinion 73: 94 (1922); 76: 774 (1924).
Deutsche Rundschau 216: 142 (1928).
Dial 67: 140 (1919); 70: 202 (1921); 75: 285 (1923).
Edinburgh Review 237: 113 (1923).
Englische Studien 59, no. 2: 193 (1925).
English Journal 14: 89 (1925).
English Review 35: 288 (1922); 37: 405 (1923); 47: 491 (1928).
Forum 65: 98 (1921); 78: 797 (1927).
Living Age 282: 392 (1914); 286: 281 (1915); 299: 624 (1918); 302: 532 (1919); 308: 789 (1921); 317: 244 (1923); 333: 728 (1927); 339: 287 (1930).
London Mercury 3: 43, 570 (1920–21); 5: 506 (1922); 18: 538 (1928); 19: 517 (1929); 22: 560 (1930).
London Quarterly Review 124: 119 (1915).
Mercure de France 194: 513 (1927).
Nation 108: 1014 (1919); 112: 266, 554 (1921); 114: 289, 721 (1922); 120: 434 (1925); 123: 536 (1926); 125: 231 (1927).
Nation (London) 33: 75 (1923); 39: 735 (1926); 40: 561 (1927).
Nation and Athenæum 40: 16, 561 (1927); 41: 17, 581 (1927).
New Adelphi 2: 121 (1928).
New Republic 1: 27 (1914); 19: 188 (1919); 25: 315 (1921); 30: 358 (1922); 35: 102 (1923); 48: 197 (1926); 49: 301 (1927); 61: 203 (1930).
New Statesman 13: 240 (1919); 17: 246 (1921); 20: 695 (1923); 23: 16 (1924); 29: 540 (1927).
North American Review 210: 122 (1919).
Nuova Antologia 250: 318 (1926); 266: 217 (1928).
Revue Politique et Littéraire 57: 340, 657 (1919).
Revue des Deux Mondes 6th period 36: 457 (1916); 6th period, 41: 445 (1917); 7th period, 41: 685 (1927).
Saturday Review 123: 3 (Supp. May 19, 1917); 128: 556 (1919); 132: 203 (1921); 135: 317 (1923); 140: 340 (1925); 142: 220, 263, 388, 617 (1926); 144: 278 (1927); 150: 118 (1930).
Saturday Review of Literature 4: 54 (1927); 5: 1177 (1929).

Spectator 135: 459 (1925); 137: 349, 539, 819 (1926); 138: 565, 757 (1927); 141: 269 (1928).
Virginia Quarterly Review 3: 127 (1927); 4: 119 (1928).
Yale Review N.S. 16: 298 (1927).

WHARTON, EDITH

Edith Newbold Jones was born in New York City on January 24th, 1862, of an old New York family. Her great-grandfather, Ebenezer Stevens, was a general in the Revolutionary War. She spent a great deal of her childhood and youth in Europe, and was privately educated. In 1885 she married Edward Wharton, a Boston banker. They lived in New York, Newport, and Lenox, and went frequently to Europe. She began her literary career with the publication of a sonnet in *Scribner's Magazine* in 1889. Her first short story appeared in *Scribner's Magazine* in July, 1891. In 1899 she collected her short stories and published them under the title, *The Greater Inclination*. Her second collection was *Crucial Instances* (1901), which led to a significant friendship with Henry James, who influenced her literary style considerably. Her first novel, *The Valley of Decision* (1902), was a story of eighteenth-century Italy. *The House of Mirth* (1905), a novel of New York society, established her reputation. *Ethan Frome* (1911), a novelette of New England, is her finest achievement. Since 1906 she has lived in France. She was engaged in relief work during the Great War and was awarded the Cross of the Legion of Honor by the French Government, while Belgium made her a Chevalier of the Order of Leopold. She has been writing steadily over a period of twenty-five years. In 1921 *The Age of Innocence* was awarded the Pulitzer Prize. Her works include novels, short stories, travel books, and a book on literary criticism, *The Writing of Fiction*.

BIBLIOGRAPHY

Novels and Novelettes

The Touchstone. 1900. (Scribner, 1900)
The Valley of Decision. 1902. (Scribner, 1902)
Sanctuary. 1903. (Appleton, 1923)
The House of Mirth. 1905. (Scribner, 1922)
Madame de Treymes. 1907. (Scribner, 1907)

Bibliography

The Fruit of the Tree. 1907. (Scribner, 1907)
Ethan Frome. 1911. (Scribner, 1919)
The Reef. 1912. (Appleton, 1932)
The Custom of the Country. 1913. (Appleton, 1932)
Summer. 1917. (Appleton, 1933)
The Marne. 1918. (Appleton, 1918)
The Age of Innocence. 1920. (Appleton, 1932)
The Glimpses of the Moon. 1922. (Appleton, 1922)
A Son at the Front. 1923. (Scribner, 1923)
The Old Maid. 1924. (Appleton, 1924)
New Year's Day. 1924. (Appleton, 1924)
False Dawn. 1924. (Appleton, 1924)
The Spark. 1924. (Appleton, 1924)
The Mother's Recompense. 1925. (Appleton, 1925)
Twilight Sleep. 1927. (Appleton, 1930)
The Children. 1928. (Appleton, 1930)
Certain People. 1930. (Appleton, 1930)
Hudson River Bracketed. 1930. (Appleton, 1930)
The Gods Arrive. 1932. (Appleton, 1932)

Short Stories

The Greater Inclination. 1899. (Scribner, 1899)
Crucial Instances. 1901. (Scribner, 1909)
The Descent of Man. 1904. (Scribner, 1904)
The Hermit and the Wild Woman. 1908. (Scribner, 1908)
Tales of Men and Ghosts. 1910. (Scribner, 1910)
Xingu. 1916. (Scribner, 1916)
Here and Beyond. 1926. (Appleton, 1926)
Human Nature. 1933. (Appleton, 1933)

Studies and Reviews

BOOKS

Björkman, E.	Voices of To-morrow.
Boynton, Percy.	Some Contemporary Americans: the Personal Equation in Literature.
Canby, H. S.	Definitions. Series One.
Collins, Joseph.	Taking the Literary Pulse.
Hackett, Francis.	Horizons: A Book of Criticism.
Halsey, F. W.	Women Authors of our Day in Their Homes.

Hind, C. L.	Authors and I.
	More Authors and I.
Huneker, J. G.	Ivory Apes and Peacocks.
Lovett, R. M.	Edith Wharton.
Melish, L. M.	A Bibliography of the Collected Writings of Edith Wharton.
Overton, G. M.	American Nights Entertainment.
	Authors of the Day.
Sedgwick, H. D.	The New American Type.
Sherman, S. P.	Main Stream.
Squire, J. C., and others.	Contemporary American Authors.
Underwood, J. C.	Literature and Insurgency.
Van Doren, Carl.	American and British Literature since 1890.
	Contemporary American Novelists.
Williams, Blanche C.	Our Short-Story Writers.

PERIODICALS

Atlantic Monthly 151: 385 (1933).
Bookman 63: 641 (1926); 72: 303 (1927).
Bookman (London) 64: 262 (1923).
Century 119: 112 (1929).
Dial 68: 80 (1920); 73: 343 (1922).
English Journal 12: 24 (1923).
Forum 68: 905 (1922); 74: 154 (1925); 78: 78 (1927).
Independent 109: 79 (1922); 111: 157 (1923).
Literary Review 2: 883 (1922); 3: 61 (1923); 4: 803 (1924); 5: 3 (1925).
London Mercury 13: 52 (1925).
Mentor 22: 41 (1930).
Nation 85: 514 (1907); 97: 404 (1913); 112: 40 (1921); 131: 654 (1930).
New Republic 2: 40 (1915); 3: 20 (1915); 10: 50 (1917); 36: 105 (1923); 39: 77 (1924); 51: 78 (1927); 65: 225 (1931); 73: 53 (1932).
New Statesman and Nation 4: 488 (1932).
North American 182: 840 (1906); 183: 125 (1906); 219: 139 (1924); 235: 65 (1933).
Outlook 71: 209 (1902); 81: 719 (1905).
Quarterly Review 223: 182 (1915).

Bibliography

Saturday Review 150: 747 (1930).
Saturday Review of Literature 1: 43 (1924); 5: 84 (1928); 9: 145 (1932).
Sewanee Review 40: 425 (1932).
Spectator 95: 470 (1905); 129: 373 (1922); 131: 514 (1923); 132: 1006 (1924); 145: 804 (1930).
Yale Review 16: 646 (1927).

WOOLF, VIRGINIA

Virginia Stephen, the daughter of Sir Leslie Stephen, the famous biographer and literary critic, was born in London in 1882. She was privately educated, and, among other studies, she learned Greek. In her childhood she was surrounded by her father's distinguished friends, artists, novelists, poets, and historians. When her father died she moved with her sister Vanessa (now Mrs. Clive Bell) to a small house in Bloomsbury. This house became the meeting place of their friends and formed the nucleus of "The Bloomsbury Group," which included Lytton Strachey, E. M. Forster, Clive Bell, and others equally famous in art and literature. In 1912 she married Leonard Woolf, and together, at Richmond, they set up a small hand press and began producing a few books, in limited editions, including her own. It was called the Hogarth Press and became so successful that it developed into a real publishing house. Her first novel, *The Voyage Out* (1915), was written when she was twenty-four. *Jacob's Room* (1922) was her first novel to achieve literary distinction. Her novels became more and more divergent from the traditions of fiction writing, and *The Waves* (1931), which portrays the sensations of a few characters, has practically revolutionized at least her own technique of fiction. In addition to her novels she has written three books of literary criticism, *Mr. Bennett and Mrs. Brown*, *The Common Reader*, and *The Second Common Reader*, as well as a psychological study of women and fiction-writing, *A Room of One's Own*.

BIBLIOGRAPHY

Novels

The Voyage Out. 1915. (Harcourt, 1931)
Night and Day. 1919. (Harcourt, 1931)

Jacob's Room. 1922. (Harcourt, 1931)
Mrs. Dalloway. 1925. (Harcourt, 1931)
To the Lighthouse. 1927. (Harcourt, 1931)
Orlando: A Biography. 1928. (Harcourt, 1928)
The Waves. 1931. (Harcourt, 1931)
A Biography. 1933. (Harcourt, 1933)

Short Stories
Monday or Tuesday. 1921. (Harcourt, 1921)

Miscellaneous Works
Mr. Bennett and Mrs. Brown. 1924. (Hogarth Press, 1924)
The Common Reader. 1925. (Harcourt, 1925)
A Room of One's Own. 1929. (Harcourt, 1929)
The Second Common Reader. 1932. (Harcourt, 1932)

Studies and Reviews

BOOKS

Bennett, Arnold.	Savour of Life.
Brewster, D., and Burrell, A.	Adventure or Experience.
Bullett, Gerald.	Modern English Fiction.
Collins, Joseph.	The Doctor Looks at Literature.
Drew, Elizabeth.	The Modern Novel. Some Aspects of Contemporary Fiction.
Gould, Gerald.	The English Novel of Today.
Holtby, W.	Virginia Woolf.
Mais, S. P. B.	Why We Should Read.
Muir, Edwin.	Transition: Essays on Contemporary Literature.
West, Rebecca.	Ending in Earnest.

PERIODICALS

Bookman   68: 625 (1929);   74: 362 (1929).
Bookman (London)   68: 214 (1925).
Books   [New York Herald-Tribune]   November 1, 1931.
Calendar of Modern Letters   1: 320, 404 (1925).
Commonweal   3: 220 (1926).
Current Opinion   68: 93 (1920).
Dial   70: 572 (1921);   75: 83 (1923);   77: 451 (1924).

Bibliography

Die neue Rundschau   40: 717 (1929).
Everyman   15: 114 (1919).
Forum   87: xiv (1932).
Les Lettres   June, 1930.
L'Européen   January 8, 1930.
Literary Review   3: 547 (1923);   5: 2 (1925).
London Mercury   14: 40 (1926).
Nation   116: 368 (1923);   120: 631 (1925);   133: 674 (1931).
New Criterion   4: 277 (1926).
New Republic   22: 320 (1920);   66: 239 (1931).
New Statesman   25: 229 (1925).
New Statesman and Nation   2: supp. x (1931).
Revue anglo-américaine   June, 1928;   April, 1930.
Saturday Review   139: 549, 588 (1925);   140: 17 (1925); 143: 712 (1927);   152: 462 (1931).
Saturday Review of Literature   1: 755, 872 (1925);   8: 352 (1931).
Spectator   129: 661 (1922);   138: 871 (1927).
Virginia Quarterly Review   4: 119 (1928).
Voices   3: 33 (1920).
Yale Review   19: 754 (1930).

WORKING SUGGESTIONS

I present here a number of subjects for class discussion or theme work by the student. The items might be multiplied almost indefinitely. In my own experience with advanced students I have found the material outlined in the first section of this book particularly suggestive. Essays that concentrate attention on form have a concrete basis to work from. The old type of undergraduate essay dwelt too vaguely on generalizations. Characterization was the main resource, but the topic was generally left hanging in the air. Definite results may be reached if the student follows some such plan as this in his report on any assigned novel:

Theme. What is the novel about?

Plot and Narrative Elements. How does the novelist marshal his material? Is there a recognizable design in his treatment?

Other elements, such as *dialogue, description,* and *analysis,* might be separately treated, with attention given to the skill with which these are combined. A *general account* might then follow of the author's particular contribution to fiction in formal arrangement or philosophy.

I append a series of questions.

1. Investigate the handling of time in Thackeray's *Vanity Fair,* or any other novel.

   (Read what Lubbock has to say in his *Craft of Fiction* on the subject of time and space, especially pp. 49 ff. Consult also Muir in *The Structure of the Novel,* Chapter III, Henry James's *Prefaces,* Mrs. Wharton's *The Writing of Fiction.*)

2. Illustrate what you consider to be dramatic methods in fiction. What American or British authors do you consider to be most dramatic?

   (Beach in *The Twentieth Century Novel* is useful here. Chapters XIII ff. should be consulted. The present book also discusses this question. See pp. 9 ff., 35 ff.)

3. Do you attach more importance to form or to content in fiction?

4. Does form necessitate a special kind of content, or does content shape the form a story takes?

   (Note Lubbock's discussion of *War and Peace* in Chapter III of *The Craft of Fiction*, and his statement, "The best form is that which makes the most of its subject—there is no other definition of the meaning of form in fiction.")

5. Indicate how development in technique has taken place from ———— to ————

   (a) in dialogue   (b) in description   (c) in analysis
   (d) in the author's attitude to his story.

6. Is American fiction independent of external influence, or what is the extent of the dependence?

7. What view do you hold of the virtue of massed detail in fiction?

   (See Virginia Woolf, *Mr. Bennett and Mrs. Brown*, in *Hogarth Essays* and *The Common Reader*, pp. 184–195.)

8. Do you support Mrs. Virginia Woolf in her criticisms of Wells, Bennett, and Galsworthy?

9. Write an essay on static characters and developing characters in fiction.

10. Name the most important multiple novels of our period. Discuss the virtues and defects of this form.

    (See Beach, *The Twentieth Century Novel*, Chapter XXI, and Elizabeth Kerr, *The Sequence Novel*, University of Minnesota.)

11. Discuss the effect on fiction of serial publication.

    (Consult Beach, *Publications of the Modern Language Association of America*, December, 1921, and Leavis, *Fiction and the Reading Public*, Chatto.)

12. Discuss the varying degrees of intelligence possessed by important characters in fiction.

    (a) Enumerate a list of such characters possessing respectively high or limited intelligence.
    (b) Make the necessary deductions from your enumeration.
    (See *Saturday Review of Literature* 5: 581[1929].)

13. Indicate some novels where a dual plot exists, and comment on the practice.
    (See Mrs. Wharton's *The Writing of Fiction*, pp. 81 f.)

14. Give examples of novels that are restricted or liberal in their space and time measure with inferences drawn from your classification.

15. Proceed similarly with novels that have a wide or a narrow range of characters.

16. In how far are mid-nineteenth century determinism and the emphasis on heredity and environment reflected in fiction?
    (Consult Myers in *The Later Realism*, pp. 28–33.)

17. What new factors in science and philosophy may be said to influence current fiction?

18. In how far can Realism, Romanticism, Impressionism, and Post-Impressionism be considered satisfactory distinguishing terms as applied to fiction?

19. Can you establish any effective relation between contemporary movements in fiction and the other creative arts?

20. Account for the increased frankness of modern fiction, its exploitation of sex, and its penchant for the crude, the primitive, and the abnormal.
    (See *North American Review* 231: 234, 232: 274; also *Atlantic Monthly* 147: 657.)

21. Henry James stressed the value of
    (1) The point of view—multiple or single, first personal or third personal.
    (2) Progressive revelation.
    (3) The principle of selection and elimination.
    (4) The principle of proportion.
    (5) Unity of theme.
    (6) Evenness of surface.
    (7) The principle of "indirection."
    (8) The submergence of the author in the story.
    (9) The need of dramatizing fiction.
    Discuss these items, and illustrate by reference to his or other books.   On (1) see Mrs. Wharton's *The Writing of Fiction*, pp. 86 f., and Lubbock's *The Craft of Fiction* and James's *Prefaces, passim;* on (9) consider Lubbock's statement, "The less

dramatic, strictly speaking, the subject may be—the less it is able, that is to say, to express itself in action and in action only—the more it is needful to heighten its flat, pictorial, descriptive surface by the arts of drama."

Lubbock has much to say of the methods whereby a skill-ful novelist may render these non-dramatic elements dramatic.

22. What seems to you the most satisfactory way of classifying fiction?

        i.e. Romantic or realistic?
        Historical, sociological?
        Novels of character?
        Novels of incident?   etc.

In case of confusion of type might it be well to define a novel by its dominant characteristic? Lubbock, for example, de-scribes Henry James's *The Ambassadors* as "a pictorial theme dramatically rendered."

23. Is there any one aspect of fiction which in your view has outstanding and permanent importance despite all variations of technique?

24. Discuss the meaning of the following terms as applied to fiction: scenic, pictorial, panoramic, dramatic. (Consult Henry James's *Prefaces*, and Lubbock's *Craft of Fiction*.)

25. Lubbock says that Strether (of James's *The Ambassadors*) "is enough to prove finally how far the intricate performance of thought is beyond the power of a man to record in his own language."

This would seem to imply that first personal narration can never be intellectual, can never, in other words, record the intellectual processes of the narrator's mind. Criticize this statement on the basis of Proust's and Dorothy Richard-son's performance. Is it not perhaps true to say that the effect of immediacy is difficult under these conditions, but that intricacy and intimacy can be readily achieved?

By "immediacy" is implied the conveying of the impres-sion that events are in progress in the present, that they are happening now, rather than that they *have* happened and are being merely recalled.

(Consult A. Maurois in *Saturday Review of Literature* 8:70 [1931].)

26. Charts and diagrams like statistics are never quite reliable. The following instructive chart survey of American fiction was prepared for me by Miss Muriel Miller, M.A. Subject it to criticism, and endeavor to produce as good a chart for the same period of English fiction.

27. Read carefully the paragraph in Chapter XXIX which summarizes James's contribution to the theory of fiction. Indicate in what respects later writers have adhered to or departed from the principles there outlined.

28. (a) Is it possible to indicate any general difference between novels by women and men? (See Woolf's *Room of One's Own* also, *Forum* 81: 179[1929] *Fortnightly* 132: 123[1929] and *American Mercury* 16: 60[1929].)
    (b) Can you account for the greater success of women in fiction than in other branches of literature and the creative arts? (Chapter XXVII.)
    (c) Write an essay on feminine characters presented by men and masculine characters presented by women.
    (d) Does the feminist propaganda, as, for instance, in Dorothy Richardson's novels, seriously impair the artistic content?

29. Do you attach more value to French or to English fiction?

30. Are there any fixed general principles underlying good fiction?

31. Is there any evidence that a new tradition is being established in fiction?

32. Study the methods of chapter arrangement in any two or three recent novelists.
    (See Beach's *The Twentieth Century Novel*, Chapter XXI, Section 3.)

33. How should fiction be taught in our colleges?

34. Are there any novelists of the past who are now unduly neglected? Substantiate your views.

35. Name a number of books concerning which it is difficult to say whether they should be classified as novels. This question will necessarily involve an attempt to define fiction.

36. It is obvious that Mrs. Wharton has been influenced by James. Indicate the extent of the influence, and the extent

of her deviation. Deal similarly with Anne Douglas Sedgwick, Ethel Sidgwick, and Hergesheimer. Deal similarly also with authors influenced by Joyce.
(See page 302.)

37. Justify or condemn the introduction of the class struggle in contemporary fiction. Does the propagandist intention impair the artistic value?
(Consult Wilkinson, Hazel, *Social Thought in American Fiction.*)

38. Is fiction a satisfactory vehicle for the conveying of general ideas?

39. Discuss the novel as affording a means of escape from crass reality.
(Consult Cabell, *Beyond Life*, also Woolf, *The Common Reader*, etc.)

40. How far do you think the novel of escape is productive of fine literature? (See Chart above.)

41. Who among our older writers (i.e. Scott, Thackeray, Reade, etc.) is the dominant influence in historical fiction? Or has historical fiction swerved away from older models?
(See Sheppard, A. T., *The Art and Practice of Historical Fiction*, also *Fortnightly Review* 135: 100[1931].)

42. Relate Hardy to other regional writers.

43. Can satiric fiction be classified, as, for example, satire of ideas, satire of types, satire of national characteristics?
(See Hall, Ernest, *The Satirical Element in the American Novel.*)

44. D. H. Lawrence, Huxley, and Maugham are known to have frequently based their characters on friends and contemporaries. Do you defend the practice? (Consult Chapter XXV.)

45. Discuss and criticize the extension of analytic methods in modern fiction. (Consult Chapter II.)

46. Compare Maugham's novel, *The Explorer*, with his play of the same name. Which form of presentation gives the more satisfactory characterization? Make similar comparisons in the case (a) of a novel that has been dramatized by the author

himself, (b) of a novel dramatized by some one else. (James has made fictions of several of his dramas.)

47. No book satisfies everybody. Every book might have been made both different and better. Subject the present book to criticism under the following heads:

    (a) Disproportion of treatment. (E.g. Is there too little Dickens and too much Huxley?)
    (b) Faulty judgments. (Is Wells, for example, under-estimated as a force in fiction? And are there other opinions in the book with which you disagree?)
    (c) Are certain authors omitted who would be more deserving of treatment than some of the authors included? Can the omission, for example, of Disraeli, Borrow, and Charles Reade be justified?

48. You have observed the prevailing tendency in serious fiction to eliminate the author as far as possible.

    (a) How far is this submergence of the author possible?
    (b) How far is it desirable? Has the novel lost certain valuable elements in the process?
    (c) Name some important novelists of today in whom the personal quality is manifest.

49. We should all be interested in the genesis of a work of fiction. Write a paper dealing with certain novels concerning whose origin we have specific information from the author, or from some other source.

    (Consult the scenarios appended to James's *Sense of the Past* and *The Ivory Tower*. See also an article by Edith Wharton in *Atlantic Monthly* 151:385[1933] and Bennett, *Old Wives' Tale*, Preface.)

50. Do you subscribe to the view that the most satisfactory art product results from the blending of separate elements to constitute a harmonious whole? If so, what criticism can be lodged against the Discontinuous Novel? Does it move here, there, and everywhere regardless of consequences, or is discontinuity a device that can achieve a unified effect?

51. Much has been said in this book and elsewhere written concerning the obvious importance of certain novels that seem to disregard the prevailing principles of composition. Is it

your view that the proved value of such novels invalidates the effort to establish principles of any kind, and that the result will always justify the means? Genius must call art to its aid in order to create satisfying men and women: beyond that does anything matter? The writer of this book would like to see this question effectively answered, for he feels that he has not adequately treated it himself. He is predisposed to attach great importance to the arrangement which covers every detail of a book, but he is compelled to admit that some of the greatest novels in the world abound in seeming carelessness.

(See *Yale Review* N.S. 22:533[1933] and *Bookman* 72:350 [1930].)

52. What has been the influence of the short story on the full-length novel? In your answer consider obvious differences of technique as well as affinities. Take into account also the fact that most important novelists have been writers of short stories. James's manner decidedly changed after the ten-year period when he was writing drama and short fiction.

53. Consider any given author from the point of view of evolution in his form.

54. We reserve our most important question for the last: It is somewhat drastic and far-reaching, for it does not suggest merely what is wrong with the novel, but what is wrong with the world. It is not, therefore, what might ordinarily be considered an academic question. Still we should like some of the younger University generations to deal with the subject. Why then, we ask, have the men who meant most for the race been in their life-time neglected, if not reviled and despised? This happened with Keats as it happened more acutely with Shelley. We know the facts, or some of them at least, of D. H. Lawrence's life. We are aware now that he is a positive force who will count for much in the spiritual and mental life of the generations that are to follow. We know also that he paid a rather severe price for his originality. People who pick his brains, the publishers and the critics, will profit by him. Is it quite playing the game that he sometimes had to ponder where and how he would get his next meal? Will you take the line that suffering of this

kind is a valuable incentive to creative work? There are a good many pros and cons to be considered, and there is much material to furnish forth your answer. Is it, perhaps, better that a man of genius should be angry rather than acquiescent and content? Is that the all-sufficient justification of contemporary neglect?

WORKING SUGGESTIONS (referring to specific chapters in this book)

CHAPTER II.

The treatment of the constituents of all fiction is perhaps complete enough to demand no further expansion by the student. The application of the various principles to particular books can always be made with profit.

CHAPTER VI.

Sterne affords a searching test of a student's capacity for literary appreciation. His work bristles with interesting problems: the qualities of his style, the peculiar art of his composition, his humor, his sensibility, etc. Comparison might effectively be made between the humor and sentiment of Sterne and of Dickens, and it would be a good exercise of ingenuity for the student to indicate the reasons for the increase of Sterne's reputation in recent years. What are the qualities in his writing that appeal peculiarly to the modern mind?

CHAPTER VII. (*Scott*)

In the case of no other great English writer except possibly Dickens is it so necessary for the student to weigh obvious defects against quite as obvious merits. A partisan survey of his work, whether it bears with it excessive praise or excessive blame, would be a prime critical blunder. Few authors need such discriminating appraisal, and to write with complete justice of Scott demands exceptional powers of judgment. Between the zealot and the devil's advocate he has severely suffered.

CHAPTER IX. (*Jane Austen and Thackeray*)

Jane Austen and Thackeray have been here presented in association rather by reason of their differences than their affinities.

The term "essential novelist" has been applied to Jane Austen, as later to Henry James. A profitable comparison might be made between them to discover whether in both cases the phrase has any justification. As applied to both of them the implication is that a sufficient but not extraordinary theme has been chosen which the author has evolved to its fullest capacity. Is there possibly more wastage of effect in James, and a less developed sense of proportion?

CHAPTER X. (*A Group of Dickens's Novels*)
It is reported that when *Old Curiosity Shop* was appearing serially many thousand New Yorkers assembled at the Battery to meet an incoming ship. The impulse that urged them was the desire to know whether "Little Nell" had died. It is obvious that nothing similar can ever recur. The question to be resolved is how far such outrageous popularity betokens a healthy condition of fiction and the fiction public. Is an author justified in considering the interests of his readers—the multitudinous, sentimental, and uncritical thousands—rather than the severer artistic demands of his theme?

CHAPTER XI. (*Hawthorne*)
The approach to Hawthorne might be made from the quoted opinion of Van Wyck Brooks—"the most deeply planted of American writers who indicates more than any other the subterranean history of the American character." Are not the artist and moralist in Hawthorne pulling in opposite directions? Given his Puritan background and the English novel tradition, what is the differentiating quality in his talent? Study also the elements of morbidity as exhibited in the art of Poe and Hawthorne. What affinities are there with the strain of romantic melancholy that had prevailed in Europe in the preceding generation?

CHAPTER XII. (*Melville*)
Are we justified in singling out *Moby Dick* as the outstanding performance of Melville? Do you find in him a profounder use of symbol than in Hawthorne? What symbolic interpretation do you give to *Moby Dick*? Have you any suggestions to offer for his late flowering and his early sterility? "Until I was

twenty-five I had no development at all." For the last thirty years of his life he scarcely wrote.

CHAPTER XIV. *(George Eliot)*
The main point to be developed here is suggested in this sentence: "She is, then, the first of our novelists to be preoccupied with ideas, and had she possessed the art of fusing these in her narrative her reputation to-day would be incontestably higher than it is."

Meredith and Wells were equally concerned with making the novel an effective medium for conveying their theories of life and society. Huxley among the younger moderns is ranked as an "intellectual." It would be interesting to study the whole group of novelists whose preoccupation is primarily with ideas. Are some of the continental writers like Gide and Mann more successful in fusing philosophy and fiction? The question is open, and it is not unimportant.

George Eliot's treatment of simple people, and her particular brand of sympathetic realism is also a provocative subject of discussion.

CHAPTER XV. *(Meredith)*
As with Hardy, so with Meredith, the poems are an essential complement of the prose. The themes of the novels will be encountered there in condensed and concentrated form: Egoism *(The Empty Purse)*; Feminism *(Ballad of Fair Ladies in Revolt, The Sage Enamoured and the Honest Lady,* etc.); Nature and Man *(The Woods of Westermain, Earth and Man,* etc.); Pagan Stoicism *(A Faith on Trial)*.

The student may add to these themes and provide further parallels.

CHAPTER XVI. *(Thomas Hardy)*
The Early Life of Thomas Hardy is important to consult for obvious reasons, not the least of which are the author's statements regarding his own work. Note the following journal jotting under date of January 22nd, 1886: "*The Mayor of Casterbridge* begins to-day in the Graphic newspaper—I fear it will not be so good as I meant, but after all it is not improbabilities of incident, but improbabilities of character that matter."

And note the implications in the following paragraph: "*The Mayor of Casterbridge* was a story which Hardy fancied he had damaged more recklessly as an artistic whole, in the interest of the newspaper in which it appeared serially, than perhaps any other of his novels, his aiming to get an incident into almost every week's part causing him in his own judgment to add events to the narrative somewhat too freely. However, as at this time he called his novel-writing 'mere journey work,' he cared little about it as art, though it must be said in favour of the plot, as he admitted later, that it was quite coherent and organic, in spite of its complication."

Consult as to the effect on fiction of serial publication Q. D. Leavis, *Fiction and the Reading Public*, and Ellen Mary Chase, *Thomas Hardy from Serial to Novel* (University of Minnesota). On Hardy's metaphysical background consult L. Abercrombie's *Thomas Hardy*, Helen Garwood's *Thomas Hardy, an Illustration of Schopenhauer*, and Brennecke's *Thomas Hardy's Universe*. Abercrombie also makes valuable comment on the dramatic and epic tendencies in Hardy's fiction.

The student might work out more closely the suggestions conveyed in this chapter connecting Hardy with Meredith by way of contrast and comparison, and elaborate the relationship of Hardy's poetry with his prose. The chapter suggests also a consideration of the conventional and original elements in Hardy's fiction, of the qualities of his prose style, and of his treatment of nature.

CHAPTER XVIII. (*Conrad*)

It cannot be said that Conrad is a master of the art that conceals art. The problem of form asserts itself in every corner of his work, and the young student of method should scan his devices with as careful attention as he bestows on Henry James. *Nostromo* was the novel chosen for exposition in this book. I suggest a careful analysis of *Chance* as an almost bewildering example of Conrad's craft. His handling of the time element and his concern for the narrative point of view are well exemplified there. Henry James has a useful chapter on Conrad in his *Notes on Novelists*. Attention should also be given to Conrad's devices for rendering character, to his descriptive powers, and the qualities of his style.

CONCLUDING CHAPTERS.

The problems arising out of our immediately contemporary literature have, for the most part, been stated if not solved in these chapters. Personal prejudice is here more likely to confuse the issues. The present book has at least given a sufficiently long perspective from which to view the subject. Exigencies of space forbade the perspective in breadth that the treatment of contemporary and recent foreign work would have afforded. The Russians from Tolstoy onward, Wassermann, Mann and Zweig in Germany, Proust and Gide in France, and Couperus in Holland are as essential as our own writers to the understanding of the English novel.

INDEX

Index